A PEOPLE'S H

OF ENGL

A PEOPLE'S HISTORY
OF ENGLAND

by

A. L. MORTON

With 15 maps by

J. F. HORRABIN

*'Ill would Change be at Whiles, were it not
for the Change beyond the Change'*

MORRIS

LONDON
VICTOR GOLLANCZ LTD
1938

First published May 1938
Second impression May 1938

*To my Father
who has helped more
than he imagines*

PRINTED IN GREAT BRITAIN BY PURNELL AND SONS LTD. (T.U.)
PAULTON (SOMERSET) AND LONDON

CONTENTS

Chapter **XIV** (*continued*)

LIST OF MAPS

Maps 6, 8, 9, 10 and 14 are reproduced from J. F. Horrabin's
An Atlas of European History.

CHAPTER I

TRIBES AND LEGIONS

I. THE IBERIANS

EARLY MAPS SHOW a world in which Britain is a remote outpost, a shapeless cluster of islands thrust out into the encircling ocean. But in some of these maps a significant tilt brings their South-western coast close to the North of Spain, reminding us that earlier still, centuries before the making of any maps that have survived, Britain lay not outside the world but on a regular and frequented trade route which linked Mediterranean civilisation with the amber-bearing North. It was by this long sea route and not across the Dover Straits or the Channel that civilisation first reached these shores.

In Cornwall, in Ireland and along the coast of Wales and Scotland cluster the monuments left by Iberian or Megalithic men who reached and peopled Britain between 3000 and 2000 B.C. A final group of such monuments in Sutherland, the last point at which their ships touched land before pushing across the North Sea to Scandinavia, makes the route and its objective abundantly clear. At this time the land subsidence which had begun a thousand or so years earlier was still going on, and the apparently shorter and safer route up Channel and along the European coast was closed, if not by a land bridge joining Britain to the continent, then by straits that were narrow, shifting, shoaling and swept by rapid tides. This is perhaps the first reason for the settlement of Iberian man in Britain.

Though little is certainly known about these Iberians of the New Stone Age, a good deal may be inferred with reasonable safety, since they have left their mark upon the face of the land more clearly than either Celt, Roman or Saxon. Further, their stock is one of the main contributors to the present population of the British Isles, especially in Ireland, Wales and the West of England. A small, dark, long-headed race, they settled especially on the chalk downs that radiate from Salisbury Plain. Below the ridges of these hills run their trackways, like the Icknield Way and the Pilgrim's Way, which are our oldest and most historic roads. On the downs and along the trackways lie the long barrows, the great earthworks such as crown Cissbury and Dolebury, and the stone circles of which Avebury is the grandest and Stonehenge the best known. It is from these monuments and from the downland terraces formed by their agriculture that we can guess what manner of people these were.

The size and splendour of their monuments speak of a numerous and well-organised people. Thousands must have worked together to raise the great earthworks, and the trackways link settlement to settlement in an orderly fashion. So, the Icknield Way joins the industrial centre of Grimes Graves, site of a large scale flint knapping on the Brecklands of Norfolk, with the religious centre at Avebury. The downland terraces indicate an intensive agriculture carried on with hoe and spade. The whole lay-out of Iberian civilisation points to a certain specialisation and division of labour which enabled the Norfolk people, for example, to mine and work flints that were traded all over the country.

More direct evidence of the social structure of the Iberians is the long barrow. Often over 200 feet in length, these barrows were burial places and prove the existence of sharply marked class divisions. On the one hand there must have been chiefs or nobles, people important enough to demand such elaborate funeral arrangements, and on the other, an abundance of the men whose cheap, possibly servile labour, was available for such works. If it could be definitely established that the huge pyramidal mounds at Silbury and Marlborough were also barrows it would

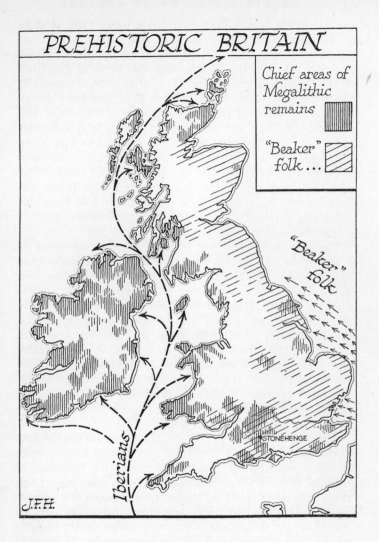

PREHISTORIC BRITAIN

Chief areas of
Megalithic
remains

"Beaker"
folk...

"Beaker"
folk

Iberians

STONEHENGE

J.F.H.

be reasonable to infer also the existence of something in the nature of kingship.

Finally, there is some evidence that Iberian culture was mainly unwarlike. Few finds that can be classed as weapons have been unearthed of an earlier date than the first Celtic invasions in the Late Bronze Age, and the downland earthworks usually have the ditch inside the rampart, and not outside as it would be if they had been constructed for defensive purposes.

The diffusion of certain types of implements and utensils shows that a considerable trade went on along the trackways and by sea between Britain and Spain and even to the Mediterranean. Whether metals, other than gold which was mined in Ireland, were known is uncertain, since it is becoming increasingly difficult to draw any clear line between New Stone and Early Bronze Ages. Soon after 2000 B.C. a new race of Alpine stock entered the country, this time from the South-east and East. From their characteristic pottery they are known as the Beaker Folk. This race was certainly familiar with the use and working of bronze. The two peoples were closely related in culture, and the new-comers spread along the East Coast, through East Anglia and up the Thames Valley. Iberian and Alpine met and fused in the Wiltshire area which is the focus of all pre-Celtic civilisation in Britain, and it is probably this fusion that produced Stonehenge sometime before 1000 B.C. Tin, copper and lead were mined in Cornwall and Wales and probably exported in considerable bulk during this period.

Although a respectable level of civilisation was reached in the Early and Middle-Bronze Ages it was spread over only a small part of Britain. The mountain areas of the West and North were, as now, thinly peopled. More remarkably, much of the lowland area which today affords the richest agricultural land was also untouched. These areas were then covered with forests of oak and ash, with a thick, impenetrable underscrub. Such forests, on heavy, wet, clay soil were an absolute barrier to men equipped only with stone or even bronze implements, and, in fact, they were not seriously attacked till the Roman occupation and not finally cleared till the Saxon period. Prehistoric man kept to the dry chalk uplands, not because they were the richest but because they were the best he could occupy with the tools at his disposal, and it is not until the advent of the great iron axe that the richer but more heavily timbered lowlands were conquered.

2. THE CELTIC TRIBES

Soon after 700 B.C., the first wave of Celtic invaders entered Britain, coming probably from the Upper Rhineland. These invasions were part of a widespread westward movement of tall, fair-haired, warlike tribes which overran the Mediterranean civilisation much as the later Teutons were to overrun the Roman Empire. The movement began in the Second Millennium B.C., when barbarian tribes had learnt the use of bronze from the Mediterranean peoples and turned their knowledge to the production of weapons far superior to those of their teachers. In Britain the most striking sign of this is the appearance of the leaf-shaped sword, replacing the less effective knives and daggers of the Early and Middle-Bronze Ages.

An early part of this movement was the penetration of the Aegean area by the Greek tribes, but the Celts proper spread as far abroad as Spain and Asia Minor. About 390 B.C. Celtic tribes sacked Rome and set up a kingdom in the fertile plain of Lombardy. The character of these invasions can be learnt from Caesar's account of his war with the Helvetii, who attempted to march across Gaul to escape attacks from the German tribes across the Rhine. They were movements of large tribes, composed of free warriors under tribal chiefs, accompanied by considerable numbers of women and children. They were, that is to say, national migrations rather than the raids of military bands, and their object was not so much plunder as conquest and settlement.

In Britain the first Celtic invaders were the Goidels or Gaels. These were followed about two centuries later by the Brythons, a branch of the Celts who had learned the use of iron, and who drove their bronze using kinsmen out of the South and East and into Wales, Scotland, Ireland and the hilly Pennine and Devon areas. A third wave of invaders, Belgae from Northern Gaul, containing probably a considerable Teutonic element, arrived about 100 B.C. and occupied the greater part of what are now known as the Home Counties.

The Celtic conquerors blended with their Iberian predecessors to varying extents in different parts of the country. While in the West the dominant strain is Iberian, the Celts were able to impose their tribal organisation, modified to some extent by the fact of conquest, throughout the whole of the British Isles.

It is necessary at this point to describe the main characteristics of this organisation, since the whole history of the next thousand years may best be understood in terms of the gradual weakening and break up of tribal society and its eventual replacement by feudalism. From this point of view the Roman occupation must be regarded as an interruption except in so far as it weakened Celtic tribal structure. This was especially the case in those parts of the country that were first reached by each subsequent invader.

The basic unit of the Celtic tribe was the kinship group, or enlarged family. These groups were in turn combined to form larger groups also based upon real or supposed kinship, rising to the tribe and the nation. But it was upon the enlarged family that the economic life of the Celts centred. They were mainly a pastoral people, but practised a rude agriculture based upon the heavy plough drawn by four or more often by eight oxen. This large plough is the technical key not only to the agriculture of the Celts but throughout the whole of the feudal period. The holding of the Celtic family group, the gwely, or as it was later called in Ireland, the bally, represented the amount of land that could be worked with one plough and ox team. The holding was the joint property of the kindred and was sub-divided among its adult males, each of whom assisted in the communal ploughing, in the upkeep of the team and in the harvest. The important point is that though the gwely might be almost infinitely subdivided it remained the property of the whole family and was carefully preserved as an economic unit. At the same time, when the pressure of population became acute a part of the family would split off and form a new gwely elsewhere. This was easy, because there was no lack of land though there might be a shortage of *cleared* land.

Celtic agriculture was in some ways crude, with a lower yield per acre than the terraced agriculture of the Iberians, and their ploughing was often no more than a scratching of the surface. Still, their better use of metal and the technical advance of the heavy plough with its iron plough-share enabled them to occupy new areas. Though the wet oak forests remained uncleared, the Celtic period sees the beginning of that valleyward movement of settlements that has now left Salisbury Plain, the Downs and the Norfolk Brecklands as almost unpeopled sheepwalks.

While Celtic tribal society cannot be described as classless, its class divisions were not sharply marked or of decisive importance. The difference between chief and free tribesman was one of degree rather than of kind, and such class divisions as existed seem to have been mainly the result of the subjection of a native population. It is unlikely that this took the form of slavery except under special circumstances. The technique of production was still too crude for slavery to be economically possible. Welsh law gives us the impression that the two peoples lived side by side in free and unfree hamlets and gwelys. The native population of the unfree gwelys was not apparently exploited by the mass of the free cultivators, but directly by the chiefs and the landlords who grew up after the settlements had taken place. It was undoubtedly their ability to exploit the labour of this large semi-servile class that formed the basis of the growing power of the chiefs, and which marked them off ever more sharply from the generality of the free tribesmen.

The coming of the Belgae opens a new and important stage in the development of Celtic Britain. Unlike the Goidels and Brythons they were mainly agricultural, and the South-east of Britain soon became, what Caesar noted it as being, a corn growing country. At the same time towns began to spring up, as at St. Albans and Colchester. These towns, if nothing better than large stockaded villages, were a marked contrast to the open hamlets and isolated homesteads of the earlier invaders. The Belgae kept up a close relation with Gaul, and a regular, if not extensive trade developed. With this came the earliest native coined money. The Brythons had employed iron bars, rather like half-finished swords in appearance, but now gold coins were struck in imitation of the Macedonian staters brought by merchants from the continent. It is curious to observe these coins becoming progressively more crude with each new minting, but it is also worth noting that no gold coins at all were struck in England between the end of the Roman occupation and the reign of Edward III. With the growth of agriculture, trade and towns, powerful chiefs began to claim kingship over wide areas, and at the time of Caesar's invasion in 53 B.C. all South-east Britain was in theory subject to a certain Cassivellaunus whose capital was probably Colchester.

3. ROMAN BRITAIN

It was the close relation of Britain to Gaul which first attracted the notice of the Romans. Having conquered Gaul, Caesar soon heard tales of the pearls and corn in which the island was reputed to be rich. At the same time the export of tin from Cornwall, which had begun possibly as early as 2000 B.C., still continued. Caesar's invasions were, however, dictated by strategical rather than by economic motives. Britain was a centre from which Gallic resistance to Roman power was maintained, British warriors crossed the Channel to help their Gaulish kinsmen, and rebels from Gaul found a refuge and encouragement among the British tribes. It is unlikely that the conquest of Britain was contemplated at this time, but some sort of punitive expedition was necessary before the Roman occupation of Gaul could be regarded as assured.

Roman Imperialism, based upon the predatory exploitation of the provinces, needed a constant forward movement to prevent a decline at the centre now becoming increasingly parasitic. But in 55 B.C. Gaul was newly conquered and assimilation and plunder by Rome's merchant and usurer capitalists had hardly begun. It was not till nearly a century later that Rome was ready to digest the new province of Britain. We shall see later that the inability to continue this process of absorption in the face of increasing resistance led directly to the decline of the Roman Empire.

In any case, Caesar's two invasions were little more than reconnaissances in force. The first was made in the summer of 55 B.C. with two legions and a body of cavalry, making a total of perhaps 10,000 men. Some successes were gained but the opposition was strong and in the following year an army of about 25,000 was landed. The Thames was crossed and the capital of Cassivellaunus stormed. Caesar then departed, taking hostages and securing a promise to pay tribute. There is no evidence that this promise was ever fulfilled.

In the ninety years between these raids and the invasion of A.D. 43, in which the actual conquest of Britain began, many changes took place. Excavations prove that during this period a thorough economic penetration of South-east Britain went on. Trade became considerable, corn and hides being exchanged for pottery and a variety of luxury articles. Traders and colonists settled in large numbers and the growth of towns was so considerable that in A.D. 50, only seven years after the invasion of Claudius,

St. Albans or Verulamium was granted the full status of a Roman municipium with civic self-government and the rights of Roman citizenship for its inhabitants. The British upper classes began to imitate Roman ways and even to build crude imitations of the Roman stone villa.

When Boadicea led the Iceni in revolt in A.D. 60 and sacked Verulamium, Colchester and London, the loss of life in these three cities was estimated by a Roman historian, possibly with some exaggeration, at 70,000. This revolt was the most serious opposition that the Romans encountered in Southern Britain, and there is no doubt that the ease with which the country was conquered was mainly due to the economic penetration of the preceding century and the consequent disintegration of the Celtic tribal organisation.

The Roman occupation of Britain lasted nearly 400 years, and sets the historian two important and closely related problems: how thorough was the process of Romanisation? And how enduring were its results?

Roman Britain divided itself into two parts: the civil districts and the military. Wales and the whole area North and West of the Peak District up to the Roman Wall which ran from the mouth of the Tyne to Carlisle composed the latter. North of the Wall the occupation was never more than occasional and haphazard. About the character of the occupation of these military districts there can be no doubt. A network of roads, strung with military blockhouses covered the whole area. North of York and West of Chester and Caerleon there are no civil towns of any importance. Three Legions were stationed here: one at York, one at Chester and one at Caerleon. The Wall was heavily garrisoned by auxiliary troops. In all a permanent garrison of some 40,000 men was maintained in the province.

The native population of the military districts were little affected by the occupation except perhaps along the Wall and around the main stations. They revolted frequently till about A.D. 200, and there is no reason to suppose

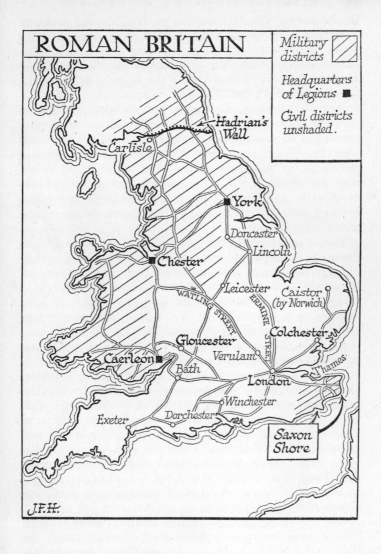

ROMAN BRITAIN

Military districts

Headquarters of Legions ■

Civil districts unshaded.

Hadrian's Wall

Carlisle

York

Doncaster

Lincoln

Chester

Leicester

Caistor (by Norwich)

WATLING STREET

ERMINE STREET

Gloucester

Verulam

Colchester

Caerleon

Bath

London

Thames

Winchester

Exeter

Dorchester

Saxon Shore

J.F.H.

that their economic or tribal organisation was seriously interfered with, since it reappears intact centuries later in the earliest Welsh laws. The whole area was poor, bleak and hilly, and, except for some minerals that were worked in Wales, it had little to attract the greed of the conquerors.

In the civil districts the situation was different. Britain was valued largely as a producer of grain, and annual shipments were made to Gaul until about A.D. 360, when their sudden ceasing is one of the most ominous signs of the decay of Roman power.

Scores of towns grew up along the Roman roads. Five of these ranked as municipia: Verulamium, Colchester, York, Lincoln and Gloucester. London, which for some obscure reason never acquired municipal rank was larger than any of these and became the most important trading centre in Northern Europe. Between the towns were the villas, country houses of the Roman or British magnates. These villas were not mere pleasure resorts, but the centres of agricultural estates. The British upper classes became completely Romanised and were transformed from Celtic tribal chiefs into Roman landowners and officials.

So much is clear: what is and must be uncertain is how far Roman customs and the Latin language and the Roman mode of production affected the mass of the people outside the towns. Roman agriculture was based on the large estate, and this was cultivated in two ways, either by gangs of slaves or by semi-servile *coloni* who were allowed to cultivate patches of land in return for fixed rents or services. The second system became common at the end of the Roman period when depopulation and the inability to open up any new sources for the supply of slaves produced acute labour problems. Almost certainly both systems were common in Britain and were found alongside of Celtic tribal agriculture even in the most settled regime.

During the Roman occupation large forest areas were opened up. Along the rivers and roads, and on the edges of the forest belts, clearings were made, and the demand for fuel to supply the elaborate central heating apparatus of the villas must have been a powerful factor in this process. We must conclude that the energy and method of the Romans radically transformed the whole of the civil districts and that the lives of all the people were moulded towards the Roman pattern. There is not the slightest evidence that any national feeling existed or that the inhabitants thought of themselves as Britons as opposed to Roman provincials.

Yet the permanent effects of Roman rule were astonishingly meagre. The roads remained. The towns remained but were laid waste and there is no evidence that any Roman town was continuously inhabited after the Anglo-Saxon inroads. It is possible that the economic structure of the villa contributed something to the make-up of the English township and the feudal manor. And, finally, Christianity, introduced by the legions, remained the religion of those parts of Britain which escaped the English conquest, penetrated thence to Ireland[1] where it acquired a curiously tribal character and ultimately played a big part in moulding the cultural development of the Anglian kingdom of Northumbria.

4. THE ROMAN TWILIGHT

The destruction of the Roman Empire was due to a unique combination of internal and external causes, some of the former especially being very deep rooted and slow in taking effect. Even at the height of its power, the Empire was suffering from profound maladies and it was when the measures which served to alleviate these could no longer be applied that a steady process of disintegration set in.

Italy was originally a land of small peasant cultivators, and her towns no more than trading centres supplying their needs. From the time of the wars between Rome

[1] But an independent, and possibly earlier, group of missionaries came into Ireland from Spain.

and Carthage (264—200 B.C.) these peasant holdings were destroyed and replaced by huge farms worked by slave gangs. The Italian peasant was driven from the land, just as the English peasant was in the period between the Sixteenth and Eighteenth Centuries. But while in England the destruction of peasant agriculture was accompanied by the growth of capitalist industry in the towns this was not the case in Italy. Industry remained at a low level of development and was carried on almost entirely by slave labour. The result was the rapid development of merchant and usurer's capital without a corresponding industrial basis. Consequently, and especially in Rome itself, there came into being a huge parasitical proletariat, with citizen rights but no settled means of livelihood. The wholesale corruption of this mob by the merchants and tax farmers who replaced the old aristocracy at the close of the Republic, involved a continuous forward movement so as to provide the series of provinces from whose plunder alone both proletariat and capitalists could exist.

These provinces were also needed to provide reinforcements for the slave army on which the whole Roman economy depended. Slave production is always wasteful and the Roman slave army always failed to reproduce itself, this failure producing a recurrent depopulation both in the provinces and at the centre. When the conquests reached the point at which it was a military impossibility to hold and assimilate fresh territories, decline was inevitable, though it was in part and for a time masked by improved methods of exploitation such as the substitution of a type of serfdom for the earlier chattel slavery. The political organisation of the Roman Empire in the form of a military dictatorship added to these weaknesses by the constant strife between rival provincial generals attempting to use their legions to secure the Imperial crown. Britain, as an outlying and isolated province, suffered especially from this, being periodically drained of man power to support the claims of such adventurers as Maximus (383) and Constantine (407).

For long the Empire persisted rather because of the absence of any outside force powerful enough to attack it than from its own strength. In the Fourth Century A.D. a series of westward migratory movements across the steppes of Asia and Europe forced the German tribes nearest to the Roman frontiers into motion. The whole sequence is obscure but at its heart we can trace the westward migration of the Huns, a Mongol tribe from Central Asia, probably the result of climatic changes turning their grazing lands into desert. At first these German tribes were allowed and even encouraged to enter the Empire, where they were absorbed and partially Romanised. Gradually, as the pressure increased, the hold of the central government on outlying provinces was relinquished and one by one they were overrun by barbarian tribes who set up independent kingdoms of varying character—some largely Roman in culture and language, others almost wholly barbarian.

Britain, as the most remote and among the most exposed of the provinces, was among the earliest to fall away and lost most completely its Roman character.

The first attacks came not from German tribes across the North Sea but from the unconquered Goidelic Celts of Scotland and Ireland. This is in itself a sign of Roman decline, since in earlier times such attackers had been beaten off without much difficulty. After a period of peace from 250 to 350 a series of inroads swept Britain right up to the walls of London. The villas were burnt and pillaged, and, after about 360, were rarely rebuilt. The walled towns held out longer, but no coins later than 420 are found, for example, in Silchester, where a rude stone found in the forum bearing an Ogham inscription proves the destruction to have been the work of Celtic and not of German tribesmen.

Even after the first invasions there was a partial recovery but in 407 two events ended the long period of Roman occupation. One was the departure of Constantine, with the bulk of the troops stationed in Britain, in an attempt to secure the Imperial purple. The other was the crossing of the Rhine into Gaul of a great host of German tribesmen which cut Britain off from the Roman world and prevented the return or replacement of the departed legions.

The year 407 is usually said to mark the 'departure of the Romans', and, in a sense, this is so. But there was no deliberate plan of abandonment. Constantine only intended to add new provinces to the one he already held, and the failure of his legions to return may be almost described as accidental. Yet it was at this date that the regular arrival of new Imperial governors and officials ceased. The people of South and East Britain, with their tribal organisation destroyed and their new civilisation already seriously weakened, were left to improvise their own government and defence against their never conquered kinsmen of the more remote parts of the islands.

When a new enemy, the Anglian and Saxon tribes from the German coast who had already made themselves feared as daring raiders, appeared about 450 as intending conquerors and settlers they found much of the work of the Romans undone already. The richest and most civilised part of the island, in which their landings were made, had been laid waste before their arrival. Centralised government had disappeared and in its place was a welter of petty principalities under the control of local landlords or magnates at the head of armed bands that were almost as ruinous to the people as the enemies from whom they claimed to provide protection. It was largely for this reason that the traces of Roman rule in Britain are so few and the English conquest so complete.

CHAPTER II

THE GROWTH OF FEUDALISM

1. THE ENGLISH CONQUEST

THE PERIOD BETWEEN the year 407 when Constantine led away the legions and 597 when Augustine landed in Kent, bringing not only Christianity, but also renewed contact with the mainstream of European events, is an almost complete blank. No written records survive except the melancholy treatise of the monk Gildas "concerning the ruin of Britain", and though he wrote as early as 560 Gildas is very remotely concerned with history. The traditions of the invaders themselves, committed to writing much later by Bede (about 731) and in the Anglo-Saxon Chronicle (begun shortly before 900), are confused, scanty and frequently misleading. Even the evidence of archæology is slight, for the low level of civilisation of the invaders has left us no trace of their early settlements except the meagre contents of their burial places. Yet it is from this evidence, supplemented by the written records and a critical use of historical geography, that a provisional account of the course and character of the invasions must be drawn together.

The bulk of the invaders came from among the most backward and primitive of the German tribes, living on the coast around the mouth of the Elbe and in the south of Denmark. These tribes, the Angles and Saxons, were closely akin in speech and customs, so that it is even doubtful if any real distinction can be drawn between them. The third group of invaders, called traditionally Jutes, were probably a Frankish tribe from the lower Rhineland. It was among these tribes that the Romans were accustomed to enlist auxiliary troops in the last

days of the Empire, and the burial places of Kent and
the Isle of Wight, where the Jutes settled, give evidence
of a people at a higher cultural level than the other invaders, and suggest some contact, if only at second hand,
with Roman civilisation. There is thus every reason to
accept the tradition that the Jutes were invited to enter
the country as allies by a British chief and afterwards
ousted their hosts. It is in Kent alone that faint signs of
continuity with the settlements and agriculture of the
Romans can be discerned. Kent has, indeed, a social
history quite different from that of the rest of England,
passing directly from small scale individual peasant
agriculture to capitalist agriculture.

In general the social organisation of the invaders was
still tribal, resembling that of the Celts as described in
the first chapter. It will be convenient henceforth to give
to the invaders as a whole the name English, though, of
course, the word does not come into use for some centuries.
The English were an agricultural rather than a pastoral
people, and even before they entered Britain their tribal
organisation was rapidly disintegrating. Vast migratory
movements were sweeping over Europe, scattering and
mixing together the settlements of kindred. By the Fourth
Century the institution of kingship was well established
in Germany. There was emerging also a class of professional warriors, distinct from and ranking higher than
the peasants, who were becoming increasingly content to
till the soil as long as they were allowed to do so in peace.
The kinship group was losing its importance, on the one
side to the war band collected round a chief and bound
to him by a personal tie, and on the other to the purely
local unit of the village.

The rate of disintegration was immensely increased by
the invasions themselves. The first raids on the coast of
Britain were probably the work of small war bands, and
their effect would be to increase the wealth and prestige
of the warrior class as compared with the homekeeping
cultivator. In the Fifth Century the raids were replaced

by something approaching national migrations. While in some cases small independent settlements may have been made along the coast it is now believed that the main invasion was the work of one or possibly two great war hosts like that of the Danes which came near to conquering England in 871. Such a host would be composed of both warriors and cultivators, and, probably, a considerable number of women and children as the Danish host often was. More cultivators and their families probably followed, but in any case the spear-head of the invasion was formed by the warriors with their superior equipment and training.

The settlements formed after the invasion represent in their variety the mixed and transitional character of the host. Here a kinship group would settle and divide the land in a rough equality. In another place a warrior would settle with a group of dependents, in a third a number of Britons might survive and be forced into slavery (often those who survived were precisely those who were already slaves). The main result of the invasion, with its involved movements and incessant warfare, was to mix and remix conqueror and conquered in an infinite variety of combinations and to strengthen the military organisation just as it weakened that of kinship. The same causes greatly increased the authority of the kings, and at the close of the period they emerge with a claim, shadowy as yet and much hedged about with the restrictions of folkright, to be sole and ultimate owners of the land.

The details of the conquest are now hopelessly lost, yet it is possible to reconstruct the main outlines and even to give a few approximate dates. The Jutes have already been mentioned. The traditional and probably correct date of their advent is about 450. Of the Angles nothing is known for certain till we find them in possession of the North-east coast and much of the Midlands by the end of the century. We can guess that the point of arrival was probably Humber mouth, and that the Trent and Ouse were their pathways into the interior.

Somewhere between these dates the host of the Saxons entered the country by way of the Wash. Sailing up the Great Ouse in their long, shallow-draught boats they passed through the Fen Country and disembarked somewhere near Cambridge. Thence they moved South-west along the Icknield Way and burst into the East Midlands and the Thames Valley. Gildas, in words that seem to choke with horror, describes the devastation that followed. For a number of years the country was harried from end to end. Whatever had survived of Roman civilisation was blotted out, and the Britons were killed, enslaved or driven into the west.

About 500 there was a pause, possibly when the cultivators began to parcel out the land and leave the warriors to carry on the fighting alone. Gildas speaks of a certain Ambrosius Aurelianus, the one reasonably probable name in a period of extraordinary obscurity, who rallied the scattered Britons and led them to success in a series of encounters. The last of these, Mount Badon, Gildas places in the year of his own birth, probably about 516. At the same or a slightly later period, there was a mass migration into Armorica on such a scale as to give that country its present name of Brittany and the Celtic character that it has retained to this day.

Later in the Sixth Century the advance of the English was resumed. A victory at Deorham in Gloucestershire brought the Saxons to the Bristol Channel. In 613 a battle at Chester gave the Mercians access to the Irish Sea. The Britons were now cut off into three sections, penned into the mountain regions of Devon and Cornwall (West Wales), Wales proper and Cumberland (Strathclyde). There their reduction was only a matter of time, though Wales held out till well into the Middle Ages.

By this time the English had settled down into a number of small kingdoms whose boundaries advanced and receded constantly with the fortunes of the never ending wars. These wars, as no doubt the initial invasion, were greatly facilitated by the still undestroyed network of

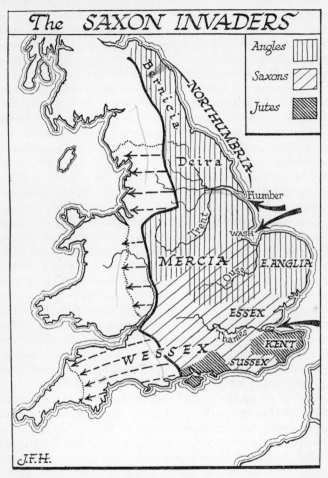

Extent of Anglo-Saxon conquest and occupation at the end of
the 6th century. The smaller arrows show the further advance
westwards by the 8th century.

Roman roads. Some of these kingdoms survive in the names of modern English shires: others vanished so utterly that we hardly know their names. By the end of the Sixth Century, seven emerge. In the North, Northumbria stretched from the Forth to the Humber. Its two parts, Deira corresponding to Yorkshire and Bernicia lying between Tees and Forth, appear at times as separate kingdoms. East Anglia covered Norfolk, Suffolk and part of Cambridgeshire. Essex, Kent and Sussex correspond roughly to the modern counties bearing the same names. Wessex lay south of the Thames and west of Sussex with a western frontier being pushed slowly into Somerset. Mercia occupied most of the Midland shires, but the Cotswold region was for long debatable ground between Mercia and Wessex.

The relation of the English to the conquered native population has been a favourite subject for dispute among historians. It has been maintained, on the one hand, that the Britons were all but exterminated, and on the other that a quite small body of conquering English settled among masses of natives. No finality has ever been reached, but certain pointers may be noted. First, there was a catastrophic fall in the total population. The towns were destroyed without exception and long remained uninhabited. London may be a partial exception, for though there is no evidence that it was continuously occupied its position at the heart of the system of roads made it the inevitable focus for trade the moment it began again, and it reappears early as a place of some importance. Apart from the destruction of the towns, the area of cultivation was greatly diminished. Most of the forest land cleared by the Romans was abandoned, and the early English settlements are strung along the rivers and cluster in one or two specially favoured areas like Kent and the Thames Valley. It is reasonable to suppose that the displacement of the British rural population either by slaughter or migration must have been correspondingly great.

Secondly, the evidence of language is opposed to the view that the invaders settled down as a small minority. In Gaul, where the Franks were in such a position, it was the language of the conquered which prevailed. In England, Celtic words and place names are few except in the West. The analogy of the Danish invasions shows that it is possible for invaders from overseas to settle in such numbers as to form their own self-contained communities. Yet there is equally no reason to suppose that the Britons were wiped out even in the East where the English settled in the greatest numbers. Early English laws make provision for Welshmen living alongside their conquerors quite as a matter of course. And in Suffolk today, after two thousand years and Roman, English, Danish and Norman invasions, the shepherd calling to his sheep still uses the Welsh word for "Come here". Many of the English brought their womenfolk, but these were certainly far fewer than the men and much intermarriage must have taken place from the start.

Perhaps it is most reasonable to conclude that in the East, at any rate, the bulk of the population was English, and that such Britons as survived in these parts were enslaved. The further west we go the greater becomes the proportion of Britons in the population. Wessex law even allows for the existence of Welsh landowners who have their own place in society and a wergild half that of their English counterparts. For the most part, however, the Britons who survived would be those of the lower classes, and villagers rather than town dwellers. This was just the section who were the least Romanised and between whom and the English the narrowest cultural gap existed.

2. THE TOWNSHIP

From the earliest times the settlements of the English were marked by a striking duality, the outcome of their transitional position between tribal and what we must begin to call feudal organisation. On the one hand we

have the hide and the hundred, forms characteristic of
the tribe, on the other the township, a purely local entity
with no necessary connection with kinship. It is the
growth and direction of growth of the township, and of
social classes within it, that forms the internal history of
the period between the English and Norman conquests.

The hide, like the Celtic gwely, was the holding of a
family. Its size was likewise based upon the cultivation
with the eight-ox plough, and can be averaged roughly
at 120 acres, more or less according to the nature of the
soil and other variations in local conditions. But while
the gwely was an economic as well as a social unit, the
economic unit among the English was not the hide but
the township. The normal township was a largish, compact village, markedly different from the hamlets of the
Celts which often contained only one family or a few
closely related families. The hamlet often coincided with
the gwely, which in any case was a self-contained whole,
complete within its own boundaries. The hide was scattered in single acre strips over the entire extent of the
township's common fields.

These fields, two or three in number, were worked in
strict rotation. If there were three, one was sown in the
autumn with wheat and barley, one with oats, beans or
peas in the spring, while the third was left fallow. Where
the two-field system prevailed one field was sown and the
other left fallow. The fields were unfenced, and the strips
divided only by narrow balks of turf left unploughed.
After harvest the whole extent of the fields became common grazing ground for the sheep and cattle of the township. Besides his 120 strips scattered patchwork fashion
over the common fields, the holder of a hide had certain
customary rights over the common meadows and the
township's waste. The latter was usually extensive, a
township being often no more than a clearing in the
middle of a large tract of wood or heath land. It was
valued chiefly for its timber and the beech mast and
acorns on which the pigs fed. So that a hide was really a

holding comprising as much land as one plough could work, plus certain well defined rights over the common meadow and waste of the township.

From the start it was treated less as the holding of a family than as the holding of the head of a family. It was not yet private property, it could not be sold and its use was hedged about with all sorts of customary restrictions, yet the germ of private property in land lay within it already. We have seen how the invasions helped to strengthen the military as opposed to the tribal organisation, and the hide was from the start a military holding, carrying an obligation to put one fully armed man into the fyrd in time of war. Its holder was still in theory a free warrior. But when wars were frequent the hide was not a sufficient holding to support a warrior, and alongside the coerl, holder of a hide, we find the thane, the descendant of the professional war man, who has been granted by the King or who has carved out for himself a much larger holding, usually not less than five hides (600 acres) and often much more. The coerl might still serve in the fyrd in a special crisis but in ordinary times the fighting was done by the thane and his personal followers. Here begins the rough division of labour between the man who fights in the wars and the man who toils in the fields that lies at the roots of the feudal system.

Very soon the thane gained an ascendancy over his weaker neighbours. Times were unsettled, the central authority of the State in its infancy, and the cultivator would undertake to perform services or pay rent in produce as a return for the protection of the thane and his band. Within the ranks of the coerls a rapid social differentiation set in. Some prospered and became thanes, more declined and the normal holding of a free man grew smaller. The hide, being based on the eight-ox plough, was easily divisible up to a point, that is, into not more than eight portions. The common holding of a peasant cultivator in later Saxon times was not the hide but the virgate or two-ox share (30 acres) or the bovate or one-ox share (15 acres). Besides this a numerous class sprang up with much smaller holdings, ranging from two to five acres. These were not and could not be part of the common fields, since they were too small to support an ox to share in the communal ploughing. They were often carved out of the waste, and cultivated with the spade or a light plough. Their holders, whom we shall meet in Domesday Book under the names of bordars and cotters, were often the village craftsmen, smiths, wheelwrights and the like, or pieced out a living by working for wages on the increasingly extensive domain lands of the thanes. It is among them that we have to look for the direct ancestors of the modern proletariat.

In time the hide ceased altogether to be a real division of land, and in the centuries before the Norman Conquest it appears mainly as a term used for purposes of taxation and administration. In the same way, the hundred, once a grouping of 100 hides or families, becomes a vague local area, a medium-sized subdivision of the shire only important as the basis of a court of justice.

As early, perhaps, as 600, the thane was well on the way towards becoming a feudal lord, the coerl well on the way to becoming a serf, private property in land was beginning to take shape and well-defined social classes were everywhere arising. At the same time the State, growing out of the military conquest and division of the country and the permanent importance of the King as war leader in a period when war was the normal state of affairs, was superseding the looser tribal organisation that had served the English in their German homeland. Such a process, marked by the acquisition of special powers by a minority and at the expense of the remainder of the people, is in fact the only way in which society can advance beyond the tribal stage and must, for all its harshness, be regarded as essentially progressive. All these tendencies were accelerated and given a precise legal form by the introduction of Christianity. Christianity added also to the existing division of labour between fighter and cultivator a third specialised activity, that of the preacher and man of learning.

3. CHRISTIANITY

Though the Welsh held tenaciously to the Christianity that they had learned during Roman occupation, it was not from Wales that the conversion of the English came. The mutual hatred between conquerors and conquered was too bitter to allow of normal intercourse, and the Welsh attitude was that the English were no more than a punishment sent upon them by God on account of their sins. It was from Rome, and a little later from Ireland by way of Iona, that Christianity reached England. The Seventh Century is taken up with this conversion, with the clash between the rival sects and with the final triumph of the Roman type of Christianity.

Augustine, who landed in Kent in 597, was sent by Pope Gregory the Great under whom a marked religious revival, accompanied by much missionary enthusiasm, was taking place. He found Ethelbert of Kent married to a Christian wife and more than half ready to accept baptism. The conversion of Kent was followed by that of Essex and East Anglia. In 625 Edwin of Northumbria married a Kentish princess and northward with her journeyed Paulinus the first Bishop of York. More speedy conversions were recorded, and after the baptism of Edwin we read that Paulinus spent twenty-six consecutive days immersing converts in the River Glen. Similar mass rites followed in the Swale and Trent.

The new religion had a resounding but hollow victory. It made little real impression on the masses and when Edwin was defeated and killed at Heathfield by the Mercian king Penda in 633, the reversion of Northumbria was even more rapid than its conversion had been. Religion was still and for long a matter upon which kings decided from policy or conviction and the people followed.

The next year a new king, Oswald, was crowned in
Northumbria. He had been brought up by the Irish monks
of Iona, and with him came Aidan who founded the great
monastery of Lindisfarne, the real cradle of Christianity
in Northern England, and set out in turn upon the task
of converting the Northumbrians. The Celtic type of
Christianity with its simple piety and its absence of
centralisation struck home much more deeply to the
rough farmer-soldiers of the North. A Northumbrian poet
of the next century writes of Christ as:

> "The young hero
> That was God Almighty,
> Strong and brave,"

and early Northumbrian Christianity was a unique
blend of the heroic paganism of the past with the milder
but still heroic faith of the Irish Christians. The result
was very different from the religion of fear and organisation
which had come from Rome and continued to make slow
headway in the South of England. When Oswald was
defeated and killed by Penda in 642 Northumbria remained
Christian and the conversion of Mercia followed within
twenty years. Meanwhile Wessex also was slowly adopting
the new faith, and only Sussex, isolated behind the Romney
marshes and the vast forest of the Andredesweald, remained
heathen.

In 664 Roman and Celtic Christians met at Whitby to
decide their points of difference. Much more was involved
than the trivialities that appeared on the surface: issues
such as the date of keeping Easter and the exact shape of
the priestly tonsure. Celtic Christianity as it developed
in unconquered Ireland had adapted itself to the tribal
mould. Its organisation took the form of monasteries that
were no more than groups of hermits living together in a
cluster of huts. It held little land, and that still remained
the property of the tribe as a whole. It never had any local
or parish organisation, and its bishops were only wandering
missionaries with the vaguest supremacy over their fellows.

Roman Christianity inherited all that remained of Roman discipline and centralisation, Roman law with its precise definition of property and its recognition of slavery, and a carefully graded ecclesiastical hierarchy. Further, it was already committed to an elaborate territorial organisation of bishoprics and parishes. The nearest Roman Christian country, and the one with the greatest influence over England, was France, and it was here that feudalism had made its greatest advances. The victory of Rome at the Synod of Whitby was therefore a victory for feudalism and all that feudalism involved.

All the qualities, good and bad, of Roman Christianity are summed up in Wilfred, who first came to the front at Whitby and was afterwards Archbishop of York. A bustling, diplomatic man, jealous of the authority of his Church and of his own authority because he was its representative, he is the first of the great clerical statesmen who loom so large for centuries to come. He intrigued incessantly, built churches, lectured kings and accumulated the great treasure that he commanded to be laid out before him in his deathbed. Nothing could be more unlike the ascetic Cuthbert of Lindisfarne, living for weeks together on a handful of raw onions or standing all day up to his neck in sea water to pray, but it was Wilfred's religion and not Cuthbert's to which the future belonged.

Because the priests of the new religion were the only literate class they became a permanent bureaucracy, easily imposing their ideas upon the slower witted kings and thanes. In no way was this more so than in the matter of property. Accustomed to absolute property rights, to written charter and to testament by will, they soon began to undermine the already weakened communal rights. We can trace the process in the institution of bookland growing up alongside of folkland. The latter, as its name implies, is land held under customary or folk rights. Even though not common property, no individual could claim absolute ownership of it, and only had possession within the framework of the township. Bookland was

B1

land granted by book or charter and its grant implied complete private ownership. The first charters were made out in favour of Church bodies, but once their advantages were realised they were increasingly sought after and obtained by the magnates.

All kinds of devices, from the invocation of the terrors of Hell to plain forgery, were adopted by the Church to secure land, and Church lands became so extensive as to be a real source of weakness to the State. They were also burdensome to the rest of the community, since they bore only a small part of their fair share of taxation and military service. These extra burdens fell on the peasantry and the endowment of the Church went hand in hand with the subjection of the cultivator.

On the other hand in its creation of a literate class, its encouragement of trade and closer contact with Europe, and, internally, by the consolidating and centralising tendency of an institution covering the whole country, the Church was a strong progressive force. The two centuries between the adoption of Christianity and the coming of the Northmen were a time of slow but solid material advance. Once more stone begins to be used for building, and if this stone was obtained mainly from the ruinous towns and villas of Roman times, and even from the roads, this was mainly because of the poverty of the more advanced parts of England in suitable building stone. Wilfred's great church at Hexam, for example, was constructed of stone taken from the Wall. The houses of the laity, even of thanes and kings, were still of timber. If rough, these houses were often spacious and well proportioned, and if they were poor as compared with the castles and manors of the upper classes after the Norman conquest the house of the Saxon peasant was probably far superior to the mud and wattle hut of the feudal serf built in a time when timber was growing less plentiful. Metal working and the illumination of manuscripts reached a high level, and a remarkable standard of learning was to be found in the best of the monasteries, especially in those of

Northumbria. It was in one of these, Jarrow, that Bede, the most learned man in the Europe of his day, and the first and one of the greatest of English historians, lived and worked.

The political history of the age is that of a series of struggles in which first Kent, then Northumbria and Mercia and finally Wessex took the lead. The fluctuations of these struggles depended in great part upon the individual capacity of the kings. Ethelbert of Kent, Edwin and Oswy of Northumbria, Penda and Offa of Mercia and Egbert of Wessex all had a big share in the temporary success of their kingdoms. Yet we can trace, if only faintly, general causes at work.

Kent's early supremacy was due to the initial cultural superiority of its Frankish invaders and its continuous contact with Europe. Its decline was due to its small area and to its failure to secure control of London and the lower Thames Valley. Northumbria's period of greatness coincides with its permeation by the advanced culture introduced by the Celtic Church, and can also perhaps be connected with the warlike character retained by its people on the bleak Northern moors. Its decline was the result of a too ambitious attempt to expand simultaneously north into Scotland and south into Mercia. It suffered also from the imperfect fusion of its two constituent parts, Deira and Bernicia, and from their internal feuds.

The reasons for the rise of Mercia are more obscure, but possibly the growth of a large and prosperous population in the rich Midland plains and the experience of war gained against the Welsh were the most important. Its weakness was the absence of good natural frontiers which laid it open to attack from all sides and exposed it to constant warfare. By contrast, Wessex was a country with good frontiers, and a hinterland in the South-west large enough to allow room for expansion but not large enough to be a menace. It had considerable areas of fertile land, and, by the end of the Eighth Century, was beginning to establish valuable contacts with the Frankish Empire of Charlemagne, just rising to its full power across the Channel.

Soon after 800 Wessex under Egbert began to draw away from its rivals, but the issue was still in doubt when the invasions of the Northmen gave a new turn to events. The full force of these invasions fell first upon Mercia and Northumbria, which were soon overrun, leaving Wessex free from its ancient rivals but face to face with a new and more formidable enemy.

4. THE NORTHMEN

In the year 793, on June the 18th, says the Chronicle, "the heathen men miserably destroyed God's church at Lindisfarne with rapine and slaughter". This brief entry opens a record of calamity and battle lasting nearly 300 years, in the course of which half England was overrun and Scandinavian ways and people had set an indelible mark upon the land.

The invaders are described indifferently as Danes or Northmen, and the two Scandinavian peoples mainly concerned are so closely akin, and their movements so interconnected that it is not always possible to be sure with which we are dealing. Their host was, indeed, often of a composite character, but in the main the Danes were the invaders of England and the Norwegians of Ireland and Scotland. These peoples, though in some ways more barbaric than the English, had developed a specialised skill that made them most dangerous enemies.

The key to their development is the great iron axe, which appears in their burial places about 600. With this they were able to clear the forests of Denmark, and to spread rapidly up the coast of Norway on the narrow strip of lowland between sea and mountain. By 700 these areas, poor and constricted at best, held almost as many people as they could support. But the axe not only made it possible for the Northmen to clear the forests, it helped them to build larger and more seaworthy ships than the North had yet seen. In these they soon made considerable voyages, and the next stage was the colonisation of the uninhabited Shetland and Faroe Islands. The first settlers were peaceful peasants, but at the end of the Eighth Century the islands began to be used as a base for piracy.

It was in one of these pirate raids that Lindisfarne was sacked, but so far as England was concerned this was an isolated episode. The movements of the Northmen are only obscure till the simple principle on which they worked is grasped. Though prepared to fight, they were not looking for fights but for loot, and their raids were always directed to that point where the greatest quantity of booty could be had with the least possibility of resistance. In 800 this point was Ireland, which had escaped both Roman and English invasions and where there was a civilisation as brilliant and rich and almost as defenceless as that of the Incas of Peru in the time of Pizzaro. It must be remembered that in early times Ireland was the chief gold-producing country of Western Europe. Though internal tribal wars were frequent, the courteous and convention-ridden Irish warriors were no match for the ferocity and cunning of the Northmen.

The first years of the Ninth Century were occupied with the pillage of Ireland. When that country had been so stripped as to cease to yield the raiders a satisfactory return for their labour, the long ships were pointed south towards the fragments of Charlemagne's great but lumbering Empire, now falling into hopeless disorder. Paris was sacked and vast tracts of France were overrun. Even more ambitious voyages were made, and in the course of one of these Rome itself was besieged in 846.

Before this date England began to occupy the attention of the Danish fleets. In 838 a large body of Danes was routed by Egbert, but in spite of defeats each year saw fresh hordes arrive. In 842 London was burned. In the winter of 850–1 the raiders wintered in Thanet instead of going home as they had previously done. From this time the raids became bolder, till, in 866, a great war host landed in a real attempt at conquest and settlement.

From the military point of view they had almost everything on their side. Iron had always been plentiful in Scandinavia, where the Swedish deposits have been worked from prehistoric times. The plunder of the previous generations gave the Northmen the means of equipping themselves with the best weapons and armour then available. They carried axes and long swords, wore iron helmets and shields, and among the pirates and professional soldiers chain armour was not uncommon.

They had also developed new methods of war. They learned to move fast at sea in their long, many-oared ships carrying up to 100 men apiece, and on land by rounding up all the horses wherever they touched and turning themselves into the first mounted infantry. In battle they learnt to combine the cohesion of the boat's crew with the flexibility of the barbarian horde. They learned also to build strong, stockaded forts, and when defeated retired behind these and defied pursuit.

The English were, in comparison, poorly armed, the mass of the fyrd having only spears and leather coats. Even the smaller body of thanes were beginning to degenerate into landowners and were not always reliable for a long campaign, while the slow moving fyrd was of little use for more than a single battle. Until Alfred built his fleet the advantage of surprise was always with the invaders. The military genius of Alfred, his capacity for learning from the enemy and then going one better, was one of the main reasons for the defeat of the Danes. The other was the undeveloped social structure of the Scandinavian peoples which made them incapable of a prolonged effort on the grand scale. The host always tended to split up into fragments when faced with unexpectedly stout resistance, each minor leader taking his men off elsewhere to look for easier game.

Yet the host that landed in East Anglia in the spring of 866 seemed formidable enough. In the next year it rode north, crushed the Northumbrians in a great battle under the walls of York, and spent the next three years

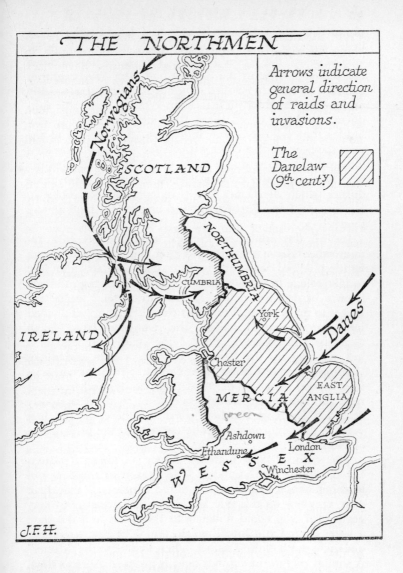

THE NORTHMEN

Arrows indicate
general direction
of raids and
invasions.

The
Danelaw
(9th cent?)

Norwegians

SCOTLAND

NORTHUMBRIA

CUMBRIA

York

IRELAND

Chester

Danes

MERCIA

EAST
ANGLIA

Ashdown

Ethandune

London

W E S S E X

Winchester

J.F.H.

plundering and subduing Mercia and East Anglia where little resistance was encountered. Early in 871, known for long after as "the year of battles", the Danes moved down the Icknield Way, as the Saxons had done four centuries before, and made a fortified camp at Reading, strategically an excellent base for an attack on Wessex. Beaten at Ashdown, their fort saved them from destruction and eight battles that followed were indecisive. At the end of the year the host made a truce with Alfred who had succeeded his brother as King in the midst of the battles. During the next four years the invasion passes through a new phase during which the Danes set up independent kingdoms in Northumbria and East Anglia and divided the land among themselves. ———

In 876 the attack on Wessex was renewed with reinforcements from overseas, and after two years of desperate fighting Alfred was surprised at Chippenham and had to take refuge in the Somerset marshes. Emerging suddenly he won a decisive victory at Ethandune and forced the Danes to make peace. From this time England was divided into roughly equal halves, the Danelaw lying north and east and Saxon England lying south and west of a line running up the River Lea to its source and along Watling Street to Chester. A renewed attempt at conquest fifteen years later was defeated more easily, and from this time the Northmen turned once more to the less stoutly defended lands of Northern France, where, in the first years of the next century, Rollo carved out the principality of Normandy.

The cultural and material havoc of these invasions can hardly be overestimated. "So great was the decay of learning among Englishmen," Alfred lamented, "that there were very few on this side Humber and I ween not many north of it who could understand the ritual and translate a letter from Latin into English. No, I cannot remember one such, south of the Thames, when I came to the throne." A similar picture in another field is given in Alfred's laws, where the scale of payments for various offences (wergild) is on the average only half that of Ethelbert's laws of two centuries earlier, a clear sign of a land stripped of its movable wealth. It is his successful efforts to arrest this decay even more than his military ability that mark Alfred as one of the greatest figures in English history.

His first task was to secure his kingdom against future invaders. To this end he had ships built superior to those of the Danes: "full nigh twice as long as the others . . . both swifter and steadier and also higher." More permanently important was his system of fortified burgs, garrisoned by trained and permanent soldiers capable of resisting minor attacks or of forming a core round which the fyrd could rally. These burgs are the earliest English towns and play an important part in the transformation of the English from a purely rural folk. Alfred's defensive arrangements enabled the mass of the people to live and work in peace and the remarkable recuperative powers of all primitive agricultural peoples had full opportunity to come into play.

Alfred encouraged learned men to come from Europe and even from Wales and in middle age taught himself to read and write both in Latin and English, a feat that Charlemagne was never able to accomplish. He sought eagerly for the best knowledge that the age afforded and in a less illiterate time would probably have attained a really scientific outlook. Constantly in ill health, never long at peace, the extent of his work is remarkable, and its thoroughness is attested by the long period of peace which followed his death. Of his successors Edward, Athelstan, Edmund and Edgar were all capable soldiers and administrators, and the period between 900 and 975 is marked by the reconquest of the Danelaw, which nevertheless kept its Scandinavian character while acknowledging the supremacy of the English kings. The two peoples were sufficiently alike in language and institutions to make tolerably good neighbours, and the Tenth Century saw the disappearance of many of the differences between them.

So far the purely destructive aspect of the Danish invasions has been stressed, but this is really only half the story. In some respects the Danes had a culture superior to that of the English. Their greater use of iron has been mentioned, and they were the introducers of the great axe into the country. We have seen that the early English settlements were restricted to narrow limits outside the dense forests that covered the richest agricultural land. When Domesday Book gives us a complete picture of English rural life we find the whole country dotted with townships. Most existing villages can be traced back to that date. It is reasonable to deduce that it was the introduction of the Danish great axe that gave the decisive impetus to forest clearing and made possible the full exploitation of the richest agricultural areas of England.

Further, as compared with the stay-at-home Saxons, the Danes were trading and town-dwelling people. When they entered England they had already travelled far. Men who had sailed the Mediterranean and seen the great city of Byzantium had no room for the superstitious dread with which the English still regarded the Romans and all their works. The Danes were traders as well as pirates, and commerce was reckoned honourable among them. "If a merchant thrived so that he fared thrice across the seas by his own means, then he was thenceforth of thane-right worthy," runs an early law, reminding us that classes among the Scandinavians as among the English were based rather upon wealth and social position than upon blood or inherited rights. The Danish invasions led everywhere to town building and increased trade, and by the time of the Norman Conquest both towns and trade had attained considerable dimensions.

5. THE END OF SAXON ENGLAND

Three generations after the death of Alfred a clearly marked degeneration of English culture and institutions set in. The now virtually complete break-up of the tribal structure had been accompanied by an advance towards feudalism, but English society seemed to be unable from its own momentum to pass beyond a certain point. It is possible that the halt was only temporary but speculation on this point is unprofitable since, in fact, two invasions, one by the Danes under Sweyn and Canute and later that of the Normans, cut short the time in which a recovery might have been made.

During the Tenth Century the consolidation of England into a single kingdom went hand in hand with the creation of an organisation into shires, often centring round Alfred's burgs or those of the Danes. While the earlier and smaller kingdoms could be administered from a single centre, there was no machinery adequate to cover the whole country and though the shire reeve or sheriff was in theory responsible to the King for the administration of the shire the actual supervision exercised from the centre was in practice slight. Above the sheriff was the Ealdorman who controlled a group of shires, often corresponding roughly to one of the old kingdoms. While the sheriff remained an official and later became the main link in the State organisation, the Ealdorman, like the Count of European countries, soon became a semi-independent territorial magnate. The powers of the Ealdorman greatly increased during the short period of Canute's Empire, when England was only a part of a much larger whole. This increase of power coincided with the adoption of the Danish title of Earl.

In the sphere of justice, also, great strides were made in the direction of feudalism by way of the delegation of royal rights to powerful individuals. The old system of shire, hundred and township courts worked fairly well only so long as no landowner in the area was so powerful as to be able to oppose their decisions. With the advent of powerful semi-feudal lords the authority of the traditional courts was weakened, and they were supplemented and in part superseded by the granting to these same lords of the right to hold courts of their own. Such rights were eagerly sought for the income produced by fines. The New Courts continued to employ the old methods of ordeal by fire or water alongside of the newer but still venerable method of compurgation or oath helping, whereby the accused brought into court a number of his neighbours, proportionate to his alleged offence, who were prepared to swear to his innocence. Private courts of justice, always among the most definite marks of feudalism, were well established in England by the time of the Norman Conquest.

The other thing which is characteristic of the manor, a servile peasantry, was also now the rule except in the Danelaw. The Danish invasions had indeed a curious dual result. In the Danelaw itself the enserfment of the cultivator was retarded while in the Saxon half of England it was accelerated. The evidence of the *Colloquies of Aelfric*, a series of dialogues written as a text-book for the boys in the monastic school at Winchester some time before 1000, is striking with its assumption that the typical cultivator was unfree.

"What do you say, ploughman, how do you do your work?" asks the teacher.

"Oh, sir, I work very hard. I go out at dawn to drive the oxen to the field, and yoke them to the plough; however hard the winter I dare not stay at home for fear of my master; and having made the share and coulter fast to the plough, every day I have to plough an acre or more."

"And what more do you do in the day?"

"A great deal more. I have to fill the oxen's bins and give them water and carry the dung outside."

"Oh, it is hard work."

"Yes, it is hard because I am not free."

The terms freeman and serf are puzzling to the modern mind, since they are used in a peculiar sense in the Feudal Age. They can only be understood with reference to the holding of land. A man without land was neither free nor unfree, he did not count.[1] A free man was one

[1] He might, of course, be a slave, but then he would be a kind of property rather than a person.

who held land on condition of military service, or of some other service reckoned honourable, or one who paid a money rent. The serf or villein was he who held land on condition of performing agricultural labour on his lord's land. He was bound to the soil, whereas the freeman could leave his land and go elsewhere or even in some cases take his land, as the saying went, and commend himself to another lord. In a time when to be landless was the worst of all misfortunes it was not so terrible a thing to be bound to the soil as it might seem today. The serf had his own rights, precisely defined by custom even where not legally enforceable. One of the results of the Norman Conquest was to draw the line between serf and freeman—a very vague line in Saxon England—higher up in the social scale and to reduce everyone below this line to a dead level of servitude.

Late in the Tenth Century the Danish invasions were renewed under Sweyn, who had managed to unite Denmark and Norway under his rule. The intervening period had been largely filled with inroads on Northern France, but with the establishment of a strong Scandinavian principality in Normandy the centre of attack shifted. The wealth and degeneration of England, of which the Danes must have been well aware, made it once more the most profitable objective. These new attacks were organised on a curiously commercial plan, a preliminary harrying being followed by a demand for the payment of money as a condition of withdrawal. Every couple of years the operation was repeated.

These payments of Danegeld, as it was called, were made seven times between 991 and 1014 and totalled 158,000 pounds of silver, equal to at least £10,000,000 in modern money, a gigantic sum for this period. When Canute became king in 1018 and paid off his army, a final geld of 82,500 pounds was extorted. From this Danegeld grew the first regular taxation. Under Canute and the Norman kings it was levied regularly, and it became the basis of a property tax that was an important part of the Budget of all kings until the Stuart period. Its social results were equally far reaching, since it came as a crushing burden upon the cultivator, driving him ever more rapidly into servitude. It increased correspondingly the power of the local magnates who were made responsible for its collection and used this office as a further lever to establish their power as lords of the land and its tillers. The feudal maxims of 'No man without a lord' and 'No land without a lord' can be fully applied to England from this time.

Another feature of these invasions was the leadership of the citizens of London in organising resistance. When the Central Government under Ethelred the Redeless collapsed miserably London stood firm. Already greater beyond comparison than any other English town, it now begins to appear in history almost as an independent political force. So great was its importance that we read that in 1016 the fyrd of Mercia refused to move against the Danes "unless they had the support of the burgesses of London". Year after year the Danes were driven back rom its walls, and it only surrendered when resistance elsewhere was virtually at an end. Its wealth can be judged from the fact that when the great geld of 1018 was levied, London had to pay 10,500 pounds of silver, more than one eighth of the total for the whole country.

When in 1018 Canute, son of Sweyn, became King of England as well as of Norway and Denmark it appeared for the moment as if the future of England was to be linked with the Scandinavian lands rather then with France. But the social structure of the Northern peoples was still largely tribal and so inadequate for the basis of a permanent empire. The unity temporarily achieved depended too much on the personality of an individual and ended with his death. It was not till Northern energy had been crossed with French feudal institutions that it was capable of advancing towards a permanent State power.

One further development under Canute was the formation of a small standing army of highly trained, paid, professional soldiers, the housecarls. A recurrent tendency within feudalism is for the feudal or semi-feudal soldier class (knights or thanes) to evolve into landowners and to become less willing to perform military duties. The formation of the housecarls under Canute is thus a close parallel to the replacement of the feudal knight by the professional mercenary during the Hundred Years' War. The one other thing that must be noted in this reign is the rise of the house of Godwin from obscurity to virtual control of all England outside the Danelaw.

When Canute died his sons were incapable of holding his dominions together and the Godwins were able to restore the old English line without opposition. The new king, Edward the Confessor, was a pious half-wit who had spent his youth as an exile in Normandy. When he returned he brought a train of Norman monks and nobles to whom he gave the best and richest bishoprics and lands. The history of his reign is one of constant struggle between the Norman influence at court and the power of the Godwins. The permeation of England by the Normans was one of the main reasons for the ease with which their conquest was carried through.

Eventually the Godwins triumphed, and established complete control over the King, a control similar to that exercised by the contemporary Capetians over the French descendants of Charlemagne. All England was now divided into six great earldoms, and of these three were held by the Godwins. When Edward died in January 1066, the Witan, or council of wise men, a body with some of the characteristics of the Teutonic folk moot and more of the feudal King's Council, proclaimed Harold, eldest son of Godwin, king. William, Duke of Normandy, also claimed the throne and began to assemble an army to enforce his claim.

The conquest of England by the Normans can be regarded both as the last of the hostings of the Northmen and the first of the Crusades. Though William was a feudal prince his army was not a feudal army but one gathered from all quarters by the promise of land and plunder. He safeguarded himself with an elaborate chain of alliances, including one with the Pope that formed the basis for many later claims and disputes. His army was not large—perhaps about 12,000—but was trained in methods of warfare unknown in England. The English had learnt from the Danes to use horses to move swiftly from place to place, but continued to fight on foot in a dense mass behind the traditional shield wall. Their principal weapon was the axe. The Normans employed a skilful combination of heavy armoured cavalry and crossbowmen which enabled them to break up the ranks of their opponents from a distance before pushing home a decisive charge. Once the shield wall was broken the effectiveness of the cavalry in pursuit made recovery out of the question. This was the military reason for William's victory, just as the political reason was his firm control over his vassals as compared with the defiant attitude adopted by the Earls of Mercia and Northumbria towards Harold.

All through the summer of 1066 Harold waited in Sussex for the Normans to land. Early in September the patience of the fyrd broke and they insisted on going home. A few days later Harold heard that his namesake the King of Norway had landed in the North and taken York. With his housecarls he rode swiftly north, and routed the invaders at Stamford Bridge on September 25th. On the 1st of October he learnt of the landing of William at Pevensey. Within a week he was back in London, waited there a few days for the fyrd to gather and moved south to take up his position at Battle, on a chalk ridge overlooking William's camp. Tactically, the speed and decision of Harold's movements was masterly, and his housecarls proved a magnificent fighting machine. Strategically, he would have been wiser to have waited longer in London. As it was, only a part of the fyrd had time to assemble, and the housecarls, who alone could be relied on to stand up to the Norman cavalry, were worn out by a hard won victory and two marches almost without parallel in the history of the time.

Yet the new military methods of the Normans made their victory all but inevitable, and one battle was enough to decide the future of England for centuries to come. The Chronicle records this battle in words moulded to a formula that had become almost obligatory when describing the warfare of the English kings, and with a curious brevity that seems to emphasise its decisiveness:

"Tidings were brought to King Harold, and he gathered then the great host and came towards him at the Hoar Apple Tree, and William came against him unawares ere his people were mustered. But the King nevertheless withstood him very bravely with the men that would follow him, and there was a mighty slaughter wrought on both sides. There was slain King Harold and his brothers, the Earls Leofwine and Gyrth, and many good men, and the Frenchmen held the place of slaughter."

CHAPTER III

FEUDAL ENGLAND

1. THE CONQUEST

At SENLAC WILLIAM had broken the power of the Godwins and laid all England south of the Thames open to invasion. The Midlands and North were still unconquered, and London once more formed the central point round which resistance was gathering and towards which Edwin and Morcar, the Earls of Mercia and Northumbria, were slowly moving. William's army was too small to make a direct assault on London. Instead, he carried out a brilliant outflanking march, crossed the Thames higher up, devastating the countryside as he advanced, and finally cutting the city off from the North and so from all hope of reinforcements.

London surrendered, a hastily summoned meeting of the Witan proclaimed William king, and on Christmas Day he was crowned at Westminster. All the land of those who had given support to Harold or fought at Senlac was confiscated and divided among William's Norman followers. The rest of England, having acknowledged William as king, was left undisturbed. By 1069 William was ready for the next stage in the conquest, Mercia and Northumbria were goaded into revolt, and received the support of the King of Denmark.

After a campaign that showed William's military genius at its best, this combination was defeated. The conqueror set to work, with a cold ferocity far more terrible than the fury of the Northmen, to make a repetition of the rising impossible. The greater part of Yorkshire and Durham was laid waste and remained almost unpeopled for a generation. It was not till the Pennine slopes were turned into great sheep farms by the Cistercian monks in the Twelfth Century that the region really recovered. Above the burnt villages of the North rose the great castle of Durham to assure the permanency of the new order. The completion of the conquest was followed by a fresh confiscation of lands and a new division among the Normans.

It is at this point that we can say that feudalism is fully established in England. We have seen how the economic basis of feudalism was evolved out of the English township, and how political organisation was taking on a feudal form even before the Conquest. Now the fashioning of a political superstructure to match the economic basis was completed with a rigid and dogmatic uniformity by the Normans. Within a few years the whole of the land of the country passed out of the hands of its old owners and into the hand of the Conqueror.

The essential political feature of feudalism was the downward delegation of power, and all power was based upon the ownership of land. The King was the sole and ultimate owner of all the land, and granted it to his tenants-in-chief in return for military and other services and for the payment of certain customary dues. With the land was granted also the political right of governing its cultivators: the right to hold courts of justice, to levy taxes and to exact services. So far as the King was concerned the most important duty of his vassals was to follow him in war, and so the whole country was divided up into areas, corresponding roughly to the older thane holdings, but much more regular and approximately equal, each of which was bound to provide and equip one heavy armed cavalryman for the Army. These areas, called Knight's Fees, tended to coincide with the economic unit of the manor.

Just because England was conquered within a few years and the political institutions of feudalism deliberately imposed from above, the system here reached a higher regularity and completeness than in most other countries. Elsewhere the King's ownership of all the land was a fiction. Here it was a fact, and the King granted land to his vassals on his own terms, terms extremely favourable to himself. As the Chronicle says: "The King gave his land as dearly for rent as he possibly could; then came some other and bade more than the other had before given, and the King let it to the man who had bidden him more. . . . And he recked not how very sinfully the reeve got it from the poor men, nor how many iniquities they did; but the more that was said about right law, the more illegalities were done."

Feudalism was always in theory a contract between king and vassal, but in England this contract was more a reality than it was elsewhere.

The very completeness with which feudalism was imposed in England created immediately the possibility of a State organisation transcending the feudal system. This State organisation was built around William's power as the military leader of a victorious army and around the pre-Conquest shire organisation of the Saxons. William was able to grant land to his followers in scattered holdings. He was, in fact, forced to do this, since the country was conquered piecemeal, and as each new area came under control he granted what his followers regarded as an instalment of the reward that was due to them. For this reason there was no baron in England, however much land he might hold in all, who was able to concentrate very large forces in any one area. Further, the Crown retained enough land in its own possession to ensure that the King was far stronger than any baron or any likely combination of barons. Apart from his hundreds of manors, William claimed all the forest lands, estimated at the time to comprise one-third of the country. It is unlikely that he did this merely because "he loved the tall deer as if he had been their father". More probably he sensed the huge possibilities of development in these still unexploited tracts.

With the exception of Chester and Shrewsbury, which were border earldoms planned to hold the Welsh in check, and the County of Durham under its Prince Bishop which served the same purpose against the Scots, no great principalities whose holders might become semi-independent princes as many of the French feudal nobles had done, were allowed to arise in England. Consequently, the sheriff, the representative of the Central Government in each county, remained stronger than any baron in his territory. And, since it was not necessary to strengthen the sheriffs unduly to enable them to control the local nobility, there was no danger of the sheriffs in their turn making themselves independent of the Crown.

England had, therefore, a development that was unique in European history. From the start the power of the State was greater and the power of the feudal nobility less. Private war between nobles was the exception rather than the rule, and private armies and castles were jealously watched by the Crown and prohibited as far as possible. The agents of the Crown were certainly oppressive, and the exploitation of the villein masses was severe. But these exactions of the Crown were to some extent fixed and regular, and a limit was set to the much more oppressive exactions of the feudal lords.

There is plenty of evidence that the English regarded the power of the Crown as a protection against their own immediate superiors. When in 1075 there was a revolt of the barons who were disappointed at the restrictions placed upon them, William was able to call out the fyrd to suppress it. The harshness of the conquest was soon forgotten by a peasantry who had been accustomed to conquest and pillage during the long Danish invasions, and who regarded William's severe but firm rule as preferable to an anarchy in which they were always the worst sufferers. The alliance between the King and the Saxon population remained a constant feature during the generations that followed the Conquest. In the reign of Henry I, when a baronial rising attempted to place his brother Robert, Duke of Normandy, on the throne, Henry was able to invade Normandy with a mainly Saxon army which defeated Robert and his feudal forces at the Battle of Tenchebray in 1105.

The century and a half between the Conquest and Magna Charta was the period during which feudalism existed in its most complete form in England. Yet it would be a mistake to imagine that at any time during these years things stood still. The common conception of the Middle Ages as a period of stability or of barely perceptible change is very wide of the mark, for not only every century but each successive generation had its specific characteristics, its important departures and developments. It is quite impossible to put one's finger on any date and to say, "At this moment feudalism in England exists perfectly and completely."

Throughout the period there was a constant struggle between the centralising power of the Crown and the feudal tendency towards regionalism. While the main trend was always towards increased central authority, this authority developed within the framework of feudal institutions which limited and conditioned it. Some of the forces at work were general forces common to all Europe, others sprang from the special conditions created by the survival of pre-feudal Saxon institutions, and others again from the geographical situation of the country. We have now to trace the progress of this struggle in the history of the time and to observe the growth of new combinations of class forces both locally and nationally.

2. THE SOCIAL STRUCTURE OF DOMESDAY ENGLAND

Twenty years after the Conquest William sent commissioners to almost every town, village and hamlet throughout England with power to call together the leading men of the townships, to examine them, and to make a complete survey of the economic life of the country.

They asked all kinds of questions: How much land? Who holds it? What is it worth? How many ploughs? How many tenants? How many oxen, sheep, swine? The inquisition was highly unpopular: "It is shameful to tell but he thought it no shame to do," grumbles a monastic chronicler resentfully. Yet nothing shows more conclusively the completeness of the conquest, nor of William's power than the carrying through of the Domesday Survey within twenty years of Senlac. It is without parallel in any other country. It would have been equally impossible in Saxon England or in feudal France, but there is not the slightest sign that any effective opposition was made to it even by the most powerful of the barons.

The survey had two objects: first to provide the necessary information for the levying of the geld or property tax, and second, to give the King a detailed knowledge of the extent and distribution of the wealth, lands and revenues of his vassals. For us it has a greater importance, in that it affords a comprehensive if not absolutely accurate picture of the social structure of England at the time when it was made. The unit of agricultural economy was the manor, which had been imposed upon and roughly coincided with the earlier township. It must be remembered, of course, that the country was still overwhelmingly agricultural. Some of these manors were held directly by the King: the rest were held from him by a number of vassals, lay and ecclesiastical. They in turn had a larger or smaller number of sub-vassals who were the actual holders of the manors. Every village, however small and remote, had to fit into this framework, and society was graded into a series of groups mounting step by step from the serf at the bottom to the King at the top.

The Domesday Survey classified the cultivators of the soil into classes, and even numbered them, so that it is possible to present a rough statistical account of the population, remembering that account is only taken of the adult males who were the actual holders of tenements. The result can be tabulated as follows:

Class.	Proportion of total Population.	Number.
Slaves . . .	9%	25,000
Bordars and cotters	32%	89,000
Villeins . .	38%	106,000
Freemen . .	12%	33,000

Multiplying these figures by five to make an average family, allowing for the classes not included (lords and their direct dependants and manorial officials, priests, monks and nuns, merchants and craftsmen, landless wage labourers and isolated cultivators who may have escaped the net of the Domesday commissioners), the total population may be estimated at somewhere between two million and one and three-quarter million.

The classes actually mentioned in the Survey were distributed unevenly in various parts of the country. Slaves were most numerous in the South-west, rising to 24 per cent of the total in Gloucestershire, 21 per cent in Cornwall and Hampshire, and 17 per cent in Shropshire. In Lincoln, Yorkshire and Huntingdon, they are not mentioned at all, and there were very few in East Anglia, or the East Midlands. Bordars and cotters were more evenly distributed, few counties having more than 40 per cent or less than 20 per cent of their population in this class. Villeins were also evenly distributed, except that they were less common in East Anglia and Lincoln where there were many free tenants, and in Essex and Hampshire where bordars and cotters were specially numerous. Free tenants were only found in the East and East Midlands, the counties of the old Danelaw. In Lincoln they form 45 per cent of the total, in Suffolk 40 per cent, and in Norfolk 32 per cent. Numerous in Nottingham, Leicester and Northampton, they hardly appear in any other counties. For convenience the closely similar group known as socmen has been reckoned as free.

To examine these classes separately and to trace their fortunes through the succeeding generations will perhaps be the best way of outlining the social history of this period.

Slaves were, by the time of Domesday, a rapidly vanishing class. For the most part they were house-servants or shepherds and ploughmen on the lord's domain. The lords were finding it more economical to hire personal attendants and to work their domain lands with the forced labour of the serfs. By about 1200 slaves have disappeared, becoming completely absorbed into the classes of villeins and cotters above them.

Bordars and cotters, who appear to have been the same kind of people listed under different names in different parts of the country, have been mentioned already. They were the holders of small patches of land outside the framework of the open-field system. Though most of them were serfs, some were reckoned as free tenants, and when the tide set away from serfdom in the Thirteenth Century they tended to free themselves more rapidly than the villeins who were bound up in the joint agriculture of the manor. Many who were craftsmen paid dues in the products of their craft, cloth, smithy or wood-work, instead of in labour on the lord's domain. This was considered less servile, and with reason, since the crafts-men did their work as individuals instead of under the direct supervision of the manor officials.

The villeins, holders of fifteen- or thirty-acre shares in the common fields, were the pivot around which the whole life of the manor revolved. Their services were regularised and most often increased after the Conquest. They were of two kinds: day work, and boon work. Day work was performed on a regular number of days a week, usually three. Boon work consisted of extra labour which might be demanded at any time. It was the more dis-liked of the two, and the harder to get free from, since it came at times, such as harvest and sheep shearing, when the serf's work was most needed both on the lord's domain and on his own land. It is clear from the amount of labour services due from the villein that the bulk of the work in his own holding must have been performed by the other members of his family, just as in Africa today the incidence of the hut tax takes the adult males away from the village and throws the work of the villages upon the women and children.

The relation of villein to cotter was close. Cotter tenements were often held by members of villein families for whom there were no shares in the common fields, while the cotters formed a reserve from which villein holdings could be stocked if they fell vacant. As time went on the two classes tended to be more and more lumped together by the lawyers under the common name of villein or serf.

Like the slaves, the freemen of Domesday were a declining class. Even in 1086 many who were free before the Conquest had come to be reckoned unfree as a result of the changes in ownership of the land, and the whole tendency of the time was to consider any peasant as a serf unless he could prove himself otherwise beyond any question. After the Domesday period the free disappeared rapidly, and when we once again find free smallholders in number towards the middle of the Thirteenth Century they are not usually the direct successors of the *libri homines* of Domesday but are villeins who, by one means or another, have managed to win a certain measure of freedom.

The Normans introduced into England a body of written and rigid feudal law which tended to force all cultivators into the one mould, that of serfs, "possessing nothing but their own bellies" as the saying went, and with no legal rights against the lord of the manor except that they might not be killed or mutilated without a proper trial. This meant an improvement of the status of the slave, but for the rest of the population it was a step backwards, and the time is one of increasing burdens and general misery.

Every trick of the lawyer was used to add to these burdens, and besides his heavy labour services the villein had all sorts of disabilities. The village mill, for example, was the lord's, and all corn must come to it to be ground. So common a ground was this privilege for abuse that there is hardly a single miller in the whole of popular medieval literature who is not a rogue. Then, just as the King claimed all the forests, the lord of the manor claimed exclusive rights over the village waste. When these rights were strictly enforced they meant no more turf or wood cutting by the villeins and no pasture for his swine. The long series of Game Laws that have lain like a blight upon rural England for centuries begin at this time. Worst of all, perhaps, all land that was won back from the waste was added to the lord's domain and was not available for extending the common fields.

On the whole, and after due allowance has been made for local peculiarities, we can apply to England the generalisation made by a contemporary of King John, the Pope Innocent III: "The serf serves; he is terrified with threats, wearied by corvées [forced services], afflicted with blows, despoiled of his possessions; for, if he possesses nought he is compelled to earn; and if he possesses anything he is compelled to have it not; the lord's fault is the serf's punishment; the serf's fault is the lord's excuse for preying on him. . . . O extreme condition of bondage! Nature brought freemen to birth but fortune hath made bondmen. The serf must needs suffer, and no man is suffered to feel for him, he is compelled to mourn, and no man is permitted to mourn with him. He is not his own man, but no man is his!"

Such was the legal view, which the lords and their clerks fought to apply universally. In practice law was modified by custom, and on the average manor and in average times the serf had a rough security. Lawyers might say that a serf "ought not to know one day what labour he will be commanded to perform the next". In practice the whole year's work was probably known with a monotonous certainty. If nothing else served, the very obstinacy and conservatism of the villein, his refusal to change his ways, was a formidable weapon with which to defend the barricade of the ancient customs. For more than two centuries a battle raged in every manor between this peasant obstinacy and the craft of the Norman lawyer. At the start the lawyer won spectacular victories, but beyond a certain point he was never able to go. Even at the worst there remained on the manor a core of rights that kept the serf a person and not a thing, a residue of freedom which served as a starting point for the gaining of new rights when, in the Thirteenth Century, economic forces began to work powerfully in another direction, transforming the serf into a free wage-labourer or a small-holder paying rent for his land instead of labour services.

This perpetual village conflict must be kept in mind when we come to interpret the political history of the period, for the one helps to explain the other, and either alone is insufficient to enable us to understand the drift of the age.

3. STATE: BARON: CHURCH

The Conqueror's two sons, William II and Henry I, continued to strengthen the power of the State at the expense of the feudal nobles. Henry, who was remarkable among the kings of his time in that he could read and write, and so knew how to value and make good use of a literate bureaucracy, was responsible for a number of changes. He began his reign with an attempt to conciliate the Saxons by compiling and reaffirming the old laws that were by now being quite mistakenly attributed to Edward the Confessor. These laws he combined as far as possible with the newer conceptions introduced by Norman feudalism.

Henry began a process which was in time to take the administration of justice out of the hands of private individuals and make it solely the affair of the State. In earlier times a crime had been merely an offence against the victim or his family, and was therefore to be settled by suitable payment to the sufferers. Now it began to be established that a crime was also an offence against the King's peace for which it was the right and duty of the State to exact punishment.

Travelling judges were sent out to hold courts, and a new form of procedure was employed—trial by jury. In its early form the jury was a selected body of men who were obliged on oath to 'present' for trial all the people in their district who were believed to have committed crimes. They were not chosen for their real or supposed impartiality but because they were believed to know the facts already. Trial by jury was not thought of as a right of the individual but as the special privilege of the King. It was a new form of judicial machinery devised to attract cases into the royal courts and no one else was entitled to make use of this machinery without paying for it. The State's interest in administering justice was mainly financial: "There's big money in justice" would be a rough translation of a legal maxim current at the time. The Crown wished to attract cases to its own courts for the sake of the fines to be levied, and if the growth of the King's courts did weaken the power of the nobility this was rather the result of accident than of design.

Almost all of Henry's innovations had a financial object, and one of the most important was the establishment of a special department, the Exchequer, to deal with the collection of revenue. Much of the King's income came from the Crown manors, the rest from the geld and the various feudal dues and tallages. All these were collected by the sheriff in each county and paid over to the Exchequer. The Exchequer was a special development of the King's Council, a feudal body which originally consisted of the tenants-in-chief or as many of them as the King thought it convenient to consult. Quite early the Council began to split up into departments. The Council itself, assembling all the chief nobles and Church dignitaries, was the origin of Parliament. A smaller body which could be consulted from day to day grew into the Privy Council and indirectly into the modern Cabinet. Other committees grew into the King's Bench, the Exchequer, and other courts. These developments mostly lie far ahead and are noted here for convenience. At the time they were not thought of as separate bodies but as different forms that the Council might take for doing particular jobs, and all in theory remained equally the King's Council. What is important is that it was out of this feudal body that a permanent bureaucracy evolved to carry out the work of the Central Government.

On Henry's death these developments were checked because he left only a daughter, Matilda, to succeed him. A powerful group of barons refused to recognise her and supported Stephen of Blois, Henry's nephew. Twenty years of war followed, neither side being able to win a complete victory. It was a time that left a lasting impression on the minds of the people. All the worst tendencies of feudalism, which had been suppressed under the Norman kings, now had free play. Private wars and private castles sprang up everywhere. Hundreds of local tyrants massacred, tortured and plundered the unfortunate peasantry and chaos reigned everywhere. "Never were martyrs tormented as these were," writes a chronicler who recorded the wretchedness of the times.

Yet what is significant about the events of Stephen's reign is not its misery but its uniqueness, the fact that such conditions, normal in many parts of Europe, only arose in England under the special circumstances of a disputed succession and a crown too weak to enforce order. This taste of the evils of unrestrained feudal anarchy was sharp enough to make the masses welcome a renewed attempt of the Crown to diminish the power of the nobles but not long enough for disorder to win a permanent hold. In 1153 the two parties met at Wallingford and a compromise was reached. Stephen was to reign during his life and Matilda's son, Henry of Anjou, was to succeed him.

In the next year Stephen died. Henry, adding England and Normandy to his own large domains, became unquestionably the most powerful monarch in Western Europe. Though in theory his continental possessions, the larger and richer half of France, were held from the French king on a feudal tenure, he was in fact their absolute ruler. He began at once to break down the power which the barons had acquired during the previous reign. Hundreds of castles were destroyed, and in their place began to be built the unfortified manor houses that were the characteristic dwelling places of the upper classes in England throughout the remainder of the Middle Ages.

The State machinery which Henry I had set up was overhauled and extended. More and more powers were given to the travelling commissioners who represented the King in all parts of the country, and Henry himself travelled unceasingly over his domains. These travels were in part necessary because much of the royal revenue was still paid in the form of corn, meat and other produce of the Crown estates. In a time when land transport was slow and costly, the only way in which this produce could be used was for the King and his court to go from manor to manor and consume it on the spot.

Increased use was made of the sheriffs as permanent representatives of the Crown. At the same time they were kept under the closest control and some sort of limits were put to their habits of enriching themselves by the double process of fleecing the population of the shires and defrauding the Crown of the payments that were due to it. In 1170 a general purge, the so-called 'Inquest of Sheriffs' was held and more than half were dismissed and replaced by others more closely connected with the royal exchequer. The interest of the Crown was to discourage unauthorised exactions so that its own revenue could be as large as possible. Almost every reform of this age has as its object the increasing and better collection of the King's dues.

Apart from the barons, the increasing power of the State had to meet the claims of the Church to be recognised as an independent, international organisation transcending all national limits. The struggle between Church and State in England was only a part of a battle that extended all over Europe with varying results. In Germany, the Emperor Henry IV was forced to make a humble submission to Pope Gregory VII at Canossa in 1177, while in France the substance of victory rested with the Crown. The dispute turned on the dual character of the Church and its officers. On the one hand, bishops and abbots were feudal lords with vast lands and revenues. On the other, they were representatives of a power with an international organisation and headquarters at Rome. The Crown wished to appoint and control them as feudal magnates: the Papacy claimed to appoint and control them as its representatives. The situation was complicated because the bureaucracy on which the Crown depended was almost entirely composed of churchmen, and, in general, the Church supported the State against the barons while pushing its own claim to independence. Later, the success of the baronial revolt against John was largely due to the exceptional support which the rebels received from the Church.

Under William I an uneasy equilibrium was maintained, but in the next reign a long battle over Investitures—the right to appoint the leading officials of the Church—opened. Not till 1106 was a compromise reached, by which the Crown won the right to choose the new bishops, who were then elected by their cathedral chapters, formally invested by the Pope, and finally did homage to the King as feudal vassals. In substance this was a victory for the Crown.

Under Henry II the struggle took a new form. While the Crown was attempting to bring more and more cases within the scope of its own courts, the Church claimed the right to try all clerics in special ecclesiastical courts. These courts operated under the Canon Law and inflicted penalties much lighter than those of the ordinary courts. It must be remembered that clerics included not only priests but also a much larger number of people in minor orders, a class so large and important that it came to be assumed that any man who could read was a cleric and was entitled to be tried under Canon Law. The central figure of the struggle was Thomas Becket, who sums up in his personality and career the curious dual position of the Church in his age. The son of a rich London merchant, he entered the King's service and became Chancellor, working with great energy to implement Henry's centralising reforms. When Henry wished to extend these to the Church he made Becket Archbishop of Canterbury, expecting him to carry out his plans. Becket had other ideas and opposed the King as vigorously as he had before worked with him.

After a long struggle Henry was rash enough to allow some of his followers to murder the Archbishop. The scandal that followed, probably deliberately worked up by the Church, was so great that Henry was forced to drop his plans and to allow the Church courts to continue to deal with all criminal charges against clerics. The practice of 'benefit of clergy' went on right up to the Reformation. Becket's murder had one curious and unexpected result. He was canonised and his tomb became the most popular of all resorts for pilgrims. Two centuries later, the first great classic of the English language, made possible by the fusion of Saxon with Norman French, was written. It was the *Canterbury Tales*, and recorded the conversation and pastimes of a group of typical pilgrims riding to the shrine of St. Thomas.

Yet the victory of the Church was not complete. The State had to surrender criminal cases: civil cases it retained. And during this period there grew up what came to be called the Common Law, a body of law holding good throughout the land and overriding all local laws and customs. This Common Law was based in the main on the principles and practice of the Anglo-Saxon law of

C1

the pre-Conquest days. Because of the strength of the Common Law, Roman Law, which became the basis of most European codes, was never acclimatised into England. As a result the ecclesiastical Canon Law, based on Roman principles, was isolated and weakened and remained alien to the main tendency of legal development. Here we meet another of the puzzling cross-currents characteristic of the class relations of the feudal period. Whereas the Church in the main supported the centralising designs of the Crown against the barons, the latter were opposed to the power of the Church courts. These courts took cases away from the local feudal jurisdiction just as much as from the Crown courts, and the barons were suspicious of any attempt on the part of the Church to introduce Roman Law because of the support which it gave to State absolutism. Reasons of this kind explain the unstable alliances and constant shifting of support which mark the three-cornered antagonism of Crown, barons and Church in the Middle Ages.

4. FOREIGN RELATIONS

After the Norman Conquest the Kings of England continued to be Dukes of Normandy and even used England as a base from which to extend their domains in France. In the same way, the large section of William's followers who were also feudal lords in Normandy continued to hold their estates in both sides of the Channel. For at least a century and a half the ruling class in England was a foreign ruling class, or, from another point of view, a class with a double nationality. Until at least the end of the Thirteenth Century French was its normal language, and when Chaucer, writing his *Canterbury Tales* as late as 1380, mildly satirises the Prioress who spoke French,

" . . . . full faire and fetisly
After the scole of Stratford atte Bowe,"

we are not intended to conclude that the French of Stratford atte Bowe was not still tolerably good.

The bi-national character of kings and barons, the fact that at first they were even more at home in France than in England, determined the main direction of foreign relations. It was no more than a matter of routine for the kings and those of the barons who had interests across the Channel to spend half their summers campaigning in France. At first England was valued, probably, more for the men and treasures it could provide for these adventures than for any other reason.

Of far greater importance than these wars, which had few permanent results and whose details are now forgotten, were the new economic links forged, the new fields of trade and articles of merchandise, the new crafts introduced by foreign artisans. Not all those who followed the Conqueror were soldiers. Many were traders who were drawn as if by a magnet to London as the inevitable centre of the commerce of Northern Europe. London's growth has been referred to already, and its pre-eminence was now assured. It was the depot for all the trade of the rich English lowlands. It lay opposite the mouth of the Rhine, main highway for trade between the Mediterranean and the North. It had already close trading connections with Scandinavia and the Baltic. By the time of Ethelred 'men of the Emperor', merchants from the Rhineland probably, had a permanent settlement there. Others from the Hanse towns of North Germany and the Baltic followed.

Now a new influx, this time of Normans and Flemings, arrived, attracted, as a contemporary writer expressly says, "inasmuch as it was fitter for their trading and better stored with the merchandise in which they were wont to traffic."

Apart from London, a lively trade across the Channel from the ports of the South coast and from such places as Lynn, Boston and Ipswich to Flanders and the Baltic grew up. If the volume of this trade was small by present day standards, it included a number of absolutely vital commodities such as iron, salt and cloth. Little iron was mined and smelted in England till the Fifteenth Century, the bulk of what was used coming from Sweden and the north of Spain. At a time when the general price level was about one-twentieth of that of to-day wrought iron cost as much as £14 a ton. The dearness of iron was one of the greatest handicaps to agricultural progress and it was used with the utmost economy in farm implements. Harrows, for example, were almost always of wood, and in the plough only the share and coulter were made of iron. Wool and cloth were also disproportionately dear. Readers of the ballad *The Old Cloak* will remember that the goodman speaks of his cloak as a lifelong possession, and garments were often handed down by will from generation to generation. Only the roughest kind of homespun was made in England, the finer cloths being imported from Flanders. Salt too, though a little was obtained from brine pans around the coast, was mostly imported from the South-west of France.

With the Norman Conquest the list of imports was considerably increased. Wine from Gascony, a greater quantity and variety of fine cloths, spices from the East, and, most surprisingly, so bulky a commodity as building stone, begin to feature prominently. Many of the Norman castles and churches around the coast and on navigable rivers were built from stone quarried round Caen. Exports, according to a list given by Henry of Huntingdon, a writer of the middle of the Twelfth Century, included wool, lead, tin and cattle. The rule of the English kings on both sides of the Channel made travel relatively safe for merchants over a wide area and discouraged piracy in the Narrow Seas.

Besides the merchants, skilled artisans also began to enter England. The Normans were skilled builders in stone, and must have needed many foreign masons to raise their churches and castles. William I, who had married the daughter of the Count of Flanders, encouraged the settlement of Flemish weavers. These settlements began immediately after, if not in some cases before, the Conquest. We find, for example, that the Suffolk village of Flempton appears in Domesday as Flemingtuna. The parish church of this village is still dedicated to Saint Catherine whose fortuitous connection with the wheel made her the patron saint of textile workers. The Flemings were scattered widely over the country till Henry I forced a great many of them to settle in South Wales.

It is in connection with these weavers that we can detect the first faint signs of what looks like a class struggle in the towns. The gilds of merchants that were beginning to grow up in the Twelfth Century often made regulations to prevent the weavers from securing the rights of burgesses. There is not, however, enough evidence to make it certain whether the merchants were attempting to keep the weavers in an inferior position as artisans or whether it was merely the opposition of the established natives of the towns to foreign intruders.

As trade grew, the centre of gravity shifted, and England grew more important to kings and barons than Normandy or Anjou. And as his English estates became more and more the centre of his interest the baron began to be unwilling to spend his summers following the King in his French campaigns. A feudal army was in any case only bound to serve in the field for forty days in any year. This might do for a war between two neighbouring European States or baronies, but was far too short for an expedition from England to France. To meet this difficulty Henry II began to allow and even encourage his barons to make a payment called scutage as a substitute for personal service in the field. The proceeds were used to hire troops for the duration of a campaign.

Scutage was an important step towards the growth of a money economy out of the essentially personal relations of feudalism. Gradually, though not to any great extent in this period, it had the effect of encouraging the barons to take money payments from their own serfs instead of the customary labour dues. Similar developments resulted from the Crusades which began in 1096.

The Crusades were wars of a transitional character, mingling some of the features of the expeditions of the

Northmen in search of plunder and lands with others characteristic of the later wars of trade and dynastic conquest. At first, especially, they were undertaken not by kings but by barons who wished to carve out new fiefs richer and more independent than those they already held. In these early Crusades the barons of the regions conquered in France and Italy by the Northmen were the most active. The regular armies were in some cases preceded by hordes of land-hungry peasants who straggled across Europe plundering and being attacked till they perished miserably.

At the same time, the Crusades were a counter-attack against a new invasion of Moslems who threatened to cut the trade routes to the East and even menaced Constantinople. A religious motive was added by setting the Holy Places at Jerusalem as the objective, but Palestine was then, as now, the strategical key to the Levant. In any case, the Moslem invasion had put a stop to the stream of pilgrims going to Jerusalem, and these pilgrimages were a highly organised business, as vital to some parts of the Mediterranean as the tourist trade is to modern Switzerland. The Papacy took the lead in organising the Crusades as a method of increasing its political power.

England took little part in the earlier Crusades in which Jerusalem was captured and a 'Latin Kingdom' set up there. The reason was, first, that the English barons were busy establishing themselves in their newly won domains, and, later, because Wales and Ireland afforded the more adventurous and land-hungry type of baron such as formed the core of the crusading armies a similar but more promising outlet nearer home.

In the Third Crusade, whose occasion was the recapture of Jerusalem by the armies of Saladin, the kings of Europe first took a direct share. Prominent among these kings were Philip of France and Richard I of England. For the first time in history English ships entered the Mediterranean, and the adoption of St. George by Richard as his patron saint was at once a symbol and a direct result of his alliance with the rising maritime republic of Genoa.

The Crusade itself was a failure, immensely costly in lives and treasure, and Richard, having spent one fortune in preparing his expedition, had to raise a second to ransom himself from the Emperor of Germany by whom he was captured while returning. Nevertheless, it led to the establishment of direct and permanent connections between England and the trading cities of Italy, that is, to her entry into world as opposed to local trade.

In England itself one of the first results of the Crusade was a pogrom directed against the Jews. They had come into the country soon after the Conquest, and were regarded as the special property of the King. They were barred from all ordinary trade and industry, and, as moneylenders, were used by the Crown as a kind of sponge to gather up wealth from their neighbours and then be squeezed by the royal treasury. In this way the exactions of the Crown were concealed and the anger they aroused turned upon the Jews instead of their master. Whenever the protection of the Crown was relaxed, as in 1189, they were exposed to massacre and pillage.

To equip so large a force as accompanied Richard on the Crusade exceptional sums of ready money were needed. They were raised in various ways, but above all by the sale of charters to the towns. At the time of the Conquest these towns, except London, were no more than overgrown villages under the rule either of the Crown or of some feudal lord or abbey. Still depending upon the cultivation of their common fields, they were organised like any other manors. As they grew, they began to make bargains with their lords, undertaking to pay a lump sum, or, more often, a yearly 'farm', to be quit of their obligations to perform labour services. This involved the grant of a charter and the creation of a corporate body collectively responsible for the payment of the farm. As the Merchant Gilds[1] grew up they tended to coincide with the town corporation and often the two became indistinguishable.

[1] See page 87 below.

Henry II had made it a policy to grant such charters. Richard's need of money led him to extend the practice, and the urgency of this need made it possible for the town to drive bargains very favourable to themselves. In any case, at a time when trade and towns were growing, a payment that was fixed in amount, and so grew lighter in proportion as the wealth of the town increased, was a certain gain to the citizens. Once more we can observe the growth of a money economy within the feudal framework.

The rise of corporate towns, 'communes', freed from the system of personal relations and services, led to the formation of new classes ready to enter the political field. Richard's short reign was thus a time of important developments. It was also a time when the bureaucratic machinery elaborated by Henry II was tested out in the absence of the King himself. Under the guardianship of the Justiciar, Hubert Walter, these institutions proved their vitality when an attempt by Richard's brother John to revolt was easily crushed. This revolt was the last occasion in English history in which any feudal magnate ever attempted to establish an authority opposed to and independent of that of the State.

5. THE GREAT CHARTER

Though the period between the Conquest and 1200 was one of growing State power, and of the growth of the power of the King as head of the State, this growth remained within the conditions imposed upon it by the character of feudalism. No king aimed at autocratic authority or hoped to override the imperfectly defined but generally appreciated limits of the feudal contract in which the existing balance of class forces was embodied. It was recognised that the King had certain rights and duties—the duty of keeping the peace, of leading the army in war, of securing his vassals in the possession of their fiefs, and the right to levy certain dues, to exact certain military and other services from his vassals and to receive their homage as the ultimate owner of the land. In the same way the vassal had his corresponding rights and duties, In particular, the dues that he paid were confined to specified occasions and amounts, and upon his death his fief must be allowed to pass to his heir after the payment of a customary fine.

Second only to these rights were those of holding a court for his tenants, these courts being an important source of income. Though, as we have seen, the royal courts had been extending their scope at the expense of private jurisdictions this had been done with discretion and rather by providing machinery that was obviously more efficient than by compulsion.

In the last resort the barons retained the right of rebellion. If the feudal contract was shamelessly violated by the King and all redress failed, the baron was entitled to renounce his allegiance and to enforce his rights by war. This was always a desperate expedient, and in England, where the power of the Crown was greatest and that of the barons least, it was almost hopeless. Even the strongest combination of barons had failed to defeat the Crown when, as in 1095 and in 1106, it had the support of other classes and sections of the population.

John, ablest and most unscrupulous of the Angevin kings, did make the attempt to pass beyond the powers which the Crown could claim without a violation of the feudal contract. He levied fines and aids not authorised by custom, he confiscated estates of his vassals, he refused to allow the heirs of others to succeed to their fiefs without exorbitant fines, he enforced the right of the Crown courts to try a variety of cases that had hitherto been left in private hands. In short, he attempted to go beyond the whole system of property relations lying at the root of the feudal system. Nor were his innovations confined to the barons. The Church was similarly treated, and the towns, which during the two previous generations had been growing increasingly conscious of their corporate rights, were made to pay all kinds of new taxes and dues.

The result was the complete isolation of the Crown from those sections that had previously been its strongest supporters. John was peculiarly unfortunate in that his attack on the Church was made when it was at one of its periods of exceptional strength under a superb political tactician, Pope Innocent III.

Even so, it is possible that he might have been successful but for the failure of his foreign policy. A dispute over the succession with his nephew Arthur led him into a long war with France. One by one he lost the provinces his father had held, including the dukedom of Normandy. The loss of Normandy meant for many of the English barons the loss of huge ancestral estates. In their eyes John had failed in his first duty, that of guarding the fiefs of his vassals. At the same time the loss of their foreign possessions made them more anxious to preserve those still held in England.

At this moment, having lost the support of the barons, John became involved in a direct dispute with Innocent III over the filling of the vacant Archbishopric of Canterbury. Ignoring the King's nominee, and contrary to the well-established custom, Innocent consecrated Stephen Langton, and to enforce the appointment placed England under an interdict. He followed this by declaring John excommunicated and deposed, and persuaded the kings of France and Scotland to make war on him. John organised a counter alliance which included Flanders and the Emperor. His forces were crushed at the Battle of Bouvines in 1214 and the English barons refused to fight. Even a last minute submission to Innocent failed to win back the support of the Church in England, and Langton continued to act as the brain of the baronial revolt.

John stood alone. It was not even possible for him to call out the fyrd, which in the past had been the trump card of the Crown in its struggles with the nobility. This fact in itself indicates that the movement against John was to some extent of a popular character. Unwillingly he submitted, and at Runnymede on June 15th, 1215, he accepted the programme of demands embodied by the barons in Magna Carta.

Magna Carta has been rightly regarded as a turning point in English history, but almost always for wrong reasons. It was not a 'constitutional' document. It did not embody the principle of no taxation without representation. It did not guarantee parliamentary government, since Parliament did not then exist. It did not establish the right to trial by jury, since, in fact, the jury was a piece of royal machinery to which the barons had the strongest objections.

What it did do was to set out in detail the ways in which John had gone beyond his rights as a feudal overlord and to demand that his unlawful practices should stop. It marked the alliance between the barons and the citizens of London by insisting on the freedom of merchants from arbitrary taxation. In other ways, as in its attempts to curtail the power of the royal courts, the Charter was reactionary. And, while its most famous clause declared that "No freeman shall be taken or imprisoned or disseised or exiled or in any way destroyed, nor will we go upon him or send upon him except by the lawful judgment of his peers and the law of the land", the second word excluded from any possible benefit the overwhelming mass of the people who were still in villeinage. Later, as villeinage declined, this clause took a new meaning and importance.

More important than all the specific points of grievance was the clause setting up a permanent committee of twenty-four barons to see that John's promises were kept. This was a real attempt to create machinery that would make it unnecessary to resort to an open revolt that could only succeed under such unique circumstances as those of 1215, or, at the worst, to ensure that a revolt would begin in a way as favourable as possible for the barons. This particular device did not work very well, but it did open a new avenue along which the barons could conduct a political struggle as a class rather than as individuals. It also prepared the way for the entry of new classes on to the political field.

It led to the development of Parliament as the instrument through which first the nobles and afterwards the bourgeoisie defended their interests.

The moment the barons dispersed, John denounced the Charter and gathered an army. The barons replied by declaring him deposed and offering the crown to Louis, son of the King of France. A civil war followed which was interrupted by the death of John in October 1216. His son Henry was only nine, and the supporters of Louis quickly deserted to the young prince. He was crowned, and government was carried on in his name by a group of barons led by William Marshall, Earl of Pembroke, and Hubert de Burgh. During this long minority the principles of the Charter came to be accepted as the basis of the law. In the following centuries Magna Carta was solemnly reaffirmed by every king from Henry III to Henry VI.

Its subsequent history is curious and falls into three chapters. As feudalism declined it ceased to have any clear practical application and passed out of memory. The Tudor bourgeoisie were too closely allied to the monarchy to wish to place any check upon it, while the power of the nobles was broken in the Wars of the Roses. Shakespeare, writing his play *King John* never mentions Magna Carta and quite possibly had never heard of it.

When the bourgeoisie entered their revolutionary period under the Stuarts the Charter was rediscovered, and, being framed in technical feudal language, was completely misinterpreted and used as a basis for the claims of Parliament. This view of the Charter as the cornerstone of democratic rights persisted through the greater part of the Nineteenth Century. It is only within the last fifty or sixty years that historians have examined it critically as a feudal document and discovered its real meaning and importance.

Just because it marks the highest point of feudal development and expressed most precisely the nature of feudal class relations, Magna Carta marks also the passing of society beyond those relations. It is both a culmination and a point of departure. In securing the Charter the barons won their greatest victory but only at the price of acting in a way which was not strictly feudal, of forming new kinds of combinations both among themselves and with other classes.

CHAPTER IV

THE DECLINE OF FEUDALISM

1. TRADE AND TOWNS

THE THIRTEENTH CENTURY in England is marked by the decline of feudalism both in the economic and political fields. In the Fourteenth this decline became a rapid and apparent disintegration. Economically, the decline took the form of an increase in commodity production in agriculture, leading to the break-up of the manor and the decay of villeinage. The large-scale production of wool for the Flemish market led to the development of trade on an international scale and of merchant capital. In the field of politics we have seen how the State assumed by degrees the functions of the feudal nobility—the administration of justice in the baronial fiefs, the protection of the cultivators and the service in the feudal host in time of war. As the barons shed these functions they were gradually transformed into landowners in the modern sense, drawing an income from their estates and tending to look to the Court and capital as the natural sphere of their political activities.

In the last chapter mention was made of the growth of towns, and the methods by which they secured charters freeing them from burdensome feudal obligations. Such charters were most easily had from the King, to whom money was always more useful than the accustomed feudal services, less easily from the nobles and with great difficulty from the great abbeys under whose walls towns had grown up in many places. The histories of such towns—St. Albans, Bury St. Edmunds and Reading—are punctuated with bitter conflicts, sometimes amounting to armed risings of the towsnmen, as at Bury in 1327. Here the townsfolk, supported by the villeins of the surrounding villages, stormed the abbey and set up a commune that lasted six months before it was suppressed. It is noteworthy that after the rising no fewer than thirty-two parish priests were convicted as ringleaders.

By the end of the Thirteenth Century almost all towns of any size, except a few under monastic rule, had won a certain measure of self-government. After gaining freedom from feudal exactions, the main object of any town was to keep its trade in the hands of its own burgesses, on the principle that only those who paid their share towards the freedom of the town had the right to share in its privileges. This object was attained through the organisation of the burgesses in the Merchant Gild. These gilds, which included all the traders in any given town (at first no clear division existed between the trader who bought and sold and the craftsman who made the goods, both functions being normally performed by the same person) were rigidly exclusive and their regulations were enforced by fines and, in extreme cases, by expulsion.

As the towns grew in size Craft Gilds came into being, in addition to, and sometimes in opposition to, the Merchant Gilds. These included only the men of some particular craft; smiths, saddlers, bakers or tailors. They aimed at regulating the whole of industry, laying down rules as to price, quality, conditions of work, and so on. They were composed of master-craftsmen, each working in his own home, usually with one or more apprentices and sometimes with journeymen or wage labourers. The latter were men who had served their period of apprenticeship but had not yet been able to become master-craftsmen.

At first the journeymen do not appear to have constituted a separate class, but were men who might expect to become masters themselves. Towards the end of the Thirteenth Century, however, clearer class divisions begin to appear. The number of journeymen increased, and many of them remained wage earners all their lives. By imposing high entrance fees and by other devices the gilds became more exclusive and harder to enter. As a result, separate gilds of the journeymen, the so called Yeomen Gilds, began to arise.

These gilds, like the first trade unions, were discouraged and often forced to work secretly. Consequently we only hear of them casually, when their members appear in court or in such cases as that when the London Gild of Cordwainers (leather workers) declared in 1303 that "it is forbidden that the servant workmen in cordwaining or other shall hold any meeting to make provisions that may be to the prejudice of the trade".

In 1387, again "John Clerk, Henry Duntone and John Hychene, serving men of the said trade of cordwainers . . . brought together a great congregation of men like unto themselves, and did conspire and confederate to hold together", and were committed by the Mayor and Aldermen to Newgate prison "until they should have been better advised what further ought to be done with them". Similar records of strikes or combinations exist for other trades and towns, as in the case of the London saddlers, 1396, weavers, 1362, and the Coventry bakers in 1484.

Beside the skilled craftsmen, covered by the gild organisation, the larger towns soon attracted a floating population of escaped serfs and others who formed a submerged class of unskilled and irregularly employed labourers. In London this section was especially large, and, while the conditions of skilled workers may have been fairly satisfactory, the medieval slum population lived in depths of filth and poverty that can hardly be imagined.

One later development must be noted which accentuated the class differentiations in the towns. This was the growth of gilds of merchants and dealers who dominated the productive crafts. Thus, by the end of the Fourteenth Century, the London Drapers control the fullers, shearmen and weavers, and of the twelve great gilds from which alone the Mayor could be chosen, only two, the weavers and the goldsmiths, were productive. The same thing took place more slowly and to a less extent in the other towns, and serves to remind us that it was in the form of merchant capital that the first great accumulation of bourgeois property took place.

The first and most important field that merchant capital found for its operations in England was the wool trade. From quite early times wool was exported from this country to be woven in Ghent, Bruges, Ypres and other towns in Flanders. By the Thirteenth Century this trade had grown to large proportions, easily exceeding in bulk and value all other exports combined. In some respects England assumed a position with regard to Flanders comparable to that of Australia and the West Riding today.

There were, however, important differences. England was not politically dependent upon Flanders as countries producing raw materials usually are upon industrial countries. This was partly due to the internal situation in Flanders, politically weakened by the constant struggles between the merchants, the handicraft weavers, the counts of Flanders and the kings of France, struggles which kept Flanders divided and, in the Fourteenth Century, had important consequences in English history.[1]

More important was the monopoly position of England as a wool growing country. Throughout the Middle Ages no other country produced a regular surplus of wool for export, and, on more than one occasion, the prohibition of the export of wool produced an instant and devastating economic crisis in Flanders. The English monopoly was the result of the early suppression of private war, noted already as one of the results of the peculiar strength here of the crown as against the barons. Sheep are of all kinds of property the easiest to lift and the hardest to protect, and only under circumstances of internal peace not normal in the Middle Ages was sheep farming on a large scale profitable.

As early as the Twelfth Century the Cistercian monks had established huge sheep farms on the dry eastern slopes

[1] See below, page 108.

of the Pennines. The Cistercians were not only large scale farmers, but financiers as well, and through their hands and those of the Lombard and Florentine merchants who acted as their agents was passed much of the revenue which the Popes drew from England, a revenue stated in Parliament in the reign of Edward III to be five times that of the Crown. Much of this revenue was collected in the form of wool rather than of currency.

Besides Yorkshire, the Cotswolds, the Chilterns, Hereford and the uplands of Lincolnshire were important wool growing areas by the Thirteenth Century if not earlier. At first the bulk of the export trade was in the hands of Italian and Flemish merchants. The former, especially, coming from cities where banking had already made great progress, were able to conduct financial operations on a scale unknown in Northern Europe. It was because the Lombards were able to finance him more efficiently than the Jews that the latter were expelled from England by Edward I in 1290. This action, often represented as a piece of disinterested patriotism, was in fact the result of the intrigues of a rival group of moneylenders who could offer the King better terms.

With the growth of the trade English exporters began to challenge their foreign rivals. Export figures for 1273, incomplete but probably reliable enough, show that more than half the trade was in English hands. The establishment of the Wool Staple marks this stage in the growth of English merchant capital. The idea of the Staple was to concentrate all wool exports in one place or a few places, both to protect the trader from pirates and to make the collection of taxes easy. First various towns in Flanders were selected, then, in 1353, a number of English towns. Finally in 1362, the Staple was fixed in Calais, which had been captured during the Hundred Years' War. From the start the Staple was controlled by native merchants.

The growth of trade on a national scale involved the loss of many of their exclusive privileges by the chartered

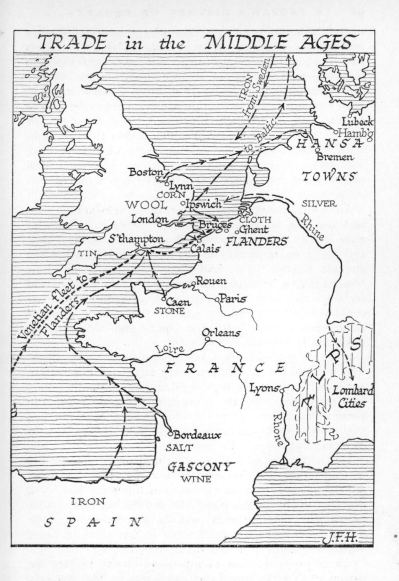

TRADE in the MIDDLE AGES

IRON from Sweden
to Baltic
HANSA
Lübeck
Hamb'g
Bremen
TOWNS
SILVER
Rhine
Boston
Lynn
CORN
WOOL
Ipswich
London
CLOTH
Bruges
Ghent
S'thampton
FLANDERS
TIN
Calais
Venetian fleet to Flanders
Rouen
Caen
Paris
STONE
Orleans
Loire
F R A N C E
Lyons
A L P S
Lombard Cities
Rhône
Bordeaux
SALT
GASCONY
WINE
IRON
S P A I N

J.F.H.

towns. Both Edward I and Edward III encouraged alien merchants and gave them concessions that led to conflicts with the burgesses of the towns. Attempts were made to improve roads and harbours and to allow trade to flow freely and safely from one part of the kingdom to another. How imperfect was even the relative peace of England at this time is strikingly illustrated by a clause in the Statute of Winchester (1285) which orders that all highways should be cleared "so that there be neither dyke nor bush, whereby a man may lurk to do hurt, within two hundred foot of the one side and two hundred foot of the other".

Another factor that helped to break down local exclusiveness was the trade done at fairs. These fairs were to some extent outside the control of the Merchant Gilds, and the more important of them attracted traders from all over Europe. They had their own legal code 'Law Merchant', an important matter when every country and every district had its own peculiar customs. Law Merchant was an international code so that traders from all parts were familiar with the rights and obligations it enforced. It was for the purpose of international trade, too, that a gold coinage was introduced alongside silver. The first gold coins (florins) were struck at Florence in 1252. In England the first regular gold coin, the noble, was issued soon after the capture of Calais in 1347. The greater compactness of gold gave it an obvious advantage, but it was some centuries before gold coins were in common internal use in England.

The decline of feudalism and the growth of trade led to changes in the character or taxation that had most important consequences. In Norman times the King was expected to 'live of his own' like any baron. Only under exceptional circumstances was it customary to raise special taxes and these taxes were at first taxes on land. With the growth of towns taxes were imposed on other forms of property, thus giving other classes besides the barons a direct interest in affairs of State. The property tax, originally based on a rough assessment, soon became fixed in amount and in its usual form of 'a Tenth and a Fifteenth' produced on an average about £40,000.

During the reign of Henry III prices rose sharply, and the ordinary revenue of the Crown became increasingly insufficient, especially as the State tended to do more and more things previously done by the barons. From this time the use made of the estate of the Crown began to be an important political issue. All classes had a direct interest in preserving the Crown lands intact, since if they were alienated the burden of taxation would be heavier. It is significant that all the kings who met with specially strong opposition—Henry III, Edward II, Richard II and Henry VI—were kings under whom the Crown lands were recklessly disposed of.

Under these circumstances the fusing of the baronial opposition to the Crown, which had led to the granting of Magna Charta, and the opposition of the rising merchants of the towns became inevitable since they had frequently a common ground for complaint if more rarely a community of positive interests. The medium through which this new opposition expressed itself was Parliament. But while this is so, the Crown itself frequently made use of the town merchants as a counterweight to the barons and in this sense their growth to political importance can be regarded as a by-product of the struggle between king and nobles, a struggle between two evenly matched powers both anxious to secure an ally. It is at any rate to this clash of classes that we must look for the origin and development of Parliament.

2. PARLIAMENTARY ORIGINS

During the minority of Henry III the baronial party which had triumphed at Runnymede administered affairs in the King's name. Willian Marshall, de Burgh and the Archbishop Langton appear to have been men of some ability, and under them, and in the absence of opposition, the barons held together and the importance of the Great Council as the core of the State apparatus increased. The barons had a training in administration which enabled them to act as a class, to aim at collective control of the State instead of at individual power in their several fiefs.

When Henry came of age and attempted to take personal control the struggle was resumed. His incompetence was balanced by a vanity that prevented him from realising his limitations, and his extravagance combined with the rising prices to force him to make constant demands for money. He was personally much influenced by his French wife's foreign friends to whom he gave lands that the barons thought should have been kept and positions that they thought should have gone to themselves. Henry was priest-ridden as no king since Edward the Confessor had been, and it was during his reign that England became the main source of revenue for the Popes: this revenue was obtained partly by direct taxation and partly by allowing the Popes to sell church offices to whoever—English or foreign—would give the best price for them.

The result was that while Henry was constantly making demands for money the administration of the State grew less efficient. Trade was interfered with and not only the barons but also the lesser landowners and the merchants were once again united in opposition. At first this opposition took the traditional baronial form.

When Henry allowed himself to be persuaded by the Pope in 1257 to accept the Kingdom of Sicily for his son Edmund, and asked the council to provide the money necessary to conquer the island from the Hohenstauffens who were in occupation, opposition came to a head. The barons refused the money and a Council at Oxford set up an elaborate system of committees responsible to the Council itself for the detailed carrying on of the Government. They also demanded the right to appoint the Justiciar, Chancellor and other officers as well as the sheriffs of the counties. It was at about this date that the Council began to be known as Parliament.

After three years the weakness of the purely baronial movement became obvious. The barons were always liable to be split by personal feuds and by the conflict of interest felt by each of the body between the new class loyalty and the old and still powerful desire to work for the strengthening of his own fief. As a result the King was able to win over a section and to begin a civil war. Those of the barons who remained in opposition under Simon de Montfort were forced to rely on the support of other classes, and when, in 1264, Simon defeated Henry at Lewes a whole wing of his army was drawn from the citizens of London.

After Lewes the desertions from the baronial ranks went on, and the movement began as a result to assume a really popular character. It included the town merchants, the lesser landowners, those of the clergy who were opposed to the growing power of the Papacy and the students of Oxford, who, drawn mostly from the middle and lower middle classes, were throughout the Middle Ages strongly radical in temper. It was under these circumstances that de Montfort summoned to his Parliament of 1265 representatives of the burgesses of the chartered towns as well as two knights from each shire.

De Montfort's Parliament, though called together in accordance with strictly legal forms, has nevertheless been correctly described as a revolutionary party assembly. It contained only five earls and seventeen barons, and the burgesses were clearly intended as a makeweight against the barons who had deserted. Yet if this Parliament of 1265 was a revolutionary body, it was also in line with the developments of preceding decades, themselves the outcome of the changing class structure of England.

The decline of feudalism had created a growing differentiation between the great barons and the lesser landowners or knights. While the former retained bands of armed followers and looked to war and politics as their natural activity, the latter were growing content to live on their estates and make the largest possible income from them. The wool trade, by providing them with a product easily and profitably marketable, confirmed them in this course and in the Thirteenth Century we can trace already the beginnings of the English squirearchy which dominated the countryside for five centuries.

These knights were early drawn into local government through the shire courts, and in 1254 representative knights of the shire were formally summoned to the Council, though only to report decisions already arrived at in the shire courts. Knights were summoned several times between 1254 and 1266 for various purposes. No very theoretically startling change was involved, therefore, in de Montfort's action, but in practice the character and balance of the Council was changed and it can no longer be regarded as a merely feudal body.

In the next year de Montfort was defeated by Henry's son Edward, after a brilliant campaign in the Severn valley, and died at the Battle of Evesham. Edward found it wiser to adopt many of the changes which the rebels had demanded and in his reign Parliament assumed permanently the form which de Montfort had given it. There is no evidence that at first the knights and burgesses took any active part in the proceedings. They were there mainly to agree to the taxes which the King wanted, to help by giving the information needed to draw up assessments and to go home and see that the shires and towns raised the money. They were also the bearers of petitions from their localities and helped the Government to check up on the doings of local officials.

Like the jury, Parliament was a royal convenience rather than a right of the subject. The expense of attending or of being represented was avoided when possible both by individuals who had to be forced to go and by towns which often petitioned not to be forced to send representatives. Parliament was developed as a tax collecting apparatus, and, if it became a focus for opposition, this was quite outside the purpose of the Crown.

Between 1265 and 1295 various experiments were made, and it was not till a new crisis took place in the latter year that the next big advance was made. In 1295 Edward was seriously involved in wars with France and Scotland and with the task of holding down the recently conquered Welsh. He therefore summoned what is known as the 'Model Parliament' because it contained all the elements which were to become recognised as necessary to make a full assembly. This Model Parliament made a large grant of money with some reluctance, but in the two following years more was needed. Edward levied a heavy property tax, tolls on wool exports and seized some of the property of the Church.

These levies were strongly resisted, and in 1297 the 'Confirmation of the Charter' was secured. Edward promised, in effect, that no new taxes would be raised in future without the consent of Parliament. The opposition was still largely of the traditional baronial type, but what is important is the new Parliamentary forms which this opposition was beginning to take. The same thing is true of the next reign. Edward II alienated the barons by the failure of his Bannockburn campaign in 1315 and by his grants of Crown lands to personal friends, commoners who were raised by these gifts to a position of equality with the older nobility. In 1327 Edward was deposed after a rising of the barons but this deposition was carried through in a regular Parliamentary manner, establishing a precedent which was to be of great importance.

It was the continued need of Edward III for money to carry on the Hundred Years' War that led to further developments of Parliamentary control over taxation. In the years between 1339 and 1344 grants were actually refused until after grievances had been dealt with. The advance was due more to the King's necessity than to the strength of Parliament; it seemed to Edward more important to continue the war in France than to quarrel with Parliament over what on the surface seemed minor questions. Consequently he agreed to allow Parliament

DE

to elect treasurers to supervise the expenditure of the money voted and to examine the royal accounts. This was in substance a recognition of the right of Parliament not only to withhold supplies, but, more vaguely, to exercise an indirect control over the way the money was spent and hence over policy.

It would be easy to exaggerate the importance of these precedents. Such parliamentary control was only nominal except in moments when the Crown was specially weak. But nevertheless precedents were established which enabled Parliament to take up a strong position on the field on which important class battles were to be fought in centuries to come.

It was during the same period that the final steps were taken which gave Parliament its modern form. At first all sections sat together as one body, and, inevitably, the proceedings were dominated by the great barons. Then came a period of experiment. Sometimes there were three 'Houses'—Barons, Clergy and Commons. Sometimes the burgesses sat alone to legislate on matters concerning trade, as at the 'Parliament' of Acton Burnel in 1283. Sometimes the knights of the shire sat with the barons, sometimes with the burgesses. Then the clergy ceased to sit in Parliament and formed their own Convocation, and the division into Lords and Commons took place on the lines which exist to-day. In this division the knights of the shire—representing the smaller landowners—took their places in the Commons with the representatives of the town merchants.

This grouping, found only in England, was an exact reflection of the unique distribution of class forces in this country towards the close of the Middle Ages. The prohibition of private war and the growth of the wool trade, as has already been pointed out, caused a sharp differentiation between the greater and lesser landowners. The latter, mainly interested in drawing an income from land, had begun to rear sheep on a large scale. They had a far greater community of interest with the merchants who also prospered from this trade than with the great barons whose outlook was still largely military. At the same time they formed a link between merchants and barons which enabled all three classes to act together from time to time.

This alliance between the merchants and the squires is the key to the growth of parliamentary power. It enabled the former to develop their strength under the wing of an already established class and it enabled the House of Commons to act at times as an independent body without the Lords. While in most parts of Europe the representative bodies which grew up about this time declined and in many cases disappeared with the decline of feudalism, in England the decline of feudalism only strengthened the position of the Commons as the non-feudal part of Parliament.

In the late Fourteenth and the Fifteenth Centuries the nominal power of Parliament was considerable. Yet it would be a mistake to overestimate its strength or that of the merchant class. If Parliament was allowed to acquire many powers it was because it was still normally led by the Lords. The decay of feudalism, while creating the class of squires, also concentrated power in the hands of a very small number of powerful noble families, mostly related to the Crown and fighting bitterly for supremacy among themselves. They saw in Parliament a convenient means through which to dominate the State machine, and its wide powers were in practice often exercised by the ruling clique of nobles. The whole period was one of transition, of a delicate balance of class forces, and Parliament became at the same time a reflection and a battle-ground of these forces.

3. WALES: IRELAND: SCOTLAND

The Norman Conquest at first only extended over the area roughly covered by England: the rest of the British Isles was still independent and was organised into a bewildering number of small kingdoms and princi-palities largely tribal in character. The attempt of the

Normans to subdue and feudalise these areas cover several centuries. Scotland, though already feudal in its southern part, never was conquered, while in Ireland it was not till Tudor times that anything more than a precarious foothold around Dublin was secured.

It was in Wales that the conquest began first and was most thoroughly carried out. The Anglo-Saxon invaders had pushed the Welsh back to a line running roughly from the Wye to the Dee but had made no real attempt to penetrate the mountains or the plain running along the southern coast. After the Norman Conquest the piece-meal reduction of Wales was undertaken, not by the Crown but by the Marcher Lords whose fiefs lay on the border. Because they were regarded as a protection against raiders from the hills these fiefs were larger and more compact than those granted to the barons elsewhere in England and there was a clear understanding that any Marcher Lord was entitled to add to them any land he could win from the Welsh.

There followed 150 years of confused warfare in which the Welsh were gradually pushed back into the hills and scores of Norman castles were built in the valleys and along the coast. Their owners reigned as virtually inde-pendent princelings—half feudal lord, half tribal chief—over just so much land as their armoured followers could protect from the Welsh up the mountain or their Norman neighbour in the next valley. By about 1200 only the princes of North Wales remained unconquered. With the Snowdon area as a natural fortress and the rich cornlands of Anglesey as a base, the house of Llewellyn ruled Gynnedd and even, in the Thirteenth Century, was able to make use of the feuds dividing the Marcher Lords to reconquer much of what had been lost.

It was this revival, reaching its highest point under Llewellyn ap Griffith (1246–1283) which led to the first direct attempt by the English Crown to conquer Wales. Edward I followed the Roman strategy of building castles at points of vantage and linking them with military roads.

Moving along the coast from Chester he cut off Llewellyn, who had retired as usual to the Snowdon range, from his food supply in Anglesey, and by 1285 the conquest was complete. North Wales was divided into counties under the direct control of Crown officials though elsewhere the authority of the Marcher Lords remained undisturbed.

This partial conquest of Wales had unfortunate political and military results. Long after England had become relatively peaceful, Wales was filled with warlike nobles, Mortimers, Bohuns and Clares, who were a constant disturbing factor in English politics. When feudalism declined elsewhere it retained a spurious vitality here and the Marcher Lords formed a large section of the gangster nobles who conducted the Wars of the Roses.

The means of war were always to hand, since the poverty of the Welsh people made it easy to recruit mercenaries from the hills of the interior. In the Scottish War and the Hundred Years' War a large proportion of the infantry were Welshmen. Further, the conditions of war in Wales helped to mould English battle tactics. The longbow, the weapon which gave the English a technical superiority over all their opponents was in the first place a Welsh weapon and it was in the endless guerilla fighting of the hills and valleys that was developed that combination of heavy armed troops with longbowmen which proved equally effective against the irregular tribal warriors of Ireland, the Scottish pikemen and the feudal cavalry of France.

It was in Ireland that the new tactics were first tested. Taking advantage of internal feuds, the Earl of Pembroke, significantly nicknamed Strongbow, landed there in 1169 with a few hundred heavy armed horse supported by Welsh archers. Their tactics, neither feudal nor tribal but wholly new at the time, were extraordinarily successful in a land of trackless bogs and hills and against a desperate but poorly sustained resistance.

Once the first stages of the conquest were past, the character of the invaders made their assimilation easy and

rapid. The majority of the invaders were Welsh tribesmen, different in no essential from the Irish among whom
they settled. Even the leaders had been influenced by a
century of Welsh conditions. The result was the creation of
a ruling class who were neither feudal nor tribal. The
Fitzgeralds became more Irish with every generation and
the de Burghs were speedily transformed into Burkes.
Apart from their stone castles and their armoured retainers
and a feudal tinge imparted to the land laws there was
little to distinguish them from the native Irish O'Connors
and O'Donnells of the West. What difference there was
was small compared to the gulf dividing them all from the
English of the Pale, the area around Dublin garrisoned
and ruled direct from England. Every attempt to use
the Pale as a base for further conquest was fiercely resisted
by Celt and Anglo-Irish alike, and it remained no more
than a foothold till the subjection of Ireland was seriously
undertaken by the Tudors.

Such attempts were probably bound to fail because
there was no means of maintaining at such a distance
the large permanent army that would have been needed
and no means of preventing new groups of settlers from
being assimilated as the first had been. In any case, after
the outbreak of the Hundred Years' War no serious attempt
was made at conquest except by Richard II who was
forced to abandon it because of the weakness of his position
at home. Ireland remained divided among innumerable
chiefs and barons, a prey to internal wars that checked
the economic development of the country and impoverished
its people. In this period the tribal structure slowly decayed
and the land came by degrees to be regarded as the
property of the chief instead of the tribe. At the same time
no effective new social organisation grew up to replace
decaying tribalism. Ireland, which in the early Middle
Ages had been one of the richest and most civilised countries
in Western Europe, became, after the successive Danish
and English invasions, one of the poorest and most
backward.

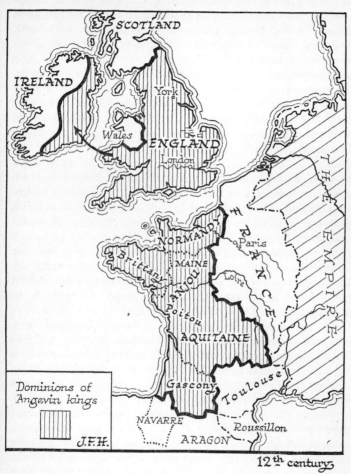

SCOTLAND

IRELAND

York

Wales

ENGLAND

London

NORMANDY

Brittany

MAINE

ANJOU

Poitou

Paris

Loire

FRANCE

THE EMPIRE

AQUITAINE

Dominions of
Angevin kings

J.F.H.

Gascony

Toulouse

NAVARRE

Roussillon

ARAGON

12th century

The methods of war developed in Wales and perfected in Ireland were first put to the test against regular opponents in Scotland. It, unlike Wales and Ireland, had become largely feudal in the centuries between 1066 and 1286, when the death of Alexander III and the extinction of his line gave Edward I the chance to push forward with the policy of extending his kingdom over the whole of Britain.

Centuries earlier invading Angles had settled among the East Coast up to the North and over the Lothian plain, and this area was for long part of the English kingdom of Northumbria. In 1018 a battle at Carham added the Lothians to Scotland. This battle did more than fix the frontier between England and Scotland in its present position. It was decisive in Anglo-Scottish history because it determined that Scotland would not be a purely Celtic country and that its most fertile and economically developed part was English in speech and race and open to feudal influences from the South. After 1066 a feudal baronage grew up closely connected with England and holding large estates in both countries. Robert Bruce, for example, had 90,000 acres in Yorkshire and his rival John Balliol held lands in Normandy and England as well as in Scotland.

For two centuries relations between England and Scotland were generally friendly, broken only by isolated Scottish interventions into English politics like that which led to the capture of William the Lion at Alnwick in 1170. The great belt of wild moorland dividing the two countries served to hinder invasions and there is little indication of anything like the continuous petty border warfare that grew up later. The claims of the English kings to be overlords of Scotland were occasionally put forward in a vague form and rather less frequently admitted. Meanwhile, Scotland was moving along lines similar to those we have traced in England, always remembering the greater poverty of the country, its distance from European trade centres and the large, sparsely peopled tribal regions still existing in the West and North.

When the death of Alexander III and his young daughter left a dozen or so nobles with claims to the throne, the barons, being as much English as Scottish, naturally turned to Edward I to settle the dispute. Edward marched a strong army to the border, announced that he was Lord Paramount of Scotland and decided to support the claim of John Balliol. His claim to overlordship was not disputed by the barons, though it is recorded that "the community of the people" made a protest the nature of which no chronicler has troubled to report.

Having made Balliol king, Edward proceeded to goad him into revolt by slights and insults, and, in 1286, he succeeded. He marched north again, took and sacked Berwick, Scotland's one important trading town with a large Flemish population, deposed Balliol and once more received the submission of the Scottish barons.

Edward left the Earl of Warenne as governor with an army of occupation, apparently regarding the conquest as complete. But if the nobles were indifferent from whom they held their lands, the Scottish masses soon found the presence of a foreign garrison intolerable. In 1297 a small landowner, William Wallace, revolted and raised an army of peasants and burgesses which defeated Warenne at Falkirk. After a few months Edward returned in person and met the rebels at Stirling. They were drawn up in the traditional Scottish circle of pikemen, a development of the Saxon shield-wall. The English archers shot gaps in the ranks through which the cavalry were able to charge. Once the circle was broken it was easy for the armoured horsemen to ride down the pikemen at pleasure.

At this point Robert Bruce, grandson of the claimant of 1286, who had been shifting from side to side with great diplomatic skill, saw the possibility of turning the popular movement to his own advantage. He had himself crowned king at Scone and for some years carried on an able guerilla war. This was possible because, though Edward could raise an army strong enough to crush all opposition, he could not, with existing transport facilities and the wild tract separating England from Scotland, keep such an army permanently in the field. The regular garrison, numbering some 2,000 men, could do no more than hold a few of the main towns and castles. In 1307 Edward died while leading another army into Scotland.

The irregular war was continued in the next reign, castle after castle passing into Scottish hands till only Stirling was left. In 1314 Edward II took the largest army that had ever left England to relieve it, and was crushingly defeated at Bannockburn. The victory was in part the result of the skill of Bruce in the choice of a battleground, but far more to the stupidity with which the English Army was handled. Relying on his great superiority of numbers, and ignoring all the lessons of the past decades, Edward launched his cavalry at the Scottish pikes without a preparatory covering fire from his archers. The limitations of feudal cavalry were as thoroughly exposed as they were later at Crécy and Poitiers.

Important though it was, Bannockburn was not the decisive event it has often been thought to be. Edward was prevented from renewing the war by the internal struggle with the baronage that ended in his deposition and murder in 1327. But it was resumed by Edward III. Feuds among the Scottish nobles and the skill of the English longbowmen gave him a victory at Halidon Hill, after which Bruce's son David was forced to seek refuge in France. The war continued for some time on the classic guerilla lines and was finally abandoned partly because it seemed impossible to bring it to any definite conclusion but mainly because the Hundred Years' War was beginning to absorb all the available English resources.

From this time no further attempt at conquest was made, but a permanent irregular war took its place which reduced a great area on both sides of the border to a wilderness, put an end to the early development of Scottish trade and industry and kept Scotland feudal at a time when feudalism in England was rapidly declining.

The result for England was less serious because only the North, which in any case was poor and backward, was affected. But it created a powerful and turbulent nobility, which, like the Welsh Marcher Lords, preserved feudal traits that were in contradiction to the development of the rest of the country and were largely responsible for the internal disorder and wars of the Fifteenth Century.

4. THE HUNDRED YEARS' WAR AND THE REVOLUTION IN MILITARY TECHNIQUE

The wars in Wales and Scotland were wars of a characteristically medieval kind, wars of simple appropriation undertaken to extend the domains of the English kings and barons. The Hundred Years' War was one of a new kind, primarily a trade war and only in form and on the surface a war of medieval conquest. Edward III, who was strongly influenced by the ideas of chivalry that only developed during the decline of feudalism, did indeed put forward a claim to the French crown, but this claim was hardly taken seriously and was little more than a mask for the real objectives of the war.

The switch of English foreign policy from Scotland to France can be accounted for by the greater wealth of France as compared with either Scotland or Ireland, but more than this is really involved. Neither Scotland or Ireland had any real importance to English trade, whereas the Kingdom of France included the two regions that were of vital importance in this respect. These were Flanders, the centre of the wool industry, and Gascony, still held by the kings of England as a feudal fief. Gascony was the main supplier of wine and salt, and was important as a base for the import of iron from Spain.

The Hundred Years' War was thus a reflection of the growing importance of merchant capital in England and of the interest of a large and influential section of the landowners in the wool trade. Its real object was to bring England, Flanders and Gascony, already bound by relations of trade, under a unified political control, and it was on Flanders and Gascony that the main military operations were based.

The origin of the war was so closely connected with the class struggle in Flanders, which in the Fourteenth Century reached a level not attained elsewhere for centuries, that this must be briefly described. By the end of the Thirteenth Century Flanders had assumed a definitely urban character and its great cities were manufacturing rather than trading centres. It has been estimated that of the 50,000 inhabitants of Ghent 30,000 were directly dependent upon the wool industry. In Ghent, Bruges, Mechlin and the other woollen towns a small class of rich merchants, who gave out wool to the working weavers to be made up into cloth, formed a close oligarchy controlling the city councils. Among the weavers strikes and armed risings were common from about 1250. In 1280 a general revolt took place, and the weavers were supported by the Count of Flanders and other nobles who wanted to weaken the power of the cities. The merchants, beaten by this combination, appealed to the King of France, who was in his turn quite ready to take the opportunity to strengthen his hold over the half independent County of Flanders.

A whole generation of bitter fighting followed. In 1303 the weavers defeated the pick of the French feudal nobility in a pitched battle outside Courtrai and for a short time gained control of the towns. An internal feud between the weavers and the fullers soon enabled the merchants to regain control in Ghent, the key town, and the Count of Flanders then turned to England for support. Bruges and Ypres, still governed by the weavers, offered to support Edward III and to recognise him as ruler of Flanders and of France.

In 1327 the English Government carried out a masterstroke of diplomacy. By prohibiting the export of wool to Flanders they produced an immediate crisis there that can be compared in its effect with the cotton famine in Lancashire at the time of the American Civil War. The result was to bring about a temporary alliance of all classes in support of their French policy in return for a removal of the embargo. Edward had now an assured base for his war.

The first campaigns were fought from Flanders, while Gascony was used as a base for a secondary attack. A series of these campaigns met with little success, and their failure soon weakened Edward's position in Flanders. Once the peculiar circumstances that had produced it ended, the unnatural class alliance in Flanders dissolved. In 1345, Philip van Artevelde, the leader of the Ghent merchants and Edward's chief supporter, was defeated and killed.

The next year saw the first big battle—Crécy. Like Poitiers and Agincourt later, Crécy was the result of the blundering strategy of the English, who marched an inadequate army into the heart of France and were cornered by stronger enemy forces. What was lost by bad strategy was regained by superior tactics. The lesson of the Scottish wars and of Courtrai had shown both the weakness of feudal cavalry and the value of the longbow and of trained and determined infantry drawn up in mass formation. For the first time feudal knights dismounted and fought on foot among the archers. The French, instead of pinning down the cornered English army and forcing it to attack, flung masses of cavalry against a prepared line and suffered total defeat. After this had happened a second time at Poitiers in 1356, the first stage of the war ended with the peace of Bretigney in 1360.

Edward gave up his claim to the French crown and was unable to secure Flanders. He received the greater part of France south of the Loire and the town of Calais which had been taken the year after Crécy. Calais was of great importance as a centre for the wool export. After a few years the war reopened under very different conditions. The English had been weakened by a futile campaign in Spain and the French were now commanded by Betrand du Guesclin, perhaps the outstanding military genius of the Middle Ages. Du Guesclin, the son of a small Breton squire, had spent the first fifteen years of his career as an outlaw chief in the hills and forests of Brittany. Here he had shed all the romanticism of chivalry and learnt every trick and ruse of the guerilla fighter. When he became Constable of France he forced the French nobility against their will to fight on foot, to refuse battle, to attack outposts and stragglers. He was the first general to grasp the value of gunpowder in siege operations, and he developed a technique of assault by which supposedly impregnable fortresses were taken in a few days.

More important still, his outlaw days had brought him into close contact with the peasants and he realised that while the English professional army could defeat the ill-disciplined feudal forces of France in the field they would be powerless in the face of a national resistance. In 1358 France had been convulsed by the *Jacquerie*, a desperate rising of peasants driven beyond endurance by the plundering of both sides and the inability of their lords to protect them. Du Guesclin insisted that his troops should be paid regularly, even if he had to find the money himself, and refused to allow them to prey on the country folk. Soon the English found themselves faced with a national resistance in which every village was full of enemies and every movement they made was instantly reported to the French forces.

In nine years (1369–1377) not a single battle was fought, but the English were driven from province after province till only Calais, Bordeaux and a few other coast towns remained in their hands. After the death of Edward III in 1377 the French were able to take the offensive and harry the English coast. The Isle of Wight was occupied and a landing in Sussex was pushed as far as Lewes.

The last events of the war, like its opening, were connected with the internal politics of Flanders. Philip van Artevelde, the son of Edward's ally, had in 1375 put himself at the head of the Ghent weavers and seized power as a partisan of the English. He was defeated and killed at

West-Roosebeke in 1382 but the next year Spencer, Bishop of Norwich, who had made a reputation by his brutality in suppressing the insurgent peasants of East Anglia, was sent to Flanders with an army to try to revive the war. This campaign, dignified with the title of a Crusade because the French supported a rival Pope against the one recognised in England, was a complete failure. The exhaustion of the country after forty years' almost unbroken war, and the growing internal conflicts among the leading noble families, put an end to the war till it was revived in 1415 by Henry V.

The direct results of the war were almost wholly disastrous for both England and France, neither of which obtained any real return for the vast expenditure of lives and treasure and the continued devastation of the countryside. Indirectly, however, it helped to accelerate the decline of feudalism. The French crown emerged stronger because of the prestige gained as the leader of a national struggle and the regular army and artillery train created during the war. In England, the failure to conquer Flanders led the Government to encourage the home woollen industry. Flemish craftsmen were aided to immigrate. Oppressed by the merchants, the weavers were told "how happy they should be if they would but come into England, bringing their mystery with them, which should provide their welcome in all places. Here they should feed on beef and mutton, till nothing but their fatness should stint their stomach". England became more a manufacturer of cloth and less a mere producer of raw wool. By the Fifteenth Century she was supplying most of her own needs and beginning to export cloth abroad.

On the battlefields of the Hundred Years' War the prestige of the armoured feudal cavalry had received its death blow. The decisive technical advance which had robbed the knight of his superiority was not, as is sometimes supposed, the invention of gunpowder, but the longbow. This placed the trained peasant archer on terms of equality with his lord, robbing the latter of his main claim to special consideration, his position as a specialist in war. Gunpowder was important at first only as a siege weapon, depriving the castle of its invulnerability. The hand gun or musket did not appear till the very end of the Middle Ages. It was used first in Germany and introduced into England during the Wars of the Roses by foreign mercenaries in the pay of Edward IV.

At first it was in most respects inferior to the longbow. It had a shorter range, a slower rate of fire and less power of penetration. But its compensating quality was that it could be used by slightly trained men while it took a lifetime of practice to turn out a skilled archer. The introduction of the hand gun coincides with the decline of the yeomanry in England at the close of the Fifteenth Century and the recruiting of armies from the landless rural population and the slum proletariat.

Finally though this takes us well outside the period covered by this section, a new kind of cavalry was evolved after a period in which the infantry was the most important arm. This new cavalry was unarmoured and mounted on lighter and swifter horses. It relied on the speed of its impact and on pistol fire to break the formation of the enemy. This is the cavalry of the Thirty Years' War and of Rupert and his cavaliers, a cavalry that, though it was mainly composed of gentlemen and their followers, reflects the structure of society in an age of transition between feudal and bourgeois. In a later chapter we shall see how this cavalry was adapted by Cromwell and the English bourgeoisie to suit the needs of their struggle for power.

While the revolution in military technique sprang from changes in the structure of society, it reacted in turn upon this society. War became industrialised, employing more complicated instruments and involving more complicated financial arrangements. The English troops in the Hundred Years' War were hired on a regular basis, the archers on foot getting 3d. a day and the mounted men 6d. "The provision of powder and firearms required industry and money, and these were in the hands of the burgesses of the towns. From the outset, therefore, fire-arms were the weapons of the towns and of the rising monarchy drawing its support from the towns, against the feudal nobility" (Engels, *Anti-Duhring*, p. 190).

Feudal wars, growing into national wars, transcended the organising capacity of the feudal system and hastened its decline.

5. THE BLACK DEATH

When, in the autumn of 1348, two years after Crécy, the Black Death began to spread in South and West England, a slow revolution had been transforming the villages for nearly a hundred years. The organisation of the manor, with its typical arrangement of serfs bound to the soil and owing labour services to their lord, has been described already. And we have seen that forces were at work modifying this arrangement: the growth of a central government, the replacement of the feudal services of the lords by money payments, the growth of towns and trade and the large scale production of wool for export. All these and other causes worked together to replace the natural, subsistence economy of the manor by a money economy.

From quite early in the Thirteenth Century began a process of commutation, of the replacement of labour services by quit rents, differing from modern rents because they are related not to the value of the holding of land but the value of the services they represent. At first day labour was commuted, then boon labour, sometimes on the initiative of the lord who needed money and sometimes on that of the villagers who felt money payments to be less servile and harsh. In the main the change was made without much friction, since it was to the interest of both parties. Above all, wage labour proved more economic than the forced labour of serfs. It required less super-vision, it enabled the lord to employ efficient beasts and implements instead of the inferior ones of the serfs and it was more regular. The disappearance of the class of slaves also led to the hiring of shepherds and other types of worker who had to be continuously employed.

Gradually the traditional structure of the manor was modified, as the dependence of the serf upon his lord became less direct. Commutation did not only involve the creation of a rent-paying peasantry, it involved also the creation, on a scale previously unknown, of a class of wage labourers, since the lords now had to pay for the cultivation of their own domain land. The two classes were not as yet clearly differentiated, nor was there a middle class of tenant farmers standing between the landlords and the working masses. Alongside of, and arising from this economic change was a legal change in the status of the villein, a tendency to concede him greater rights and to interpret more broadly the obligations of serfdom.

Between 1066 and 1348 the population had risen from less than two million to about three and a half million, a rise that was remarkable under medieval conditions and reflects the abnormal security of life in England. Commuted and uncommuted services existed side by side, even in the same village, the old system steadily declining but still very widespread. Into this England came the Black Death, transforming the speed of development and setting ablaze the latent class antagonisms of the countryside.

The Black Death was the name given to a violent epidemic of bubonic plague, coming from the East and sweeping all Europe. The first English outbreak was at Melcombe Regis in August. In the spring of 1349 it had reached East Anglia and the Midlands. In 1350 Scotland and Ireland were devastated. Like all epidemics entering new territory it was peculiarly deadly. The death roll has been variously estimated at a half and a third of the population. Probably about one and a half million people perished, and the disease seems to have been more fatal to men than to women and children. In some areas whole villages were wiped out. Two thirds of the parish clergy of the Norwich diocese died, a third of the burgesses of Colchester, half the population of Leicester.

The disorganisation of agriculture was complete. Fields were left unsown and unreaped, and prices doubled in a single year. The rise in prices caused an instant demand for higher wages, and even by the harvest of 1349 they had increased in full proportion to the cost of living. So great was the mortality that the labourers were able to dictate their own terms to the lords and to secure an increase that in most cases meant a rise in real wages.

In 1350 Parliament, composed almost entirely of land-owners, attempted to check this rise by the Statute of Labourers ordering:

"Every person able in body under the Age of Sixty Years, not having [wherewith] to live, being required shall be bound to serve him that doth require him, or else committed to Gaol, until he find surety to serve.

"If a Workman or servant depart from service before the time agreed he shall be imprisoned.

"The old wages and no more shall be given to servants.

"If any . . . take more Wages than were wont to be paid he shall be committed to Gaol.

"Victuals shall be sold at reasonable prices."

The complete failure of the Statute is proved by the fact that it was necessary to re-enact it repeatedly, as in 1357 and 1360, each time with more severe penalties. The lords might pass laws, but when their harvests were rotting in the fields they ignored their own laws and made what terms they could with whatever labour was available. The failure was openly admitted in 1376 by the 'Good Parliament' which declared:

"If their masters reprove them for bad service, or offer them the said service according to the terms of the Statutes, they fly and run suddenly away out of their services and out of their own country, from county to county and town to town, in strange places unknown to their said masters. And many become staff-strikers and lead wicked lives.

. . . And the greater part of the said servants increase their robberies and felonies from day to day."

If the Black Death brought higher wages and greater freedom to the wage labourers it brought equal advantages to the peasant cultivators. Those who had already commuted their services for fixed payments found the value of these payments halved by the rise in prices. Those who still owed labour services were able to press for them to be commuted under the most favourable conditions. It was round this issue that the main struggle was fought. The lords naturally tried to force those who paid quit rents back to labour and opposed any demands to extend commutation where it did not already exist. But the value of an estate depended solely upon the amount of serf labour that would be exploited upon it, and in practice lords who attempted to drive hard bargains found themselves without tenants. The fugitive serf was liable to heavy penalties if caught, but the chances of being caught were slight and the chances of bettering himself elsewhere good. Some went to the towns, others joined the ranks of the wage labourers and others found lords who were prepared to grant empty holdings upon favourable terms.

The old village community in which families lived generation after generation upon the same land began to break up and a migratory class of labourers and peasants moving from one job and holding to the next arose. The attempt to counter the effects of the Death by direct coercion were unsuccessful, though no doubt many peasants were forced into accepting unwelcome conditions.

The lords did, however, find two methods of counterattack that were more successful and that led to profound economic changes. The first was the enclosure of arable land for sheep pasture. The huge profits to be made from selling wool encouraged this move, and sheep farming required far less labour to the acre than arable. When villages had been badly depopulated by the plague or by subsequent flights these enclosures could be easily made.

In villages where the lord's domain had already been separated from the open field cultivation it was also easy. In other cases it meant evictions, considerable displacement of population and much local hardship.

In the main, however, the large amount of land left empty prevented the enclosure of the Fourteenth Century from having the same disastrous social consequences as those of Tudor times. Their immediate effect was to reduce the demand for labour, and within twenty years of the Black Death the abnormal scarcity of workers was a thing of the past. In 1377 Commissioners of Justices of the peace were set up to fine and imprison those who still demanded high wages and it was now more possible to enforce such penalties. The enclosures were not spread evenly over the country, being mainly confined to East Anglia and the North Midlands, but the migratory character of labour gave them an effect throughout a much wider area.

The second method by which the lords tried to escape from their dilemma was the introduction of a new kind of land tenure—the stock and land lease. Here the tenant took a holding for a certain number of years and the landlord provided the seed, cattle and implements. In return he received a rent calculated to cover both the value of the land and of the stock, and at the end of the lease this stock had to be returned in good order. This was a transitional form leading to the modern type of tenant farming. At first the holdings rented in this way seem to have been usually small but in time many of them grew and the tenants themselves began to employ labourers.

Both the stock and land lease and the enclosure of land for sheep farming were important steps towards a capitalist agriculture, to making the land a field for the investment of capital from which a regular return could be obtained. They led to the progressive breaking down of the personal relations which had characterised the subsistence farming of the manor and their replacement by a simple money relation. It is, therefore, not surprising to find in the Fourteenth Century the beginnings of a class struggle on a national scale in England. The peasants and labourers had had a taste of prosperity and freedom and were now menaced by a determined counter-attack from the lords. The lords had been forced to be content with a smaller share in the produce of the soil than they had hitherto received and were trying to recover their lost position. It was out of this situation that the great agrarian rising of 1381 sprang.

6. THE PEASANTS' RISING

Faced with an attempt to drive them back into the serfdom from which they were slowly climbing, the villeins had three weapons. One, already mentioned, was flight. This was the first and most obvious recourse, but it was a purely individual remedy and for a man with a family it had many disadvantages. There remained two others, organisation and armed revolt.

The flight of the most active and determined of the villeins and their dispersal over the country helped to weld the primitive and spontaneous local unions that grew up everywhere into an organisation on a national scale. The preamble of the Statute of 1377 reflects the terror of the lords at this new development. The villeins, it declares "do menace the ministers of their lords in life and member, and, which is more, gather themselves in great routs and agree by such confederacy that one should aid the other to resist their lords with strong hand: and much other harm they do in sundry manner to the great damage of their said lords and evil example to other". Many villages must have had their local organiser, like the Walter Halderby in Suffolk, who was charged in 1373 because he "took of divers persons at reaping time sixpence and eightpence a day, and very often at the same time made various congregations of labourers in different places and counselled them not to take less than sixpence or eight-pence". The Statute of Labourers had fixed the wages of reapers at twopence or threepence a day.

It was from the labour of these nameless pioneers that the 'Great Society' arose, a nation-wide body with an organisation that included the collection of money to pay the fines of its members in its activities, and prepared a programme of demands that gave a unified character to the rising of 1381.

This rising has features which mark it off sharply from the majority of the peasant risings of the Middle Ages. While the *Jacquerie*, for example, was a revolt of despair, a movement of hopeless men without plan and with little purpose other than to do all the harm they could to their oppressors, the revolt of 1381 was the work of men who had already won a certain measure of freedom and prosperity and were demanding more. The villeins who declared, "We are men formed in Christ's likeness and we are kept like beasts", were growing conscious of their human dignity. Many of them had fought in the French war and were fully aware that a well shot arrow could bring down a gentleman as well as a common man. The English peasantry normally possessed arms and were accustomed to their use. As G. G. Coulton says: "Here, more than in any other great country, every man was his own soldier and his own policeman."

Quite apart from the immediate demands of the peasants, which were the abolition of serfdom and the commutation of all services at a flat rate of fourpence an acre, the rising had a background of primitive Communism, strongly Christian in character. It was spread by the poorer parish priests, by the friars, who, Langland wrote,

"Preach men of Plato and prove it by Seneca
    That all things under Heaven ought to be common",

and to some extent by Wycliffe's Lollards, though their responsibility for the rising was probably smaller than is often supposed.

Of all these preachers of Communism only one, John Ball, has come down to us as a living figure. Though a North Countryman, he worked mainly in London and the surrounding counties, deducing the equality of men from their common descent from Adam and declaring in Froissart's often quoted words that "things cannot go well in England, nor ever will until everything shall be in common". The personal prestige of Ball among the rebels of 1381, one of whose first acts was to release him from Maidstone Gaol, was unquestionably great, though there is no trace of Communism in the demands they presented. These demands were probably a minimum upon which all were agreed.

By the spring of 1381, the Great Society had passed from mere organisation on the economic field to preparing an armed revolt on a national scale. The revolt when it came had all the signs of having been carefully planned, as is shown by its widespread character and the unanimity of the demands presented. Cryptic but well understood messages went from village to village when the moment arrived.

"John Schep, sometime Seint Mary's priest of Yorke, and now of Colechester, greeteth well John Nameless and John the Miller and John Carter, and biddeth them that they beware of guyle in borough, and stand together in God's name, and biddeth Piers Plowman goe to his werke and chastise well Hob the Robber, and take with you John Trewman and all his fellows and no moe; and look sharp you to one-head [unity] and no moe" ran one of these messages, and another, clearer in language, declared: "Jack Trueman doth you to understand that falseness and guyle have reigned too long."

Apart from the general economic causes of revolt special grievances existed in this year. The long war with France, now bringing defeat after defeat, had forced the government to levy taxes harsher than ever before. While Edward III was in his dotage and Richard II was a child the government had been carried on by a greedy and corrupt nobility of whom John of Gaunt, Richard's uncle, was typical. With them were allied a new class of tax farmers and moneylending merchants like John Lyons and John

Leg, both of whom were executed, during the revolt. Much of the money raised never reached the royal treasury at all.

> "Tax has troubled us all,.
> Probat hoc mors tot validorum,
> The King thereof hath small
> Fuit in manibus cupidorum,"

ran a popular rhyme of the period.

Further, taxation was being deliberately imposed by the landowners in Parliament as a means of attacking the new prosperity of the villeins. "The wealth of the nation," Parliament declared, "is in the hands of the workmen and labourers," and, in 1380, a poll tax was imposed with the object of taking away some of this wealth. The labouring classes were assessed at sums varying between fourpence and one shilling a family. It was this poll tax, intended and resented as an oppressive class measure, that precipitated the inevitable revolt in the spring of 1381 rather than at some other time.

Late in May the inhabitants of villages in South Essex attacked and killed tax collectors. They took to the woods and sent out messengers asking for support to other parts of the county and to Kent. On June 5th there was a revolt at Dartford. On the 7th Rochester Castle was taken and on the 10th Canterbury. By this time the revolt was general all over the Home Counties and East Anglia and a concerted march on London began. One army of rebels camped at Blackheath and another to the north of the city.

Inside, the rebels had many supporters. The apprentices and journeymen had their own quarrel with the Government and with John of Gaunt, whose financier friends formed a ruling oligarchy in the city. Besides these were the numerous slum dwellers, reinforced during the past two or three decades by hundreds of runaway villeins. Even sections of the well-to-do citizens, including two aldermen, Horn and Sybyle, were friendly. On Thursday, June 13th, the London supporters of the rising opened

London Bridge and Aldgate and the villeins poured into the city unopposed and took complete possession.

John of Gaunt's palace of the Savoy was burnt, but there was little disorder. The rebel leaders tried to prevent plunder and when it took place it was probably largely the work of the slum population. The King and his Ministers took refuge in the Tower, and on Friday they met the rebels at Mile End and promised to grant all their demands. At about the same time the Tower was forced and the Treasurer and Archbishop Sudbury, who as Chancellor was regarded as responsible for the poll tax, were taken out and executed. On the next day there was a massacre of the Flemings living in London. This, too, was probably the work of the Londoners, since the peasant rebels had no interest in what was purely an internal London feud.

After the Mile End meeting the majority of the peasants returned home, satisfied that their cause was won. Others, who realised that the Government was only playing for time, stayed to see that the pledges given were carried out. It was now that the weakness inevitable in any peasant rising began to show itself. The peasants could combine for long enough to terrorise the ruling class but had no means of exercising a permanent control over the policy of government. A peasant State was impossible because the peasants were bound sooner or later to disperse to their villages leaving the landlords in control of the apparatus.

On Saturday the King again met the rebel leaders at Smithfield, and, under circumstances still obscure, their spokesman Wat Tyler was struck down by one of Richard's followers. An immediate clash was only prevented by the King hastening to reaffirm the promise made at Mile End. The rebels then left London, most to go home, a few of the more far sighted to prepare for resistance in the provinces.

While London was the centre of revolt, it was not confined to the Home Counties. All England south and east of a line drawn from York to Bristol had risen. Manors were stormed and lords and lawyers who had made themselves specially hated were killed. The monasteries, which had been the slowest to commute the services of their villeins, suffered most. At St. Albans the Abbey was sacked. At Bury the head of the Prior was set up in the market-place alongside that of the Lord Chief Justice. Even after the rebels had left London the pacification of the provinces was still a formidable task.

The gentry and their followers, who had crept into hiding during the rising, now gathered in London to take their revenge. The promises twice made by the King were repudiated and the common people of England learnt, not for the last time, how unwise it was to trust to the good faith of their rulers. The royal Army began a bloody progress over the disturbed areas. Hundreds were slaughtered with or without trial, and when the people of Waltham pleaded the promises made at Mile End they were answered brutally, "Serfs you are and serfs you will remain".

But, though the rising had failed, there was no complete return to the old conditions. The lords had been badly scared. In 1382 a new poll tax was voted by Parliament, placed only on the landowners on a plea of "the poverty of the country". In 1390 the attempt to keep wages at the old level was abandoned when a new Statute of Labourers gave the Justices of the Peace the power to fix wages for their districts in accordance with the prevailing prices.

The decades after 1381 saw a series of minor risings and the villein unions continued to exert pressure for higher wages and for the commutation of services. Commutation went on steadily, and the Fifteenth Century was probably the period of the greatest prosperity for the labouring population of rural England. Peasant agriculture on small, compact farms began to replace the open field system, and, though enclosures for sheep farming continued to cause local and temporary hardships, it was not until about 1500, when the population had returned nearly to the level reached before the Black Death, that it began to drive the peasants off the land on a large scale. The period was one of slowly falling prices masked in part by a lowering of the weight of silver in the coinage, and real wages were consequently high and tended to rise.

These favourable conditions were not the result of the revolt so much as a general economic trend, but the revolt did give the peasantry a new independence and a sense of their power and common interests as a class. After 1381, even more than after Crécy, it was impossible for the ruling class to treat them without a certain respect springing from a very real fear. The serf became a free peasant farmer or a wage labourer.

7. THE POLITICAL SIGNIFICANCE OF
THE LOLLARD HERESY

In the first centuries after the fall of the Roman Empire the Church had been the sole guardian of learning and of the traditions of the ancient civilisation. Its monasteries were centres of scholarship, poor in quality as a rule but eminent amid the surrounding ignorance. The great monastic orders, Benedictines, Cluniacs, Cistercians, not only helped to keep alive learning and the fine arts but also a knowledge of agricultural and industrial technique. But by the Fourteenth Century, the influence of the Church had declined. Churchmen were neither generally respected nor generally deserved to be. For this there were a number of reasons, some universal, some peculiar to England.

The first was a direct result of the influence the Church had gained in the Dark Ages, which it had used to secure its endowment with vast estates and great wealth. As the monastic orders became great landowners they ceased to be anything else and they shared to the full the hatred felt by the masses for their class. By reason of its endowments the Church was an integral part of the feudal system and shared in its decline.

The collection of tithes was another constant source of dispute and there was a general feeling that the priests were more interested in their tithes than in the instruction

and relief of their flock. This belief is supported by a list
of sins typical of the peasantry drawn up to assist the priest
when hearing confessions. The first sin listed is refusal to
pay tithes and the next two are neglect to pay promptly
and in full. Almost all of the other nineteen sins are
breaches of ecclesiastical discipline or failure to render
dues and services to the lord of the manor. A German
medieval writer expresses a common view when he says:
"I saw a man singing and celebrating Mass. It was Money
who sang and Money who chanted the responses. I saw . . .
how he laughed up his sleeve at the people whom he was
cheating."

It is difficult to be certain that the Church was more
corrupt and worldly in the Fourteenth than in earlier
centuries, but its faults were more apparent because of the
higher general standard of civilisation. The clergy were
now no longer the only literate class. Laymen were beginning to express views on religion and to criticise uneducated
and negligent priests in a way their ancestors would not
have been capable of doing. Langland complains that the
upper classes argue about theology over their dinner and
"carp against clerks crabbéd words".

Such changes were common all over Europe. England
had special reasons for being anti-clerical. Few countries
were so heavily taxed by the agents of the Papacy. One of
the main causes of the unpopularity of the monks was the
fact that much of their wealth was sent out of the country
to Rome. In 1305, the dislike of Papal taxation was intensified by the transference of the Holy See to Avignon. From
then till 1378 the Popes were all French at a time when
England and France were usually at war and when
national sentiment in England was beginning to take
shape. From 1378 to 1417 there were two rival Popes, one
at Avignon and one at Rome, each cursing and waging
war on the other to the general scandal of Christendom.

Inside the English Church there had quite early
developed a Papal and anti-Papal party. The first consisted mainly of the monks, the latter of the bishops, who

were almost all part of the State machine and doubled their ecclesiastical posts with positions in the higher ranks of the civil service, and the parish priests. These, though orthodox in theology, resented the payment of taxes to Rome and the appointment of Italian priests to the best English livings.

Englishmen who had visited Rome reported the luxury and corruption of the papal court. Those at home had the opportunity of observing the same traits in the papal agents who flooded England, collecting taxes, selling pardons and doing a busy trade in false relics of saints. In the Thirteenth Century the last serious attempt to reform the Church from within was made by the Friars. At first they made a deep impression by their poverty, their simplicity and their democratic teaching. But they were hampered by their close connections with Rome and by the Fourteenth Century their early enthusiasm had gone and they were at least as rich and worldly as the older monastic orders.

When about 1370 Wycliffe began to preach the confiscation of the wealth of the monasteries he was encouraged both by the great lords who hoped to profit by this and even by many of the parish priests who felt their own poverty in strong contrast with the wealth of the monastic orders. He based his attack on a theoretical Communism which declared all right to wealth and authority to depend on the righteousness of the individual. All things must be held in common by the righteous, he argued, for all the righteous possess all. His attacks on the "Caesarean clergy" who held State offices was equally welcome to the nobles, who were beginning to regard themselves as the most suitable persons to fill such offices.

Wycliffe's connection with John of Gaunt, who protected and encouraged him as a weapon to despoil the Church, prevented him from applying his Communist theories to secular affairs. "The fiend," he wrote, "moveth some men to say that Christian men should not be servants and thralls to heathen (i.e., ungodly) lords . . . neither to Christian lords."

Some of his followers, who were not, like him, subtle theologians, drew the social conclusions he was unable to draw. It was in his purely theological heresies that Wycliffe himself was boldest and most revolutionary, and every one of these heresies had a political significance, all being anti-clerical, anti-feudal and democratic in implications and content if not in form. They insist on the right to private judgment in religion, on the idea that the righteous layman is as near to God as any priest can be. Hence the attack on transubstantiation and on the practice whereby the layman received only the bread in communion, the wine being reserved for the priest. Like all Protestants Wycliffe tended to regard sacraments as of minor importance as compared with preaching and a study of the Bible. He or his immediate followers produced the first English translation of the Bible and groups of Lollards all over the country were soon at work reading and interpreting it. Finally, he declared that it was better for a man to lead a good and active life in the world than to shut himself up in a monastery.

These ideas soon alienated Wycliffe's highly placed supporters and his theory was condemned and he himself expelled from Oxford, the first centre of Lollardry. This had the effect of scattering Lollard preachers all over the country, of transforming them from academic theologians to mass evangelists. They found support among the lesser gentry, the yeomen farmers and above all among the weavers of East Anglia—the classes from which Cromwell was to draw most of his followers in years to come.

The Lollards made such rapid progress that in 1382 the House of Commons insisted on the withdrawal by the King and the Lords of an ordinance they had passed to facilitate the arrest of heretics. Their resolution declared:

"Let it be now annulled, for it was not the intention of the Commons to be tried for heresy, nor to bind themselves or their descendants to the prelates more than their ancestors have been in times past." This attitude was probably at least as much due to the contempt in which the Church was held as to active sympathy with Lollard doctrine.

In spite of this stand an energetic persecution of the Lollards soon began. In 1401 the Statute De Heitetico Comburendor ordered the burning of obstinate offenders and a number of executions followed. In 1414 an attempted rising failed and its leader, Sir John Oldcastle, was burnt. The movement soon lost its respectable adherents and became more and more one of the poor and illiterate. In the generations after Wycliffe the Lollard preachers developed all the bourgeois and democratic tendencies latent in his teaching. They came to value poverty and thrift, to despise display and worldly pleasure. Throughout the Lancastrian period the sect lived on, savagely persecuted and driven underground, yet counting many followers above all among the weavers. It was the Lancastrian persecution that made the East of England solid in support of the more tolerant Yorkists during the Wars of the Roses.

When Lutheranism began to reach England early in the Sixteenth Century the Lollards were still in existence ready to welcome their new allies. In 1523 Tunstall, Bishop of London, wrote to Erasmus that Lutheranism was not "some pernicious novelty; it is only that new arms are being added to the great band of Wycliffite heretics". It was in the same classes and in the same areas in which Lollardry had been strong that the Protestant Reformation took the quickest and firmest root.

CHAPTER V

THE END OF THE MIDDLE AGES

1. A CENTURY OF PARADOX

THE FIFTEENTH CENTURY was an age of violent contrasts which are reflected in the diverse and contradictory views expressed about it by historians. To some it has appeared a period of general decline, of ruined towns and political chaos. Others have pointed to the real increase of prosperity of the mass of the people, to the growth of trade and industry and to the development of parliamentary institutions in the period from 1399 to 1450. The key to the proper understanding of the age is that both views are correct but neither complete, that while feudal relations and the feudal mode of production were decaying, bourgeois relations and the bourgeois mode of production were developing rapidly.

The decline of feudalism did not only affect the baronage and agriculture, it affected also the towns and the gild organisation. The Black Death and the heavy taxation entailed by the Hundred Years' War dealt a heavy blow at the chartered towns. Contemporary records are full of the complaint of their decay, of ruined houses and streets unpaved, of harbours silted up and of population in decline. Even allowing for some exaggeration these records cannot be wholly disregarded. In 1433 Parliament allowed a rebate of £4,000 when voting a tenth and a fifteenth "in release and discharge of the poor towns, cities and burghs, desolate and wasted or destroyed or over greatly impoverished or else to the said tax greatly overcharged" and such remissions are common.

There is evidence, too, that the raids of pirates were more frequent as a result of the continued wars and there

EE

are many cases of towns as important as Southampton and Sandwich being stormed and burned by such raiders. Inside the towns the gilds were growing more exclusive and the apprenticeship system was ceasing to be a normal stage in the development of a craftsman and was being used to keep the gilds in the hands of a select minority. Under Henry IV it became illegal for any but free-holders with twenty shillings a year to apprentice their children.

The heavy burden of taxation and the rigid gild restrictions in the chartered towns had the effect of driving industry outside them into the village and suburbs. The weaving industry in particular, growing rapidly at this time, developed outside the towns and outside the gild organisation. So that while many of the older towns were in a state of decay new towns were growing with a new capitalist or semi-capitalist production, and trade was finding a new freedom. The medieval restrictions on usury were by now plainly outmoded and were generally disregarded.

Equally marked were the contrasts in the countryside. The nobles, who lost all those social functions that had been their justification in the earlier Middle Ages had acquired in the French wars settled habits of violence. They were evolving on the one hand into modern landowners and on the other into gangster chiefs, each with his band of armed retainers, drawn from unemployed soldiers and those of the lesser gentry who had been unable to adapt themselves to the changed conditions, men who regarded work as beneath their dignity and whose job was to terrorise weaker neighbours. In the feudal age the nobles had their own courts of law. Now they used their armed followers to overawe and defy the local courts. Great nobles undertook to protect their followers from justice, and this practice, known as maintenance, became a permanent scandal. Nobody from Parliament down to the obscurest bench of magistrates, was secure from the menace of these bands, whose open intimidation prevented verdicts being given against the interests of their employers.

When a suit brought two such nobles into conflict the proceedings often ended in a pitched battle.

The situation is vividly portrayed in the *Paston Letters*, with their mixture of hard business sense and gangster politics. The same men who are growing rich by sheep farming are seen carrying out armed raids against their neighbours and using every device known to the lawyer to trick these neighbours out of their estates. One of the most characteristic features of the age, and one which marks it off sharply from the age of feudalism was the wholesale perversion of the law by the ruling class for the ends of lawlessness rather than the open disregard of law.

As they shed their social functions the new nobility developed a fantastic if superficial refinement of manners, an elaborate mask of pseudo-feudal behaviour hiding the reality of decay. Clothing and armour became increasingly ostentatious, gold and silver were made into plate and ornaments as the lords vied with each other to produce the most magnificent effect at court. Heraldry, the tournament, the elaboration of the code of chivalry reached their highest pitch just at the time when they were losing all relation to the business of war. This extravagance was at bottom the result of the gradual displacement of land by money as the prevailing form of property. While tenacious of their land and as eager as ever to add to their estates, the nobility were mere children where money was concerned as compared with the great merchants. The extravagance of the age enabled many of these merchants to secure a financial hold upon the nobility through usury, and some were able themselves to enter the ranks of the nobles. The de la Pole family, for example, were originally Hull merchants.

Both merchants and nobility were far more literate than their ancestors had been. Humphrey Duke of Gloucester collected one of the greatest libraries of the time, and the Earl of Worcester, famous even in the Wars of the Roses for his brutality, was equally noted for his culture and scholarship. It was this new literate class, coming into existence all over Euorpe, that provided the conditions necessary for the invention of printing. The former literate class, the clergy, was self-sufficing in the production of books, the copying of manuscripts being one of the main occupations of monastic life. The lay reading public of the Fifteenth Century, besides being much larger, was composed of people who were far too busy to produce their own books and the professional copyists were too slow and too few to keep pace with the steadily increasing demand.

The first books produced by Caxton in England were mainly of a leisure type to suit the needs of this new public. His first book was the *Histories of Troye* and *The Dictes and Sayings of the Philosophers* (1477); the first book printed in England, Malory's *Morte d'Arthur* and Chaucer's poems, were all of this class. In the next generation the bourgeoisie began to use the press as a weapon, and during the Protestant Reformation a torrent of religious and political polemical works appeared, spreading the ideas of the reformers among a far wider circle than would have otherwise been reached.

The disorder and internal feuds of the Fifteenth Century seem to have been curiously limited in their scope. While the nobles and their followers fought among themselves the rest of the nation was but little disturbed, even at the height of the Wars of the Roses. The Chief Justice Fortescue, writing in exile after the Battle of Towton, compares the general insecurity and misery in France with England, "where no man sojourneth in another man's house without the love and leave of the good man". Perhaps, as exiles will, he exaggerates the happiness of the land he was forced to leave, but it is clear that the wars which bulk so large in the history of the time were the work and the concern of a very small minority of professional fighters.

There was probably at this time a larger proportion of small peasant farmers, cultivating their lands as freeholders or tenants, than at any other time in English history. Their prosperity can be judged from the steady rise in the price of land, doubling during this period from ten to twenty years' purchase. The increase in population, the expanding market for wool and the generally steady level of prices all contributed towards the prosperity of the peasantry.

The labourers also enjoyed relatively high wages. Under the Statute of Labourers they were fixed at threepence or fourpence a day, and the wages actually paid may have been even higher, though there is no means of telling how regular was the employment obtainable at these rates. A man hired by the year received 20s. 8d. in addition to his food and lodgings and a woman was paid 14s. Both the labourers and the peasant farmers were taking up spinning and weaving as domestic industries, and it is probably this at least as much as the condition of agriculture that made the age one of greater prosperity for them than those which preceded and followed it.

Thus, both the chaos and the prosperity of the Fifteenth Century were equally real and arose from a common cause, the transition from feudal to bourgeois society. The temporary growth of peasant agriculture was the result of the decline of the manorial organisation, taking place in a period when the accumulation of capital was insufficient to allow of the development of a fully capitalist agriculture. Once this accumulation reached the necessary level, as it did in the next century, the extinction of the peasant farmer was inevitable. With the increase of the wool industry and of merchant and usurers' capital this accumulation was going on rapidly and began to make itself felt even before the close of the Fifteenth Century.

In the same way, the anarchy of the period was due to the decline of feudalism and of the form of State power which had developed out of feudalism. The bourgeoisie, though becoming more numerous and wealthy, were not yet strong enough to form the basis for a powerful, bureaucratic monarchy, and the local administration was not strong enough to stand up to the great nobles, a few of whom were more powerful individually than any of the feudal barons had ever been in England. The internal wars that resulted had the effect of destroying the power of these nobles, who perished in an unsuccessful attempt to secure control of the State apparatus. The struggle left both Crown and bourgeoisie relatively and absolutely stronger than before and ready to form an alliance very much to their mutual advantage.

2. PARLIAMENT AND THE HOUSE OF LANCASTER

For some years after the rising of 1381 the government was carried on in Richard's name by the Council, that is, by the ruling clique of nobles grouped around John of Gaunt. But Gaunt's authority had been weakened by the evidence the rising had given of his universal unpopularity and by the intrigues of rival nobles. An opposition party soon began to gather round the King, challenging the supremacy of Gaunt. To a large extent the grouping was personal, composed of the King's friends and those who found themselves shut out from the spoils of office. It included a number of the younger nobles like the Earl of Oxford and of recently ennobled families like that of Michael de la Pole, the Hull merchant. There was also an important cleavage among the London merchants. The drapers, that is those concerned with the wool and clothing trade, supported John of Gaunt while those dealing in foodstuffs supported the King. It is probable that the lines of this division were connected with the fact that the royal party were opposed to the continuation of the French War, in which the wool merchants were naturally the most interested.

Some years of struggle between the two parties culminated in 1386 in the impeachment of the King's Chancellor, the Earl of Suffolk. Impeachment was a new procedure, in which the House of Commons acted as accusers and the House of Lords as judges. It was developed mainly as a method of limiting the royal power by attacking the King's servants and was a primitive method of securing the responsibility of Ministers to Parliament. The impeachment of Suffolk was followed by the setting up of a committee of control, the Lords Appellant, after the pattern that had become traditional with the barons in their conflicts with the Crown. It differed from earlier attempts of the kind by its close relation to Parliament, to which it was directly responsible for its actions.

For a short time the Lords Appellant were able to hold power, but in 1389 Richard executed a *coup d'état* and assumed control. The period that follows is one of the most obscure in English history, both because the motives of the parties are quite unknown and because of the complicated cross-currents resulting from personal feuds and the shifting of allegiances from side to side. But it was a period in France and elsewhere of growing royal absolutism and there is reason to believe that Richard was working on a deliberate plan of establishing dictatorial power.

For the first years after his *coup d'état* he was careful to conciliate the Commons and they in turn worked with him fairly harmoniously. The period is important because for the first time the House of Commons begins to appear as a political force independent of the great nobles. This alliance between King and Commons is easily understandable. The King had seized power in defiance of the bulk of the nobility and could not afford to lose the support of the lesser gentry as well. At the same time no Government of the period could exist without the financial backing of a strong party among the London merchants and Richard was able to secure for his friends the control of the City of London.

The position of the small landowners was also insecure. On one side they were menaced by the demands of the peasants and labourers, on the other by the growing power and violence of the great nobles who threatened to engulf them. On this basis an uneasy alliance was formed, in which both sides were aware of the extent to which the other depended upon them and determined to exploit the situation to the full.

An undercurrent of opposition to Richard soon developed as a result of his extravagance in dissipating the Crown estates and his ruthless suppression of all opposition. The banishment of Henry Bolingbroke, John of Gaunt's son, and the seizure of his estates when Gaunt died, alarmed even those nobles who had remained friendly or neutral. The merchants were alienated by the illegal taxation and by the failure of the Government to suppress piracy. In this situation Richard took a step which has never been adequately explained. He secured a packed Parliament by manipulating the elections, and, to make doubly sure, summoned it to meet at Shrewsbury away from a possible outbreak in London, and overawed it with an army of Welsh archers. From this Parliament he secured a vote of taxes for life and persuaded it to transfer its powers to a committee under his personal control. For a year his power appeared to be absolute, but it rested on nothing but his Welsh mercenaries, and, when Henry Bolingbroke landed in 1399 to claim his forfeited estates, Richard found himself without supporters.

For the second time a king was deposed by Parliament after an armed seizure of power. This time Parliament went farther than in the case of Edward II. Then Edward's son had succeeded without question: now a new king was appointed by Parliament who was not by hereditary right the next in succession and whose title depended only on conquest and a parliamentary vote.

The new king, Henry IV, was thus committed to a policy of conciliating the gentry and the town middle class, and during his reign Parliament reached its high-water mark for the Middle Ages. If the support of the Commons was to be secured, some attempt had to be made to end the anarchy of the great nobles. But it was largely by their support that Henry had come to the throne and they expected in return an even greater licence. As a result the King was faced in 1403 with a general revolt of the wild Marcher Lords of the North and West, led by the Earl of Northumberland and Mortimer, Earl of March, whose descent from Edward III was nearer than Henry's own. They were supported by the Scotch and by the Welsh, who had risen under Owen Glendower and enjoyed a generation of independence. It was only the mutual suspicions of these allies and their consequent military blunders that enabled Henry to defeat them in a battle at Shrewsbury.

For the rest of his reign he displayed a diplomatic ability in the avoidance of issues that prevented him from meeting serious opposition. He had added to the estates of the Crown those of the Duchy of Lancaster and so was able to avoid making excessive demands for money, demands that would certainly have been resisted. It became customary during this reign for the different taxes to be earmarked by Parliament for specific purposes. The Crown estates went for the upkeep of the royal household, tunnage and poundage, a tax on imports, to maintain the navy and the coast defences which were considerably improved. The custom on wool was used for the defence of Calais and other taxes for the general defence of the kingdom.

Election to Parliament was now a privilege rather than a burden, and in the shires a struggle began to keep the control of the elections in the hands of the gentry. The rising class of free peasant farmers began to take an active part in the elections in the shire courts, and, in 1429, an Act was passed to limit the franchise. It states its object with a remarkable frankness. Whereas, it declares, elections "have now of late been made by very great and excessive number of people . . . of the which most part was by people of small substance, or of no value whereof every one of them pretended [i.e. claimed] a voice equivalent, as to such elections to be made, with the most worthy knights and esquires", in future the right to take part shall be confined to those who "shall have free [hold] tenement to the value of forty shillings by the year at the least above all charges". The forty shilling freeholders continued to have a monopoly of the county franchise till the Reform Bill of 1832. In the towns there was no uniform franchise, each conducting elections according to its local custom. The Act of 1429

E1

was followed in 1445 by another requiring that those who were elected to Parliament should be gentlemen by birth.

For long before this, elections had been rigged and Parliaments packed, but now, with the number of electors reduced and as the anarchy of the Fifteenth Century grew more profound, the manipulation of Parliament became the regular practice. The great lords came to Westminster with bands of retainers and Parliament degenerated into a mere instrument for carrying out the desires of the ruling group of the moment. The House of Commons had deprived itself of the mass basis that alone could have made resistance to such pressure possible.

The change is marked by the substitution of the Bill of Attainder for the older practice of Impeachment. By a Bill of Attainder the group controlling Parliament could have its enemies condemned and sentenced by legal enactment without any form of trial. Throughout the Wars of the Roses every turn of fortune was followed by a wholesale destruction of the defeated.

In these struggles Parliament became a cypher and lost almost all of its practical importance. Yet the fact that it was kept and manipulated and used as an instrument was a reflection of the place it had won. All over Europe similar bodies were in decay because there was no middle class powerful enough to keep them alive. In England the middle classes—gentry and merchants—were strong enough to be valued as allies by both sides. The very fact that Parliament proved pliable was an argument against reducing its powers and, at the end of the Fifteenth Century, these powers were if anything greater in theory than ever before. As a result Parliament was retained by the bourgeoisie as a weapon ready to hand whenever they were strong enough to use it.

3.   THE HUNDRED YEARS' WAR — II

No clear economic motives such as led to the outbreak of the Hundred Years' War can be discerned in its renewal by Henry V in 1415. Here, as often during the Fifteenth Century, we are left with a sense of parody, of a dying class following a policy blindly for no better reason than that it had been tried before. It is almost as if an inner compulsion was driving Crown and nobility into a course of action inevitably fatal to themselves but unavoidable because no course more immediately hopeful could be found. It was a situation characteristic of an age on the edge of a great social transformation and can be paralleled by the equally blind and suicidal impulse driving the bourgeoisie to-day towards war and Fascism.

Such an impulse can usually be defended with plausible political reasoning, and there were an abundance of satisfactory political reasons for the renewal of the attempt to conquer France in 1415. At home Henry's position was still insecure and a campaign in France was the most obvious way both of conciliating and finding employment for the great nobles. For them such a war meant the opportunity of unlimited plunder and in their eyes Richard's peace policy had been one of his main offences. A claim to the French throne, however baseless, meant an immediate strengthening of Henry's position as King of England, diverting attention from the flaws in his own title.

At the same time there was considerable social unrest that was to culminate in the Lollard rising led by Sir John Oldcastle three years later.

In France the ally without whom no attempted conquest could possibly be successful was provided by the civil war that had broken out between the Dukes of Burgundy and Orleans. The Orleanist faction controlled the imbecile king, Charles VI. In the summer of 1415, Henry, having concluded an alliance with the Burgundians, landed with an army in Normandy.

Just as the war was an unoriginal copy of an old policy so the strategy pursued in the first campaign followed slavishly the pattern set by Edward III in his Crécy campaign. After a siege in which disease carried off half the invaders, Harfleur at the mouth of the Seine was captured.

Henry then plunged recklessly into the interior, only to be cornered at Agincourt by an army that outnumbered his by about six to one. Here in their turn the French repeated all the old errors and suffered a defeat even more crushing than that of Crécy. Henry was too weak to follow up the victory and returned to England.

Two years later he began a more systematic invasion which had as its object the piecemeal reduction of Normandy. This was done by a methodical seizure of one district after another, each gain being consolidated and the inhabitants of the new territory conciliated so that it formed a base for a further advance.

This realistic strategy, together with sweeping successes by his Burgundian allies, enabled Henry to secure, at the Treaty of Troyes in 1420, a recognition of his claim to the French throne to which he was to succeed on the death of Charles VI. At the time of Henry's death in 1422 half France was under his direct control. His brother the Duke of Bedford continued the war along the same lines and by 1428 the French were desperately defending their last important stronghold at Orleans.

It was at this moment that the curious figure of Joan of Arc appears, throwing a light on one of the obscurest aspects of medieval history. The bare outlines of her career are remarkable enough. A peasant girl from Lorraine, she persuaded the French authorities to give her a position of authority in the army that was attempting to relieve Orleans, an army that had ceased to believe even in the possibility of victory. Her arrival disheartened the English and encouraged the French to such an extent that the siege was quickly raised. Further successes were followed by the crowning of the Dauphin, son of Charles VI, as King of France at Rheims in 1430. Less than a year later, after some futile campaigns that there is every reason to believe were deliberately sabotaged by the French military authorities, Joan was captured and burned as a witch by the English in the Rouen marketplace.

Her acceptance by the French authorities appears to

have been the result of a court intrigue, but this does not explain the extraordinary effect she had on the common soldiers of both French and English armies. She acted as a trigger force, releasing an energy hitherto latent and giving the war against the English, previously only an affair of the nobility, a popular, national character. Against this national resistance the professional armies of the English were as powerless as they had been in the age of du Guesclin.

It is impossible to be certain about the character of the force released by Joan, but all the evidence there is points to its connection with the witch cult, which existed through the Middle Ages as a secret religion of the exploited masses. The social history of the cult has been lost because it was a religion mainly of the illiterate and because it was savagely persecuted and forced to exist underground. In part it was a survival of pre-Christian nature worship, in part a direct negation of Christianity. Men who felt that Church and State were leagued against them turned for consolation to the old enemy of the Christian mythology, the Devil. The French historian Michelet declares that "the medieval peasant would have burst but for his hope in the Devil".

The cult was strongest where the peasantry was poorest and most wretched—very strong in France and Germany, for example, and stronger in Scotland than in more prosperous England. Fragmentary references indicate that it was often connected with political unrest and conspiracy. Its organisation, in local groups, or covens, and districts with coven and district leaders whose identity was unknown to most of the members was curiously like that of an illegal party.

It was this force that appears to have been swung by Joan or by whoever the persons were who were responsible for her actions, against the English. Her appearance implies a recognition by the tormented French peasantry that the expulsion of the English was the first step towards a mitigation of their misery. Joan's connection with the cult would explain the eagerness of the French authorities to get rid of her as soon as possible when she served their turn, their failure to make any attempt to rescue her from the English and her close association with Gilles de Rais and the Duke of Alençon, both of whom were afterwards proved to have been connected with the cult.

The continued success of the French after the death of Joan was due to other factors besides the enthusiasm that she released. A quarrel between the English and the Burgundians united the two warring factions against the invaders and is probably the main cause of their defeat. The French armies also made an important tactical innovation—the use of artillery in battle as well as for siege operations. The Battle of Chatillon in 1453 exposed the limitations of the traditional English methods when used in attack on a prepared position defended by even the crude cannon of the period.

But long before the Battle of Chatillon the war had been virtually lost. The difficulties of the army in France had been increased by dissensions at home after the death of the one really capable commander and politician, the Duke of Bedford, in 1435.

The corruption and mismanagement of the nobles who ruled in the name of Henry VI—an infant when he came to the throne and later half-witted—led to the army being starved of supplies and reinforcements. After the Battle of Chatillon the war was finally abandoned and only Calais remained in English hands.

4. THE WARS OF THE ROSES

Barely two years after the close of the French war the long continued anarchy and violence of the nobles burst out into open civil war. The Wars of the Roses, which occupy thirty years from 1455 to 1485, brought the period to a bloody close and completed the self-destruction of the nobles as a ruling class. The defeat in France had brought back the most warlike nobles, more dissatisfied than ever and eager to recoup their losses, with bands of soldiers in their pay unfit for any peaceful employment. Under such circumstances a general outbreak of civil war was inevitable.

In form, however, this war was a dynastic struggle between descendants of Edward III who had rival claims to the throne. To this extent it was the outcome of a policy that had been initiated by Edward III who had married his children to the heirs of the most powerful nobles in the hope of strengthening his family. In this way immense lands and wealth were concentrated in the hands of a small group of men all connected with the royal house and all politically ambitious. In the long run, instead of strengthening the Crown it had had the effect of concentrating the opposition and making it doubly dangerous.

The early part of the reign of Henry VI was filled with a constant struggle between these groups, carried out by methods of intrigue, assassination and judicial terror.

By 1445 the King was under the control of a group headed by the Earl of Suffolk, while the opposition was led by Richard Mortimer, Duke of York, and the nearest claimant to the throne. During this long period the corruption of the Ministers of the Crown reached its highest point. In 1433 the revenue from the royal estates had dwindled to about £9,000 a year, a tiny fraction of what found its way into the pockets of the ruling clique. The cost of government therefore fell more than ever upon the taxpayers.

Even before the end of the Hundred Years' War the general discontent aroused by this misgovernment had found expression in the Kentish revolt led by Jack Cade. This revolt had a double character. In part it was a kite flown by the Duke of York to test the popular feeling and the strength of the Government. From this point of view it can be regarded as the first phase of the Wars of the Roses. But it was also a genuinely popular rising of the middle classes, merchants, and country gentry and yeomen farmers, against the misgovernment of the great nobles.

It was a very different movement from that of 1381. Serfdom was now almost extinct, and in Kent had long been extinct. The demands of the rebels, set out in the "Bill of Complaints and Requests of the Commons of Kent", are wholly political in character, while the composition of Cade's army, which included many squires and well-to-do people as well as peasants and labourers, was far wider and more varied than that of the earlier rising.

The main grievances listed were the inclusion of "persons of lower nature" in the King's Council, the mismanagement of the French war, a specially sore point in Kent, which, lying on the direct lines of communication, usually prospered in wartime, and the rigging of elections. The rebels demanded that the Duke of York and his party should be brought into the Council and the followers of Suffolk should be dismissed and punished.

Early in 1450 a strongly Yorkist Parliament had met and impeached Suffolk who was banished. On his way to Calais he was seized by sailors on board ship, beheaded and his body thrown on Dover beach. This murder was the signal for revolt and on June 1st an army of 50,000 men from all parts of Kent marched on Blackheath to place their demands before the Council.

They were refused a hearing and a royal army moved out to Greenwich against them. They retired in good order to the wooded country around Sevenoaks. A panic then seized the Government. Its army melted away and Cade's followers entered London, where they had many supporters, on July 2nd Lord Saye, one of the most unpopular ministers, and Crowmer, sheriff of Kent, were captured and executed. The rebels kept good order and there was little looting, but this restraint soon created a real problem. To feed so large an army demanded considerable funds and Cade proposed to levy the rich London merchants for this purpose. They had hitherto supported the rebels, sharing the general hatred of the Government, but now they began to wonder what this popular army would do next.

On July 5th they suddenly seized London Bridge, shutting off Cade and his men, quartered in Southwark, from the City. All next day a battle was fought for the Bridge, but the rebels were at last driven back. On the 6th, while they were disheartened by this reverse, envoys from the Government came offering a free pardon to all and promising to consider their demands. They dispersed, only Cade and a few of his followers remaining in arms. Cade was hunted down and killed and in a judicial progress through Kent, known as the 'harvest of heads' many of the most active rebels were executed.

The rising had exposed the weakness of the Government, and in 1455 the Wars of the Roses opened with a victory for the Duke of York over the royal party at St. Albans. The war that followed was not feudal in character, that is, it was not waged by barons who wanted to enlarge their domains and make themselves independent of the central authority, but by rival groups of nobles fighting to gain control of the State machine. This is the main reason for its ferocity. In feudal war one of the main objects was to capture opponents and hold them to ransom and only those who were too poor to pay were slaughtered. The Wars of the Roses were wars of extermination, every victory being followed by a crop of murders and by the confiscation of the lands of the defeated to the Crown. Hence they were extremely destructive to the participants though they hardly affected the country as a whole. The numbers engaged were usually so small that the economic life of the time was little disturbed and the mass of the people seem to have been generally indifferent as to the result.

The war was in form a battle between rival gangs of nobles, but underlying the struggle was another real though hardly apparent issue. Supporting the Lancastrians were the wild nobles of the Scottish and Welsh borders, the most backward and feudal elements surviving in the country. The Yorkists drew most of their support from the progressive South, from East Anglia and from London, even if this support was not usually very active. The ultimate victory of the Yorkists was therefore a victory of the most economically advanced areas and prepared the ground for the Tudor monarchy of the next century with its bourgeois backing.

Towton, the one great battle of the war, standing out among a welter of skirmishes, underlines this fact. The Lancastrians had advanced south with a great army of Northerners plundering as they went. They reached St. Albans but London closed its gates and prepared for a siege. Edward, the son of Richard Duke of York who had been killed in 1460, marched swiftly from Gloucester and entered the city. The Lancastrians retired and were caught in a violent snowstorm at Towton on March 29th, 1461. Their defeat was as much a victory of the South over the Northern specialists in fighting as of Yorkists over Lancastrians and brought the first phase of the war to a conclusion.

Edward IV, who came to the throne immediately after the battle, anticipated many of the characteristics of the Tudor absolutism. He maintained friendly and intimate relations with the merchants of London, Bristol and other great trading cities. From the beginning the Yorkists had found the support of the Hanse towns of immense value, securing them the command of the sea and enabling them to land at any point on the coast. At the same time, since his claim to the throne was made good in the face of the Parliamentary title of the House of Lancaster, Edward ignored Parliament almost entirely and, like Henry VII, preferred to raise money by direct negotiations with his merchant supporters. Not only did Edward establish intimate relations with the merchants, but he embarked upon trade himself on a grand scale. The forfeiture of the estates of his enemies made him richer than any English king before him, and he built whole fleets in which wool, tin and cloth were shipped abroad as far as the Mediterranean. He anticipated the Tudors, also, in devising new and arbitrary methods of taxation.

He also reduced as far as possible the power of the great nobles, creating a new nobility directly dependent upon himself as a counterbalancing force. But he was unable to do much to end the anarchy of internal disorder. His attempts to curb the nobility, including those who had been his supporters, led to a dangerous rising headed by the Earl of Warwick. This was suppressed, but after Edward's death in 1483 the older nobles under his brother Richard had little difficulty in ousting the new men whom he had left to govern for his young son. Richard made himself king after having Edward's sons murdered but in his turn found himself involved in a struggle with the nobles who had helped him to power. This inevitable struggle involved all the kings of the period in a contradiction that remained insoluble till almost all the great families had become extinct.

When Henry Tudor, who produced a remote claim to the throne landed at Milford Haven, the treason and desertion that had been a constant feature of the age reasserted itself and Richard found himself almost without supporters. The Battle of Bosworth, fought on August 22nd, 1485, by a mere handful of men on either side, ended the Wars of the Roses and with them a whole historic epoch in England.

The new monarchy founded by Henry VII was of a totally new kind, based upon a new relation of class forces.

It is not often possible to fix a date for such events, but in 1485, so far as this country is concerned the Middle Ages can be said to have ended.

CHAPTER VI

THE NEW MONARCHY AND THE BOURGEOISIE

1. THE CLOTHING INDUSTRY

IT WAS DURING the political turmoil of the Fifteenth Century that England passed definitely from being a producer of wool to being a manufacturer of cloth. Though employing far fewer people than agriculture the clothing industry became the decisive feature of English economic life, that which marked it off sharply from that of most other European countries and determined the direction and speed of its development. During the Middle Ages England was more rural than, for example, France. Its towns were smaller, never succeeded in winning so full a measure of self-government, never came into so sharp an opposition to the feudal lords or the mass of the peasantry. But rural England was more developed, its peasantry freer and less exploited. It was this evenness of development, this relative weakness of a specifically urban and so partially feudal production of manufactured goods, which made the development of a capitalist textile industry, inevitable in any case once a certain technical level had been reached, so easy and rapid.

This textile industry developed first in East Anglia, around Norwich and in the towns and villages of the Stour valley where the tall Perpendicular churches and the many-windowed houses of the rich clothiers remain as evidence of a peculiar and long departed prosperity. East Anglia had always stood in a special relation to Flanders facing it directly across the narrow sea. While other parts of England had developed a large scale export of wool, East Anglia had exported little. Instead it shipped corn to feed the industrial population of Ghent and Bruges, where, as a poem written about 1436 says:

"Alle that groweth in Flaunderes greyn and sede
May not a moneth fynde hem mete and brede.
What hath thenne Flaunderes, be Flemmynges leffe or lothe
But a lytelle madere and Flemmyshe clothe?
By drapynge of our wolle in substaunce
Lyvynge here [their] comons, this is here governaunce
Wyth out on to wych they may not lyve at ease
There moste hem sterve or wyth us most have peasse."

East Anglian agriculture was of a mixed character, sheep being reared as part of an arable tillage instead of on the large sheep walks of the exporting areas. Their wool was inferior in quality, that of Suffolk being ranked last of a list of forty-four brands drawn up in 1454, and valued at only 52s. the sack against 260s. for the best Hereford wool. Norfolk wool was not even considered worth a place on the list. This wool was not of such quality as to be welcome abroad and so it was woven at home into coarse fabrics from an early period. Probably the fact that it was not produced for export or in bulk led to less effort being made here than elsewhere to improve the breed.

Geographically, East Anglia was the area into which Flemish craftsmen tended to settle, and, as we have seen, such settlements began immediately after the Norman Conquest. Gradually the new-comers taught the natives their superior methods, and by the beginning of the Fifteenth Century great improvements had been made in the variety and quality of the cloths woven. Villages now quite obscure, like Kersey and Worsted, gave their names to cloths that were known all over the country and even began to compete with Flemish products in the European market.

At first exports were mainly in the form of half-finished cloth which went to Flanders to be sheared and dyed, the greater part of the profit remaining in Flemish hands. Their proverbial saying that they bought the fox's tail from the English for a groat and sold them the tail for a guelder was still almost as true as in the days when exports were confined to raw wool. This trade was at first carried on by the merchants of the Hanse towns who had been ousted from the wool export by the Merchants of the Staple but were able to gain control of this newer branch. But just as the Staplers had been able to challenge and defeat the Italians in the Fourteenth Century, a native body known as the Merchant Adventurers wrested the cloth export from the Hansards in the Fifteenth. Establishing a 'factory' at Antwerp in 1407, they prospered in spite of the hostility both of the Flemish clothing towns and of the old-established Staplers who still used Calais as their headquarters.

Among their advantages was a free and uninterrupted access to the supply of raw materials, which they could buy cheaper than the Flemings who had to pay a heavy duty. When in 1434 Flanders prohibited the import of English cloth a retaliatory prohibition of the export of wool was far more damaging. After normal trade relations were re-established under Henry VII in 1496, by the treaty known as the "Great Intercourse", the industry of Flanders continued to decline. In the Tudor period the Spanish invasion of the Netherlands and the fierce wars that followed completed the process, impelling a new wave of craftsmen to settle in England. Holland, which succeeded in winning its independence, was the less industrialised part of the Netherlands and became rather a commercial than an industrial rival in the Sixteenth Century.

The two-sided development is illustrated by figures showing the decline in wool exports alongside the increase in exports of cloth. In 1354 cloth exported was estimated at less than 5,000 pieces. In 1509 it was 80,000 pieces and in 1547, 120,000. On the other hand the duty on exported wool, which averaged about £68,000 in the reign of Edward III, had fallen to £12,000 in 1448—a decline that was certainly not the result of decreased production or a lower duty.

Most important of all, the cloth industry developed almost from the start on capitalist lines. Once the production of cloth was carried out on a large scale for the export market the small independent weaver fell inevitably under the control of the merchant who alone had the resources and the knowledge to tap this market. Wool growers had also long been accustomed to sell their clip in bulk. The minute division of labour and the large number of processes between wool and cloth made it almost impossible to organise the industry on a gild basis. The Norwich gilds appear to have made persistent efforts to control the weavers of the surrounding villages but with little success.

The clothier, as the wool capitalist came to be called, began by selling yarn to the weavers and buying back the cloth from them. Soon the clothiers had every process under control. They bought raw wool, gave it out to the spinners, mostly women and children working in their cottages, collected it again, handed it on to the weavers, the dyers, the fullers and the shearmen, paying for each process at fixed piece rates in preference to selling and rebuying at each stage. A Statute of 1465 gives a detailed picture of the whole process and complains of the frauds perpetrated by the weavers in giving false weight. This Statute is also notable as the first Truck Act, ordering that wages shall be paid in "true and lawful money" and not in "pins, girdles, and other unprofitable wares". The rate of profit was generally high and the accumulation of capital rapid. As the industry spread from East Anglia to Somerset, to the West Riding and to other parts of the country the clothiers began to form the nucleus of a capitalist class more enterprising, more unscrupulous and more ready to explore fresh channels of investment than the conservative gildsmen of the older towns. Bristol, Hull and above all London became centres of far-reaching commercial activity and their great merchants began to rank with the nobility in wealth and influence.

A higher stage of concentration was reached when the clothiers began to collect a large number of artisans under a single roof and to carry out the whole industrial process there. This practice, vividly described in the novels of the Norwich weaver Thomas Deloney (1543–1600), became fairly common in the earlier part of the Sixteenth Century and roused general protest from the weavers. Some of its evils are described in the preamble of an Act of 1555 which aimed at limiting it.

"For as much as the weavers of this realm have as well at this present Parliament as at diverse other times complained that the rich and wealthy clothiers do many ways oppress them, some by setting up and keeping in their houses diverse looms, and keeping and maintaining them by journeymen and persons unskilful, to the decay of a great number of weavers, their wives and households, some by engrossing of looms in to their hands and possession and letting them out at such unreasonable rents as the poor artificers are not able to maintain themselves, much less their wives, family and children, some also by giving much less wages and hire for the weaving and workmanship of cloth than in times past they did. . . ." The Act went on to limit the number of looms that a clothier might keep in his house, and the development of the industry out of the domestic stage appears to have been checked. Probably the extra profit to be gained by this concentration was not sufficient to drive the domestic weavers out of existence, while the machinery used was not so expensive as to enable the clothiers to secure a monopoly control.[1]

The rising rate of profit, the increase in commodity production and of international trade that were common to a greater or lesser extent through most of Europe at this time, created a serious currency crisis in the later part of the Fifteenth Century. There was a correspondingly increased demand for gold and silver money as the only satisfactory medium of exchange when credit was still in its infancy. Europe itself could not meet this demand.

[1] See below, page 326.

Small quantities of gold reached it from time to time, but more was exported, was lost in the wearing of coin or was immobilised as plate or jewelry. There was probably less gold in circulation about 1450 than during the Roman period. And while silver was mined, especially in Germany, the amount was not sufficient to meet the greatly increased demand.

A real famine of the precious metals, and especially of gold, the most convenient medium for international trade, began to act as a check to the continued increase of commerce. All European countries attempted, without the slightest success, to prevent the export of bullion, which in England was actually made a felony during the reign of Edward IV. It was the shortage of gold and the desire to find new sources of supply that gave the general impulse to the geographical discoveries which, in the Sixteenth Century, opened vast new territories for European exploitation.

Columbus himself who wrote that "Gold constitutes treasure, and he who possesses it has all he needs in this world as also the means of rescuing souls from Purgatory and restoring them to the enjoyment of Paradise", was fully aware of the nature of his objective. His voyage was the signal for the commencement of the first, the greatest and, in its effects, the most far-reaching of the world's gold rushes.

2. THE DISCOVERIES

It was in 1492, seven years after Bosworth, that Columbus reached the West Indies. Six years later still Vasco da Gama cast anchor at Calicut after his voyage round the Cape of Good Hope. These events were the climax of a long series of changes and essays, transforming the relations between Europe and the East and beginning its relation with the continent of America.

During the Middle Ages trade between Europe and Asia was carried on along several routes. The most easterly was by way of Trebizond, up the Don and Volga and into the Baltic, with the Hanse towns at its northern extremities. A second was by way of the Persian Gulf, Bagdad and Aleppo and thence by sea to Constantinople, Venice and Genoa. A third was up the Red Sea and overland to the Nile, where Italian galleys awaited their cargoes at Alexandria. All these routes had one thing in common: they involved the transhipment of goods and their carriage overland on horse or camel back, in most cases for considerable distances. The sea voyages were purely coastal, and, in their Asiatic part, were carried out by Arab sailors and shipping. All goods were passed on from merchant to merchant along the route, each taking a substantial profit.

The high cost of land transport made it unprofitable to carry any but the least bulky merchandise. So for Europe the East became 'gorgeous', a land yielding silks, spices and precious stones, an Eldorado of incredible richness. And, in the main, the trade was a one way trade, since Europe had no commodities small enough in bulk to export and was compelled to pay for goods in gold and silver, diminishing her already inadequate store of bullion. The Eastern trade was frowned upon by the statesmen as immoral, wasting treasure in return for luxuries, but the merchants of Italy and the Hanse, who received goods by a continuation up the Rhine of the Mediterranean routes as well as through Russia, found it exceedingly profitable. Each route was the jealously guarded monopoly of a city or group, which kept out all competitors, if necessary by armed force.

During the Fifteenth Century these routes were threatened by invading Mongols who overran much of Russia and by Turks who drove the Arabs out of Asia Minor and in 1453 captured Constantinople. The Egyptian route, though not cut, was threatened. The overland routes were not rendered impossible but the risk was much greater, freights rose and profits declined. Further, nation States were growing up, with strong central governments, which had no share in the old routes and were anxious to develop routes of their own and so destroy the trade monopoly of Venice and Genoa. These States included Spain and Portugal, created out of the struggle to expel the Moors, France, created out of the struggle with England, and, a little later, the Hapsburg monarchy which arose from the defence of Eastern Europe against the Turks. The new routes were all opened by State and not by private enterprise and could not, perhaps, have been developed at this time in any other way.

Finally, the Fifteenth Century had seen a great advance in the technique of ship building and of navigation. The typical merchant ship of the Middle Ages was a basin-shaped affair with a single mast in the middle. It was quite incapable of sailing against the wind, and, in rough weather, was almost unmanageable. In England, at any rate, ships larger than 100 tons were seldom built before 1400. After this rapid progress was made. A list of ships used by the Government in 1439 for the transport of troops included eleven between 200 and 360 tons. Another similar list made in 1451 contains twenty-three ships of 200 to 400 tons. A little later William Canynge, a famous Bristol merchant, owned 2,853 tons of shipping, including one vessel of 900 tons.

Corresponding advances were made in seaworthiness. The Spanish and Portuguese developed the caravel for coastal trade in the Atlantic. It was a longer, narrower craft, with a high forecastle and three or four masts. The compass, known since the Twelfth Century, was perfected and came into general use, the astrolabe was adapted for the calculation of latitude and map makers were beginning to replace mythical cities and dragons with a certain measure of accurate information. It was at last technically possible to leave the coasts and to undertake transoceanic voyages.

The first attempts were made by Portugal, whose seamen, under Government control, began a systematic exploration of the coast of Africa. Cape Bojador was reached in 1434, Gambia in 1446, the Congo in 1484. When Vasco da Gama returned to Lisbon from India, with a cargo that is said to have repaid sixtyfold the cost of his voyage, the effect was shattering. Even under the most favourable circumstances imaginable the old routes with their high freights and the score of merchants who handled the goods in transit could never compete. The power of the Italian merchant towns was destroyed and the whole centre of gravity of Europe shifted towards the Atlantic coast. (Incidentally the decay of the German trading towns that followed upon the disuse of the Rhine route was a major cause of the Reformation.)

The Cape route was a Portuguese monopoly. Rivals had to find others and so Spain led the way to the West, discovering a new continent where a short cut to the Indies had been expected. The new continent proved to be rich in gold and silver beyond anyone's dreams. From Mexico, from Chile, from Potosi came a river of bullion carried by treasure fleets, that, even after pirates and shipwreck had taken heavy toll, still provided huge profits for the German, Italian and Flemish financiers, the Fuggers and Grimaldis, who equipped and insured them.

For in fact, neither Spain nor Portugal had sufficient capital resources to exploit their new possessions or to absorb the wealth they produced. The Spanish governments made attempts to keep their precious metals at home but they flooded irresistibly over Europe, sending prices soaring and stimulating the commerce of Spain's rivals. Of these, France, Holland and England became the most important.

Not strong enough as yet to challenge Spain and Portugal in the regions where they were established, English seamen were forced to seek ways of their own. In 1497 John Cabot, a Genoese sailor in English pay, sailed from Bristol, discovered Newfoundland and sailed along the coast of Labrador. Gradually the existence of a great land mass forming a barrier between Europe and the East was realised, and, since this bleak coast gave no

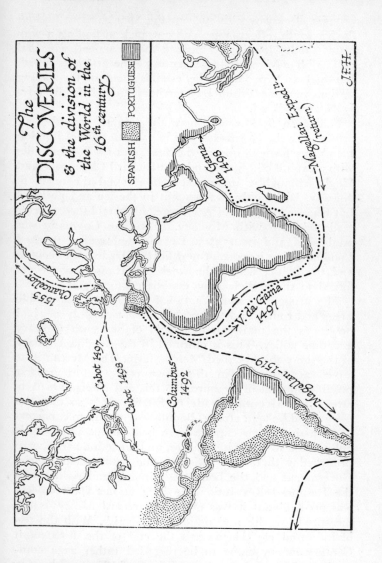

The

DISCOVERIES

& the division of
the World in the
16th century

SPANISH PORTUGUESE

da Gama
1498

V. da Gama
1497

Magellan Exped.ⁿ
(return)

Magellan 1519

Columbus
1492

Cabot 1497

Cabot 1498

1553 Chancelor

J.E.H.

promise of easy wealth such as the Spanish were finding further south, efforts were concentrated on finding a way round—that North-west Passage that remained the goal of English navigators for a century. The attempts failed, but had as byproducts the establishment of fur-trading stations in the Hudson Bay territory and of the fisheries in Newfoundland.

Failing to find a way here the English turned their attention to the North-east and in 1553 a group of London merchants formed one of the first joint-stock companies with a capital of £6,000 and sent Richard Chancellor and Hugh Willoughby in an expedition round the north of Norway. Willoughby was caught in the ice and perished but Chancellor reached Archangel and established regular trade relations with Moscovy. A Russian Company was established and in 1557 a Russian ambassador reached London. Other important new fields of trade were Iceland and the Baltic, where the weakened Hanse towns were forced to share their long established monopoly.

The struggle to secure national monopoly of profitable areas and routes and to break up the monopoly of rival powers is the main characteristic of Sixteenth Century maritime policy. This is reflected in the dominant theory of the time, the so-called Mercantilism. The Mercantilists aimed at amassing in their own country the greatest possible amount of treasure. To this end Navigation Acts attempted to confine trade to English ships so that the navy could be kept strong. Bounties were paid to exporters of corn since corn exports were held to encourage agriculture and to bring in treasure, and home industries were protected with tariffs. This was the theory held by the Government and the bourgeoisie in England right up to the Industrial Revolution. So long as merchant capital was predominant it was natural to regard money as the measure of wealth and national prosperity. With the rise of industrial capital towards the end of the Eighteenth Century money came to be regarded rather as a commodity among other commodities and the wealth of a nation to be measured by the volume of its production of commodities of all kinds.

In the Sixteenth Century England's main export was cloth and the two main objects of exploration, in accordance with the Mercantile theory, were the securing of gold and silver and the finding of new markets for English cloth. If Hakluyt was allowing imagination to run ahead of practical possibility when he wrote: "Because our chief desire is to find out ample vent of our wollen cloth, the natural commoditie of this our Realme, the fittest place which in all my readings and observations I find for that purpose are the manifold islands of Japan and the regions of Tartars next adjoining," the century certainly saw a great increase in this export and those regions which failed to provide a market for cloth were generally turned to some account by English merchants.

The quest for gold and silver involved England in a generation-long conflict with Spain, which must be dealt with elsewhere. Bullion certainly came pouring into the country fast enough to satisfy the most ardent mercantilist and its coming brought new problems, great misery to the masses as well as great riches to the traders. But it came not by conquest or pillage but as the natural consequence of increasing trade. So far, two of the main features of the economic life of Sixteenth Century England have been considered—the growth of the cloth industry and the geographical discoveries. There remains a third, no less important and having an even greater immediate effect on the lives of the people. This was the revolution in agriculture, leading to the creation of large scale unemployment and the beginnings of a modern proletarian class.

3. THE AGRARIAN REVOLUTION

We can err, when considering any historical period, as much by fixing our eyes too resolutely upon the future as by fixing them too obstinately upon the past. Especially is this so in a clearly transitional age like the Sixteenth Century when feudal and capitalist traits jostle one another to form a total world that is neither feudal nor capitalist. What we have been describing in the last two sections is not the formation of capitalist society but the development of the conditions out of which it necessarily arose, the creation of the free market for the production and sale of commodities. In nothing was a free market more important than in land and in human labour, and, since England was still overwhelmingly agricultural, the two things went hand in hand.

Feudal agriculture had been largely collective, based on the plough team and the joint cultivation of the common lands that were both legacies of a distant tribal past. Such a collective agriculture could not pass directly to capitalist agriculture, and we have seen how the individual peasant cultivation of the Fifteenth Century was a transitory form arising from the break up of the manor. The peasantry had to be atomised, broken up into solitary and defenceless units, before they could be reintegrated into a mass of wage labourers taking part in capitalist production. Here lay the importance of the enclosures of the Tudor period.

Enclosures were not new. They had been going on ever since the Black Death and it is doubtful if the rate of enclosure in the first half of the Sixteenth Century was greater than in the middle of the Fourteenth Century. They were not carried out in all parts of the country and in no part was the enclosure of the land complete. Much land remained to the open field system till the end of the Eighteenth Century. Yet the Tudor enclosures have a decisive importance. The quantitative transfer of land from open field to enclosure and from arable to pasture, proceeding continuously up to this time, assumes the qualitative character of a widespread dispossession of the peasantry. The change coincided with the growth of population to perhaps five million, which may be regarded as the maximum which the land would support under the hitherto existing mode of production. Under these circumstances enclosures of an extent which earlier might have passed almost unnoticed were bound to involve sweeping social changes. Further, these changes coincided with the beginning of a rise in prices, the result of the influx of precious metals into Europe, that had the effect of doubling profits and almost halving wages by the end of the century. The 'prosperity' of the later Tudor period was in fact a vast transfer of wealth from the labouring masses to a small class of merchants and capitalist farmers. The rise in prices became in its turn an inducement to speed up enclosure, since the land now became immensely more valuable. Rents and wages lagged far behind prices till it was almost impossible for the farmer to avoid making a fortune.

The results of these enclosures have been described by More in his Utopia with an unsurpassed passion and a wealth of detail:

"Your shepe that were wont to be so meke and tame, and so small eaters, now, as I hear say, be become so great devourers and so wylde that they eat up, and swallow downe the very men themselves. . . . Noblemen and gentlemen: yea and certyn Abbottes, holy men no doubt. . . . leave no ground for tillers, thei enclose al into pastures: they throw downe houses: they plucke downe townes and leave nothing standynge but only the churche to be made a sheephowse. . . . The husbandmen be thrust owte of their owne, or else either by coveyne and fraude, or by violent oppression they are put besides it, or by wronges and injuries they be so weried that they be compelled to sell all: by one means or by other either by hook or by crook they must needs depart awaye, poore selye, wretched soules, men, women, husbands, wives, fatherless children, widowes, woful mothers with their yonge babes, and their whole household small in substance and much in number. . . . And when they have wandered abrode tyll that be spent, what can they else do but steale and then justly pardy be hanged, or else go about a begging."[1]

The army of landless and propertyless men created by the enclosures was reinforced by two other contingents, one at the beginning of the period and one towards the middle. After the Wars of the Roses Henry VII set to work to break up the bands of retainers kept by the great nobles, a policy necessary to prevent the continual revival of civil war. He was able to succeed in this partly because the nobles had been too weakened by the long struggle to offer effective resistance and partly because, as the country began to be less disturbed and the nobles turned to the peaceful management of their estates, these armies of retainers seemed to them superfluous, an unnecessary expense to be got rid of as soon as possible.

These discarded retainers formed the most disreputable section of the unemployed. They were for the most part proud, idle, swashbuckling ruffians who turned naturally to robbery where the expropriated peasantry tried if possible to find new employment. It was these men who provided some justification for the savage laws directed against beggars.

The third stream poured in when the dissolution of the monasteries in 1536 and 1539 turned thousands adrift. The monks themselves mostly received pensions, but the far larger number of monastic servants were less fortunate. The relation of the dissolution of the monasteries to the enclosure movement has not always been properly appreciated. It is not true that the abbeys did not enclose lands on their estates. The evidence available shows that there was little difference between monks and lay landowners in this respect. But after the dissolution the greater part of the monastic lands fell into the hands of landlords of a new type, men who had already accumulated considerable capital and bought these estates at bargain prices with the intention of exploiting them to the utter-

[1] The Chronicler Hollingshed states that 7,200 thieves were hanged in the reign of Henry VIII.

most. These new owners of the Church lands were the men who set the pace and gave their more conservative neighbours an example they were ready enough to follow.

For all these reasons England in the first half of the Sixteenth Century was faced with the problem of a huge army of unemployed for whom no work could be found. In time they or their children were absorbed by the growing cloth industry or the commercial enterprises of the towns, but this was a slow process and one which the Government could do nothing to hasten. They tried two remedies, legislation to check enclosures and ferocious penal laws against the victims. Neither proved effective and their frequent repetition is an indication of their failure. As early as 1489 an Act forbade the destruction of houses to which at least 20 acres of land belonged. Other Acts attempted to fix a proportion between corn and pasture land or to limit the number of sheep that a single farmer might keep. All were ignored or evaded for the excellent reason that the men who were charged with enforcing them, the Justices of the Peace, were the actual landlords who benefited by the enclosures. In any case, what the nascent capitalism required, consciously or otherwise, was not a free and prosperous peasantry— "the plough in the hands of the owners" in Bacon's phrase—but "a degraded and servile condition of the mass of the people, the transformation of them into mercenaries, and of their means of labour into capital!" (Marx, *Capital*, I. 744.)

For this purpose the series of penal laws against the unemployed were more effective, however useless they might be as a remedy for unemployment. In 1536 it was decreed that 'sturdy vagabonds' should have their ears cut off, and death was made the penalty for a third offence. In 1547 anyone who refused to work was condemned to be the slave of whoever denounced him. He was to be forced to work with whip and chain, and if he tried to escape was to be hunted down, brought back and branded. In 1572 unlicensed beggars of fourteen or over were to be flogged and branded unless someone was willing to employ them. For a second offence they were to be executed unless someone would take them into service. For a third offence they were to be executed without mercy as felons.

Towards the end of the century a change can be noticed. The industries of the towns had absorbed a large part of the unemployed and the very growth of these towns had created an increased demand for bread, meat and other foodstuffs. The result was that arable farming became more attractive and enclosures for sheep were checked. But it is important to notice that the movement was not merely from arable to pasture and back to arable again. It was from peasant, small-scale, arable farming to large-scale sheep farming and then back to arable on a large scale, to capitalist arable farming.

In the last decades of the century there was even a certain shortage of skilled agricultural labour, the result of the enclosures which had driven men from their farm to find work in the towns. In 1563 the Statute of Artificers ordered that all able-bodied men and women not otherwise employed were to work in the fields if required. At the same time the Justices of the Peace were to meet annually and to fix maximum wages according to "the plenty and scarcity of the times". It has sometimes been claimed that this Act was not intended to keep down wages, though what it actually did was to place with the representatives of the employing classes the power to fix maximum wages and to inflict penalties on all paying or receiving wages above the rates.

A few years later in 1572 the first Act for the levy of a compulsory poor rate was passed. Each parish was made responsible for its poor and anyone falling on the rates could be sent back to his place of birth. The more famous Poor Law of 1601 did little more than regularise existing practice and included arrangements for setting the poor to work upon "a convenient stock of flax, hemp, wool, thread, iron and other necessary ware and stuff" and for the apprenticing of pauper children. From this Act developed the whole system of Poor Rate, Workhouse, and settlement by parish that remained till the shock of the Industrial Revolution destroyed it.

The character of the social legislation of the late Sixteenth Century shows that the problem has changed, that the period of the primary accumulation of capital, of the violent and predatory seizure of land, is over. The bourgeoisie have now secured a firm basis, a sufficient capital to ensure a continuous and automatic accumulation by the legal and peaceful exploitation of the propertyless class that has been created. Their victory was not won without desperate struggles, however, and some account of the peasant risings of the Sixteenth Century must be given in concluding this section. The first of these, and the most misleading in appearance, was the Pilgrimage of Grace, 1536. In form it was a reactionary, Catholic movement of the North, led by the still half feudal nobility of that area and aimed against the Reformation and the dissolution of the monasteries. But if the leaders were nobles the mass character of the rising indicated a deep discontent and the rank and file were drawn in large measure from the dispossessed and from the threatened peasantry. The Government had no standing army to take the field against the rebels and were saved only by two things. One was the support of the South and East, the result perhaps of old memories of the days of Towton. The other was the extreme simplicity of the rebels, who entered into long negotiations with the Government, during which their forces melted away and those of their enemy collected till they were faced with overwhelming numbers and quickly dispersed. In the terror that followed leaders and rank and file suffered alike and for the rest of the reign of Henry VIII England was cowed by force and by an elaborate system of spies and informers.

In the reign of the young Edward VI dissensions among the Council weakened the hand of government and a number of risings took place. The most important of these were a rebellion in Devon and Cornwall and another in Norfolk, both in 1549. The first of these, like the Pilgrimage of Grace, was in form Catholic but was of a more popular character, the upper classes being by this time too gorged with Church land to wish for a Catholic restoration. The West was still strongly opposed to the Reformation and in Cornwall, where the people still spoke a Celtic dialect, the new English Prayer Book was specially unpopular, being just as unintelligible as and less familiar than the Latin missal it replaced. This rebellion was put down by German mercenaries after hard fighting outside Exeter.

The Norfolk rising was quite different in character and is, after the revolt of 1381, the most important of all the English peasant wars. Norfolk was probably the most Protestant county in England and the rising was entirely directed against the enclosures. Eastern England, with its well developed domestic industries, had a peasantry that was still relatively prosperous, that had held its land for generations and was quick to resist any attempt to take it away. There is clear evidence that the rebellion was brewing long before 1549, and when it began out of a quite trifling incident it spread with extraordinary rapidity.

On the night of June 20th a party of men at Attleborough pulled down fences that a landowner named Green had placed round land he had enclosed. Next day Green advised them to pull down the fences of his neighbour Kett against whom he had a grudge. Kett met the party at the boundary of his land, admitted his fault, expressed sorrow and offered to lead a revolt against the whole system of enclosures.

His part in the rising is obscure. He was a landowner, a member of an old Norfolk family, and throughout the rising we can see that his influence was thrown in the direction of moderation, of toning down its class character. It would appear that he had some feud with members of his own class which he hoped to use the rising to forward. However, he proved a capable organiser and an army of 20,000 men soon gathered for a march on Norwich, the second city of the kingdom. Such a body meant that the whole county was under arms. This is shown clearly when the total is compared with the estimates made later by the Government of how many men Norfolk could provide for the Army in case of war. In 1557 the number was put at 2,670. In 1560 it was put at 9,000, and this is the highest estimate ever recorded. It was an optimistic guess, men on paper not men under arms.

On July 22nd, Norwich was taken and shortly after a force of 1,200 men under the Marquis of Northampton was routed. The Government prepared a great army of 12,000, under the Earl of Warwick, known later as the Duke of Northumberland, a capable general and perhaps the greatest scoundrel who ever governed England. After a battle lasting two days Warwick's German cavalry broke the peasants and Kett and his brother rode out of the battle, leaving his followers to shift for themselves. The remnant of the rebels drew together behind a barricade of waggons and held out so stoutly that they secured a personal undertaking of safety from Warwick before laying down their arms.

The Ketts were pursued, taken and hanged, as were hundreds of others. The Norfolk gentry who had been terrified at the openly class character of the rising clamoured for a wholesale slaughter and not even Warwick's brutality could satisfy them. The chronicle which tells the story of the revolt says that he was forced to remind them that the rebels were the source of all their wealth, asking pointedly, "Will ye be ploughmen and harrow your own land?"

Though suppressed, the rising had some striking results. It helped to stay the progress of the enclosures and to give East Anglia the predominantly peasant character which it long preserved and which made it a stronghold for Parliament in the Civil War and of the most advanced

section of the New Model Army. Its immediate effect was
to bring about the fall of the Government of the Protector Somerset, an aristocratic demagogue who had
shown himself inclined to treat with the rebels rather
than to suppress them, and whom the nobles suspected
of wishing to halt the enclosures. He was replaced by
Warwick, but four years later he, too, paid dearly for
his brutalities in Norfolk. When Edward VI died in
1533, Warwick proclaimed Lady Jane Grey queen in
place of Edward's sister Mary. Mary took refuge in
Norfolk, where, so intense was the hatred of Warwick,
this most Protestant of English counties rallied to the
support of a Catholic queen against the self-styled
champion of the Reformation.

4. THE TUDOR MONARCHY

Henry VII, founder of the new monarchy[1] was in the
fullest sense a symbolic figure. Winning his kingdom by
force of arms he consolidated it by the homespun qualities
of thrift, cunning, diplomacy and double-dealing. A
capable soldier, he hated and avoided wars because war
cost money. A capable business man, he administered
and exploited his kingdom as scientifically and thoroughly
as the new capitalist landowners did their estates. He was
the living embodiment of all the virtues and vices of the
thrusting bourgeoisie who prospered under the protection
of the Tudor regime and to whose support it owed its
stability.

He began his reign with the disadvantages of a strong
opposition party, a title to the throne by no means strong
and openly disputed, and the persistence of the general
disorder which had characterised the whole period of the
Wars of the Roses. But he had certain compensating
advantages. The relative strength of the Crown and the
nobility had been greatly altered to the advantage of
the former, not only because of the physical extinction

[1] See page 147 above.

of many noble families in the wars and the passing of many peerages into the hands of minors, but because the wholesale confiscations of the lands of the defeated had added immensely to the estate and income of the Crown.

Above all, Henry had the support of the merchants, the clothiers, the town artisans, of all those who valued security and feared above all things the resumption of civil war. With this support he was able to go forward steadily to destroy every possibility of opposition and to lay the foundations of an absolutism that lasted a century. The Tudor monarchy rested on the fact that the bourgeoisie were strong enough in the Sixteenth Century to keep in power any Government that promised them the elbow room to grow rich, but not yet strong enough to desire direct political power as they did in the Seventeenth.

Two main objects presented themselves to Henry. The first was to destroy the power of the nobility. The second was to accumulate such a treasure as would make him independent. How successful he was in the latter project is shown by the fact that in the twenty-four years of his reign he only had to summon seven parliaments, and only two of these in the last thirteen years. His first step against the nobles was a law prohibiting the keeping of retainers. This was backed by a royal monopoly of artillery, an arm which had been much improved in the latter part of the Fifteenth Century and was now capable of reducing almost any medieval fortress. He also created the Court of the Star Chamber, a committee of the Privy Council which had powers to deal summarily with offenders who were powerful enough to defy the local courts. The Councils of Wales and of the North carried this machinery right into the heart of the most disturbed parts of the country. These courts, being mainly used against the nobles, were generally popular and through their influence the ordinary local machinery of justice, which had almost broken down under the anarchy of the preceding decades, was gradually restored.

Besides weakening the old nobility Henry began to create a new nobility drawn from the upper middle classes and directly dependent upon the Crown. Such families as the Cecils, Cavendishes, Russells, Bacons and Seymours were all new creations of the Tudors. A lawyer, Dudley, one of the instruments of Henry's financial policy, was the father of that Duke of Northumberland whom we have seen as the butcher of the Norfolk rebels.

To Dudley, as to the Chancellor, Archbishop Morton, was given much of the responsibility of collecting the money which Henry desired above all things. The most diverse methods were used. Parliaments were induced to vote taxes for wars that Henry never intended to fight, heavy fines were inflicted upon law-breaking nobles, old laws were revived, and forced loans and gifts made the merchant classes pay heavily for royal protection. By these means, and by the utmost economy, Henry left at his death some £2,000,000—a vast sum equal to at least fifteen years' ordinary revenue at the time.

In only one direction was Henry prepared to spend with some freedom, on the building of ships. As Bacon said, he "loved wealth and could not endure to have trade sick". The importance which he attached to the development of English shipping is shown by the infrequency with which he sold exemptions from the Navigation Laws, though this would have been an easy source of revenue. The policy of giving bounties on the building of ships, begun by Henry VII, was continued throughout the Tudor period, developing into a fixed allowance of 5s. a ton on all new ships of 100 tons and over.

It was this meagre, thin-faced, calculating man far more than his spectacular successors who established the Tudor monarchy on a firm basis and brought England into line with the general consolidation of centralised nation States going on throughout Europe. France, Spain and the looser grouping of South German States around the Hapsburgs were taking something like their modern shape. With their rise European politics, as distinct from feudal politics, may be said to begin. The new States, instead of being mainly concerned with preserving their internal stability, of checking the disruptive forces of the feudal nobles, began to struggle among themselves for European supremacy. And England, which in the Middle Ages had stood apart from Europe, launching attacks now and then from the outside, became a part of Europe and involved in the complication of its political struggles.

The early years of the Fifteenth Century were full of confused wars, but in essence the battle lay between France and Spain, struggling for the control of the rich territories of Italy and Flanders. England was far inferior to either of these States in wealth and population and developed gradually a policy, the preservation of a balance of power, that has since become a fixed tradition among English politicians. The basis of this policy was to prevent any Power in Europe from becoming overwhelmingly strong by creating and maintaining two roughly even groups, by supporting first one and then the other and by never allowing either side to count with certainty upon the continued support of England.

The first and one of the most astute players of this game was Cardinal Wolsey, chief minister during the first half of the reign of Henry VIII. From 1509, when Henry came to the throne, England usually supported Spain and was at war with France. These wars had few outstanding events, but a by-product was the terrible defeat inflicted upon the Scots at Flodden in 1513. After the battle of Pavia (1525) which made Spain the master of Italy, the European situation changed. Spain, now united with the Hapsburgs, completely dominated Europe and it became clear that England, now unnecessary, was to have no share in the spoils of victory. Wolsey and Henry therefore began to gravitate towards France, precipitating a political situation at home that determined the course and character of the Reformation in England.

Before tracing the course of the Reformation, however, something must be said of the nature of the machinery through which the Tudor monarchy governed.

Though relying on the bourgeoisie as their main supporters the Tudors made little use of Parliament. Parliaments were called from time to time to vote taxes or when they were needed for some special purpose such as legalising the break with Rome. But they showed little independence, aroused little interest and the long intervals between their meetings were not resented. Nevertheless the constitutional forms were duly observed and just because the Tudors had nothing to fear from Parliament its theoretical powers even increased. Writing in 1589 Sir Thomas Smith declared:

"The most high and absolute power of the realm of England consisteth in the Parliament. . . . The Parliament abrogateth the old laws, maketh new, giveth order for things past and for things hereafter to be followed, changeth rights and possessions of private men, legitimateth bastards[1] establisheth forms of religion . . . condemneth or absolveth them whom the prince will put on trial. And to be short, all that ever the people of Rome might do either in *centuriatis comitiis*—or *tributis*, the same may be done by the Parliament of England which representeth and hath the power of the whole realm, both head and body."

Parliament, in fact, lay fallow under the Tudors, accumulating reserves of strength for the great struggles of the English Revolution. The direct power of the bourgeoisie was exercised much more forcibly by the citizens of London, whom the Tudors were always careful to flatter and conciliate. London, a great and turbulent city, was always a force to be reckoned with by a government that never possessed a standing army, and the influence of Sir Thomas More was far less the result of his reputation as a scholar than of his position as the chosen mouthpiece of the London merchants.

[1] Mary and Elizabeth were both declared illegitimate and legitimated again by Act of Parliament.

The day to day work of government fell upon the Privy Council. When the feudal Great Council developed into Parliament[1] the Lesser Council remained, sometimes as a small body of the King's chosen advisers, sometimes as an assembly of the greater barons. During the Fifteenth Century the composition of the Council was a hotly disputed point, the nobles claiming the right to be summoned, the Crown claiming the right to select what advisers it chose. In the Tudor period the addition of the word 'Privy' to the Council's title indicates its character. It was a body chosen by the Crown and consisting of the chief Government officials, resembling somewhat the modern Cabinet except that it was responsible not to Parliament but to the King.

It developed a whole series of committees for special purposes, some settled at Westminster, some moving about the country. These bodies kept their fingers upon every detail of administration, so that the Council and its offshoots besides forming a rudimentary Cabinet contained in itself the first elements of a bureaucracy.

Closely attached to the Council, which guided and controlled their work with minute care, were the Justices of the Peace. Drawn mainly from the lesser landowners, these Justices, who had existed at least from the time of Edward III, grew in power with the weakening of the nobility, who were not now able to act politically in opposition to the Crown. The Justices were powerful because they represented a rising class and because they had behind them the wholehearted support of the Council. They have been called the "Tudor maid of all work" and their functions were far wider than those which they exercise today. Besides holding the sessions they had to fix wages, levy poor rate and administer the poor law, repair highways and regulate trade and industry. A stream of directives constantly poured upon them from the Council and they became virtually the executive part of the machine of government, an unpaid civil service

[1] See page 70 above.

with vast and undefined powers and duties. The responsibilities placed upon the Justices added immensely to the political weight of the squirearchy in the localities and gave them an experience which they soon learnt to use for their own ends.

By modern standards Tudor government was cheap government. There was no standing army and only a small paid bureaucracy. But by medieval standards it was costly enough and soon outran the old sources of revenue that had changed little since the Middle Ages. Henry VIII started with the immense accumulation of funds left by his father but soon spent it. The extravagance for which he is notorious was not merely a personal weakness, it had political motives. The kings of Europe in this period aimed at attracting the nobles to court, and, by turning them into courtiers, weakening them as political rivals. For this purpose a lavish expenditure was necessary and kings and nobles competed in display on an ever increasing scale. Where the feudal nobles had shown their importance by the size of their armed following, their descendants were judged by their dress and the style of their houses. Politically sound, this policy was very costly and Henry, always apt to develop political necessity to the point of mania, seemed to take a positive delight in squandering his resources. In addition, the wars to which the balance of power policy committed him proved expensive and brought no return. Finally, as the century went on, the influx of gold and silver from America began to increase prices without bringing any corresponding increase in revenue.

Henry soon faced a financial crisis. He could not reduce his expenditure and so had to find new sources of income. His first was the plunder of the Church lands (1536–1539) but these were treated as income instead of as capital and dissipated in a few years. His last and most disastrous recourse was what is today politely termed inflation but was then called debasing the coin of the realm. Each debasement gave the Government a certain immediate profit, but was followed by a rise in prices which made the situation worse than ever before and necessitated a further debasement. In 1527, 11 $\frac{1}{12}$ oz. of silver and $\frac{11}{12}$ oz. of base metal had been coined into 37s. By 1551 3 oz. of silver and 9 oz. of base metal were coined into 72s. That is, the coinage was diminished to a seventh of its value in a single generation. Trade was thrown into confusion, prices rose rapidly and real wages fell. The new coinage became a byword. Latimer, even when preaching before the King and Council in 1549, could not refrain from gibing openly at it:

"We have nowe a prety litle shilling, in dede a very pretye one. I have but one, and the last daye I had put it away almost for an old grote, and so I trust some will take them. The fyneness of the silver I can not se. . . ."

By the middle of the century the debasement had had its effect of plundering the mass of the people and was becoming increasingly inconvenient for the trading and landowning classes. One of the first acts of Elizabeth's Government was to call in the whole coinage in 1560. It was paid for at approximately its silver value in new coins and the Government actually made a profit on the transaction. The effect was not to reduce prices but to stabilise them at the existing high level. This stabilisation, coming at the end of the period of enclosures and of the plunder of the Church, marks a definite stage in the consolidation of the position of the bourgeoisie in England, at the opening of an era of armed struggle with Spain for the more intensive exploitation of the world market.

5. THE REFORMATION IN ENGLAND

The medieval Papacy was a centralised, international organisation which succeeded in establishing a highly profitable monopoly in the grace of God. Even in feudal times, as we have seen, this monopoly was often resented by kings and princes. With the coming of centralised nation States it was bound to lead to a general and open conflict, for the breaking of the papal monopoly was a necessary step in the creation of the absolute monarchies. At the same time the degeneracy and great wealth of the Church combined to make it an easy and attractive prey both for kings and landowners. The Protestant Reformation was, therefore, in essence a political movement in a religious guise, a part of the long struggle of the European monied classes for power.

The antagonism to the papal monopoly expressed itself in varying ways, not always in open conflict. The greatest powers, France and Spain, never broke with the Papacy because they hoped to be able to control and exploit it for their own ends as the French kings had done while the Popes lived at Avignon. In the Sixteenth Century the struggle between France and Spain in Italy was to a large extent a struggle to control the Papacy. At the worst they were strong enough to extort a large share of the spoil. Both Charles V of Spain and Francis I of France, for example, received large sums for allowing the sale of indulgences in their dominions. Similarly, the Hapsburgs needed the support of the Pope to maintain their hegemony over the medley of principalities composing the Holy Roman Empire. It was the poorer and more backward States, Scotland, the Scandinavian countries, and the petty kingdoms and duchys of North Germany, which were forced into open revolt and in most of these countries the Reformation had a broad popular character and assumed democratic forms.

Midway between these extremes in power and wealth stood England. Wolsey and Henry VIII began by believing that they could compete with France and Spain for the control of the Papacy and it was not till they were disillusioned that they took the first steps towards freeing England from papal control. In England the Reformation was not at first a popular movement and in some of its aspects it was certainly opposed by the majority of the population. Three strands can be separated out, not necessarily dependent upon each other and not appealing to the same classes. The first was the break with Rome, involving the cessation of the large revenue paid to the Popes, the second was the confiscation of the property of the Church in England itself and the third was the victory of the body of theological dogma known as Protestantism.

The break with Rome was almost universally welcomed. We have already seen that the exactions of the Papacy were disliked even by large sections of the clergy and when Henry in 1531 declared himself head of the Church there was little opposition except from the monks. The seizure of the monastic lands, on the other hand, was the work of the Crown and of the landowning class and was much less popular, leading even to armed risings of which the Pilgrimage of Grace was the most important. The theological changes were the work of the middle and lower classes, who had kept alive the teachings of Wycliffe and welcomed those of Luther. Protestantism was the body of ideas inspiring the popular mass movement, and, since the Reformation in England began from above, it made slow progress at first. The majority of the people remained Catholic in belief until Catholicism was politically discredited by its connection with the hostile power of Spain.

About 1526 Henry became anxious to obtain a divorce from his wife, Catherine of Aragon, or, strictly speaking, a papal declaration that his marriage was invalid since Catherine had previously been the wife of Henry's brother, Arthur. For this divorce there were two excellent political reasons. First, Catherine was a Spanish princess and in the Sixteenth Century royal marriages were a recognised method of cementing alliances between States. At a moment when Henry was contemplating an alliance with France this Spanish marriage was highly inconvenient. The second reason was that Catherine had failed to produce a male heir and did not now seem likely to do so.

Henry applied to Pope Clement VII for a divorce and in the ordinary way it would no doubt have been granted. But in 1527 Rome had just been sacked by an army of

Germans and Spaniards and Clement was virtually a prisoner in the hands of Catherine's nephew Charles V. He temporised as long as he dared, hoping to find some compromise. But for Henry this was a test case, a test of his power to coerce the Papacy. When he found that this was impossible he determined on a break with Rome. It was a test also of Wolsey's diplomatic capacity and when he failed he was stripped of his offices and died only just in time to avoid execution. Henry turned to a rougher adviser, one who would be less scrupulous in carrying out the plans he was beginning to form for the plunder of the monasteries. This was Thomas Cromwell, a typical 'new' man, born and brought up no one quite knew where and enriched by the most questionable methods of the age.

For seven years—1529 to 1536—the Reformation Parliament sat, passing without opposition a series of Acts which cut off the Church in England from Rome and brought it under the control of the State. Appeals to the Pope were forbidden. Payments such as annates and 'Peter's Pence' were forbidden. The King was made head of the Church with power both to appoint its leading officials and to determine its doctrine. So far as England was concerned the Church was now no longer part of an international organisation but was part of the apparatus of the State and its fortunes were bound up with those of the Crown. One paradoxical result of this change was that from this time leading churchmen played a part in State affairs not more but less prominent than formerly. Before Wolsey few leading ministers had been laymen. After him no cleric held high office under the Crown. The Church which in the Middle Ages had been an independent power in some respects equal to the State was henceforth subordinated and rigidly confined to its own limited sphere.

In 1536 the direct attack on the monasteries began. A Commission had been sent out to gather or concoct enough scandal to justify confiscation on moral grounds. On the strength of their report, received by the landowners in Parliament with delighted shouts of 'Away with them!'

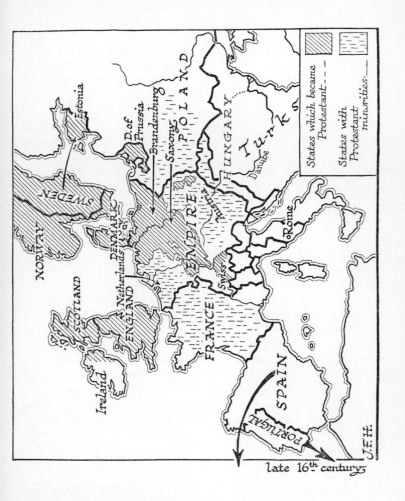

late 16th century

J.F.H.

States which became Protestant ----

States with Protestant minorities ——

NORWAY
SWEDEN
Estonia
DENMARK
D. of Prussia
Brandenburg
Saxony
POLAND
EMPIRE
HUNGARY
Turks
Danube
Rome
Swiss
FRANCE
Netherlands
ENGLAND
SCOTLAND
Ireland
SPAIN
PORTUGAL

376 of the smaller houses were suppressed. In 1539 the rest followed. The reasons for the dissolution of the monasteries and some of its results have been noted already. The monks were too isolated to resist, the old antagonism between them and the parish clergy depriving them of much support even from churchmen.

A few schools were founded out of the spoil, a little was used to endow six new bishoprics. The rest was seized by the Crown and sold to nobles, courtiers, merchants and groups of speculators, mostly at far less than its real value. Much was resold by them to smaller landowners and capitalist farmers, so that a large and influential class was created who had the best of reasons for maintaining the Reformation settlement. This squandering of the Church lands by the Government was poor economics, but politically it was a master-stroke, ensuring with absolute certainty the permanence of the Reformation as far as it had gone up to that time.

So far the changes had been only political and economic. Henry still, and for the rest of his life, regarded himself as a pious Catholic whose religious beliefs were not altered by his political quarrel with the Pope. As for the monasteries, they had been dissolved in the interest of morality and true religion. This view was ultimately untenable, especially as it was by no means shared by the Pope or by the Catholic Powers. Cromwell, realising this, tried to push Henry along the road to complete Protestantism and an alliance with the Lutheran States of North Germany. For some years progress was made in this direction but Henry became alarmed at a policy that would have isolated England from all the great European Powers. Cromwell, like Wolsey, overestimated his power to determine Henry's policies and in 1540 he was accused of treason and beheaded. Henry reverted to the old balance of power tactics and found that Charles V was now quite prepared to accept the support of a heretic against his French enemies.

At home there was a corresponding reaction. The Statute of the Six Articles made denial of the main Catholic

doctrines punishable by death. Latimer and other prominent Protestants were deprived of their positions. For the
rest of his reign Henry quite impartially executed
Protestants for denying the doctrine of transubstantiation
and Catholics for denying that he was head of the Church.
With very few exceptions the bishops and clergy took the
required oath of obedience to the King and remained in
their places. The old forms of worship continued unchanged
and only here and there did a reforming cleric preach the
new doctrine.

One innovation did have an immense though delayed
effect. This was the publication of an English version
of the Bible. Once the Bible was common property and
not a book in an unknown tongue available only to
the priests, the key to the mysteries lay in the hands of
any man who could read. Protestants made the Bible the
text-book of their party and its study the centre of their
practice. For the men of the Sixteenth and still more the
Seventeenth Century it was a veritable revolutionists'
handbook, making the priestly monopoly of grace for ever
untenable.

A more powerful and immediate force spreading
Protestantism was the thousands of holders of Church
lands. They realised that their possession of these lands
could only be guaranteed by a wide diffusion of
Protestantism among the masses and that its growth
might enable them to secure the still considerable wealth
remaining to the Church. In London and the Eastern
Counties especially, the upper classes became fervent
if not disinterested advocates of "a thorough godly reformation", drawing behind them numbers of their tenants,
apprentices and workpeople.

So affairs stood at the death of Henry in 1547. The
break with Rome was complete. The appropriation of
Church property was partially carried out. The revolution
in doctrine had hardly begun. The Protestant section of
the population was still a definite minority, but a minority
vocal and influential out of all proportion to its numbers,

a minority whose desires coincided precisely with the natural course of historical development.

6. THE COUNTER-REFORMATION AND THE ELIZABETHAN SETTLEMENT

When Henry died he left a Council of Regency to govern in the name of his young son Edward VI. This Council was strikingly composed of the 'new' nobility, not one of its sixteen members having a title that dated so far back as the beginning of the century. Its leading figure was the King's uncle, Edward Seymour, afterwards Duke of Somerset, and nearly all its most active members were ardent reformers, men who had profited much by the spoiling of the Church and who hoped for more.

Under their rule the extreme Protestant party gained ground rapidly. A new Prayer Book was issued in 1549, differing only in detail from the one in use today. Its chief merit was the extreme vagueness of its formulations which enabled men of all parties to read their own interpretations into it. The property of the chantries and other religious bodies that had been spared in the previous reign were forfeited to the Crown and passed rapidly into the hands of the Council and its supporters. The considerable proportion of the endowments of the gilds which were devoted to religious purposes went the same way. Only the London gilds were spared because they were too powerful to be attacked with safety, and throughout the country this confiscation was fatal to the already declining gild organisation. Under the pretext of suppressing idolatrous images and superstition there was a general plunder of the parish churches.

In this plunder their rich plate, ornaments and vestments were taken, much carving and stained glass that could not be removed was destroyed and in many cases even the lead was stripped from the roofs. All pretence of moderation and decency was abandoned, so that even the Protestant Bucer wrote in 1550:

"For as yet sacrilegious persons hold and plunder the parishes, and often one, four, or six, or more: and it is said that there are not a few who bestow two or three benefices upon their Stewards or Huntsmen, yet on condition that they themselves retain a good part of their ecclesiastical revenues: and they present to livings vicars, not whom they know to be best fitted for their office but whom they can hire the most cheaply."

The Edwardian Reformation was the work of a predatory minority, watched sullenly by the mass of the people. The identification of Protestantism with a government so manifestly corrupt repelled many who might otherwise have been attracted to it. Only the Protector Somerset managed to escape to some extent the contempt in which the Council was held. He is a curious figure, eager himself to secure Church property, often descending to discreditable intrigues, ruthless enough to his enemies, he yet seems to have had a genuine desire to remedy the misery caused by the enclosures and to have been ready to take real risks with this object. He alienated the nobles by appointing a Commission to enquire into the evasion of the laws against enclosures and in 1548 introduced three Bills, based on the findings of the Commission, all of which were rejected by Parliament.

Somerset's hesitation in suppressing the Norfolk rebels in 1549 completed his loss of credit with the nobility and his chief rival Dudley (afterwards Duke of Northumberland) prepared a *coup d'état*. Relying on the popular dislike for the lengths to which the Reformers had gone he carefully disguised his attempt as a movement to restore Catholicism. He remained in the background and used Southampton, Arundel and other Catholic lords as his instruments. When Somerset had been overthrown Northumberland disowned these dupes and allied himself with the extreme Protestant party. With these he planned an attack on the still untouched revenues of the bishoprics. Northumberland himself was determined to secure the immense wealth of the See of Durham, and much of his attention in the following years was taken up with a series of complicated intrigues having this as their object. Doctrinaire Protestants like Hooper, who spoke of "that most faithful and intrepid soldier of Christ, the Earl of Warwick", were quite ready to see the nobles swallow up the episcopal revenues in return for support in imposing Calvinism upon England.

All these schemes depended for success upon the life of the King, and it soon became obvious that Edward was dying. The next heir was Mary, daughter of Catherine of Aragon, a Catholic and a bitter enemy of Northumberland. If she succeeded Northumberland was finished, so he prepared for a new coup. He married his son to Lady Jane Grey, a granddaughter of Henry VII, and forced the Council to declare her the lawful heir to the throne. When Edward died in July 1553 Northumberland proclaimed Jane Grey queen in London. Mary took refuge in Norfolk and received support from all over the country, since most people were hostile either to Northumberland or to the Reformation or to both. Northumberland's men refused to fight and he was arrested and brought to London to be executed.

"And after he came onsse to Shordych," says a writer of the time, "alle the pepulle revyled hym and callyd hym traytor and herytycke, and would not seyse for all they were spokyn unto for it", a passage which shows that even London was far from being wholly Protestant at this time. Northumberland's last act was a cringing recantation of a Protestantism that had never been more than a mask for his greed. His career is of some significance since he sums up both the ignoble side of Protestantism and the unresting cupidity of a class. Yet we shall fail to understand Protestantism if we look only at the greed of Northumberland and forget the courage and single-mindedness of Latimer. This yeoman's son become bishop, with his contempt for compromise and passion for social justice, carried the radicalism of More into the Protestant Reformation and remains as the true voice of the nameless

weavers and peasants who formed its genuinely revolutionary wing.

Though Northumberland's conspiracy had collapsed
at the first touch Mary was still a hostage in the hands
of the landowning class. She could restore the Mass and
burn heretical weavers but she could not force a single
squire to disgorge a single acre of Church land. Short
of this, her position was a strong one and her first actions
in bringing the Reformation back to the point reached at
the death of Henry VIII were generally popular. Such a
compromise could hardly have been permanent, and in
any case Mary was unique among the Tudors in possessing
both genuine religious convictions and a complete lack of
political judgment. The rest of her reign was filled with
blunders which destroyed whatever slight chance there
was of a restoration of Catholicism in England.

The first of these was the announcement of her intention
of marrying Philip of Spain. In the existing European
situation this meant the complete subordination of
England. In spite of strong opposition, including a rebellion
that was put down without much difficulty, the marriage
actually took place in 1554. It was especially unpopular
as an offence against what was now just becoming a constant
if unformulated principle of English foreign politics—
that the most dangerous commercial rival should also be
the main political enemy. This principle, applied in turn
to Spain, Holland and France, was one which for centuries
ahead no Government could ignore without disaster.

The next step was a reconciliation with Rome, taking
the form of a 'supplication' from Parliament entreating for
pardon and the admission of a Papal Legate. The old
laws for the burning of heretics were revived and plans
were made for the execution of the most prominent
Protestant churchmen. The persecution which followed,
and which was begun in spite of the advice of the more
realistic Spanish, proved fatal because of its ill-directed
character. After a group of leading clergy, Latimer,
Hooper, Ferrar and finally Archbishop Cranmer, its

victims were all obscure men, mainly artisans and small farmers. About 300 were burned, chosen apparently at random but probably for the most part Calvinists and Anabaptists. Five out of six came from London, East Anglia and Kent.

Not a single layman of the upper classes suffered, for they were prepared without exception to profess any faith so long as their property was untouched. Nevertheless the persecution was alarming to them, leaving them in doubt as to what Mary and her advisers might do next. Nobody in the Sixteenth Century objected to a moderate amount of persecution, but the wholesale burnings of the last four years of Mary's reign were generally felt to be excessive and led to a belief that the Inquisition, with whose workings in Flanders people were fairly familiar, was to be introduced into England.

In 1557 the Spanish connection led to a war with France, in which Calais was lost after being in English hands for three hundred years. The wool staple that had once made it important had now dwindled to small proportions, but its loss was bitterly resented, especially by the merchant class who were in any case strongly opposed to any alliance with Spain. Only the knowledge that Mary was dying prevented a rising that would have probably been followed by the invasion of England by a Spanish army.

It fell to the Government of Elizabeth to make a religious compromise characteristic of the Reformation movement in England. Elizabeth herself had no particular religious interests and the only concern was to arrive at a settlement that would be accepted by as many people as possible. The authority of the Pope was once more abolished, and a slightly modified form of royal supremacy, that is of the subordination of the Church to the State, was substituted. At the same time, the form of organisation existing in the Catholic Church, government by bishops and an elaborate ecclesiastical hierarchy was preserved. The more uncompromising and democratic forms of Protestantism were avoided. Both in organisation and doctrine the Church of

England claimed to be 'Catholic', that is, to maintain the tradition of the universal church, but also 'reformed', that is, to have shed a number of corrupt practices and beliefs that had crept in during the Middle Ages. So far as possible the formulation of doctrine was kept vague, and, as in 1549, the services of the Church were carefully drawn up so as to be capable of alternative interpretations.

"The Church of England as by law established" owed its form to the political needs of the time. It was regarded by many as a temporary arrangement, few were enthusiastically in its favour. But even fewer found it so repugnant that they were prepared to take up arms against an otherwise popular government to bring about its destruction. In the Elizabethan settlement Protestantism assumed the form most compatible with the monarchy and with the system of local government created by the Tudors. The parson in the villages became the close ally of the squire and almost as much a part of the State machine as the Justice of the Peace.

The Reformation in Scotland took a different course. There the Church was even more corrupt and discredited than in England and the movement against it was of a broader character. It triumphed when it was able to ally itself with national sentiment and to assume the form of a movement of national liberation. In England the Reformation subordinated the Church to the State: in Scotland there were moments when the State seemed likely to be altogether subordinated to the Church. Scottish Protestantism drew its inspiration from Geneva, where Calvin did for a time set up a dictatorship of the righteous. The Scottish Kirk was always democratically organised, and it was indeed only inside the Kirk that democratic ideas took root in Scotland.

In the time of Henry VIII the irregular warfare in which England and Scotland were engaged after the battle of Flodden prevented the Reformation from making much headway, since it was everywhere identified with the cause of the English enemy. Somerset wished to bring the quarrel to an end by marrying Edward VI to Mary, daughter of James V, who had died in 1542 when she was only a week old. To hasten the negotiations he marched an army into Scotland, won a battle at Pinkie and burnt Edinburgh. This made an Anglo-Scottish alliance unthinkable and Mary was hurried off to France where she married the Dauphin.

From this time the situation began to change. The Queen's mother, Mary of Guise, ruled Scotland with the help of a French army. Scotland was treated as a French province and gradually the Protestants assumed the role of patriots while the Catholics were forced into appearing as supporters of the French occupation. Many of the nobles, who had had the opportunity of observing how profitable Protestantism in England had been for their class, joined the party of the reformers. In 1559 open war broke out and in the following year, with the help of an English army and fleet, the French were expelled and Protestantism was established.

In 1561 Mary Stuart returned to Scotland, a widow of nineteen and a Catholic, ruling over a country now fanatically Calvinist. The story of her misadventures has been told often enough and it is not necessary to repeat it here. Eight years after her arrival she was deposed and only with difficulty made her escape to England where she appealed to Elizabeth for protection. Her presence in England was extremely unwelcome, since she was not only the heir to the English throne but, as all Catholics considered Elizabeth illegitimate, was regarded by many people as the rightful monarch. Elizabeth shut her up in a castle and, as was her way, began to put off as long as possible any decisive action. From this point Mary's career belongs not to Scottish history but to the history of the struggle just beginning between England and Spain.

CHAPTER VII

ORIGIN OF THE ENGLISH REVOLUTION

IN THE STRUGGLE WITH SPAIN

IN THE STRUGGLE between England and Spain which occupied the last third of the Sixteenth Century both sides were on the offensive though both were anxious to avoid an open war if they could accomplish their ends by any other means. England, that is to say the English merchant class backed by the Government, was determined to break through the colonial monopoly that Spain had established in the West. This ambition was shared by other North European sea-powers, especially the Dutch. The fortunes of English and Dutch were inseparably linked during this period, and the revolt of the Netherlands played a decisive part in the general struggle. It was only at the expense of Spain and Portugal that English and Dutch commerce could grow, since in Spanish and Portuguese hands lay all the areas outside Europe which seemed at that time to offer any possibility of profitable trading. And for both England and Holland, small countries with no hope of expanding by land and with prosperous and pushing merchant classes, such colonial expansion was a condition of national development.

On the other side, Philip's marriage to Mary Tudor had seemed for a moment to promise Spain that control over England which was a necessary condition for the success of Spanish plans for world empire. The accident of Mary's death had frustrated these plans and at first Philip hoped to recover the lost ground by a second marriage to Elizabeth. For as long as she dared Elizabeth allowed him to believe this possible though she and her advisers were far too astute to repeat Mary's blunder. When Philip realised that his marriage plan had failed he began very slowly and dubiously to try other methods, diplomacy, intrigue and finally war.

Closely allied with Spain was the Papacy. The Church reorganised its forces at the Council of Trent (1546–1551), had created in the Jesuits a body of highly trained and disciplined storm troops, had perfected the Inquisition as an instrument of repression and was working steadily and with apparently good prospects of success towards a counter-reformation which would stamp out heresy and restore the supremacy of the Pope throughout Europe. In the main the interest of the Papacy and the Spanish monarchy coincided, since the heretics were also the most determined opponents of Spanish power, and, although the allies quarrelled sometimes about the expenses of the campaign and the division of the spoils, they managed to work fairly closely together. Consequently, the struggle had also a religious character, was a struggle between Protestantism and the Counter-Reformation.

This struggle was complicated in every country by a minority problem. England contained a large number of Catholics who were always thought likely to rise in revolt. Spain had an interminable and never suppressed rising of her Protestant subjects in the Netherlands to deal with. France was even more unfortunate and a bitterly contested civil war between Catholics and the Protestant Huguenots, intensified by a dynastic conflict, made her a negligible factor in European politics during the whole of this period and completely upset the balance of power. A superficial observer looking at Europe in 1570 would have seen no possible rival to Spain, which controlled not only Southern Italy, Austria, Hungary and the Netherlands but also a vast colonial empire.

But in the Channel and the North Sea, with its head-quarters at Dover, where it was unofficially encouraged by the English authorities, was a nondescript fleet, part Dutch, part English with a sprinkling of Huguenots, who dominated the Straits and made raids in all directions upon Spanish and French shipping. Other raiders put out from the ports of Devon and Cornwall and from the Huguenot stronghold of La Rochelle, seizing Spanish merchant ships and even threatening the West Indies. In theory England and Spain were at peace but the English Government shared the plunder taken by these privateers and even at times lent them ships from the Royal Navy. When at last, in 1572, Philip demanded that the Channel fleet should be expelled from English harbours it was given time to gather its full strength for a sudden and brilliantly successful attack on the Dutch town of Brill. The capture of Brill was the signal for a general rising along the coast of Holland and the revival in the Netherlands of a war which the Spanish thought had been ended some years before. In this war the best generals and the best troops in Europe failed to overcome the resistance of the Dutch burghers and peasants so long as these were able to keep open a sea way by which trade and help from abroad could reach them.

In England meanwhile, Elizabeth and her ministers were facing the situation created by the unwelcome arrival of Mary Stuart in 1568. Almost at once the Catholic Earls of Northumberland and Westmorland had started a revolt in the North to free Mary, marry her to the Duke of Norfolk and place her on the throne. The rising was partly spontaneous and partly provoked deliberately by the Council. It collapsed at the first approach of a strong royal army and the ease with which it was suppressed is an index of the striking decline of the power of the semi-feudal nobility of the North since the superficially similar Pilgrimage of Grace only thirty years before.

For eighteen years Mary was the centre of a whole series of plots, all involving the assassination of Elizabeth. Just as the English Government encouraged the activities of the privateers on Spanish shipping and towns, the Spanish ambassador and the Jesuit priests who were sent in large numbers to reconvert England encouraged these plots.

Elizabeth was, as often during her reign, in a position where every possible course of action was full of danger. Neither she nor Cecil, her chief minister, believed that it was possible as yet to challenge Spain in an open conflict, though such a conflict was clearly inevitable sooner or later. So long as Mary lived there would be plots, one of which would probably succeed. The assassination of Elizabeth would be almost certain to precipitate a civil war and give Philip the chance for which he was waiting. On the other hand, so long as both Mary and Elizabeth remained alive war was improbable. Philip was not anxious to go to war to make Mary queen since she was half French by blood and more than half French in outlook and would be more likely to govern England in the interests of France than of Spain. Also, so long as there was a possibility of removing Elizabeth by assassination, Philip preferred to wait.

Year after year passed, with each side looking for an opening. Philip sent help to the rebel Irish. Drake, Hawkins and other privateers grew bolder in their exploits. Jesuit priests preached sedition among the Catholic nobles and gentry and were hunted down and hanged. In 1577 Drake set out on his voyage round the world, to return with an immense cargo of booty. In 1580 a Spanish force landed in Ireland and was captured and massacred at Smerwick. Elizabeth sent just enough men and money to the Dutch to keep their revolt stirring but not so much as to commit herself beyond possibility of drawing back.

In 1584 Elizabeth had to face a new dilemma. William of Orange, the leader of the revolt in the Netherlands, was assassinated and the Dutch sent ambassadors asking for their country to be incorporated with England. To agree meant open war. To refuse meant that in all probability the Dutch would submit to Spain and England would be left without an ally. As usual, Elizabeth delayed giving a definite answer as long as she could. When she finally decided to refuse she sent a stronger force of

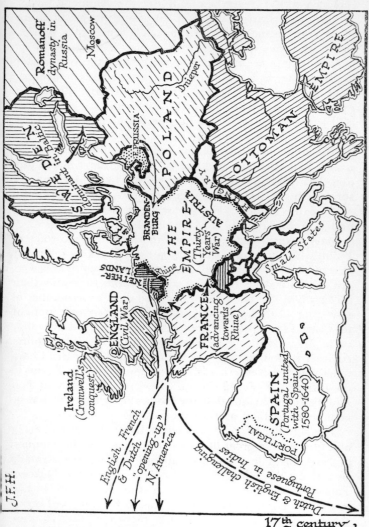

Romanoff
dynasty in
Russia

Moscow

POLAND

Dnieper

E. PRUSSIA

OTTOMAN EMPIRE

SWEDEN

D. in Baltic

Swedish power

BRANDEN-BURG

THE EMPIRE
(Thirty Years' War)

AUSTRIA

HUNGARY

Small States

NETHER-LANDS

Rhine

FRANCE
advancing towards Rhine

Ireland
(Cromwell's conquest)

ENGLAND
(Civil War)

SPAIN
(Portugal united with Spain
1580-1640)

PORTUGAL

English, French
& Dutch
"opening-up"
N. America

Dutch & English challenging
Portuguese in Indies

J.F.H.

17th century

'volunteers' than ever before, under the command of her favourite, the Earl of Leicester, to ensure the continuance of the war. In the autumn of the same year Drake harried the West Indies with a fleet of twenty-five ships.

As war became more and more certain the reasons for keeping Mary Stuart alive were correspondingly weakened. Walshingham, who represented the extreme Protestant section on Elizabeth's council, advocating an alliance of all the Protestant forces of Europe, with England at their head, for open war on Spain, set to work to trap Mary into complicity in one of the plots to kill Elizabeth. As usual, Walshingham had a spy among the conspirators and their whole correspondence to and from Mary passed through his hands. By September, 1586, he had all the evidence he needed. The plot was exploded prematurely and in February, 1587, Mary was beheaded.

Mary bequeathed her claims to the English throne to Philip who had now every reason for embarking on a war from which he alone would benefit. It was fought, however, under political conditions less favourable to Philip than if Mary had still been alive, since, while a large number of moderate Catholics would have been prepared to fight to place Mary on the throne, only the small minority under Jesuit influence were likely to do as much for Philip. Another reason for war was the continued failure of Spain to subdue the Netherlands. The original plan had been to do this as the prelude to an attack on England: it had now become obvious that the Netherlands never would be conquered as long as they received English help.

The summer of 1587 was spent by Philip in gathering and fitting out a great fleet—the Armada—for the conquest of England. The plan of campaign was for the Armada to sail up the Channel to Dunkirk, where the Duke of Parma, Spanish commander in the Netherlands, had assembled an army. This army was to be convoyed across the Straits for a landing in the mouth of the Thames. It was an excellent plan on the assumption that no serious resistance was likely. The sailing of the Armada was delayed by a raid in which Drake destroyed a mass of shipping and stores in Cadiz, by the death of its commander and by the poor quality of its equipment which made it necessary to put in at Corunna to refit, but by the end of July, 1588, it had reached English waters.

The defeat of the Armada has often been regarded as something of a miracle: in fact, it would have been a veritable miracle if it had succeeded. From the time when the Persians were beaten at Salamis till the beginning of the Sixteenth Century naval warfare had not changed in principle. Ships were treated primarily as carriers of troops and the aim was always to grapple and board the ships of the enemy. This conception of naval war still dominated the Spanish, whose soldiers were then the best in the world. But in the generation before the Armada the English and Dutch had evolved a totally new method of war. They treated ships as floating batteries and their objective was to outsail their opponents and disable them from a distance by artillery fire. They built smaller, faster ships, capable of sailing into the wind and they mounted guns at the portholes instead of only on deck. Their ships were superior both in the volume and the direction of fire. The mere bulk of the Spanish galleons, packed as they were with troops, only made them the better targets for broadsides to which they had no power to make effective reply. Their superior numbers and tonnage meant exactly nothing in the conditions under which they were forced to fight.

After a running battle lasting about a fortnight the Armada was hustled up the Channel, stampeded out of Calais by fire ships, driven past Dunkirk and out into the North Sea. The damage done was limited only by the shortage of ammunition in the English fleet, and once in the North Sea the Armada could not work back down the Channel against the wind but was forced to sail round Scotland and Ireland, on whose coasts scores of ships were wrecked. The English lost no more than 100 men killed in the whole action.

After 1588 the offensive passed into the hands of the English who continued to raid the coast towns both of Spain and the West Indies and to attack enemy shipping. Two contending strategical theories arose. The first advocated the seeking out and destruction of the enemy's battle fleet, the second, and this view mainly prevailed, urged the plunder of his colonies and the cutting of his trade routes. This method of war, followed in the Seventeenth and Eighteenth Centuries, laid the foundation of the British Empire in a series of wars whose burden was thrown chiefly upon England's continental allies. In 1589 Corunna was taken and sacked but an attempt on Lisbon failed. Fleets were sent to raid the West Indies in 1590, 1591 and 1595 while in 1596 a fresh raid on Cadiz did immense damage. At the same time the Spanish were beginning to adopt the new technique of shipbuilding and naval tactics and the struggle developed into a prolonged skirmishing in which neither side could secure any decisive success.

The war with Spain, especially in its earlier stages, was less a national war than the struggle of a class against its class enemies at home and abroad. It was carried on mainly by the English merchant class both against Spain as the centre of the reactionary and feudal forces in Europe and against their allies in England, the Catholic section of the nobility. Nothing is more surprising than the depth and sincerity of the religious convictions of many of the English seamen of the Sixteenth Century. Their Protestantism was the religion of a class in arms. Out of the memories of the Marian persecution, kept alive by Foxe's *Book of Martyrs*, published in 1563 and the most popular book of its time, out of the activities of the Jesuits and the cruelties of the Inquisition the English bourgeoisie concocted a picture of Catholicism as the fountain of all evil and the enemy with which they were committed to grapple in a life and death struggle. Religious fanaticism reinforced commercial interest to give them an enemy who was not only fought but sincerely hated, and it was in fighting Spain that they came to a consciousness of their own strength.

Up to 1588 the English bourgeoisie were fighting for existence: after that they fought for power. For this reason the defeat of the Armada is a turning point in the internal history of England as well as in foreign affairs. It was the merchants, with their own ships and their own money, who had won the victory and they had won it almost in spite of the half-heartedness and ineptitude of the Crown and Council. The victory transformed the whole character of the class relations that had existed for a century. The bourgeoisie became aware of their strength and with the coming of this awareness the long alliance between them and the monarchy began to dissolve. It might still need their support but they no longer needed its protection. Even before the death of Elizabeth, Parliament began to show an independence previously unknown.

The war with Spain, therefore, can best be understood as the first phase in the English Revolution. First, because it was a defeat for feudal reaction in Europe and consolidated the victory of the Reformation in those areas where it had already triumphed. And, second, because the classes inside England which defeated Philip were exactly those which afterwards led the opposition to Charles. It was a striking fact that at the opening of the Civil War the whole Navy and every important seaport was found to be on the side of Parliament. It was in the war with Spain that these classes had been tempered and mobilised and had developed that sense of being a special people, 'the elect', which made their Puritanism so formidable as a political creed.

2. THE CHARTERED COMPANIES

Between piracy and honest trade no very clear line was drawn in the Sixteenth and early Seventeenth Centuries. The merchant was always prepared to fight for his market or for the right to buy goods in places where his rivals had established a monopoly: the privateer was always ready to dabble in trade if his proper occupation languished. In the dubious territory through which the line meandered lived and thrived such men as Hawkins, founder of the great trade of supplying the Americas with negro slaves from West Africa.

In a little over a generation the native population of the West Indies, showing a perverse disinclination to labour in the mines and plantations of their Spanish conquerors, had been exterminated. The settlers found themselves so short of labourers that they were ready to buy from anyone in spite of the prohibitions of their Home Government. In 1562 Hawkins carried his first cargo of slaves to San Domingo, beginning a lively and profitable connection in which Spanish settlers and English traders combined to evade Government warships and customs officers. The slave trade remained on a small scale till after the middle of the Seventeenth Century, when negro labour began to provide the basis for the vast fortunes made from sugar and tobacco plantations, but the right to supply slaves to Spain's American colonies was always one of the most desired objects of English traders. For some time trade with these colonies was regarded as of greater importance than independent colonising.

The first English settlements in America were political in object, the idea being to establish bases for the struggle against Spain and to prospect for gold and silver. The colonists were mostly adventurous and impoverished gentlemen, anxious to make quick fortunes but incapable of working the land or of any sustained effort. When cut off for any length of time from England they usually starved to death. Colonies planted in Virginia in 1584 and 1587 were complete failures. The first colony to survive was one established at Jamestown in 1607 and after this settlements of two new kinds were made in considerable numbers and developed rapidly. The first kind were in New England, where groups of Puritan farmers and artisans, driven abroad by the religious troubles of Stuart times, brought with them the qualities of industry and thrift that had marked them at home. Further south in Virginia settlers with larger capital established considerable plantations for the growth of tobacco, worked by indentured labour, partly convict, partly unemployed, from England, and, in far larger numbers, drawn from the Irish peasants who had been evicted from their land and replaced by newcomers from England and Scotland. Early in the Sixteenth Century the Bermudas and Barbados were occupied and used for sugar growing with labour similarly obtained. After 1660 all these colonies, and others established later, began to replace their white indentured labour with negro slaves.

But it was Ireland which was the first important English colony, the place where they learnt all the tricks of governing subject races. In Ulster especially, where the tribal structure persisted longest, the complete conquest of the country was followed by the wholesale confiscation of the land which was sold to English and Scottish merchants and landowners at nominal prices. The native cultivators were driven out and replaced by immigrants from England and Scotland whose condition soon became little better than that of the Irish they had superseded. The whole county of Derry was taken over by an association of London merchants and divided into twelve estates one of which was assigned to each of the twelve great Companies. It proved easier, however, to ruin Ireland than to enrich England by such means, and in general the colonies of the Sixteenth Century were small affairs. There was neither the surplus capital nor population to permit of large-scale ventures, and what spare capital there was tended to be attracted into trade which promised a far higher return.

Consequently, the most significant economic development of the late Tudor and early Stuart period was the birth and consolidation of a number of chartered companies, each engaged in the promotion of trade in some specific area. Such companies were not new. The Merchant

Adventurers had been formed in the Fifteenth Century to export cloth to North Europe and continued to do so all through the period, moving their headquarters from Antwerp to Hamburg or Emden as the political situation altered. In 1578 their long struggle with the Hanse merchants ended with the withdrawal of the latter from London and the closing of their factory, the Steelyard. But toward the end of the Sixteenth Century chartered companies began to spring up in all directions. The Eastland Company (1579) traded in the Baltic and Scandinavia, the Turkey Company was established in 1581 and in 1588 an African Company was formed to organise the slave trade.

These companies were, with few exceptions, London companies and had to meet the competition not only of foreign rivals but of merchants from other English ports. The Newcastle traders, for example, fought a long and partly successful battle with the Merchant Adventurers, claiming prior rights granted to their own Merchant Gild in the Middle Ages, and the merchants of Bristol and the West Country ports strongly opposed the attempt of London to monopolise the Spanish and French trade, which, in 1604, was declared open to all Englishmen. Though London was never able to eliminate the competition of the 'outports', there is no doubt that the formation of the chartered companies, with their special privileges and their power of protecting their members, helped to concentrate the foreign trade of the country into one centre and so increase the political weight of the great London merchants.

One of the most important of the chartered companies was the Turkey Company. Individuals trading to Constantinople and the Levant ran great risks from the ships of the pirate states of the Barbary coast of northern Africa, whose ravages appear to have increased considerably with the decline of Spanish sea power and who even began to appear off the English coast early in the reign of Charles I. There was also the organised opposition of the Venetians and of a French company which had established itself in the Levant as early as 1535. The eastern Mediterranean, one of the main spheres of French activity from the time of the Crusades, witnessed the first stages of a colonial conflict that was to reach far greater dimensions a century later in Canada and India. The Turkey Company had the great advantage over the private trader that it could send out a powerful fleet each year, capable of resisting all attacks. In 1601 it was reconstituted and from this date regular trade relations with Turkey really began. The Company preserved a virtual monopoly till 1753, exporting cloth and importing silk, drugs and other Eastern produce.

None of these companies had such a long life as, or ever reached anything like the dimensions of, the East India Company, the real founder of British rule in India. From the start it was a company of a new kind, better adapted for large scale trade and making a more flexible use of its capital. Such a body as the Merchant Adventurers was not a company at all in the modern sense. It was rather an association of merchants doing a similar trade in a particular area and combining for mutual aid and protection. Inside the association each merchant traded with his own capital, making his own profit and bearing his own losses. It was, in fact, somewhat the commercial counterpart of the simple association of labour that marked the manufacturing stage of industry. The East India Company was the first important Joint Stock Company, its members investing so much capital to be pooled and used jointly and receiving a proportionate share of the common profit. At first the shares were taken only for a single voyage, after which the whole proceeds were divided out and fresh shares subscribed for a new voyage. Very soon they were left in from one voyage to another, forming a permanent capital. This gave the Company obvious advantages over the older kinds, allowing a continuous development and making possible large scale enterprises. The Company could afford to wait for a return on its activities where the private trader could not.

G1

The Portuguese had early been followed to the Spice Islands of the East by the Dutch, whose superior ships and more efficient business methods had soon driven their predecessors out of the East Indies and forced them to confine themselves to India proper. By the close of the Sixteenth Century Holland had replaced Portugal as the great importer of spices. How important spices, and especially pepper, were to Europe at this time will only be understood when we remember that the whole population had to live on salted meat during the greater part of the winter months. Turnips and artificial grasses were little used and shortage of fodder made it necessary every autumn to kill off and salt all the animals not needed for breeding. Salt being dear and scarce, and, in England, imported from abroad, the salting was often indifferently carried out so that a liberal amount of seasoning was needed to make the meat even palatable. Spices accordingly fetched high prices, and a monopoly such as the Dutch established was extremely profitable to themselves and extremely vexatious to their customers and rivals.

The first English seaman to reach the Indies by the Cape route was Sir James Lancaster in 1592. In 1600 the Dutch took advantage of their monopoly to set up a kind of pepper pool, raising the price at one sweep from 3s. a pound to 6s. and 8s. It was as a direct reply to this move that the East India Company was set up at the end of the year, and in 1601 Lancaster again visited the East Indies with a fleet of five ships, returning with a rich cargo of spices and earning a substantial profit for the Company. The Dutch soon proved to be too strongly established in the Islands for the new company to secure a permanent foothold there. A Dutch fleet of twelve ships, permanently stationed in the Indies, made trading hazardous and after a naval struggle lasting some twenty years they were able to wipe out a factory that the English had set up at Amboyna in the Moluccus. It was as a result of this struggle in the Far East that Holland began to replace Spain as England's chief rival at sea.

Driven from the Islands by the Dutch, the East India Company found the opposition of the Portuguese in India less formidable. Four large ships under Captain Thomas Best visited Surat in 1612 and defeated a Portuguese squadron which tried to bar their way. After this they had little difficulty in getting permission from the Mogul to establish a permanent depot or factory at Surat. A second naval victory in 1614 confirmed the superiority of the English in Indian waters. Factories were set up at Madras in 1620 and at Hoogli near Calcutta in 1633. Later, when Charles II married a Portuguese princess, Catherine of Braganza, he received the island of Bombay as part of her dowry. This was leased to the Company in 1680 and gave them a large and easily defended base from which to trade. It was not till the Eighteenth Century that the Company became an important political force in India, but long before this it had established a large and immensely profitable trading connection. Its activities were not confined to India but extended as far afield as Persia and even Japan, where it had a factory from 1613 to 1623.

Elizabeth, like all the Tudors, appreciated the importance of trade and of securing the support of the merchant class; James I, coming from Scotland with its undeveloped industries and negligible foreign trade, failed to realise the political importance of the London merchants and quickly alienated them by his cautious and finally pro-Spanish foreign policy.

In 1604 the war with Spain was ended with a peace treaty that was criticised because it did not specifically secure the right of trade with the Spanish colonies. Though it was unpopular its terms were probably as good as could be obtained and the alternative, a continuance of the long and indecisive war, would have been costly and could have produced little result. After the death of Cecil, peace with Spain passed over into a policy of actual alliance which infuriated the merchants and Protestants in general and brought no compensating gain. The navy was allowed to decay, old ships being laid up and no new ones built. Traders complained of the attacks of pirates even in the English Channel. In 1618 Sir Walter Raleigh, the leader of the party pressing for war against Spain, was allowed to go to South America at the head of an expedition in search of gold. He returned unsuccessful and was beheaded at the demand of the Spanish ambassador to the great disgust of the trading classes who regarded his activities as natural and praiseworthy.

This change in foreign policy led to a complete reversal of the situation at home. Under Elizabeth and up to the time of the Gunpowder Plot (1605) the Catholics had been in active and often treasonable opposition to the Crown. After 1605 there was a short period of persecution, chiefly aimed at the extreme or Jesuit wing of the Catholics. But with the development of friendly relations with Spain and, later, following the marriage of Charles I to the French Henrietta Maria, the Catholics enjoyed a period of toleration and even of court favour. Henceforward they became the most constant and active supporters of the monarchy, and the only large section of the population on whom the Stuarts could always rely.

The Puritans, drawn from the classes which had been the main supporters of the Tudors, were correspondingly driven into opposition to a regime which they believed, not altogether correctly, was working to restore Catholicism to England. In this way opposition to the Crown became identified with patriotism and the monarchy with the section of the population widely believed to be in league with foreign enemies. By their foreign policy the Stuarts abandoned what had been the main source of the Crown's strength—its alliance with the most historically progressive class in the country.

3. CROWN AND PARLIAMENT

Six years before the death of Elizabeth the long working agreement between Crown and Parliament was disturbed by an attack on the practice of granting monopolies. The subject of dispute is highly significant. Monopolies were grants to individuals or companies of the exclusive right to manufacture or sell some particular article, paper, for example, or soap. Sometimes they were given to reward or encourage invention but more often were sold to raise additional revenue or used as a cheap way of rewarding courtiers or servants who had a claim on the royal purse. So, the Earl of Essex was given the monopoly of the sale of sweet wines for ten years, and the refusal of the Queen to renew this monopoly in 1600 was more responsible than anything else for his crazy rebellion early in the next year.

These grants were defended on the ground of the Crown's right to make ordinances for the regulation of trade. The attack on them was in essence an affirmation of a new principle of the highest importance to the bourgeoisie, the principle of their freedom to buy and sell to their best advantage without interference. It was a claim totally at variance with the whole medieval conception of the national and local organisation of trade. The question was raised in 1597 and an inquiry promised. When nothing was done a new and sharper attack was made in 1601. The Government at once saw that it would be wise to give way and the reign closed with the friendly relations between Crown and Parliament apparently undisturbed.

When James I came to the throne in 1603 the whole atmosphere seemed to change with a dramatic suddenness. While the change was at bottom the reflection of changed class relations,[1] its sharpness can only be attributed to personal causes. First, James was a foreigner, half Scottish, half French, brought up in a country filled with bitterly hostile factions and accustomed to maintain himself among them by the policy of complicated trickery he called kingcraft. Scotland had no Parliament in the English sense and James had learnt to regard its one democratic institution, the Kirk, as the chief enemy of royal power.

[1] See section 5, below.

Second, the atmosphere of theological pedantry in which he had been reared made him over apt to theorise about his position, to demand explicitly as a divine right what the Tudors had been content to take quietly in the absence of explicit opposition. And he made these demands in the most tactless and blundering way at a moment when even the Tudors would probably have had to make concessions.

Third, and perhaps most important, James came from a very poor country to one moderately rich and regarded the resources of his new kingdom as unbounded. In fact, they were far from it, since the national finances had remained medieval in character and were increasingly inadequate to the complexity of national organisation. Elizabeth had been able to make ends meet on a revenue rarely higher than £400,000 a year only by the most extreme parsimony and by using the upper classes as an unpaid civil service. In the Sixteenth Century prices were still rising and James found a revenue of about £450,000 inadequate even in time of peace. Of this sum perhaps £300,000 came from the estate of the Crown and the recognised customs dues. The rest had to be cajoled from the merchants and landowners in the form of a parliamentary grant. In relation to the wealth of these classes taxation was very light, but the mere fact of their increasing wealth made them more and more reluctant to vote increased taxes except in exchange for substantial increases in political power. The situation created by the rise in prices was not generally understood and the inability of the Stuarts to balance their budgets was put down entirely to what were only contributory causes—their extravagance and bad management.

James' first Parliament set the tone that was to prevail for the next forty years. Only part of the money he demanded was voted and the Commons spent much time discussing his domestic and foreign policy. James ordered them to leave affairs of State to the King and Council who alone were qualified to understand them. "As to dispute what God may do is blasphemy," he declared, "so it is sedition in subjects to dispute what a king may do in height of his power. I will not be content that my power be disputed on." Parliament replied by affirming its right "to debate freely all matters which properly concern the subject and his right or state," and was dissolved in 1610.

From 1610 to 1621 only one Parliament was called, the 'Addled Parliament' of 1614. It at once began to criticise the policy of the Government and was dismissed before any business had been transacted. During this period James tried a variety of expedients to balance his budget. They included forced loans, new customs duties and the sale of titles. So long as peace was maintained these sources of revenue were just sufficient to stave off a crisis. After the death of Cecil, son of Elizabeth's chief minister, in 1612, James began to fall more and more under the influence of Spain and for some years the Spanish ambassador, Gondomar, was the real power behind the Government. In 1620 the Thirty Years' War in Germany created new difficulties. The Elector of the Rhenish Palatinate, one of the leading Protestant princes and son-in-law to James, had accepted the crown of Bohemia, whose people were in revolt against the Emperor. The Elector was quickly driven out of Bohemia and his own Palatinate and appealed to his father-in-law. James was anxious to help and the Puritan City of London was eager for war. James, however, preferred to attempt to restore his son-in-law to his dominions by negotiation with Spain, proposing a Spanish marriage for his son Charles and the toleration of the English Catholics as a return for the evacuation of the Rhineland by the Emperor's troops.

Such negotiations could only succeed if backed by a show of force and James was compelled to summon a Parliament in 1621. He asked for £500,000. Parliament voted about £150,000, demanded war against Spain and impeached the Lord Chancellor, Francis Bacon, on a charge of corruption. In the next session James asked

for £900,000 and was voted only £70,000 while the
Commons openly attacked the proposed Spanish marriage.
In January, 1622, Parliament was dissolved.

At this time the Council was completely dominated by
George Villiers, Duke of Buckingham, whose only
qualifications for governing were his immense vanity
and his personal attractiveness to James. Completely
ignorant of European politics he did not realise that the
Spanish were bluffing and had no intention of making
any real concessions. When he did come to realise this
after a visit to Madrid, he swung violently towards a
war policy, regardless of the fact that the navy was completely decayed and that there was no army or any means
of creating one. The Commons were equally ill informed,
and when a new Parliament met in 1624 it was enthusiastic
for war and voted the large sum of £300,000—nearly
half of what was demanded.

The war that followed was a fiasco and Buckingham
quickly lost his sudden and temporary popularity. Wretched
armies of untrained conscripts, drawn from the slum
population or the rural unemployed, were sent abroad to
be butchered or to die of fever. The decayed and ill-
appointed ships failed repeatedly to reproduce the naval
exploits of the previous generation. Out of sheer incapacity
Buckingham soon involved the country in a second and
even more pointless war with France. When he was
stabbed in 1628 by a dismissed officer the people of London
celebrated his death in the streets like a victory, and, after
a final defeat at La Rochelle, Charles made peace with
Spain, France and the Emperor as speedily and un-
ostentatiously as possible.

Meanwhile the struggle with Parliament had continued
after the death of James in 1625. The first Parliament
of the new reign, meeting in June, 1625, refused to vote
money for the war they had demanded a year earlier
unless Buckingham was removed from control. The baronial
opposition of the Middle Ages had sometimes enforced
the removal of ministers they disliked, but no such attempt

had been made for over a hundred years and from the Commons such a demand was quite new. Parliament was dissolved in August but Charles still needed money and had to call a new Parliament in February of the next year.

In spite of attempts to pack it, the new Parliament was as stubborn as the old one had been and began at once to prepare for the impeachment of Buckingham. In a few months it too was dissolved. In place of the unvoted taxes the Government raised a forced loan, systematically levied like a regular subsidy. Those who refused to pay were imprisoned or pressed into the Army. War was still going on and detachments of untrained and undisciplined soldiers were scattered over the country. Often unpaid and billeted in private houses for the sake of economy, they became a terror to their unwilling hosts who found that complaints of robbery and violence often went unheeded at the military tribunals to which the troops were answerable.

The forced loan was not a success and in 1628 Charles was compelled for the third time to call a Parliament. It met in an even more uncompromising mood than its predecessors and with a clearer idea of the political demands it intended to make. A contemporary noted of this Parliament, probably justly, that the House of Commons was able to buy up the Lords three times over. In the Fifteenth Century the Commons had been content to follow the lead of the Upper House but their wealth and social standing and that of the classes they represented were now such that it was they who took the leading role. The Lords at this time hardly existed as an independent force, acting only as an intermediate body inclining by turns towards King and Commons.

Under the leadership of a Cornish squire, Sir John Eliot, the Commons at once formulated their demands in the document known as the Petition of Right. It avoided all attempts to theorise, confining itself to four specific points. Two, the billeting of soldiers and the abuse of martial law, were of mainly immediate importance. The others were wider in scope. The Petition demanded that the practice of keeping arrested persons in prison "without being charged with anything to which they might make answer to the law" should cease and that "no man hereafter be compelled to make or yield any gift, loan, benevolence, tax, or such like charge, without common consent by Act of Parliament."

Most of the things complained of in the Petition had been done without question by the Crown for many generations. The important point was that they had been formulated and forbidden just at the time when the Crown was claiming to do them by absolute, sovereign right. The Petition was in fact if not in form an answer to the royal attempt to establish a theoretical basis for a practical absolutism.

Diplomatically, the Commons had sweetened the pill with the promise of the large vote of five subsidies—about £350,000. After some characteristic haggling Charles assented to the Petition but when Parliament went on to demand the removal of Buckingham it was prorogued. In the interval before the next session Buckingham was murdered. Parliament met again in January, 1629, and followed up the Petition of Right by granting Tunnage and Poundage for one year only instead of, as always before, for life. Indirect taxes at recognised and customary and traditional rates had always been regarded as part of the ordinary revenue of the Crown. This new move meant a far more strict interpretation of the Petition of Right than Charles had anticipated and he indignantly rejected a claim that would have given the Commons complete financial control. He refused to accept the vote for one year and continued to collect the customs as before. In a tumultuous last session, with the Speaker held down in his chair by force, the Commons passed three resolutions, declaring that anyone who attempted to introduce Popery, who advised the levy of any tax not authorised by Parliament or who should "voluntarily yield or pay" any such tax was an enemy of the kingdom and commonwealth and of the liberty of England.

Parliament was then dissolved, not to meet again for eleven years. Eliot and other leaders were thrown into prison, where Eliot died in 1632. The hatred of the King pursued him even after death, for when his son asked to be allowed to take away the body for burial he was met with the reply: "Let Sir John Eliot be buried in the church of that parish where he died."

After the dissolution of Parliament the wars with France and Spain were quickly brought to an end and Charles and his advisers set to work to devise means of raising sufficient revenue to meet necessary expenses. In accordance with the final resolution passed by the Commons the London merchants at first refused to pay the unvoted customs duties. Such resistance could not be kept up indefinitely; and after business in London had been brought almost to a standstill for six months it died down. Perhaps the most unwise of all the financial expedients employed by the Council at this time was the revival of claims to land that had anciently been royal forest. Much of this land had been in private hands for generations but the occupiers were forced to pay heavy fines before their ownership was confirmed. Much of this land was held by the most powerful nobles and by offending them Charles left himself for a time without supporters except for the Catholics, the Court clique and a handful of High Church clergy.

Money was also raised by the sale of monopolies, by increasing the customs which, in any case, were rising with the expansion of trade, and, last of all, by the levy of ship money. It had long been a recognised obligation of the seaports to provide ships for the Navy. Now the development of naval war had made most ordinary merchant ships unsuitable for this purpose and a sum of money was demanded in place of actual tonnage. In 1634 ship money was collected from the coast towns and was actually used for the repair of the Navy. So far there had been no opposition. In the next two years the levy was extended to inland places as well and it became obvious that it was intended to treat ship money as a regular tax bringing in about £200,000 a year. This would have made the Government permanently independent of Parliament and it was on these grounds that Hampden refused to pay in 1636. The trial that followed was important as a focus of opposition but Hampden's example was not widely followed and the levy was collected in each of the following years.

Apart from the protests of individuals there had been singularly little opposition to the Government during this period of arbitrary rule. During the whole time there was hardly so much as a riot throughout the whole country. The feudal conditions which had made armed rebellion a common resort in the Middle Ages had passed. The nobles were no longer served by bands of armed men. The former peasants had developed into separate classes —yeomen, tenant farmers and wage labourers—with different interests. Most of these had little direct concern in the political struggle and with the slowing down of enclosures there was less agrarian unrest of the kind that had led to Kett's rebellion. The merchants and landed gentry who led the opposition to the Crown were weak as individuals and needed the focus of Parliament and of a political party to unite them into concerted action. Lacking such a party they could do little at this time but sit at home and grumble and hope that the King would some day be forced to call a new Parliament.

The impetus for a renewal of the struggle had to come from the outside, from Scotland, where medieval conditions had persisted to a much greater extent and the pre-requisites for a successful armed rising still existed.[1] The dispute that blazed up in Scotland at the close of 1637 was religious in character, the result of an attempt by Laud and the Anglicans to remodel the Scottish Kirk.

[1] This is a striking example of the way in which the *uneven* development of capitalism creates the conditions leading to revolutions.

To understand this dispute it is necessary to know something about the nature of Puritanism and about its relation to the political struggle of the Seventeenth Century.

4. THE PURITANS

The word Puritan, when James I came to the throne, had not acquired any very exact meaning but was applied loosely to a variety of things and people. It was, first, a tendency within the Established Church. Most Puritans were still inside this Church, from which they had few important theological differences and only wanted minor changes of ritual and discipline to enable them to stay there. To the left of these and far less numerous, was a group that wished to replace the Anglican State Church by a Presbyterian State Church on the model of the Scottish Kirk. Finally, there was a fringe of small sects who were the anarchists of religion, wishing to leave every congregation free to settle its own affairs, the fathers of the Quakers, Congregationalists and Baptists of later times.

In the main Puritanism was not a matter of theological dissent as of a peculiar attitude towards morals and behaviour, a different conception of Church discipline and of civil government. The political radicalism of the Puritan grew naturally from his relation to God and to society. He was one of the Lord's chosen people, the elect. In all his activities he was encompassed by the grace of God, so that every event from the greatest to the most trivial could be classed as a trial or a leading, a mercy or a judgment. A lively faith in the doctrine of predestination divided him and his fellows from the vessels of wrath who composed the world. As God's chosen people the Puritans felt their triumph inevitable and their enemies to be God's enemies. Against any man, be he king or priest, who ventured to lay burdens or chains upon them they felt entitled to fight with any weapon that the Lord put into their hands—and sometimes the Lord gave them very curious weapons indeed. All of which is really saying, in the Biblical language of the Seventeenth Century, that they were conscious of their mission as a historically progressive class engaged in a revolutionary struggle.

When such a temper was allied, as it often was, to considerable wealth, or when it became the common property of a large organised group like the citizens of London or the artisans of the East Anglian clothing towns, it was formidable indeed. Butler's malicious picture of the Puritans, drawn to amuse the victorious Cavaliers after the Restoration of 1660, is true to at least this extent that the Puritans who:

> " Found their Church upon
> The holy text of pike and gun "

were the possessors of a fighting religion. Butler in this does not contradict Milton, whose 'true warfaring Christian' had no use for a fugitive and cloistered virtue.

It is perhaps worth remarking here that the Puritan did not as a rule (there was, of course, a small eccentric minority) speak through his nose or crop his hair. He did, however, tend to wear clothes of a sober colour and homely cut and to despise the vanities of the flesh. A description of Cromwell, making his first speech before the Long Parliament, sets the well-to-do provincial Puritan vividly before us.

"I came one morning into the House well clad," writes Sir Philip Warwick, "and perceived a Gentleman speaking (whom I knew not) very ordinarily apparelled; for it was a plain cloth-sute, which seemed to have bin made by an ill country-taylor; his linen was plain and not very clean; and I remember a speck or two of blood upon his little band, which was not much larger than his collar; his stature was of a good size, his sword stuck close to his side, his countenance swoln and reddish, his voice sharp and untunable, and his eloquence full of fervor. . . . And yet I lived to see this very gentleman (having a good taylor and more converse among good company) appeared of a great and majestick deportment and comely presence."

Cromwell was in many ways typical of the best kind of Puritan squire. Related to Henry VIII's minister, he belonged to a family that had grown rich on Church lands, yet he had a good reputation in his own country of Huntingdon as a defender of the rights of his poorer neighbours. Later, when many members of the Long Parliament, including the Speaker Lenthall, were involved in ugly scandals arising from the sale of the lands of expelled Royalists, he was among those whom even their enemies never even suspected of personal corruption. It is also interesting to remember that the speech described above was in defence of the republican Lilburne, later one of his stoutest opponents.

At the beginning of his reign James was presented with a petition from some hundreds of Puritan clergy of the Church of England asking for a moderate liberty to accept or reject certain minor points of ritual such as the wearing of the surplice and the use of the sign of the cross in baptism, for the encouragement of preaching and of the stricter observance of Sunday and the non-observance of saints' days. In 1604 a conference at Hampton Court, at which James presided in person, discussed the petition. Here the reason for James' opposition to Puritanism became plain; it was not theological—James himself was a Calvinist—but political. "A Scottish Presbytery agreeth as well with monarchy as God and the Devil," and "No Bishop no King," was his crystallisation of the issue. His bitter experience with the Kirk in Scotland had taught him to welcome a church governed from above and subordinated to the State. The Scottish Kirk, organised from the bottom through a series of representative bodies, rising to an Assembly composed of ministers and delegates from congregations, was indeed the logical embodiment of the democratic spirit inherent in Puritanism and James was right in thinking that this was incompatible with royal absolutism.

His next step was to institute a purge of the Church, in which 300 clergy who refused to conform were deprived of their livings. It had the effect of weakening the Church by depriving it of a large proportion of that minority of its ministers who cared more for truth than for tithes and leaving it in the hands of place-seekers and of the small and isolated but influential group of High Anglican enthusiasts who gathered around Laud. Some cleavage was no doubt inevitable, but James and his advisers drew the line so far to the right that for half a century the Established Church lost much of its popular appeal and the Crown forfeited the support of many who might otherwise have rallied to it when the day of actual war arrived.

Laud, honest but quite out of touch with reality, tried to dragoon the Church into what to many people looked like Papistry at a time when Papistry was wildly unpopular. A rigorous censorship embracing both press and pulpit and backed by the Court of High Commission, a sort of ecclesiastical Star Chamber, was imposed. The claim of the clergy to regulate morals and behaviour, which had lapsed with the Reformation, was revived. The use of parish churches as places of meeting and business was prohibited and a strict uniformity of ritual was imposed. Between 1628 and 1640 some 20,000 Puritans emigrated to New England to escape from a land that seemed to them doomed to revert to Catholicism. Others were driven to form secret groups for private worship, groups that became centres of political disaffection. Others conformed outwardly, waiting for better times.

By 1637 Laud, apparently feeling that the situation in England was well in hand, began to turn his attention to Scotland. James would have known that to attempt to create in Scotland a counterpart of the Anglican Church was futile and dangerous but Charles shared the blank ignorance of Scotland and things Scottish then general in England. A new prayer book, based on the English one, was compiled and sent over the border but every attempt to use it met with riotous resistance. The signing of the Solemn League and Covenant for the defence of religion soon raised this resistance to the level of a national revolt and Charles was faced in the spring of 1638, with the necessity of reconquering Scotland by force of arms.

His financial position made it quite impossible to raise an adequate army. His one capable minister, Sir Thomas Wentworth, afterwards Earl of Strafford, could only advise the calling of a Parliament. Strafford had been out of England during most of the Eleven Years, acting as Governor of Ireland where he had put into practice on a smaller scale the system of absolute government at which Charles was aiming in England. By a combination of ruthless repression and the encouragement of trade and industry he had solved the problem of finance and managed to raise an efficient army. Now he had returned to England determined to apply his system there also.

In April, 1640, the Short Parliament met, to sit for just a fortnight. Instead of voting supplies it began under the leadership of Pym to organise a petition against the Scottish war and was at once dissolved. An army of sorts was collected and marched north to find the Scots already in occupation of all Northumberland and far too strong to be attacked. Their army was stiffened by many old soldiers who had fought as volunteers in the Thirty Years' War and even Charles realised that his half trained and half mutinous troops could not attack it without certain disaster. A truce was made by which Charles promised to respect all Scottish political and religious liberties and to pay a large indemnity for the withdrawal of the Army from Northumberland. Pending its payment the Scots remained at Newcastle.

The discomfiture of Charles was completed by the exhaustion of his credit in the city. Without calling a Parliament to vote taxes that could be used as security he could borrow no more. The last serious attempt of the Crown to govern in opposition to the monied classes was ended. Once more the writs went out for the summoning of a Parliament, in an atmosphere of extreme tension with Strafford planning the arrest of leading figures in the Commons and the occupation of London by an armed force, and some of the Parliamentary leaders engaged in secret negotiations with the Scots.

The meeting of the Long Parliament in November, 1640, was the signal for a renewal of the struggle between King and Commons on a higher plane than before. Events moved rapidly toward an armed conflict and the Parliament, though summoned with due legal form, soon became in fact a revolutionary tribunal. For two years the opposing forces faced each other, waiting for the inevitable break and manœuvring to force each other into a false position. The English Revolution may be said to begin in November, 1640, with the impeachment of Strafford. In this and the preceding sections the events leading up to this, one of the decisive events in European history, have been traced in outline: it is time to pause and consider briefly the nature of the issues involved.

5. FUNDAMENTAL ISSUES IN THE ENGLISH REVOLUTION

The Tudor absolutism had been one of a most peculiar kind—an absolutism by consent. The Tudors had never possessed a standing army, a police force or more than the barest skeleton of a bureaucracy. They had never commanded a revenue that was more than sufficient for the most pressing immediate needs. Their rule was therefore of necessity based upon a temporary balance of class forces which gave them the consistent support of powerful and progressive classes, above all of the merchants and a decisive section of the landed gentry. The squires as Justices of the Peace were content to perform the work of a civil service. The monied interests were able to tide the Government over its most pressing financial crises. In particular the relations of Elizabeth's Government to the London goldsmiths, who were already beginning to do business as bankers, were friendly and intimate.

Such a balance was in its nature precarious, arising from the fact that in the Sixteenth Century the monarchy had a positive historical role to play in the destruction of the remnants of feudalism. So long as it continued to do this the middle classes were content to forgo the exercise of direct political power in return for a guarantee of the ending of disorder and the establishment of a stable government. In alliance with the bourgeoisie the Tudors destroyed the power of the Church and the nobility and created the preconditions for the development of a capitalist economy.

But the monarchy was itself too much the product of feudalism and contained within itself too many feudal survivals to be able to carry the revolution to its completion. Once a certain point had been reached, and with a startling suddenness, its objective character underwent a complete transformation, and it appeared as the main obstacle to the bourgeois revolution and the centre around which the forces of reaction gathered for the decisive struggle. In this connection the reversal of the attitude of the Catholics and Puritans to the Crown in the first decades of the Seventeenth Century becomes full of significance. It is now apparent that the bourgeoisie could no longer go forward in alliance with the Crown but only in opposition to it. To the men of the Seventeenth Century that was not, of course, obvious in so simple a way, but the necessity forced itself upon them in countless apparently unrelated dilemmas, driving them to decisions that in their totality constituted the forward movement of a whole class.

When, about 1600, the conditions creating the Tudor equilibrium came to an end, history offered, or seemed to offer, alternative paths and the one ultimately followed was not that which would have seemed most likely to a contemporary observer. The State machine which had served for the last century was growing increasingly inadequate to the complexity of national life. The question was, who would create and control the new kind of State apparatus that was needed? All over Europe feudalism was giving way to bureaucratic despotisms, of which France offered the most perfect example. The power of the nobility had there been undermined without the rise of any other class capable of stepping into its place, while continuous wars had given the kings powerful standing armies.

The Stuarts, fully aware of this tendency abroad, were consciously determined to follow the example of the French kings. Parliament, also, if less fully aware of this danger, was determined to avert it. And certain peculiarities in the situation in England worked powerfully in their favour.

First, England was less continuously involved in foreign wars and her wars had been more often fought at sea so that the creation of a standing army, without which a true absolutism could not exist, had never been possible. Second, the fact that the Tudor monarchy was actually founded upon a genuine alliance in which each partner needed the support of the other had preserved and adapted the parliamentary forms which had been created in the Middle Ages under different conditions and had left the revenues of the Crown largely feudal in character and inadequate in amount. The middle classes had been prepared to do almost anything for the Tudors except pay heavy taxes. Parliament which had begun as a check on the theoretically absolute power of the feudal king to dispose of the property of his subjects had become in time the guardian of the absolute right of the individual to the enjoyment of his private property.

The belief in the sanctity of private property had grown in strength as the bourgeoisie grew tall in the Sixteenth Century. Only by a direct attack on it could the Stuarts create the new State apparatus needed for a thorough despotism and any such attack could not but lead directly to a decisive class battle. Here is the kernel of the whole conflict and the reason why the Stuarts and their Parliaments were always at odds over the question of taxation. The Crown claimed the right to levy such taxes as it thought necessary for the administration of the State. The Commons claimed the right to pay no more than they thought necessary for the same purpose. Essentially this was a demand for direct political power, since in practice they were only prepared to allow the Crown enough to govern in the way they wanted, and, if it refused, to allow it nothing at all.

The case for the King was clearly stated by Justice Finch during the trial of Hampden for his refusal to pay ship-money:

"Acts of Parliament to take away his Royal power in the defence of his kingdom are void. They are void Acts of Parliament to bind the King not to command his subjects, their persons and goods and I say their money too, for no Acts of Parliament make any difference." The divine right of kings was squarely opposed to, and finally broken upon, the divine right of private property.

While the Stuarts were fighting with a clearly envisaged objective and a fully developed theoretical position, the bourgeoisie were guided largely by instinct. Theoretical clarity came only, if at all, in the process of struggle but at first they were content with vague affirmations of the liberty of the subject and the conception of a fundamental law which stood above the Crown, a law which could not be set aside without doing violence to the constitution. No one in 1640 foresaw or could foresee the parliamentary monarchy which emerged finally from the compromises of 1660 and 1688.

Nor was it apparent that a minor revolution had been accomplished when the Long Parliament abolished the Star Chamber, the Court of High Commission and the other prerogative courts. All that was intended was to destroy bodies that had become instruments of royal tyranny. Yet what was done was to cut the main artery of the old State apparatus. Crown, Council, Prerogative

Courts, Justices of the Peace had formed a living chain. Now the link between the central organ and the extremities was removed and neither Council nor Justices ever recovered anything like their old importance. A new State apparatus had to be created, not around a Council responsible to the King but around a Cabinet responsible to the bourgeoisie in Parliament and having a new and more adaptable system of finance and local government.

Again, few of the members of the Long Parliament in 1640 were republicans or dreamed of doing more than limiting the powers of the Crown. Such republicans as there were at this time probably anticipated not a democratic republic but a plutocratic republic on the model of Holland, whose commercial prosperity made her the ideal State in the eyes of many of the merchant class. The radicalism that emerged at the close of the Civil War was still hidden among obscure and persecuted sects, spiritual heirs of the German Anabaptists, apocalyptic dreamers awaiting the coming of the Kingdom of Heaven.

The practical men, the Pyms, Vanes, Fairfaxes and Cromwells, were content to defend their earthly possessions and, at first, to see no more than one step ahead at a time. Their profound religious convictions were important here because they helped to give them confidence in the divine justice of their cause and the courage necessary to take each step as it appeared. In their own desires they saw the hand of the Lord of Battles, leading them as certainly as He led the Israelites through the wilderness. It was perhaps largely the absence of theory and of clear objectives which cast the political movement and thought of the Seventeenth Century so often into religious forms.

In spite of all that has been said to the contrary it cannot be too strongly insisted upon that the Civil War *was* a class struggle, *was* revolutionary and *was* progressive. A Royalist victory would have meant a dead hand imposed upon the development of the country, feudal forms devoid of real content ossified into a monarchical tyranny, the persistence of a less advanced form of social and political organisation. We do not need to idealise the bourgeoisie of the Seventeenth Century, who had most of the faults common to their class in all ages, but it is possible to say that just because they were the historically progressive class of their time, they could not fight for their own rights and liberties without also fighting for the rights and liberties of humanity as a whole.

CHAPTER VIII

THE ENGLISH REVOLUTION

I. THE LONG PARLIAMENT:
CLASSES AND PARTIES

THE COMMONS IN the Long Parliament had a
cohesion and a conscious purpose new in English history.
In earlier parliaments members were elected as individuals,
for their standing in their own shires and boroughs rather
than for their political alignment. But in the interval
since the Parliament of 1628 the first political party had
begun to take shape. It was the work of a group of Puritan
squires and nobles, of Pym, a leader of the last Parliament,
of Hampden, whose stand against ship-money had made
him a nationally known figure, of the Earl of Bedford,
the grandfather of all the Whigs, of the Earl of Essex
who had, like his father, an unbounded influence among
the London citizens.

During the elections, in the autumn of 1640, Pym,
Hampden and others toured the country, urging the
return of known Puritans and strengthening their claim to
leadership of the opposition. The result was an overwhelming electoral victory for the party of the big
bourgeoisie, the landowners and merchants, not republican
but determined for the most part to make the Crown
subordinate to a Parliament of which they were complete
masters.

In the first session of the Long Parliament the new
party met with no real opposition. Charles had alienated
almost all classes and there was as yet no Royalist Party.
Men like Hyde and Falkland, who were not Puritans and
later fought for the King in the Civil War, went with the
majority in attacking royal absolutism and demanding

the removal of Strafford. In November 1640 it appeared as if the battle was won without a blow being struck. Strafford and Laud were arrested, other unpopular ministers escaped abroad and the Commons, protected on one side by the Scottish Army encamped at Newcastle and on the other by the London masses, appeared irresistible. London became the great centre of revolutionary ferment and discussion. The Laudian censorship once removed, pamphlets and preachers began to debate openly the fundamental questions of Church and State government, and scores of sects, hitherto unknown or obscure, grew rapidly in numbers and influence. Popular demonstrations to Westminster often exercised decisive political effect, coercing the King and driving the Parliamentary Party into more aggressive action. Pym and his fellows were at times terrified by the violence of the forces they had set in motion but were too much in need of popular support against the Crown to venture to restrain it.

In March Strafford was impeached for high treason. Since treason had in the past always been a crime against the King, and since Strafford had acted throughout on the King's behalf, a new conception of treason had to be put forward, treason against the State and the liberty of the subject. It was a crime unknown to law, but Pym and his followers knew that as long as Strafford was alive there was danger of a counter-revolution in which they would be lucky to escape with their lives. When the Lords seemed unlikely to find Strafford guilty, the procedure was suddenly changed and a Bill of Attainder introduced. It was significant of the state of opinion at this time that only fifty-nine votes were cast against the Bill in the Commons, and many of these were given because of disapproval of the procedure rather than from a feeling that Strafford ought not to die.

A crisis had been precipitated by the discovery of a plot among the officers of the Army at York to march on London, release Strafford and dissolve Parliament. It was encouraged by Charles and the Queen and organised by

HE

the most unscrupulous and irresponsible courtiers and adventurers, men like Goring, a Seventeenth Century Roem, of whom the Royalist historian Clarendon wrote later that he "would without hesitation have broken any trust or done any act of treachery, to have satisfied an ordinary passion or appetite, and in truth wanted nothing but industry . . . to have bene as eminent and successful in the highest attempt in wickedness of any man in the age he lyved in".

The discovery of the plot produced a panic in London. The Attainder was rushed through the two houses early in May and presented to the King for his signature. With it went a Bill to prevent the dissolution of Parliament without its own consent. For some days huge demonstrations surrounded Westminster and threatened to storm and sack the royal palace of Whitehall. Charles gave way and on May 12th Strafford was beheaded on Tower Hill before a crowd which contemporary writers have estimated at 200,000. From this time two things were clear. First, that a decisive conflict had opened in which both sides were fighting for absolute supremacy, and, Second, that the Parliamentary Party must triumph or perish because Charles would never be satisfied with less than their complete destruction.

After the death of Strafford began a process of differentiation in which the moderates, those who had believed in the possibility of a divided sovereignty, passed one by one into the Royalist camp. This differentiation, however, did not become marked till the next session, and before it separated Parliament passed a series of measures in which the various forms of extra-parliamentary taxation were declared illegal and the Star Chamber and other prerogative courts were abolished. Charles dared not oppose these measures openly but continued to intrigue with the officers and the Catholics, at the same time collecting the nucleus of a party within Parliament itself.

In August the Commons were really divided for the first time over the Root and Branch Bill to abolish bishops and to organise the Church under a commission of laymen appointed by Parliament. The question was a political one because the bishops sitting in the House of Lords formed a block appointed by, and attached to the interests of, the Crown. The Root and Branch Bill was therefore an attempt to check the formation of a Royalist Party inside Parliament.

When the Houses reassembled in the autumn a new external crisis raised directly the question of power, of armed force, and divided the Commons into two nearly equal camps. This crisis was the rebellion of the Irish, driven from their lands and coerced by Strafford and now freed from the restraint imposed by his autocratic government. Horrible and exaggerated tales came over the Irish Sea of the wholesale massacre of Protestant settlers. To Puritans and Royalists alike the Irish catholics were savages to be harried and crushed without mercy, but to crush them would require a considerable army. Who was to control this army? The Puritans knew that Charles would be at least as likely to turn it against Parliament as against the Irish. The Royalists were so afraid to trust the Puritan leaders of the Commons with an army, and in any case, the raising and control of any armed force had always been the right and duty of the Crown.

In November the Puritans drew up the Grand Remonstrance, a frankly party document, designed as an appeal to Protestant prejudices and an assertion of the unfitness of the King to be trusted with an army. So even were the parties at this time that the Remonstrance was passed by only eleven votes. If Charles had been content to stand on his ancient rights and the letter of the law he would perhaps have been successful at this point. He preferred to trust to his gentleman bravos, who formed armed bands which swaggered about the London streets provoking brawls with the citizens and apprentices. The latter, at any rate, were only too ready to retaliate. Finally, Charles threw away the advantage of his legal position by his attempt to arrest Pym, Hampden and three other parliamentary leaders. On January 4th he entered the House of Commons with some hundreds of armed followers to demand the arrest of the five members. They had been warned and had taken refuge in the City. Pym, always a master of political tactics, was quick to grasp the advantage. The alarm was sounded, the London train bands were called out to protect Parliament from massacre and it transferred its session to the Guildhall in the heart of the City. On January 10th Charles fled to York, whither about one third of the Commons and two thirds of the Lords drifted in twos and threes during the winter. Both sides began at once to raise the forces necessary for an armed struggle.

Yet it is important to notice how the terms of the struggle had been dictated by the work of the Long Parliament. Charles was no longer able to take his stand on divine right or to fight openly for his real objects. Instead he was forced to talk the language of his opponents, using the talents of the constitutional Royalist, Hyde, to draft proclamations in which he declared:

"I desire to govern by the known laws of the land and that the liberty and property of the subject may by them be preserved with the same care as his just rights. And . . . I do solemnly and faithfully promise, in the sight of God, to maintain the just privileges and freedom of Parliament . . . and particularly to observe inviolably the laws consented to by me this Parliament."

While there is no reason to suppose that this was more than a pretence it is worth comparing the language used with that of Justice Finch a few years earlier.[1]

This moderation of language certainly attracted to the King many who would not otherwise have supported him, so that when war came his supporters were no longer confined to the Gorings but included such men as Falkland, a passionate enemy of both tyranny and war, or Sir Edmund Verney, constrained by a sense of loyalty "to preserve and defend those things which are against

[1] See page 221 above.

my conscience to preserve and defend", men in every way as honest and disinterested as Hampden or Lilburne. And on the side of Parliament, to offset the Gorings, there were plenty of hypocrites, corrupt self-seekers, oppressive squires and land enclosing noblemen, like the Earls of Bedford and Manchester, both of whom Cromwell had opposed in the interests of the East Anglian yeomen. So much is self-evident: what is sometimes forgotten is that in a revolutionary struggle what counts is not the noble or ignoble motives of individuals but the alignments of classes and the objects for which these classes are struggling. Nevertheless it is important to remember that while the Falklands were the least wholehearted on the side of the King, were constantly tortured by a divided loyalty, it was the best and most progressive of the Parliamentarians who were most determined to bring the war to a victorious conclusion and most fully conscious of what they were fighting about.

On the side of Parliament was first of all London, then relatively larger and more decisive politically than today. With some 300,000 inhabitants it was at least ten times the size of the next biggest cities—Bristol and Norwich. London was the stronghold of the right wing of the Parliamentary forces, the Presbyterians, as the party of the landowners and rich merchants came almost accidentally to be called. The masses in London were politically under the leadership of the merchants. Organised in their train bands or militia, the best infantry at the command of Parliament, the Londoners were fanatically attached to the moderate leader, the Earl of Essex, until, and to some extent even after, his blundering incompetence had led them to disaster in the humiliating surrender of Lostwithiel. With them were the bulk of the smaller, but still rich, prosperous and commercially minded gentry of the East, South and Midlands. The connections between gentry and merchants were always close; merchants often bought estates and set up as country squires, while the younger sons of the gentry constantly entered the ranks of the merchants. Lilburne, for example, was the son of a Durham squire who was apprenticed to a London draper, and it was perhaps through the apprentices, many of whom came from well-to-do families, that the merchants were able to influence the London masses as a whole.

Over against these stood the Independents, the left wing, drawn mainly from the yeomen farmers and the tradesmen and artisans of the country towns. They were the most democratic and revolutionary section and from them came the splendid fighting material out of which the New Model Army was later created. They were unable however, to throw up a leadership of their own class, and had to rely, to their own ultimate undoing, upon a group of the most active and intelligent gentlemen.

In the main, Parliament was strong in the towns and in the East and South, the richest and most economically developed parts of the country. It had also the support of the Navy and controlled almost all the seaports and therefore the foreign trade. Here lay its greatest advantage, in that it was able to raise heavy and continuous taxation and to finance the war in an organised way, whereas the King had to rely on the generosity of individual supporters and was cut off from the possibility of any help from abroad. In a long war such an advantage was almost certain to be decisive, though at first Parliament, while having the money to raise and equip armies, found it difficult to secure soldiers with military experience.

The King's forces were such that his best chance lay in a speedy victory. He was strong in the West and North, the poorest but most warlike parts of the kingdom. With him were the Catholics who remained strong in those parts and the great, half feudal nobles of the borders who could still, with the backing of the royal name, call out strong levies of their tenants and dependents. Among these were the Earl of Newcastle who formed a splendid body of infantry, the 'Whitecoats' out of the wild fighters of the Scottish border, the immensely wealthy Catholic

Earl of Worcester and the Earl of Derby, owner of vast domains in Lancashire.

While the country gentry were divided, the supporters of the King were in the main those with military traditions, volunteers in the Thirty Years' War, swordsmen and dashing riders to hounds, men from whom excellent cavalry could be, and, under the able leadership of the King's nephew Rupert, quickly was formed.

Whether we look at the division by classes or by geographical area it adds up to the same thing, a struggle between the most advanced classes and areas, using Parliament as their instrument, and the most conservative gathered round the Crown. There were, of course, countless exceptions, every county and town having its minority, and in many areas the first stage of the war was a struggle for local supremacy between the rival parties. Only in the East and the Home Counties on the one side and in the far North and West on the other was there a heavy disproportion of forces. In Lancashire the local struggle developed into a particularly bitter feud between the Puritans of the clothing towns and the Catholics of the villages.

Finally, this war was one waged between two minorities. Whole classes, the tenant farmers and wage earners especially, stood outside and only fought if conscripted, while in all classes many individuals remained neutral or gave only passive support to one side or the other. This is proved by the fact that there were at no time more than about 150,000 men under arms on both sides and that a high proportion of these were pressed men. Desertion was common throughout the war. The neutral classes had grievances of their own, high rents and prices and low wages, but the war did not seem to them to be, and in fact was not, waged about these grievances. It was essentially a war between two would-be ruling classes and the lowest strata of the population took little or no part in it.

2. THE CIVIL WAR

From January to August 1642 the King at York and the Commons in London were engaged in gathering their forces and securing the castles, arsenals and other strong points in the areas under their control. Open war was preceded in most parts by local conflicts. In August Charles moved south to Nottingham and made a formal declaration of war. His forces were still small and ill-disciplined, while Parliament, with the ample resources of London at its disposal, was able to equip a considerable army, strong in infantry, to which the London train bands contributed the best elements. A determined thrust in the last weeks of August would probably have finished the war at a single blow.

But the Earl of Essex, commanding the Parliamentary Army, a quiet, honest, slow-witted nobleman, failed to move. He was an essentially moderate man, believing implicitly that the war must end in a speedy compromise and as much afraid of decisive victory as of defeat. His attitude was an exact reflection of the temper of the Presbyterians who controlled affairs in the first years of the war, a temper that had disastrous military consequences and brought the Parliamentary cause to the verge of ruin.

Charles found recruiting poor in the Midlands and moved west into the Severn Valley where he soon gathered an army composed largely of Welsh infantry and cavalry drawn from the landowners of the western shires and their dependents. With this Army he began a march on London, and on October 23rd encountered Essex at Edgehill. The drawn battle that followed revealed both the superiority of the royal horse and the steadiness of the London infantry. Charles was able to continue his advance on London, but was too weak to attack it in the face of the strong and well-equipped train bands which met him at Turnham Green. He retired to Oxford and there fixed the headquarters of his main Army. The possession of London was clearly of decisive importance, and in the spring of 1643 a concerted advance was begun by three Royalist armies.

In the North the Earl of Newcastle drove Fairfax out of Yorkshire, laid siege to Hull and advanced into Lincoln. In the West, Hopton, perhaps the King's most capable all-round soldier, defeated Parliamentary armies at Lansdown Hill and Roundway Down. Bristol was captured in July and in August Charles began the siege of Gloucester. This converging advance on London was sound enough strategically: it failed because the Royalist armies were not disciplined enough to carry out such a movement. Both the northern and western Royalist forces were essentially local, ready to fight in their own shires but unwilling to engage in a long campaign far from home. Their uneasiness was increased by the existence of the unconquered strongholds of Hull, Plymouth and Gloucester, whose garrisons threatened their communications and might attack their estates. The farther the Royalist armies advanced the more frequent desertions became. Moreover, it was in Lincolnshire that they first came upon cavalry that could stand up to their own in open battle. They were the men of Cromwell's regiment, the germ of the New Model Army, yeomen farmers from the Eastern Counties who were the equals of Charles' gentlemen riders in courage and infinitely their superiors in discipline.

Nevertheless the situation seemed desperate in London during the summer of 1643 and a strong party in Parliament and in the City began to demand peace on almost any terms. The turning point of the whole war was, perhaps, the resistance and relief of Gloucester. A fiery crusade was preached in the City and a great force of militia, such as had never taken the field before except for a few days at Turnham Green, marched out across England, fought their way to Gloucester in the teeth of Rupert's cavalry and raised the siege. On their return journey they had rather the better of a fierce fight at Newbury and returned in triumph to London after a five weeks' campaign that had altered the whole face of the war.

Such an episode was in its nature exceptional. The war was not yet won and could not be won except by the creation of a regular army of a new kind, and above all of a body of first rate horse.

Cavalry was the decisive arm in all Seventeenth Century wars. Cavalry tactics had been revolutionised by the Swedes during the Thirty Years' War, so that horsemen no longer charged in column, halting when within pistol range to exchange shots with their opponents and then, perhaps, drawing away, but in lines three or four deep, closing at top speed and holding their fire till they were actually engaged in the mêlée. Such were the tactics of Rupert's cavaliers and at first they carried all before them. But these tactics had their own disadvantages. Once a charge had been carried through the victors scattered in pursuit or rode for the enemy's camp to "kill the baggage". They could not carry out an order in the field and rarely were available for more than one charge. Cromwell mounted his men on slower but heavier horses and taught them to advance at a fair pace in line knee to knee, relying rather on the weight of their charge than upon mere impetus. They were trained to halt at command, to wheel, to fight either as a mass or in separate troops, forming a force at once solid and flexible. And they were well paid so that it was possible to prohibit looting without danger of mutiny or desertions.

Drawn from, and in many cases officered by, the yeomen farmers and more prosperous artisans, this cavalry set the tone for the whole Army. Under their influence the infantry, who were at first, except for some London regiments, mainly unwilling conscripts or unprincipled mercenaries, gradually acquired a determination and purpose which welded the whole of the New Model Army into a first-rate fighting machine and a formidable political instrument. The New Model was more than an army, it became a political party, the party of the Independents, the revolutionary lower middle class, just as the Presbyterians were the party of the upper middle class.

Soon the New Model created its own political machinery. Delegates, known as 'Agitators', were appointed by the rank and file to present their grievances and look after their interests. These delegates came to form regular soldiers' councils, and in the prayer meetings which were held at frequent intervals political and religious discussion were inextricably tangled. In these meetings, as was so usual in the Seventeenth Century, politics in fact took the form of religion and they were in practice extremely democratic institutions, the private being as free to speak his mind as the colonel since both were considered equally likely to be vehicles of divine inspiration. In these meetings and in more intimate discussion the Army worked out its theories of Church and State. The majority of the cavalry, and, in time, of the infantry as well, were Independents, wishing for each religious group or congregation to settle for itself the form of worship and discipline it preferred. For the first time the idea of religious toleration was powerfully voiced, toleration, that is, for all forms of worship that were not actually offensive to the Puritan mind, and it must be remembered that Catholics, High Anglicans, Unitarians and Freethinkers would all have found themselves outside any line the Independent would draw.

Such an army Cromwell and the Earl of Manchester were commissioned, on the strength of the former's successes in the spring, to raise in the Eastern Counties during the late summer of 1643. In October they cleared Lincolnshire, relieved Hull and joined hands with the Northern Army of Fairfax. The immediate threat to London was now removed and at the same time the English Presbyterians secured powerful new allies by a treaty with the Scots. In return for a promise to establish Presbyterianism in England and to pay the expenses of the campaign, a Scottish army 20,000 strong crossed the border early in 1644 and began to clear the Royalists from the northern shires. The Earl of Newcastle found himself caught between the Scots and Fairfax and Cromwell advancing from the South and was closely besieging in York.

The fall of York would have meant the passing of the whole of the North into Parliamentary hands, and Rupert was sent from Oxford with a picked force to raise the siege. He swung through Lancashire, reducing some minor strongholds on the way, crossed the Pennines by the Aire Gap and succeeded in joining forces with Newcastle. In the battle that followed on Marston Moor Cromwell's new cavalry regiments met and routed the pick of the Royalist horse and then wheeled to surround the infantry in the centre. Newcastle's Whitecoats were annihilated and the victory was complete. For the first time in the war the Parliamentary Army had been successful in a pitched battle. Two Royalist armies had been destroyed, but the moral effect of the victory of Marston Moor was even more important: up to that time it had seemed that the King must win, now his ultimate defeat seemed probable. And, above all, Marston Moor was a victory for the Left, for Cromwell and his 'Ironsides' of the New Model Army.

The immediate military effect was somewhat offset by a disaster in the West. Essex had led the main Puritan Army on a blundering campaign into Devon and Cornwall. Every day's march carried him farther into the heart of the enemy's territory and in September he found himself cornered at Lostwithiel. The cavalry cut their way out, Essex abandoned his Army and escaped by sea, but the whole of the foot had to surrender with their arms and stores.

The defeat was less serious for Parliament than Marston Moor had been for Charles for two reasons. First, their resources were so much greater that they had little difficulty in raising fresh forces. One of the permanent effects of the Civil War was the complete overhaul and modernisation of the system of national finance. The bourgeoisie were prepared to tax themselves through Parliament at a rate they would never have dreamed of under the monarchy. A far-reaching excise duty was placed upon most articles of consumption and the old property tax, that had ossified into the payment of so many 'subsidies' of £70,000, raised on a traditional and now quite arbitrary assessment, was revised and new and more equitable assessments made. These taxes became the mainstay of the national budget, giving the State apparatus a new stability even in the heat of the struggle. Charles, with only the poorest parts of the country under his control, was unable to raise any regular taxes at all. The result was that as the war went on his armies became less and less disciplined and in some areas degenerated into a plundering rabble, while the Parliamentary forces, paid with fair regularity, grew more disciplined and were brought more directly under central control.

Secondly, the Lostwithiel fiasco discredited the right wing and forced Parliament to reorganise its forces in such a way as to put increased power into the hands of the New Model Army and its Independent leaders. A fierce attack in Parliament on both Essex and Manchester led to the Self Denying Ordinance, by which all members of both Houses gave up their army commands and the whole Army was centralised under the command of Fairfax. In this attack Cromwell played a leading part and secured from it the greatest advantage. As a member of Parliament he should have resigned but Fairfax—probably acting at Cromwell's suggestion—insisted that he was indispensable and must be allowed to remain as general of the horse and second in command of the whole Army. This gave him a unique position. Speaking in the Commons for the Army and in the Army for the Commons he was in a position to dominate both. Fairfax, who was a capable officer but no politician and quite unambitious, soon became no more than a figurehead. Cromwell's position as virtual commander of the Army was strengthened because the New Model was built around the nucleus of his own Army of the Eastern Counties and took its political complexion, rapidly in the cavalry and more slowly in the infantry.

With the change in leadership came a change in strategy. Cromwell had justly accused Manchester of being afraid of victory: "I showed him evidently how this could be done . . . but he obstinately refused; saying only, that if we were entirely to overthrow the King's Army, he would still be King, and always have another army to keep up the war; while we, if we were beaten, should no longer be anything but rebels and traitors, executed and forfeited by the law." The fact that this view was held by the Parliamentary leaders was the reason for the planlessness of their movements, since they had no clearly defined objective before them.

Cromwell altered all that, determined to meet and destroy the King's principal Army. In the spring of 1645 the investment of Oxford began. To avoid being trapped in his headquarters Charles slipped out, intending either to attack the Scottish Army in the North and join hands with Montrose who was creating a diversion in their rear or to meet reinforcements which were expected from Ireland. But the pressure on Oxford forced him to abandon his northward march and return through the Eastern Midlands. On the way he was met by Fairfax and Cromwell who had moved suddenly from Oxford. The two armies met at Naseby, near Northampton, on June 14th. The course of the battle was very like that of Marston Moor. Rupert's cavalry on one wing swept away the force opposed to them but scattered wildly and played no further part in the day's fighting. Cromwell on the other wing, after a successful charge, wheeled round and caught the Royalist infantry in the rear. Charles escaped but his Army was destroyed and the victors captured a mass of papers proving that the King was negotiating to secure the help of various foreign armies, besides the Irish, to defeat Parliament.

Though fighting went on for another year the issue was now certain. The operations that remained amounted to little more than the rounding up of isolated detachments of Royalists and capturing a series of castles and fortified towns held by the King's supporters. The New

Model Army proved adept at siege warfare and met with little resistance except in the West where Goring still commanded a large body of irregular troops.

It was in the West and South-west that the one mass organisation that arose out of the war flourished. This was what was known as the 'Clubmen', peasant defence forces banded together for the sole purpose of defending their property against raiders of either party. In the spring of 1645 the Clubmen became an organised force, thousands strong, entering into negotiation with both King and Parliament as an independent body. Essentially neutral, they were called into action most often against the Royalists, since these, unpaid and under the leadership of the ruffianly Goring, were most given to looting. When they found that the Parliamentary forces were prepared to pay their way and appeared able to restore peace and security, the Clubmen helped them, in the last months of 1645 and the first of 1646, to make an end of the Royalist bands.

In May Charles fled from Oxford and surrendered to the Scots at Newcastle. So ended the first phase of the Revolution, the phase of armed struggle with the forces of reaction. In the next phase the differences in the ranks of the Puritans developed into a new struggle of classes and parties, with the Presbyterians, the party of the big bourgeoisie, pitted against the petty bourgeois Independents and their organisation the New Model Army. This struggle centred around, and gave significance to, the struggle for the possession of the King.

3. REGICIDE

Though Charles had been defeated he was still a king and remained a problem. Few men of any influence were Republicans, yet few believed that the King could be trusted. The problem therefore was to find means of restoring him to his throne under conditions which would make it impossible for him to renew the war or to enjoy any measure of real power. Charles had no intention of submitting to any such conditions. He explained his policy frankly enough to Digby, a member of his Council: "I do not despair of inducing the Presbyterians or the Independents to join me in exterminating the other; and then I shall be King again." For three years he faithfully followed this line of action, playing off Army against Commons and the Scots against both till he had destroyed his credit and ruined his friends and made his execution both a political necessity and an act of justice.

For the first few months after the ending of hostilities the Commons appeared to be supreme. They took it for granted that the Army was in practice as well as in theory the mere instrument of a victorious Parliament. To the Presbyterian majority in the Commons the Revolution was over and nothing was left to do but consolidate its gains. Royalists all over the country were deprived of their estates or heavily fined, many of the victors profiting by buying the forfeited lands at nominal prices. Presbyterianism was established as the State religion and savage laws were passed against the Independent sects. Finally, with an almost inconceivable disregard for political reality, the Commons proposed to disband the New Model Army without paying the considerable arrears of wages due to it. At one stroke the conversion of the Army to the tenets of the Independents was completed.

Simultaneously, negotiations had been carried on with the Scots, who had presented a bill of £700,000 for their services, "without mentioning the enormous losses which Scotland has suffered in consequence of her alliance with England and of which they left the valuation to the equity of Parliament". This was altogether too much for their brethren the English Presbyterians, who, after some haggling, offered them £200,000 down and as much again in two years' time. For this they agreed to leave England and to hand over Charles, which latter they were quite ready to do as they had found him completely intractable.

The Commons now planned to use the authority of the King against the New Model Army, to collect a fresh army from the regiments scattered in the South and West of England and not deeply tainted with Independency, to seize the train of artillery lying at Oxford and to coerce the Independents into surrender. But the Army was fully aware of the plot and prepared its own counter measures. In the period since the end of the war the regimental committees of Agitators had been welded together, and with the leading officers, had formed a body, 'The Council of the Army' which was qualified to speak for the whole and to act with authority and decision. Cromwell, who had been trying to mediate between the Army and the Commons, now decided that this was impossible and flung his influence on the side of action. A body of horse was sent out on May 1st 1647 to secure the artillery and remove Charles from Holmby House, where he had been lodged by Parliament, and bring him to the camp at Newmarket. The Council of the Army now opened negotiations with Parliament as one equal to another, and, in fact, the Army was in every real sense a more democratic and representative body than the House of Commons. After two months of such negotiations the Army began to move slowly on London.

The Presbyterians played their last card, their influence over the London masses. A demonstration was staged, a large and unruly mob of apprentices, watermen and disbanded officers who invaded the Commons and 'forced' them to pass the very measures against the Army that they were eager but afraid to pass on their own responsibility. After this the Army waited no longer, but marched into London, where no one ventured to oppose them, camped in Hyde Park, expelled the leading Presbyterians from Parliament and forced the rest to annul the Acts passed under the coercion of the London mob. A second revolution had taken place, and the Independents of the New Model Army, the party of the lower middle class, were for the moment masters of the situation.

Up to this point the Army had acted as a whole, and Cromwell and the group of high officers nearest to him, nicknamed the 'Grandees' had been accepted as the spokesmen of the rank and file. As late as March 25th the Left leader Lilburne had written to Cromwell: "I have looked upon you as among the powerful ones of England, as a man with heart perfectly pure, perfectly free from all personal views." But on August 13th he is writing: "If you despise, as hitherto, my warnings, be sure I will use against you all the power and influence I have, and so as to produce in your fortune changes that shall little please you." The Army, that had acted as the left wing of the Revolution, now developed within itself a left wing which soon came into violent conflict with the Grandees.

Cromwell's position in the English Revolution has often been oversimplified by regarding him either as a man of the Left or the Right. On the one hand, he was by birth and training a member of the class of large landowners, yet he had to suppress the Presbyterian Party. On the other, he began by standing out as the chosen leader of the Independents yet had to resist their radical and democratic demands. In spite of this, he retained, till his death, the support, decreasingly enthusiastic it is true, of the Army, and after he had established a stable regime he regained in some measure the support of the landowners and merchants.

The truth appears to be that at a moment of peculiarly delicate class relations Cromwell alone had sufficient political realism to comprehend and master them. He saw that both the Presbyterian policy and that of the Levellers would lead inevitably to a Royalist restoration, the first by alienating the revolutionary lower middle class, the second by isolating it. When the Levellers demanded a free Parliament and a wide electoral franchise Cromwell resisted them, partly because as a landowner he was sceptical about democracy but more because he knew that in such a Parliament the revolutionaries would be in a small minority. To Cromwell abstract principles were always infinitely less important than the practical necessity of maintaining power, whereas the Levellers were guided by little else than abstract principles.

After the occupation of London the political programme of the Levellers was embodied in *The Agreement of the People*. This programme, which passed through a number of transformations, and only took final shape after the execution of Charles, will be discussed in the next section. The rank and file were deeply suspicious of the negotiations between Charles and the Grandees, negotiations which culminated in a treaty, *The Heads of Proposals*, offered to Charles by Cromwell and Ireton in the late summer. The terms, better than any the Commons had put forward, included the ending of the confiscation of the Royalists' estates, the retention of bishops but the toleration of other forms of religion, guarantees for the control of the Crown by Parliament and a wider franchise than had hitherto prevailed. Charles refused these terms, and in November escaped from Hampton Court to the Isle of Wight.

A few days later Cromwell was faced with a mutiny among the troops at Ware. Two regiments, one of which was commanded by Lilburne's brother Robert, demonstrated with copies of *The Agreement of the People* stuck in their hats, demanding to be rid of the King and the carrying out of a radical social and political reform. The mutiny was soon suppressed, but the strong feeling in the Army, combined with the hopeless dishonesty and unreason of Charles, forced Cromwell into a complete change of policy. He broke with the King and declared in general terms his sympathy with the programme of the *Agreement*. Charles, meanwhile, was preparing to launch a new war, in which Presbyterians and Royalists were allied against the Army. The conspiracy was aided by a factor which has received too little attention. The five years from 1646 to 1651 were years of famine, high prices and general misery. The withdrawal of labour

caused by the war had combined with a run of wet summers to produce an unusually long run of bad harvests.
The worst year of all, 1648, was that in which the Second
Civil War actually broke out, and it is perhaps not wholly
a coincidence that hostilities actually began in May, the
month in which prices in famine years always reached
their highest point. There can be no doubt that the general
discontent caused by the famine was naïvely turned
against the Government.

The thoroughly opportunist alliance between Royalists
and Presbyterians was backed by a Scottish invasion.
Two of the counties most affected were Essex and Kent,
which had previously been Parliamentary strongholds
but were influenced by the Presbyterianism of London.
The rebellion here was crushed by Fairfax. Cromwell,
after accounting for a local rising in South Wales, marched
swiftly north to meet the Scots. In what was technically
perhaps the most brilliant of all his campaigns he completely destroyed an army twice the size of his own. He
advanced through Yorkshire and crossed the Pennines,
caught the Scots by surprise while they were straggling
slowly south in a long column between Wigan and Preston,
rolled them up from the rear, each blow driving them
farther from their base in Scotland, and, finally, forced
almost the whole Army to surrender at Ashborne on
August 25th.

The war had temporarily shelved the struggle between
Cromwell and the Left, and the whole Army marched
back to London determined to settle accounts both with
"that man of blood, Charles Stuart" and with the
Parliamentary Presbyterians who were still carrying on
interminable and fruitless negotiations with the King.
Colonel Pride was sent to Westminster with a strong
body of troopers. A hundred and fifty Presbyterian members were excluded from the Commons or imprisoned,
leaving less than one hundred who were no more than
an echo of the will of the Army.

On January 4th 1649 the 'Rump', as the Independent

remnant in the Commons was called, passed a resolution declaring: "That the people are, under God, the original of all just power: that the Commons of England, in Parliament assembled, being chosen by and representing the people, have the supreme power in this nation: that whatsoever is enacted or declared for law by the Commons in Parliament assembled, hath the force of law, and all the people of this nation are concluded thereby, although the consent of the King or House of Peers be not had thereunto." Passed by the Commons at its moment of least actual power, this resolution would be meaningless if it were not for the fact that both the tone and language are those of *The Agreement of the People*. Parliament speaks, but the words are those of the Levellers.

In accordance with the spirit underlying this Resolution the House of Lords was abolished and a Commission set up to try the King. Kings had been deposed before and murdered afterwards, but this time it was the Crown itself, the institution of monarchy, that was challenged. The execution of Charles was the work of the Independents alone, acting in opposition to both Royalists and Presbyterians. The Presbyterians and Cromwell were both right in a sense, the former in thinking that there was no essential incompatibility between a monarchy and bourgeois democracy, the latter in the knowledge that to ensure the success of the revolution so far as it had then gone a direct attack on the Crown was a present necessity.

For the men of the Left, the Levellers, the execution of Charles had further significance. It was a symbolic act of justice, an apocalyptic deed, ushering in the Fifth Monarchy, the rule of the saints, that is, the rule of the Army as the party of the revolutionary petty bourgeoisie. It was for them only the prelude to a social revolution. To Cromwell and the Grandees it was the culmination of the revolution and the beginning of a period of stabilisation.

4. THE LEVELLERS

Within a few weeks of the execution of Charles, the Levellers' agitation had blazed up to new heights. The crisis of the Second Civil War had forced Cromwell to make apparent concessions to the Left and had given its leaders a status and a freedom to put forward their ideas such as they had not previously enjoyed. In 1648 *The Agreement of the People* had received its final form at the hands of a committee consisting of Lilburne and three other leaders of the Levellers, four high officers of the Army and four Independent members of Parliament.

The Agreement was a remarkable programme, anticipating in many respects the Charter of two centuries later. It demanded the election every two years of a Parliament chosen freely by all males over the age of twenty-one with the exception of those receiving wages. The reservation serves as a reminder that the movement was one of the lower middle class, the small independent men, and was in fact less undemocratic than it appears. The wage-earning class, although perhaps numbering nearly half the population, had not yet begun to appear as a political force, and wage earners were regarded as servants of the rich, who would be under their influence and would vote at their dictation. Their exclusion from the franchise was thus regarded as necessary to prevent the employers from having undue influence, and there is every reason to think that the Levellers were correct in this judgment. Complete religious toleration, democratic control of the Army, whose regiments were to be raised in appointed districts with officers chosen by the votes of the inhabitants, the abolition of tithes and of all other taxes except a tax on property were the other main points of *The Agreement*.

The acceptance in principle of *The Agreement* by Cromwell and the Grandees was the high-water mark of the English Revolution. If the Levellers' movement looks forward to the demands of the Chartists in the Nineteenth

Century it also looked back towards the peasant Communism of the Middle Ages. It was the movements of a doomed class, the yeoman farmers, who were being slowly crushed out by the growth of large scale capitalist farming, and, though it stretched out its hands to the town craftsmen, especially in London, it made no contact with the wage-earning masses. While we cannot but admire the courage of the Levellers and sympathise with their desire for a democratic Republic, it is impossible not to see that Cromwell was right in thinking that no basis existed in 1649 for a left ward extension of the Revolution. The rôle of the Levellers, like that of the Jacobins in the French Revolution, was to carry the movement to positions which could not be permanently held but whose temporary seizure safeguarded the main advance.

It was soon clear that Cromwell and the Parliamentary Independents intended to allow *The Agreement* to remain on paper and that the Rump and the officers were going to carry on the Government as before but without a royal figurehead. A temporary body, the Council of State, was set up to act as an executive. The Levellers withdrew in disgust from the Committee which had been at work formulating *The Agreement*. Lilburne, Overton and other leaders were arrested, examined before the Council of State and committed to the Tower. Riots and protests broke out in London where the Levellers now had a strong following. Ten thousand signatures were collected in a few days to a petition demanding the release of Lilburne. This was soon followed by a second petition signed and presented entirely by women.

The Army was equally affected by the ferment, and when the Council of State decided to send the most disgruntled regiments to Ireland some refused to move. During April a regiment of Dragoons in London mutinied but were surrounded and disarmed by troops still loyal to the Government. One of the mutineers, Robert Lockyer, was court martialled and shot and his funeral was the occasion of the greatest mass demonstration of the time. Thousands of citizens followed the coffin, their sober Puritan hats decked with ribbons of sea-green, the colour of the Levellers.

From the Tower Lilburne wrote an open letter declaring "that it is both treason and murder for any General or Council of War to execute any soldier in time of peace by martial law". This letter, on top of Lockyer's execution, was followed at once by a mutiny on a far larger scale. Four regiments rose at Salisbury and 200 men of Lockyer's regiment, who had been moved to Oxfordshire, refused orders and put themselves under the leadership of a Captain Thompson, whose brother was one of the leaders of the Salisbury mutineers. The latter marched north to join hands with the Oxford rising, which they probably imagined to be more widespread than was actually the case. They had to swim the Thames, and the two bodies met at Burford. Here they camped for the night. Troops sent in pursuit by Cromwell, who had covered ninety miles in two days and whom the mutineers supposed to be miles away, caught them by surprise while still asleep. After a short and desperate battle some scattered and others surrendered. A remnant, perhaps 200 strong, broke through under Captain Thompson and finally reached Northampton where they were surrounded and forced to surrender. Out of the destruction of the Levellers, which revealed Cromwell as the protector of property and the friend of order, began a reconciliation between his group and the Presbyterians. This was symbolised by a splendid banquet which the City merchants gave to Cromwell and Fairfax to celebrate their victory in the Burford campaign.

The mutiny was smashed, and with it ended any hope there might have been of the success of the political movement, now confined almost entirely to a section of the London masses. In August Lilburne was brought to trial on a charge of treason. Lilburne, who if he was no politician was a superb agitator and pamphleteer, completely fearless and assured of the justice of his case, browbeat the judges and secured a verdict of 'Not Guilty' from the London jury. In 1652 the Rump Parliament banished him by a special Act. Next year he was back again in England, challenging the legality of the order, and, for a second time, was acquitted amid general rejoicing. But though the agitation seemed formidable it was disarmed and declining. Disillusion set in and its essential weakness was revealed in its development towards Quaker pacifism and a naïve Utopian Communism. Overton alone, one of the first of English free-thinkers, carried on the struggle to the end, being imprisoned in 1659 and again after the Restoration in 1663.

Lilburne, like many of the former soldiers of the New Model Army, became a Quaker, as did Jerrard Winstanley the Digger. The Diggers were a small group who preached and attempted to practise a primitive Communism, based on the claim that the land belonged to the whole people of England. This claim was supported by the interesting historical argument that William the Conqueror had "turned the English out of their birthrights; and compelled them for necessity to be servants to him and to his Norman soldiers". The Civil War was thus regarded as the reconquest of England by the English people. In the theological language of the time Winstanley urged that this political reconquest needed a social revolution to complete it and that otherwise the essential quality of monarchy remained:—"For you must either establish Commonwealth's freedom in power, making provision for every one's peace, which is righteousness, or else you must set up Monarchy again. Monarchy is twofold, either for one king to reign or for many to reign by kingly promotion. And if either one king rules or many rule by king's principles, much murmuring, grudges, trouble and quarrels may and will arise among the oppressed people on every gained opportunity," wrote Winstanley in his pamphlet, *The Law of Freedom in a Platform*.

Cromwell's alleged comment on such reasoning is revealing. "What," he asks, "is the purport of the levelling principle but to make the tenant as liberal a fortune as the landlord. I was by birth a gentleman. You must cut these people in pieces or they will cut you in pieces." For all his flirtations with the Left, Cromwell was and remained a landowner with the landowner's outlook and interests.

The Diggers tried to set up a model community on St. George's Hill in Surrey in 1649 but were soon ejected. Their movement never became strong in the number of its actual adherents but is important as a diffused influence, representing a considerable if vague aspiration among the mass of the Levellers. It was the backward turning face of the Leveller movement that we see in the Diggers, and their pacifism was a cause of hesitation and inactivity in moments of crisis.

The suppression of the Levellers left Cromwell and the Army officers holding the balance of power between two parties, both of which were hostile to the new regime but which were unable to combine against it. It was a victory for the centre, but a costly victory, since it weakened the Commonwealth's mass backing among the very class whose energy and sacrifices had done most to bring it into being. From this time Cromwell was forced to balance and manœuvre, to shift his ground constantly so as to find new supporters or to regain old ones. Yet it is worth noting here that Commonwealth did bring some solid gains to the working classes. Wage assessments for this period, covering both agricultural and town workers, are something like 50 per cent higher than in the preceding reign and somewhat higher than after the Restoration in 1660. Most of the ground gained appears to have been kept, and the drop in wages actually paid after 1660 to have been less than the drop in the assessments. Prices which had risen steadily up to about 1660, became stationary in the latter part of the Seventeenth Century and even tended to fall, mainly as a result of the great improvement in agricultural technique.

So far as the Army was concerned the Levellers were unable to make any headway after the defeat at Burford, and Cromwell's departure in August 1649, to reconquer Ireland gave their movement its death blow. All the most disaffected regiments were sent to Ireland where a large proportion of the mutineers perished or remained as settlers. The war in Ireland was indeed one of Cromwell's most effective strokes, since it not only removed one set of opponents to a safe distance but gave him the means to conciliate a second, the merchants and landowners, who profited by the huge confiscations of land which followed the defeat of the Royalists in Ireland.

CHAPTER IX

COMMONWEALTH AND COMPROMISE

I. IRELAND: SCOTLAND

DURING THE FIFTEENTH CENTURY English authority in Ireland reached its lowest point and the English Pale shrunk to a small tract immediately around Dublin. Outside the Pale a measure of order and unity began to take form out of the hegemony of the Norman-Irish family of the Fitzgeralds, Earls of Kildare, and when under Henry VII the second conquest of Ireland was projected it was only found possible to establish a nominal rule by giving to the Earl of Kildare the additional title of Deputy.

After some thirty years of Fitzgerald supremacy new tactics were adopted. The Fitzgeralds were provoked into rebellion in 1534 and their power destroyed. The basis of the new English policy was the utter destruction of the chiefs who showed any signs of independence and the systematic corruption of the rest by transforming them from Irish tribal leaders into English landlords. They were given titles, encouraged to speak English, to dress in English clothes and to send their sons to be educated at the English Court. In return they were recognised by English law as sole proprietors of the lands which under Irish law belonged to the whole tribe. To abolish Irish law, with its conception of communal property, out of the very memory of the people became one of the prime objects of the conquerors. If the clansmen revolted against the new authority of the chief-turned-landlord all the power of the Government stood behind him, while if he should revolt the whole clan was deprived of its land as punishment.

This policy met with fair success, but it was slow and it left few opportunities for the English ruling class to profit by the exploitation of the Irish peasantry. About the middle of the century it was abandoned for a more forward policy of direct confiscation, the forced sale of Irish land to English speculators and, in some cases, the establishment of colonies or plantations of English settlers. Fifty years of ferocious and almost continuous war, accompanied by famine and massacre and followed by confiscation, reduced large tracts of Ireland to an empty wilderness. Out of a total of just under £5,000,000 spent on foreign wars in Elizabeth's reign nearly half went for the Irish wars. Shane O'Neill (1559–1567), Desmond (1579–1583) and Hugh O'Neill (1598–1603) headed rebellions which stand out among a welter of lesser conflicts.

The situation was complicated by the Reformation, which reached Ireland only as part of the English attempt to destroy native customs and institutions. When Spain and the Papacy were in alliance against England and attempted to exploit the grievances of the Irish for their own ends, the priests were welcomed not because the Irish had any particular affection of the Popes but because the Catholic Church appeared as the avowed enemy of the invading English.

In the first years of the Seventeenth Century the conquest was completed by Lord Mountjoy, who followed the practice of the Romans, and later of Edward I in Wales, in building lines of forts from which the countryside could be systematically devastated and any rebellion threatened from the rear. There followed the series of wholesale confiscations of land already referred to,[1] and the establishment of plantations, especially in Ulster. The economic resources of Ireland were recklessly plundered. Mrs. J. R. Green writes:

"Enormous profits fell to the planters, who could get three times as much gain from an Irish as from an English estate by a fierce exploiting of the natural resources of

[1] See page 199 above.

the island and its cheap outlawed labour. Forests of oak were hastily destroyed for quick profits: woods were cut down for charcoal to smelt the iron which was carried down the rivers in cunning Irish boats, and what had cost £10 in labour and transport sold at £17 in London. The last furnace was put out in Kerry when the last wood had been destroyed.[1] Where the English adventurer passed he left the land as naked as if a forest fire had swept over the country."

The object of Strafford, who became Deputy under Charles I, was to organise this exploitation while at the same time creating a model despotism which could later be extended to England. His establishment of the linen industry was an attempt to counter the efforts of English clothiers who had begun to transfer their industry to Ireland attracted by the cheapness of labour there. In the interests of the English wool industry as a whole this was prohibited and linen weaving, which did not threaten any established English interest, was substituted. The linen industry was temporarily destroyed by the rising of 1641 and the wars which followed and when it was resumed was confined to Ulster.

The rising, resulting from the weakening of the Government after a period of intolerable oppression was marked by savage massacres of the new settlers and even more savage reprisals by the English and Scottish troops brought over to suppress it. While the Civil War was proceeding in England an independent war waged in Ireland. The Deputy Ormond was engaged in suppressing the native Irish in the King's name, while Charles was carrying on secret negotiations with the rebels. After the end of the war in England both sides combined against the victorious Commonwealth.

As early as 1641 the financial magnates in the City had begun to buy up the yet unconquered lands of the rebels as a speculation, estates being sold at the rate of £100

---

[1] This destruction of the forests took place mainly in the later Seventeenth Century.

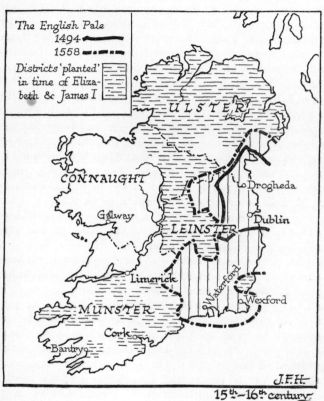

The English Pale
1494 ▬▬▬
1558 ▬ ▬ ▬

Districts 'planted'
in time of Eliza-
beth & James I

ULSTER

CONNAUGHT

Galway

LEINSTER

Drogheda

Dublin

Limerick

Waterford

MUNSTER

Wexford

Cork

Bantry

J.F.H.

15th–16th century

for 1,000 acres in Ulster and 600 acres in Munster. Cromwell therefore landed in Ireland in August, 1649, not only to reconquer the country for the Commonwealth but also for the speculators of the City of London.

After Drogheda and Wexford had been stormed and their garrisons slaughtered the invaders met with little resistance except at Clonmel, where Irish tribalism gathered under Hugh O'Neill for its last desperate battle, a combat between the past and the future. The Levellers and democrats who formed the bulk of Cromwell's Army can have had no idea that they were meeting men whose belief held unexpected parallels with their own or that in destroying them they were helping to place England as well as Ireland in the hands of the money lords, but they did perhaps recognise and respect the stubborn courage that drove them back after a hard day's fighting with the loss of some 2,500 men. It was Cromwell's only serious military reverse, partly atoned for by the abandonment of the defence later upon honourable terms.

The Cromwellian conquest was followed by the Cromwellian settlement. The bulk of the land in the three provinces of Ulster, Leinster and Munster passed to English landowners. Some were London speculators, others were officers in Cromwell's Army. Much land was allotted to the soldiers for arrears in their pay, and it was intended to replace the native Irish with English settlers throughout the three provinces. But the majority of the privates were too poor to take up their holdings which were bought at low prices by officers and others, who thus became possessed of large estates. The Irish peasants remained as labourers or as rackrented smallholders. Many died in the wars, many were shipped to virtual slavery in the American plantations—20,000 in the one year 1653 alone —and many of the upper classes went to Europe to become soldiers of fortune. The population of Ireland, which was about 1,500,000 in 1641 had decreased by 1652 to 850,000 Of this total about 150,000 were English or Scottish settlers. Many of these settlers were smallholders who sank within a generation or two to the common level of misery of the Irish around them.

Ireland now became, what it has since of necessity remained, a source of cheap food and raw materials for England. At first cattle were reared, and by 1660, some 500,000 head were being exported annually to England. When these exports were found to be causing a fall in agricultural prices and rents, an Act was passed in 1666 forbidding the export of cattle, meat or dairy products. This Act crippled the Irish cattle industry and when cattle began to be replaced by sheep a further Act forbade both the export of wool to any other country and the export of anything but the raw wool to England. Later still, the Irish cloth industry was deliberately destroyed when it became a dangerous competitor.

By May 1650 Cromwell had reduced Ireland except for the West, and returned to England leaving Ireton to finish his work. The Commonwealth Government was still threatened both from Scotland and from the sea, where a part of the Navy had gone over to the Royalists and was attacking English shipping in the Channel. On his father's death Charles II was proclaimed king in Edinburgh and in the spring of 1650 landed in Scotland at the invitation of the Presbyterians, taking the Covenant and going through all the motions of Protestant piety. The Army that was collected to support him was carefully purged of all Cavalier elements and, indeed, of all but the most orthodox Covenanters. Officered by "ministers' sons, clerks, and other such sanctified creatures, who hardly ever saw or heard of any other sword than that of the Spirit", it was a poor military instrument with which to oppose Cromwell's veterans.

Marching north in July Cromwell broke the patience of the Covenanters by a series of flanking marches, each calculated to force it to give battle at a tactical disadvantage. For a time the caution of the Scottish general, Leslie, prevailed against the instinctive desire of the Covenanters to fall headlong upon the Amalekites, but at Dunbar on

Ie

September 3rd they could be restrained no longer and
Cromwell secured a crushing victory. During the winter
a second army collected largely from the elements that
had previously been excluded, took up the struggle.
Taking up its position at Stirling it drew its supplies from
the fertile North-Eastern Coast plain. Not strong enough
for a frontal attack, and fearing a long campaign that
would have given his enemies at home an opportunity to
grow strong again, Cromwell slipped past his opponents
to Perth, in one stroke cutting them off from their base
and leaving the way open into England. This way they
had no alternative but to take. As they marched south,
with dwindling forces and Cromwell in pursuit, converging
armies edged them into the Severn valley away from the
direct road to London, and at Worcester, on the anni-
versary of Dunbar, they were surrounded and defeated.

At the same time, the Commonwealth admiral, Blake,
was rounding up the Royalist privateers and reducing
their last strongholds in the Channel and Scilly Islands.
With the success of these operations all possibility of internal
resistance to the Commonwealth regime came to an end
for the time being. The problem now was to consolidate
and stabilize, to find a class basis broad enough to ensure
its permanency and to allow the military dictatorship to
transform itself into a genuinely popular government.
Viewed from this angle the story of the nine years between
1651 and 1660 is one of persistent and heroic effort and
of unrelieved failure.

2. THE COMMONWEALTH

The Army, returning victorious from Worcester in the
autumn of 1651, found England and Holland on the verge
of war. For over a generation English and Dutch traders
had been at odds in the East Indies and the merchants
of London had looked enviously at the vast trade of their
rivals. In 1651 the Rump passed the Navigation Act,
ordering all goods imported into England to be brought

in English ships or the ships of the country where they were actually produced. This was an attempt to deprive the Dutch of some of their carrying trade, which they had obtained because of the number, size and efficiency of their ships and the perfection of their commercial organisation and which had made Holland a centre for the re-distribution of commodities brought from all over the world. In itself the Navigation Act did not lead necessarily to war. Similar Acts had been passed before from the fourteenth century onwards, and neither then nor afterwards, apart from short occasional periods, had they been strenuously enforced.

The Rump was, however, determined on war and followed the Navigation Act by a series of provocations. When war came it was a trade war, the work of the merchants alone, and was disliked both by Cromwell and the Army as a whole. As it dragged on it became more and more unpopular in spite of some naval successes. It proved costly, making necessary increased taxation and seriously interfering with foreign trade which was just beginning to recover from the chaos of the Civil War and the ravages of the Royalist privateers.

For Holland the war was disastrous, as any war with England was bound to be, for the simple geographical reason that England lay right across all the trade routes upon whose maintenance the majority of the Dutch people depended for their livelihood. Starvation rather than the naval victories of Blake forced Holland to conclude a peace in 1654, a peace in which England gained nothing tangible which had not been obtainable before the war began.

The stamp of the amateur lies over the Dutch war as over the whole foreign policy of the Commonwealth. Whether that policy was the Rump's or Cromwell's it was marked by a complete ignorance of European and world affairs and of the means by which the class interest sought could best be served. It was marked, too, by a revolutionary truculence, born of the possession of an army and fleet that had no superiors in Europe and a feeling that these splendid weapons must be continuously employed.

Since Buckingham's unfortunate essays, early in the reign of Charles I, England had taken no part in European politics, at first because Charles's attempt to govern without Parliament made economy essential and then because of the absorption of all parties in the internal struggle for power. The old trained diplomats had died or were in opposition or in exile and their places were taken by country squires, lawyers and merchants who had little knowledge or opportunity for acquiring knowledge of what was happening outside England. Naïvely they looked for a rival to fight, with no clear idea of what consequences their actions were likely to have.

The war with Holland was the first blunder, justified in part at least by the fact that Holland had now actually become England's main commercial rival. The war with Spain, which lasted from 1665 to the end of the Commonwealth, was little more than a reversion to a traditional Protestant policy that had long ceased to reflect reality at all. It followed the customary lines of an alliance with France and an attack on the Spanish treasure fleets and American colonies. A badly-equipped expedition of inferior troops failed expensively to take San Domingo but secured Jamaica as a consolation. In Europe Cromwell was led by the nose by the French minister Mazarin. An English army helped to defeat the Spanish and to capture Dunkirk, which was then ceded to England. Dunkirk was not at this time a French town, could not have been captured from Spain without English help and was quite useless to its new holders both from the military and the economic point of view. Its occupation, and the importance popularly attached to it, was a reversion to a yet older policy, belonging properly to the age of Calais and the Wool Staple.

The foreign policy of the Commonwealth reacted unfavourably upon the stability of its position at home.

With a revenue far larger than any English government had ever had before, it was constantly in financial difficulties and was forced to impose special taxes and to levy fines upon the estates of the Royalists. Since these included both the Cavalier Royalists of the First Civil War and the Presbyterian Royalists of the Second, the whole landowning class was alienated, a fact which accounts in part for the violence of the reaction of 1660. The bitterness aroused by the first of these levies, made in 1652 to finance the Dutch war, was intensified by the corruption with which it was carried out. The Rump soon became notorious for taking bribes and for the place-hunting of its members, and its unpopularity became a danger to the whole regime.

The Army demanded its dissolution: Cromwell, as often before, occupied a middle position and attempted to secure a compromise so long as this was possible. When the Rump proposed to extend its life indefinitely by co-opting only such new members as it approved, Cromwell could compromise no longer and the Rump was forcibly dissolved on April 20th, 1653. Its departure was the signal for a new turn towards the Left.

Under the influence, temporarily, of General Harrison and the Fifth Monarchy Men, and disgusted by the war policy of the merchants, Cromwell agreed to the calling of an Assembly of Nominees (known later as Barebone's Parliament) consisting of 140 men chosen by the Independent ministers and congregations. It was a frankly party assembly, the rule of the Saints, of that sober and respectable Independent lower middle class which, in the country districts, had not been deeply influenced by the Levellers and remained to the end the most constant force behind the Commonwealth. The Assembly soon proved too revolutionary and impractical for Cromwell and the Council, preferring to discuss such questions as the abolition of the Court of Chancery and of Tithes to the voting of supplies and the transaction of other immediately pressing Government business. After sitting five months it was dissolved in December, 1653, to make way for a new

Parliament for which the right wing group of officers around Lambert had prepared a brand new paper Constitution—the Instrument of Government.

This constitution aimed ostensibly at securing a balance of power between Cromwell, now given the title of Lord Protector, the Council and Parliament. The latter included for the first time members from Scotland and Ireland and there was a redistribution of seats to give more members to the counties. Against this, the franchise was restricted to those who possessed the very high property qualification of £200 and by the disqualification of all who had taken part in the Civil Wars on the Royalist side. The new Parliament was thus anything but a popular or representative body, but this did not prevent it from refusing to play the part assigned to it, that of providing a constitutional cover for the group of high officers now controlling the Army. The Parliament of the Right proved just as intractable as the Parliament of the Left had and was dissolved at the earliest possible moment in January 1655.

For nearly two years Cromwell abandoned all pretence of constitutional government as hopeless, all the more readily because of the discovery of a series of Royalist plots, one of which culminated in an actual rising at Salisbury. Charles in exile was, as the Commonwealth's spies knew, corresponding not only with the secret Royalist organisation, "The Sealed Knot", but with the Presbyterians and even with now demoralised remnant of the Levellers. The country was divided into eleven districts, each under the control of a major-general. Strong measures were taken against the Royalists, and it is from this period that much of the repressive legislation traditionally associated with Puritan rule dates. This open military dictatorship was efficient but increasingly unpopular, especially when the war with Spain at the end of 1655 led to new taxation. In spite of this taxation, imposed as arbitrarily as in the time of Charles, a deficit of £800,000 and the poor credit of the Government made it necessary to call a new Parliament in September 1656.

A quarter of the members elected were prevented from taking their seats, but this Parliament was even more markedly a body of the Right than its predecessor. A revised Constitution, the Humble Petition and Advice, was drawn up which increased the powers both of Parliament and the Protector at the expense of that of the Council of State where the Generals were strongly entrenched. The House of Lords was restored and Cromwell was offered the title of King. He refused, mainly because of the strong disapproval of the Generals who on this occasion at least certainly reflected the feelings of the rank and file of the Army. However inclined Cromwell may have been to go with Parliament at that moment he knew that it was upon the Army that his authority ultimately rested.

This move to the Right was not a success, although it gave the Government a temporary increase of stability. The old opponents of the Commonwealth were not conciliated by this apparent return to traditional institutions, while these very innovations, and above all the talk of a return to monarchy, alarmed and disgusted the Left, which, though it might differ from Cromwell on many points had yet supported him in the main as the alternative to a Stuart restoration. The Commonwealth rested on the uneasy support of two antagonistic groups, the merchants and the lower middle class, both of which together still formed only a small minority of the total population. Its efforts to find a basis acceptable to both consistently failed and both were in turn alienated by efforts to seek a backing in other classes. The last years of the Commonwealth were marked by a steady loss of mass support, an increasingly precarious balance of the Generals and the Army, only held together by the prestige of Cromwell.

Its end, like its beginning, coincided with a prolonged period of famine, lasting from 1658 to 1661. In addition, the Spanish war was proving both costly and ruinous to trade. Shipping was seriously interfered with, the export of cloth declined and there was much unemployment among the weavers. The collection of taxes became more difficult and as a consequence the credit of the Government fell so that loans had to be negotiated on increasingly unfavourable terms. However popular the Spanish War may have been among the merchants at the beginning its effects soon turned them against both it and the Government. Neither Blake's victory at Santa Cruz nor the capture of Dunkirk were able to outweigh the losses and discomfort of a prolonged war.

This unrest was reflected in the second session of Parliament, where Cromwell's influence had been weakened by the transfer of many of his supporters to the newly constituted House of Lords. After a few weeks it was dissolved and for the last seven months of his life Cromwell returned once more to an open military rule. Yet he was unable to solve any of his problems, and, above all, that of finance. Although the national finances had been modernised by the Long Parliament they were still quite inadequate to maintain a large standing army. Yet without such an army the Commonwealth could not exist. Here lay the technically insoluble dilemma which made its fall ultimately inevitable.

Cromwell's death on October 3rd, 1658, exposed the whole weakness of the regime and brought it to an abrupt conclusion, but it was the economic stresses and political contradictions which have been outlined that gave his death its instantaneous and decisive effect. The urban middle classes had proved too weak by themselves to afford a permanent basis for a government and the Restoration of 1660 was in effect a re-combination of class forces to establish a government more in harmony with the real distribution of strength. It was less a restoration of the monarchy than a new compromise between the landowners and the upper classes in the towns.

3. THE COMPROMISE OF 1660

On the death of Cromwell, his son Richard—-"Tumbledown Dick"—was declared Protector with no better recommendation than his great name and the support of a group of discredited politicians who saw in him a convenient instrument. The Army under Lambert and Fleetwood refused to recognise him and he resigned. To give their rule a semblance of legality the Generals re-assembled what was left of the Long Parliament. Within a few months it had been dismissed and recalled once again. The Army itself began to split into fragments, each general playing for his own hand. The Commonwealth disappeared in a welter of conflicting factions.

Finally, Monk, commander of the garrison in Scotland, marched south in the beginning of 1660, joined Fairfax at York, entered London and persuaded or coerced the Rump into dissolving itself after making the arrangements for a new election. At the same time he began negotiations with the exiled Charles who made his recall virtually certain by the issue on August 14th, 1660, of the Declaration of Breda, a document in which the hand of Hyde is plainly visible. In it Charles promised a general pardon except for those directly concerned in the execution of Charles I and undertook to allow religious toleration and to respect existing property relations.

The new Parliament which met on the same date was predominantly Royalist and Presbyterian, and one of its first acts was to invite Charles to return. When the excitement had died away and the loyal addresses had been forgotten, the French Ambassador in London wrote shrewdly to Louis XIV: "This government has a monarchical appearance because there is a King, but at bottom it is very far from being a monarchy." Charles I had claimed to be King by Divine Right: Charles II knew that he was King by permission of the landlords and merchants in Parliament and could be dismissed as easily as he had been summoned. The only way in which the Crown could secure any measure of real power was by exploiting the antagonisms between the various sections of the ruling class. Charles was quite ready to do this, but, for the moment, he kept his intentions to himself.

I1

The character of the Restoration is most clearly shown
in the land settlement which followed it. The Church and
Crown lands that had been confiscated during the Commonwealth were restored. As a set-off the landowners freed
themselves from all the remaining feudal dues owed by
them to the Crown, giving Charles as an equivalent an
Excise Duty and thus shifting their obligations on to the
rest of the nation. By this action, Marx says, they "vindi-
cated for themselves the rights of modern private property
in estates to which they had only a feudal title". In this
respect the Restoration was a completion rather than a
reversal of the Revolution.

The settlement of private claims was more difficult.
The landowners were not united but divided roughly into
two sections, the old or Cavalier Royalists and the new
or Presbyterian Royalists, who had transferred their
allegiance from Parliament to King in or about 1647.
But it was before this, in the period between the First and
Second Civil Wars, that the greatest bulk of the land
had changed hands and many estates now held by the
new Royalists had been confiscated from exiled Cavaliers
or sold to pay the heavy fines inflicted by the Long Parliament. The estates which had actually been confiscated
were now returned to their original owners: those, far
more numerous, which had been lost as the result of forced
sales were not. It was a solution which, while it displeased
many of the Cavaliers, had the effect of uniting the landowners in support of the Crown, at any rate for the time.

In May 1661 a new Parliament met. The Royalist
gentry had now re-emerged to dominate local politics in
all but a few of the large towns, while the people who had
been politically most active under the Commonwealth
found it wiser to withdraw from public notice. The
"Cavalier Parliament" of 1661 saw the eclipse of the
Presbyterians as a political party. It was "a parliament
of lewd young men, chosen by a furious people in spite
to the Puritans", and all the more eager for revenge
because of their dissatisfaction with the land settlement.

The work of its first sessions, known later as the *Clarendon Code* after Hyde, Earl of Clarendon, who had returned from exile to become Chancellor, was in form a religious settlement. In substance it was a series of Acts designed to drive the Puritan Party into illegality. Since the towns were the centre of Puritan strength the first step, in the Corporation Act of 1661 was to restrict their governing bodies to those who were prepared to accept the dogma and discipline of the Anglican Church. Next year, by the Act of Uniformity, some 2,000 Puritan clergy who would not declare their complete agreement with the Prayer Book were expelled from their livings. A similar conformity was demanded from all teachers. In this way the Puritans were ousted from the apparatus of the State and the State Church. The Conventicle Act of 1665 was intended to prevent them from reforming outside, prohibiting all public worship save that of the State Church. Finally the Five Mile Act (1665) prohibited the expelled ministers and teachers from coming within five miles of any corporate town, thus cutting them off from the mass of their supporters.

The Clarendon Code destroyed Presbyterianism, which was an organised national church or nothing. The Independent sects, since they were purely local and since their adherents were generally less conspicuous, were able to survive as semi-secret organisations of the lower middle class. The well-to-do Presbyterians soon found their way into the Church of England where they later formed one wing of the Whig Party. In the country districts the decline of the yeomen farmers and the growing stratification of the rural population into the groups of squires, tenant farmers and landless labourers deprived Puritanism of its social basis, and led to the complete predominance of the squirearchy, first Royalist, then Tory and always strongly Anglican. In the late Seventeenth and the Eighteenth Centuries the struggle between Whig and Tory became to a considerable extent a struggle between town and country.

In one respect the Royalist Parliaments of Charles II were as unaccommodating as those of his father had been. At the opening of the reign excise and land taxes estimated to bring in £1,200,000 a year were voted. Actually they realised little more than £500,000 and additional votes were made grudgingly and only after delays. The question of finance was soon complicated by quarrels between Charles and Parliament over foreign policy. In 1665 a war with Holland developed out of trade disputes and unofficial conflicts in North America and the East. As before the fighting was indecisive but it resulted in the capture of what afterwards became New York. Both Parliament and City, however, were coming to regard the rising power of France as the most serious enemy, while Charles was anxious to develop friendly relations with the French king, Louis XIV, from whom he hoped to get the financial help that would make him independent of Parliament.

The strength of the anti-French party forced the Government to conclude a Triple Alliance with Holland and Sweden in 1668, but two years later Charles was able to neutralise the effect of this by a secret treaty in which he promised to join Louis in a war for the partition of Holland and to declare himself a Catholic when he could do so with safety. In return Louis was to give him an annual subsidy which would make him financially independent of Parliament. A third Dutch War, in which England and France were in alliance, was begun in 1672. Charles was unable to intervene very effectively because the Parliamentary dislike of the war was expressed in an extreme reluctance to vote supplies. The Government at this time was accustomed to borrow from the London goldsmiths on the security of future taxes. Its difficulties in 1672 had become so great that it was forced to repudiate the whole of its outstanding debt, which then amounted to £1,328,526. This caused a real panic in the City. In 1677 payment of interest at the rate of 6 per cent instead of the usual 8 per cent was resumed for a few years, but it was not till much later that the capital sum was incorporated in the National Debt. By this, more than perhaps by any other action, the Government of Charles lost the support and confidence of the London financiers.

It is at about this time, at any rate, that we can place the ending of the alliance between the squirearchy and the upper classes of the towns, an alliance that had given strength to the Tudor monarchy and to the opposition to the early Stuarts, whose dissolution had weakened the Commonwealth and whose temporary revival had produced the Restoration. It was now passing for good except for a moment when an overmastering panic blotted out customary hostilities in 1688.

The long life—1661 to 1678—enjoyed by the Cavalier Parliament gave full opportunity for the professionalising of politics, for the growth of organised political parties acting under recognised leaders and for the beginning of that undisguised corruption that developed into a system in the Eighteenth Century and makes many of the detailed changes of policy and alignment so complicated, and, on the long view, so insignificant. On the one hand stood the Tory squires, restored to political influence by the restoration of the monarchy and seeing in the preservation and strengthening of the monarchy the best way of maintaining that influence. Behind them stood the Anglican Church and the yet unawakened masses of the rural population. Against them the Whigs, a more curious combination of the merchants and rising finance capitalists with a section of the most powerful of the landed aristocracy, magnates like the Dukes of Bedford and Devonshire who were sufficiently conscious of their own strength not to feel the need their lesser neighbours had to lean on the Crown. These two wings formed the 'respectable' face of Whiggery. Behind them, and far more radical, stood the largely Puritan lower middle class of the towns, and, from the Earl of Shaftesbury onwards, the Whig leaders developed great skill in stimulating and directing the passions of the slum population. At times this dangerous ally was, however, used against them by the Tories with terrible effect.

The last years of the Cavalier Parliament passed in indecisive struggles in which Shaftesbury and Whigs and then Danby and the Tories gained small advantages.[1]

But its final session was held in the midst of the panic created by the exposure of the alleged Popish plot. An ex-Jesuit, Titus Oates, declared that the Jesuit Congregation of England had met in the White Horse Tavern, London, on April 24th, 1678, and had there plotted the murder of the King and the restoration of Catholicism in England. Actually the Congregation *had* met on that day, in the rooms of Charles' brother James. Oates did not know this, and though Charles did, he had the very best of reasons for keeping his knowledge to himself.

The story was instantly believed and a reign of terror began in which a number of Catholics were executed and many more imprisoned. The intense popular feeling against Catholicism at this time is inexplicable unless it is remembered that it was largely political and social. "Popery and wooden shoes" was a current phrase to describe the conditions existing in France, and by it men meant that with Catholicism went political absolutism and a low standard of living. The fact that James was known to be a Catholic, that Oates was able by accident to implicate his secretary in genuinely treasonable activities and that considerable Court favour had been shown to Catholics during the previous decade made it all the easier for any crazy story to gain credence, even one so absurd as that the Catholics were plotting the death of Charles, their most influential patron.

Charles, Danby and the Tories knew that the story was absurd but were afraid to say so. Shaftesbury and his friends who also knew it to be absurd, seized it with delight as a weapon with which to destroy their political enemies. The great majority of the population believed it absolutely,

[1] The names Whig and Tory were not actually used till a few years later in the great crisis of 1680 but the parties they denoted had then existed some years.

and so probably did a majority of members of Parliament. Under these conditions even the Cavalier Parliament went over to the Whigs, demanding the disbandment of the Army which was believed to be permeated with Catholics and which the Whigs thought, not altogether unjustly, that Charles intended to use to establish an absolutism like that of Louis XIV. The last act of the Cavalier Parliament was the impeachment of the Tory minister Danby.

Elections held in February 1679 resulted in the return of a Parliament overwhelmingly Whig. It was the first of three short lived Parliaments (March to July 1679, October 1680 to January 1681 and March 21st to 28th, 1681) in which the efforts of the Whigs were centred upon preventing James from succeeding his brother as king. These efforts failed, partly because Charles disclosed extraordinary tactical ability, playing for time while slowly rebuilding the shattered Tory party, and partly because the Whigs were unable to agree among themselves whether they wanted to replace James by his Protestant daughter Mary and her Dutch husband William of Orange, or by the Duke of Monmouth, a reputed son of Charles' whose illegitimacy was as certain as his paternity was doubtful. The majority decided for Monmouth, most unwisely because though he was personally popular the classes on whom the Tories normally relied but who had been stampeded by the Popish Plot would never have been prepared to accept him as heir to the throne.

For all these reasons, and because the absurdities and hysteria of the Popish Plot had produced their inevitable reaction, the parties were much more nearly even in the Parliament that met on March 21st, 1681. Charles seemed at the end of his resources, the Treasury empty, his credit exhausted, the Army unpaid and almost mutinous. He summoned Parliament to meet at Oxford, away from the fiercely Whig masses of London, and offered a compromise by which James should succeed but William and Mary act as joint regents and govern in his name. Confident of success the Whigs, as Charles expected, refused this offer

which had in fact only been made to impress moderate
men with the King's reasonableness. His opponents did
not know that he had just concluded a new alliance with
Louis which guaranteed him an income sufficient to make
him financially independent of Parliament.

Without warning, and so suddenly that the Whig
leaders had no opportunity to assemble their followers or
to make any plans, Parliament was dissolved. Away from
London no resistance was possible and a contagion of
alarm scattered them in hopeless and confused flight to
their homes in all parts of the country. Freed from immediate danger, Charles passed over to the offensive. In the
Tory gentry, the Church and the Army he had a force
too formidable to be directly challenged, and, for the last
four years of his life, he ruled with a more absolute power
than any of his family had enjoyed before him.

4. THE COMPROMISE OF 1688

The events of 1681 appeared at first sight as a complete
and successful counter-revolution, undoing at one stroke
the work of the Long Parliament, the Civil War and the
Commonwealth, and their sequel seemed to confirm this
view. Charles followed his victory with a reorganisation of
the machinery of local government. Whig Justices of the
Peace were everywhere replaced by Tories, and the
Clarendon Code, which had fallen into some disuse during
the Whig supremacy, was once more vigorously enforced.
Tories were elected to the key posts of Sheriff in London,
and, since the Sheriffs chose the juries, this made it possible
for the Government to be certain of securing convictions
against any Whig leaders who might be brought to trial.

Shaftesbury, Russell, Algernon Sidney and other Whigs
began to plan a desperate insurrection, and a parallel
scheme for the assassination of Charles and James was
prepared by a group of old Cromwellian soldiers. Hopeless
of success and fearing arrest, Shaftesbury fled to Holland
in November 1682. In the following June both plots were

betrayed to the Government and their leaders, including Russell and Sidney were captured and executed. The Whig supporters were driven to silence and even in London the streets were dominated for a time by the Church and King mob.

During 1683 and 1684 the Tories attacked the last stronghold of the Whigs, the corporate towns. The Charter of the City of London was declared to have been infringed, was forfeited and only restored on conditions that put the control of the Common Council in the hands of the Crown. Many provincial towns hurried to surrender their Charters before worse befell: others were revoked on a variety of pretexts. That employed at York, where it was declared that "The Lord Mayor had refused a mountebank, that had the King's own recommendation, to erect his stage there" was perhaps as good as most of the rest. Since the borough corporations in most cases chose the members of Parliament, Charles was now assured of a Tory House of Commons if ever he should need to call one together. The Whig Party was dispersed and appeared to be destroyed.

Yet the counter-revolution was neither so complete nor secure as it appeared. The social basis of the Whigs in the class of prosperous merchants was in fact stronger than ever before. The period between 1660 and 1688 had been one of rapid commercial expansion. The alliance with Portugal and the establishment of closer trade relations with Spain and her colonies had opened new markets for English goods. The plantations in the American colonies and the West Indies grew steadily and provided both markets and raw materials, while the East India Company became not only an important trading concern but a force in English internal politics. The exploitation of the colonial areas was already placing a great accumulation of capital in the hands of the Whig merchants.

Considerable as were the social forces Charles had been able to rally behind him in his bid for absolutism, they were not the disposers of decisive masses of capital,

The Crown was temporarily and accidentally independent owing to the subsidies that Louis was prepared to grant Charles for political reasons of his own: but these subsidies could not be counted on indefinitely and the most Tory of Parliaments would not have been prepared to grant the Crown a revenue adequate to maintain the large standing army which a despotism demanded. In practice, the country gentry almost always proved especially tight fisted because their conservatism and limited outlook made it impossible for them to appreciate the increasing needs of the complicated State organisation that was developing in this era. Sooner or later the Government would have been forced to come cap in hand to the financial interests of the City for help that would have only been given on terms.

Things did not actually happen in this way because James played into the hands of the Whigs by trying to push the counter-revolution farther and faster than his Tory supporters were prepared to go. By his attempt to restore Catholicism in England he was thrown back upon the support of the most reactionary elements in the country, the Jesuits and the more reckless and short-sighted of the Catholic gentry. His attempt was unwelcome even to a large proportion of the Catholics who foresaw a failure which would leave them in a worse position than before.

It was all the less likely to succeed because it coincided with the revocation, in 1685, of the Edict of Nantes, under which the French Huguenots had enjoyed a limited toleration. The revocation was followed by an intense persecution and the desperate flight of hundreds of thousands of Huguenots who dispersed all over Western Europe. Fifty or sixty thousand settled in England, almost all of them skilled artisans. Silk weavers and hatters, paper-makers and glass-blowers, they brought with them both their industrial skill and tales of Catholic atrocities that lost nothing in the telling. A general conviction was soon abroad that a concerted plot was being hatched to destroy Protestantism throughout Europe. The width as well as the intensity of the opposition to James was to a large extent the result of contemporary events in France.

Yet the reign opened favourably enough with generous votes of supplies from a Parliament packed with Tories by the earlier manipulations of the borough corporations. In July a rising in Somerset on behalf of the Duke of Monmouth was defeated without difficulty. Monmouth had landed at Lyme Regis and his arrival in the Somerset clothing area had been the signal for a mass rising of the peasants and weavers more general than anything that had been seen since the days of Kett. The causes of this curiously spontaneous movement are obscure, but it may have been connected with a depression in the West Country cloth industry, just beginning to suffer from Irish competition. It is certain at any rate that a decade later the Taunton clothiers were complaining bitterly of this competition and of the low wages and cheap wool which made it formidable.

Monmouth's rebellion was hopeless from the start, as any such rebellion must have been so long as the Government maintained its hold on London, the centre of the great semi-circle in which the strength of the Whigs was concentrated and in relation to which the Taunton area was an outlying pocket surrounded by hostile or indifferent territory. The rebels were shot and ridden down by the Government's regular troops at Sedgemoor and in the man hunt that followed hundreds were executed and more transported to the West Indian plantations.

The Government even turned the rebellion to advantage by making it the excuse to increase the standing Army. At the Restoration Cromwell's Army had been quickly disbanded, except for a few regiments of guards. Other regiments were afterwards raised for garrison duty at Tangiers, and in Scotland a force of 20,000 men was permanently maintained. But every attempt made by Charles to keep a large standing army in England was strongly resisted. Now James brought the strength of the

Army up to about 30,000 and stationed 13,000 men at Hounslow Heath to overawe London.

So far as was possible this Army was, contrary to law, officered by Catholics. The rank and file remained over-whelmingly non-Catholic and the rather clumsy efforts that were made to convert them only aroused resentment. In Ireland James' Lord Lieutenant, the Earl of Tyrconnel, was able to form a considerable Catholic Army.

James now began to replace his Tory but Anglican ministers with Catholics, re-established the Court of High Commission abolished by the Long Parliament, appointed Catholics as magistrates and even as bishops. Realising that even his Tory Parliament would never agree to remove the legal disabilities under which the Catholics still suffered he determined to attempt to remove them by a special exercise of the royal prerogative. In 1687 and again in April 1688 a Declaration of Indulgence was issued, suspending all laws by which Catholics were barred from military and civil office. In an attempt to win new allies, the Dissenters were also included in this dispensation, but the old Puritan fear and hatred of Popery was so strong, and it was so obvious that religious toleration was being used as an instrument for creating a political absolution, that they remained unmoved.

The Anglican clergy refused to carry out the royal order to read the Indulgence in their churches and they were supported by the bishops. When seven bishops were arrested, tried and acquitted, they found themselves, as no members of the episcopal bench had ever been before, the heroes of a Puritan London crowd. In breaking with the Church of England James was also breaking with the Tory squirearchy, whom Charles with his greater political acumen had seized on as the one class upon whose support an absolute monarchy might possibly still be based. This made failure absolutely certain.

Whigs and Tories joined to open negotiations with William of Orange, and, on June 30th, a definite invitation was sent by a group of leading peers promising active support in a rebellion against James. All the summer William gathered a fleet and an army, waiting anxiously in case Louis should make it impossible for him to sail by a direct attack on the Netherlands. James and his ministers hesitated between advance and retreat, and in the end, William was able to land unopposed at Torbay on November 5th. One by one James' supporters escaped abroad or deserted to William. The decisive desertion was perhaps that of a certain John Churchill, already the most influential of the officers of the Army and soon to be better known as the Duke of Marlborough. Without the Army James was helpless and his flight in December left William, gathering strength day by day as he moved towards London, as the only possible remaining authority.

A Convention met in February and offered the throne jointly to William and Mary. The Convention declared itself a Parliament and proceeded, in the Bill of Rights, to lay down the conditions upon which the Whig bourgeoisie was pleased to allow the monarchy to continue to exist. The King was no longer, in effect, allowed to control either the Army or the judges. He was specifically forbidden either to dispense with the laws or to suspend them. The control of finance passed once and for all to Parliament which must be called at least once in every three years and must not be kept in existence for longer than that time.[1] On these terms the Whigs became loyal and enthusiastic monarchists, since the monarchy was now their monarchy and depended upon them for its existence. In this they differed from the Tories, who had rather felt that their existence depended on that of the monarchy and who were consequently far less exacting in the terms upon which their support was given.

"The 'Glorious Revolution'," as Marx said, "brought into power, along with William of Orange, the landlord

---

[1] In 1716 the Whigs extended the life of Parliament to seven years because an election at that time would have probably produced a Tory majority. In 1911 the duration of Parliament was fixed at five years but nothing can prevent any Parliament prolonging its own life indefinitely as happened during the Great War.

and capitalist appropriators of surplus value. They inaugurated the new era by practising on a colossal scale thefts of State lands, thefts that had hitherto been managed more modestly. These estates were given away, sold at a ridiculous figure or even annexed to private estates by direct seizure. All this happened without the slightest observation of legal etiquette. The Crown Lands thus fraudulently appropriated, together with the Church estates, so far as these had not been lost again during the republican revolution, form the basis of the today princely domains of the English oligarchy. The bourgeois capitalists favoured the operation with the view, among others, to promoting free trade in land, to extending the domain of modern agriculture on the large farm system, and to increasing their supply of agricultural proletarians ready to hand. Besides, the new landed aristocracy was the natural ally of the new bankocracy, of the new-hatched *haute finance* and of the large manufacturer, then depending on protective duties."

The 'Revolution' of 1688, placed in the hands of the Whigs for the next century, apart from short intervals, the control of the central State apparatus. For the exercise of this control they quickly evolved the necessary financial machinery and the appropriate political methods. Yet their victory was not complete. They were forced to leave in the possession of the Tory squirearchy the control of local government in the country districts, thus creating a kind of dualism round which much of the political conflict of the Eighteenth Century turned.

William himself was prepared to accept any conditions providing that he could secure the wealth and man power of England for use against France, with which Holland was then entering a period of prolonged wars. But before these resources were available he had to secure his hold, not only upon England but upon Scotland and Ireland. In 1689 James landed in Ireland, where he had an army ready to hand, and was easily able to stir up a national rising of the native Catholics against the Protestant 'garrison'.

In July 1690 William defeated the Jacobite Army at the Battle of the Boyne, and in October 1691 the last Irish general, Sarsfield, surrendered at Limerick after a brilliant but hopeless struggle. As a condition of surrender William promised religious toleration for the Irish Catholics, a promise that was immediately broken by the passing of severe Penal Laws which deprived them of all civil and religious rights. The new conquest of Ireland was followed by fresh confiscations of land, the greatest beneficiary being William's Dutch favourite Lord Bentinck, and henceforward the country was ruled more brutally and openly than ever before as a colony which existed for the exclusive benefit of the English bourgeoisie.

In Scotland the new regime was accepted with much opposition, a rising in the Highlands fading out after an initial success at Killiecrankie. The Covenanting lowlands were only too ready to welcome the expulsion of James, and by 1692 William's sovereignty was undisputed throughout the British Isles. In the coming period the centre of interest shifts from internal politics to the struggle with France and the economic changes leading to the Industrial Revolution.

CHAPTER X

WHIG ENGLAND

I. WAR FINANCE

THE WARS WITH France, to which England was
now committed almost as a part of the Whig settlement
and the connection with Holland, were fought under
conditions created by two factors, the rising power of
France and the rapid decomposition of the Spanish Empire.
After almost dominating Europe in the Sixteenth Century
Spain had been sinking during the Seventeenth into a
position in which she could no longer defend her vast
possessions, strung out half across Europe and occupying
more than half America. In Europe these possessions
included a great part of Italy and an area corresponding
roughly with the modern Belgium. Both France and
Austria were beginning to look on Italy as lawful prey while
the seizure of the Spanish Netherlands, lying between
France and Holland, was a necessary preliminary to any
attack on the latter country. Holland itself, which was
just passing the peak point of its commercial greatness,
would hardly have been able to defend its frontiers without
the accession of strength obtained by William's accession
to the English Crown.

The decline of Spain had in fact created a kind of
vacuum in Europe, and France, which had now become
a highly centralised bureaucratic and military State, seemed
destined to fill this vacuum and to seize and exploit the
domains that Spain was now incapable of exploiting for
herself.

Apart from the connection with Holland, the English
ruling class had a considerable direct interest in this
conflict. First because the conquest by France would

upset the balance of power in Europe. Second because a French victory would reverse the whole work of the Revolution of 1688, would destroy the power of the Whigs, and, in all probability, involve the restoration of the Stuarts and the substitution of a military despotism for the rule of "a commercially minded aristocracy and an aristocratic mercantile class".

In the third place, the Spanish colonies in America were fast becoming one of the choicest fields for English traders. Spain was too weak to enforce the regulations prohibiting foreigners from trading with these colonies but it was most unlikely that this happy state of affairs would continue if they fell into French hands. Consequently, the two great wars of this period, the War of the League of Augsburg (1689–1697) and the War of the Spanish Succession (1701–1713) were also trading and colonial wars, though not to the same extent as the wars of the middle and end of the Eighteenth Century. As yet, the establishment of colonies was left to the private enterprise of the Chartered Companies and the State only intervened to protect them from foreign attacks when necessary and to ensure that the full benefit derived from them came to the English merchant class. The period in which wars were waged with the deliberate intention of building a colonial empire still lay some fifty years ahead.

The technical character of war had been revolutionised since the time of Cromwell, chiefly by the invention of the bayonet and the improvement of the musket. The bayonet had the effect of almost exactly doubling the efficiency of the infantry, since each soldier now did the work of a pikeman as well as a musketeer. The pike disappeared from the battlefield, and with the introduction of the ring bayonet which made it possible to fire without unfixing, the cavalry once more lost their supremacy and battles were now decided mainly by the fire power and steadiness of the foot regiments.

At the same time artillery was greatly improved and fortifications and siege operations played a more important part in war. Armies now tended to be slow moving, to cling closely to carefully prepared lines and to require more elaborate equipment and vast baggage trains. The secret of Marlborough's success as a general lay in his ability to break through the paralysis that seemed to have overtaken strategy. While the Dutch were masters of slow-motion warfare, defending their positions stubbornly but unwilling to move a foot outside them, Marlborough could take half Europe for his field of manœuvre and draw his reluctant allies into combinations and movements which alone they would never have dared to dream about.

Yet the most important fact about the changed mode of warfare was that it was so costly that no nation which was not rich and industrially well developed could wage a long war with good hope of success. Here lay the advantage of the combination of England and Holland and the disadvantage of France whose financial organisation was weak and whose industry had been wilfully undermined by the expulsion of the Huguenots. Further, the wars were immensely profitable to the English financiers and contractors, and by adding to their wealth, consolidated the triumph of Whiggery.

The Bank of England and the National Debt were thus both the necessary financial means for carrying on the wars of the Eighteenth Century and the natural harvest reaped by the City for its labours in bringing about the Revolution.

From the later Sixteenth Century the London goldsmiths had performed some of the functions of bankers. They accepted deposits, made and arranged loans and issued notes on the backing of their assets. Under the Stuarts they made frequent loans to the Crown on the security of forthcoming taxes. These loans, however, were short term loans, repaid at the first possible date. We have seen already how Charles II, by the repudiation of 1672, ruined the credit of his Government.

After 1688 Government credit remained poor. The new regime was by no means secure, its fall would almost certainly be followed by a repudiation of its debts, and consequently, it could only borrow at very high rates of interest. In 1694, to raise a loan of £1,200,000, special concessions were offered to the lenders, who were allowed to incorporate themselves as the Bank of England with a monopoly of the power to issue notes. "The Bank of England began with lending its money to the Government at 8 per cent; at the same time it was empowered by Parliament to raise money out of the same capital, by lending it to the public in the form of bank-notes. It was allowed to use these notes for discounting bills, making advances on commodities, and for buying precious metals. It was not long before this credit-money, made by the bank itself, became the coin in which the Bank of England made its loans to the State, and paid on account of the State the interest on the public debt. It was not enough that the bank gave with one hand and took back more with the other; it remained, even whilst receiving, the eternal creditor of the nation down to the last shilling advanced. Gradually it became inevitably the receptacle of the metallic board of the country, and the centre of gravity of all commercial credit." (Marx, *Capital*, I, 780).

Recognised from the start as the instrument of the dominant Whig financial clique, the Bank of England met with considerable opposition. The goldsmiths finding their business threatened, selected a date in 1697, when recoinage operations had produced a temporary shortage of currency, to present for payment a quantity of bank-notes, carefully collected, far exceeding the reserves of the bank. A year earlier the Tory squires had attempted to launch a rival Land Bank. The resources of the State mobilised behind the Bank of England enabled it to defeat all these attacks, to become increasingly powerful and more and more closely connected with the Government.

Politically its effect was not unlike that of the confiscation of the Church lands during the Reformation, in that it created a great vested interest whose safety and profit lay in supporting the existing regime. The steady backing which the City gave to William and afterwards to the Hanoverians was due not so much to the preference for one dynasty over another as to fears of repudiation which would follow the restoration of the Stuarts. Economically the growth of banking meant a vast extension of credit, the possibility of employing masses of capital easily and quickly where its employment was most profitable, and the growth, alongside of ordinary trade, of a system of speculation both in stocks and commodities. The import of saltpetre, for example, important in time of war as an essential ingredient of gunpowder, was made the foundation of large fortunes at this period.

The growth of banking and speculation was paralleled by the growth of the National Debt, which began so modestly with the loan of £1,200,000 already mentioned. The War of the League of Augsburg cost the then unprecedented sum of £18,000,000 (compare the total war expenditure of £5,000,000 for the whole reign of Elizabeth). The War of the Spanish Succession cost £50,000,000 of which nearly half was added to the National Debt. By 1717 this stood at £54,000,000 and in 1739, after twenty years of peace and ceaseless efforts to liquidate it by means of a Sinking Fund, it was still £47,000,000. The Seven Years' War (1756-1762) cost £82,000,000 of which £60,000,000 was raised by loans. On the eve of the American War the National Debt stood at £126,000,000 and at its ending in 1782 had risen to £230,000,000. The wars against Napoleon brought it from £237,000,000 to £859,000,000.

These figures speak for themselves, but it is necessary to remember that they involved a rapidly increasing taxation, transferring wealth continuously from the masses to the minority who profited by these wars. And, even more important, they formed an immense concentration of capital, one of the many streams flowing from various sources to constitute to vast pool which made the Industrial Revolution possible. The holders of the bonds issued by the Government for these loans were the possessors of capital

resources on the strength of which they could, while still
enjoying the income from them, obtain credit to undertake
new enterprises. The growth of the National Debt, therefore, meant the growth of fluid capital.

Some of it was used rashly, as in the South Sea Company
of 1720 or its less unsavoury Scottish precurser the Darien
Scheme. The crisis of 1720, which was closely paralleled
by a similar crisis in France arising from the failure of
Law's Mississippi Scheme, was the result of wild speculation
typical of a period when merchant capital was still predominant. Under these circumstances crises were not
usually due so much to over-production as to over speculation.

The South Sea Company began as a quite legitimate
venture in slave trading and whale fishery, but its directors
held out the wildest expectations and even promised to
take over the whole National debt. Shares rose from £120
to £1,020, the whole affair becoming more fraudulent as
the fever of speculation rose. All sorts of bogus subsidiary
companies were formed and leading members of the Whig
Government as well as the Prince of Wales were criminally
involved. When the crash came thousands of investors
were ruined and popular fury reached such a pitch that
it was solemnly proposed in the House of Lords that the
directors should be sewn up in sacks and thrown into the
river Thames, a revival of the old Roman punishment for
parricides.

Similar financial crises on a smaller scale took place in
1763, 1772 and 1793 but in all cases it was the weaker
concerns that were involved. The Bank of England and
the great commercial houses stood firm and even profited,
and these crises were, in fact, only the inevitable accompani-
ment of the rapid increase in trade that marked the whole
century.

The first of the great European wars of this period, the
War of the League of Augsburg, was indecisive, notable
only for the successful defence of the Spanish Netherlands
by the Dutch and the penetration of the Mediterranean

by the British Navy which now secured a permanent superiority over that of the French. It proved, too, the efficiency of the financial apparatus which William's Chancellor, Montague, had built up. It ended in 1697 with the Treaty of Ryswick, a treaty that left all the major issues in dispute undecided.

Soon after, the King of Spain died without direct heir, and a grandson of Louis XIV succeeded him. Holland and England which were unwilling to allow France to control the Spanish Empire, and Austria which had a rival candidate in the field, at once declared war. French armies overran the Spanish Netherlands and Italy and a French alliance with Bavaria threatened Vienna.

On the death of William in 1702 Marlborough took his place at the head of the Anglo-Dutch armies. For two years his Dutch colleagues kept him on the defensive. Then, in 1704, when a French army was actually on the Danube, Marlborough made his famous march up the Rhine and across country into Bavaria. The French, taken by surprise, were checked in their advance on Vienna and the conquest of Bavaria was followed by their defeat at Blenheim, a battle that proved the turning point of the war. From this time it was mainly a question of how long both sides were prepared to hang on till they could agree on terms. Marlborough cleared the Spanish Netherlands in a series of campaigns lasting till 1708. The Austrians occupied Italy. In Spain a small British army, skilfully exploiting the national grievances of the Catalans, met with some success and captures, but was unable to hold, Madrid.

By 1710 both sides had fought themselves almost to a standstill. The Whigs were not anxious to make peace because a continuation of the war seemed the most likely means to keep themselves in power but in the end the Tory squires for whom war meant only a higher land tax were able to use the general war weariness to oust their opponents. The Whigs were weakened by internal feuds and their fall is interesting as an example of the part court intrigues were still able to play in English politics. At this time a general election usually followed rather than preceded a change of government. Once in office the Tories had no difficulty in using their official command of patronage and corruption to obtain a parliamentary majority.

At the end of 1711 Marlborough was dismissed and the next year the war was ended by the Treaty of Utrecht. The French candidate remained King of Spain, from which country it had proved quite impossible to dislodge him, but Austria took Italy and the Netherlands, thus preserving the balance of power and giving the Dutch a secure southern frontier. The Catalans, to whom the most extravagant promises had been made, were left to the vengeance of the Spanish Government.

Britain kept Gibraltar and Minorca, keys to the naval domination of the Mediterranean. In America, Nova Scotia and the Hudson Bay Territory, which had been occupied by the French early in the century, were acquired. The danger to trade that was anticipated from a firmer government of Spanish America was removed by a clause in the treaty which gave Britain the monopoly of supplying the Spanish colonies with slaves, and a virtual though not formally admitted freedom of trade in other goods. The importance of this slave trade can be judged from the estimate that between 1680 and 1786 an average number of 20,000 slaves were shipped from Africa each year.

The Treaty of Utrecht stands at the beginning of a long period of peace. In the thirty years that followed it British exports increased by at least 50 per cent. The American and West Indian plantations grew in wealth and population, producing sugar, timber, tobacco and rice in ever increasing quantities. The plunder of India poured in and the Nabob, the possessor of a great fortune made by trade and graft in the Far East, began to be a familiar figure. Holland declined in wealth and power and in France the recovery from the ravages of war was slow and retarded by the stranglehold of the bureaucracy. England now definitely took the lead in European commerce and the conditions necessary for the establishment of an empire were created. The Treaty of Utrecht was the work of the Tories but it was the last thing they did for half a century, and ironically enough, it ushered in the heyday of the Whigs.

2. PARTY POLITICS

The victory of the Tories in 1710 had been in part the result of their opposition to a war that had become unpopular, but also of the uncertainty about the future existing in political circles. In 1701 the Act of Settlement had fixed the succession to the throne in the house of Hanover if Anne, who was to follow William, should die without leaving children. Anne's reign thus formed a sort of interregnum. The Tories were prepared, in the main, to accept her as a genuine Stuart and to prepare quietly for future eventualities. Almost all the leading politicians on both sides reinsured themselves by carrying on secret negotiations with the Stuarts while openly accepting the Act of Settlement. Among these political hedgers were Marlborough and Godolphin, the general and the financier of the war party, who occupied a position midway between the Whigs and Tories. The existence of this intermediate group and the reluctance of politicians to commit themselves irrevocably created a curious situation in which there was an instantaneous and disproportionate stampede towards which every side appeared to have an advantage.

Thus the question of the succession became important not so much because of the persons involved as because the fortunes of the political parties—and in all probability the heads of the politicians—depended upon it. Bolingbroke, the Tory leader, a charlatan with a wealth of inflated platitudes which he managed to pass as a political philosophy, began, when he saw that the succession of the Hanoverians would destroy his party, to prepare for a *coup d'état*. First the moderate Tories were ousted from the control of the party and replaced by Jacobites. Then he began to make similar changes among the Army and Navy officers, the magistrates and Government officials.

Before the purge was well begun Anne died suddenly (August 1st, 1714) and the whole scheme collapsed. Even if circumstances had been more favourable, it is doubtful if Bolingbroke ever possessed either the realism or the resolution to be the leader of a successful counter-revolution.

From 1714 to 1761 the Whigs held office without interruption or serious challenge, and the Tory Party that triumphed at the end of that time was very different in policy and social composition from the Tory Party of the reign of Anne. In the intervening period the Tory squires retired to their estates—to grumble, but also to share the prosperity that the Eighteenth Century brought to all landowners. A few appeared in Parliament as representatives of the counties but they never became an effective opposition. Round their necks hung a half-hearted Jacobitism, a creed for which they were unwilling to fight or make sacrifices but which prevented them from being possible administrators of the Hanoverian regime. Jacobitism was politically dead in England after 1715 but it long remained as the skeleton in the Tory cupboard.

In Scotland it had greater practical importance, especially in the Highlands where it had deep social roots in the struggle of the clans to preserve their tribal organisation and culture against the bourgeois and partly English culture of the Lowlands. It was also kept alive by the feud between the dominating Campbell clan and the clans which resented its supremacy. Since the Campbells had long been Covenanting and Whig their opponents naturally adopted Jacobitism. The rest of Scotland was not Jacobite in the real sense but a long-standing hatred of England and things English weighed against covenanting memories of Stuart persecution to produce a rough neutrality.

Nothing illustrates the anti-English feeling in Scotland better than the events leading up to the Act of Union, secured by the Whigs in 1707 as a piece of military and party strategy. In 1703 the Scottish Parliament passed an Act of Security, aimed against the Hanoverian succession.

KE

The Whigs were thus faced, in time of war, with the possibility of a complete break with Scotland and of a regime that might be actively hostile. The English Parliament countered in 1704 with an Aliens Act banning all imports from Scotland till the Hanoverian settlement had been accepted. This robbed the Scottish cattle breeders of their chief market. Troops were moved north to the border and war seemed possible. The corruption of the Scottish lords and Parliament proved more effective and the Act of Union was passed amid rioting and the drilling of irregulars. Scotland gained the right to trade with English colonies: on the other hand her undeveloped industries suffered from English competition. Politically, as has been said, Scotland became "one vast rotten borough" controlled by the Duke of Argyle, the head of the Campbells.

The Jacobite rising at the accession of George I in 1715 was doomed from the start by half-hearted leadership. In the years that followed military roads were built across the Highlands and throughout a long period of peace revolt was impossible. But in 1745, when England and France were again at war, the 'Young Pretender', grandson of James II, was landed in Scotland to create a diversion. The '45 although far more spectacular, had really less solid support than the '15 and an even slighter hope of success. An army of 5,000 Highlanders marched as far south as Derby without serious opposition, created a panic in London and retired as swiftly as they had come. Pursued by a strong force of regulars they were caught and defeated at Culloden near Inverness.

The defeat of the Highlanders was followed by the total destruction of the clan system. Chiefs who had taken part in the rising were replaced by others and all alike were transformed into landowners. The tribal courts of justice, tribal costume and even bagpipes (classed as "an instrument of war") were suppressed. Secured in the possession of the tribal lands, the chiefs-turned-lairds began the systematic eviction of the crofters. In the Eighteenth

Century vast tracts were turned into sheep farms; 40,000 Highlanders emigrated to America; more went to Glasgow and the new industrial towns. In the middle of the Nineteenth Century a final degradation began when the sheep with the shepherds who had remained to look after them gave way to deer which required no labourers at all. When the great influx of Australian wool after about 1870 sent prices down, deer forests actually became more profitable than sheep and the rate of change was greatly increased. In the Highlands, as in Ireland, the extreme suffering of the masses was largely due to the passing of society at a leap from the tribal to the bourgeois stage, concentrating in a few generations what elsewhere was spread over many centuries with feudalism as an intermediate stage.

In England the whole quality of Whiggery was summed up in the commanding person of Robert Walpole. Enterprising Norfolk landowner, financial genius with an understanding of the needs of commerce as keen as any City merchant's, colleague and leader of the great Whig peers, shrewd, predatory and wholly unidealistic, he symbolised the interests and character of the unique alliance which governed England.

The policy of the Whigs was simple enough. First to avoid foreign wars as being harmful to trade. Then to remove taxes, so far as was possible, from the merchants and manufacturers and place them upon goods consumed by the masses and upon the land. But, as the leading Whigs were themselves landowners and it was considered dangerous to rouse the active hostility of the squirearchy, the land tax was kept fairly low and agriculture stimulated by protection and bounties. By avoiding war Walpole was, indeed, able to reduce the land tax considerably. All the politically active classes were thus satisfied and the masses, in this period between the age of spontaneous armed rising and that of organised political agitation, had no effective means of expressing any discontents that may have existed.

It was in the age of Walpole that the Cabinet system began to take shape. Up to this time Parliament had contented itself with passing laws, voting, or, on occasion, refusing to vote supplies and had left the detailed direction of affairs, the executive power, to the Crown. Now the ruling section of the bourgeoisie took over from the Crown the actual control of administration through the Cabinet, which is, in actual fact, no more than a committee formed by the leaders of the party representing this ruling section at any given time. Nominally controlled by Parliament, it really controls Parliament so long as the party has a majority there.

Today a Cabinet must hold a working majority in the House of Commons, must be united by a collective responsibility, that is, all its members must have, in public, a common policy and it must have at its head a Prime Minister who has a controlling voice in its decisions.

In the age of Walpole none of these conditions existed fully. It was still not certain whether the Cabinet was responsible to Parliament or to the Crown (today in theory the Government is still 'His Majesty's'). A Cabinet was still sometimes composed of openly hostile individuals fighting out their differences in public. And Walpole never took the name of Prime Minister, which was then regarded as something foreign to the English constitution, though he exercised most of the powers of a Prime Minister. Nevertheless we can say that it was at this time that the decisive steps were taken towards that direct rule of England by the bourgeoisie for which the Cabinet has proved so suitable an instrument. The change was made easier because both George I and II were petty, rather stupid German princes, more interested in Hanover than in England, ignorant of English affairs and of the English language and quite ready to let Walpole and the Whigs govern for them so long as they received their due amount of pickings and flattery.

The question of a parliamentary majority rarely arose, because such a majority could usually be obtained by the

Government in office. The open rule of the bourgeoisie found its exact and natural expression in a systematic corruption openly practised and freely avowed. Some modern historians object to the word corruption in this connection because votes in Parliament were not (often) actually bought for cash down. Instead they were secured by sinecures, jobs, contracts, titles, favours to the family or to friends of members. The vast government patronage was freely used for party purposes.

In the constituencies things were no better. The total number of voters in the middle of the Eighteenth Century has been estimated at 245,000: 160,000 in the counties and 85,000 in the boroughs. But a Tory historian, J. B. Namier, declares that, "taking England as a whole, probably not more than one in every twenty voters at county elections could freely exercise his statutory rights". The counties, the largest and freest of the constituencies, "constitute the purest type of class representation", returning almost always landowners and usually members of a few county families.

In the boroughs things were even worse. Out of 204 boroughs returning members to Parliament only twenty-two had over 1,000 voters. Another thirty-three had from about 500 to nearly 1,000 and of these many were thoroughly and notoriously corrupt. The rest were mainly places where the franchise rested in the hands of the Corporation or of a privileged minority of the inhabitants or property owners (rotten boroughs) or places so small as to be completely controlled by some local magnate (pocket boroughs). As far as possible elections were avoided because of their expense, and often a general election would see only three or four contests in the counties. The fact that each constituency returned two members facilitated bargaining between the various interests concerned. If an actual poll took place votes were freely bought or obtained by fraud or intimidation.

On such a basis party politics became less and less a matter of policies and more one of simple personal acquisitiveness. It came to be normal and respectable for a gentleman "to get his bread by voting in the House of Commons" and the main concern of such ministers as the Duke of Newcastle was "to find pasture enough for the beasts that they must feed".

For nearly fifty years the Whigs fed and grew fat, and, in absence of any real opposition party, split into warring factions, constantly combining and recombining under this or that distributor of largesse. It was as a result of one of these internal feuds that Walpole fell from office in 1742. The groups that combined to oust him were certainly corrupt place-hunters, but they represented the aggressive, war-seeking section of the bourgeoisie, just as Walpole represented its more conservative and peaceful section. The latter saw that their wealth had grown amazingly in twenty-five years of peace. The former saw their strength and the possibilities of an even vaster accession of wealth through a policy of open colonial war.

They focused popular attention on the frequent disputes arising from the trade with the Spanish colonies, and by a combination of appeals to greed and adroit atrocity mongering created a demand for war to which Walpole unwillingly gave way in 1739. The 'War of Jenkin's Ear', soon to be swallowed up in the general European conflict of the Austrian Succession, ended the Walpole age and began the age of Pitt, though it was not till a decade later that Pitt reached the height of his power. Like Walpole Pitt was an eminently symbolic figure. The grandson of a great Nabob, a bitter, arrogant, thrusting imperialist,[1] he cut through the respectable rottenness of the Whigs to complete the disintegration that the long peace had begun.

In the middle of the Eighteenth Century England stood on the verge both of the Industrial Revolution and of another round of great wars. In them party distinctions

---

[1] The word imperialist is used here and throughout the chapter in its popular sense rather than in the technical sense given it by Lenin and in which it is used in the later chapters of this book.

were erased and new lines of demarcation drawn. But for a time it seemed rather as if political parties had vanished in a welter of sects.

3. COLONIAL WAR

Pitt is supposed to have stated his intention of conquering Canada on the banks of the Elbe: he might more justly have spoken of conquering it in the Bank in Threadneedle Street. Behind the naval superiority of which so much has been heard, behind the exploits of Wolfe and the victories of Frederick the Great, was the power of British finance, able to supply the best arms and equipment then available and able to buy European allies and to maintain them in the field with vast subsidies. It was British banking which enabled Prussia, an industrially and commercially undeveloped country, to win resounding victories and establish itself as a great European power.

The ground plan of British grand strategy was this: first, a European ally had to be bought, Austria in the War of the Austrian Succession (1740-1748), Prussia in the Seven Years' War (1756-1763), as a counterweight to the main European enemy, France. By means of this ally and of small expeditionary forces sent to the Continent, the main attention of France was distracted so that, behind the screen of the navy, Britain was able to concentrate on the more profitable war upon the French colonial possessions.

Although the War of the Austrian Succession and the Seven Years' War were nominally divided by a period of eight years of peace they form in fact one whole, since the war in the colonies went on without interruption. The details of the progress of these wars in Europe, the seizure of Silesia by Prussia and the extraordinary campaigns in which Frederick defeated vastly superior French, Austrian and Russian armies are important rather for European than for English history. Attention can therefore be concentrated on the colonial struggle.

French and British possessions lay alongside each other in three main areas of European expansion outside South America which remained a Spanish monopoly. These were India, North America and the West Indies. In the last area there was little fighting of importance. The islands held by the rivals were interspersed but it was difficult to carry war from one island to another and the British naval superiority made it possible to seize many of the isolated French possessions without resistance. The main seats of war were therefore India and North America.

The East India Company had grown steadily throughout the century and by 1740 had a capital of £3,000,000 on which a dividend of 7 per cent. was paid to the shareholders. But this represented only a small part of the profits taken from India. It was the practice of the Company to pay its servants only a nominal wage: their real, and in the higher grades vast, incomes were derived from bribes, extortion and private trade. The Company kept a monopoly of the trade between India and Britain but left the internal Indian trade entirely to its servants. Clive once stated that the temptations held out to adventurers in that part of the globe were such as flesh and blood could not withstand. Even the Directors of the Company were forced to condemn a system which they themselves had created and which finally threatened the profits of the shareholders. They complained of the "deplorable state to which our affairs are on the point of being reduced, from the corruption and rapacity of our servants, and the universal depravity of manners throughout the settlement. . . . We must add that we think the vast fortunes, acquired in the inland trade, had been obtained by a series of the most tyrannic and oppressive conduct that was ever known in any country."

The French, arriving in India only at the beginning of the Eighteenth Century when the Company was already powerfully established, were forced from the start to secure their position by armed force. A naval base was established at Mauritius and a small army of native troops, armed and

The CONQUEST of INDIA

British gains under Clive

Areas brought under British influence during same period

AFGHANS

Indus

MOGUL
Delhi

EMPIRE

OUDH
Ganges

MAHRATTAS

BENGAL
Chandernagore (FR.)
Calcutta

Bombay

NIZAM
Hyderabad

Masulipatam

ORIGINAL FRENCH SPHERE

Goa
(PORTUGUESE)

MYSORE

Madras

Mahé
(FR.)

CARNATIC

Pondicherry (FR.)

CEYLON (Dutch)

J.F.H.

trained in the European manner, was raised. The English Company soon followed by creating its own private army. Since the main French depot, Pondicherry, was close to Madras and a second, Chandernagore, close to Calcutta, a clash was almost inevitable.

India in the Eighteenth Century was in a state of exceptional weakness and confusion. The Mogul Empire was breaking up and its local officials were establishing themselves as independent rulers. The general situation was not unlike that of Europe at the beginning of the Middle Ages. The immense superiority of the weapons possessed by the private armies of the French and English made it possible for them to intervene in the local wars of native rulers with decisive effect. Both began to play at king making, setting up puppet princes whom they could control.

This policy first led to open war around Madras, which the French captured in 1746 but gave up at the treaty which ended the War of the Austrian Succession in 1748. In the next year English and French intervened on opposite sides in a war in the Carnatic, of which province the English became the virtual rulers after the victory of Clive at Arcot and of Coote at Wandiwash. In 1760 Pondicherry was captured.

The battle of Plassey, in 1756, was followed by the conquest of the rich province of Bengal. Plassey was preceded by the incident that gave rise to the most famous of all atrocity stories, that of the 'Black Hole of Calcutta'. The facts are that the 'Black Hole' was merely the ordinary prison of the East India company and that a number of English, imprisoned because of a dispute between the Nawab of Bengal and the Company, died there owing to the place being overcrowded in the hot season. It was a case of callousness paralleled by the English prison train in which eighty Moplah prisoners were suffocated in 1921.

Hostilities ended in 1763 with the Treaty of Paris, which left the East India Company rulers of a great part of the country and confined the French to a few trading stations which they were forbidden to fortify. From this time there was no limit to the possibilities of exploitation. From Bengal alone the Company and its servants extorted over £6,000,000 in bribes between 1757 and 1766. In Madras and the Carnatic things were much the same. Trading monopolies in important commodities like salt, opium and tobacco yielded immense fortunes. In 1769 and 1770 the English created a famine over wide areas by cornering rice and refusing to sell it except at exorbitant prices. Clive himself amassed one of the largest fortunes known up to that time by taking bribes and 'presents' from native rulers.

In 1767 the British Government insisted on taking a direct share of the plunder, and the Company was forced to pay £400,000 a year into the Exchequer. The Regulating Act of 1773 took the further step of securing to the Government a partial control over the administration of the conquered provinces. Ostensibly aimed at checking the oppression of the Company's rule the real effect of the Act was to systematise the exploitation of India, which was now too profitable to be allowed to continue in private hands. It marks the beginning of the transition from the first stage of British penetration, in which India was a source of certain valuable commodities which could not be produced at home, to the second stage in which it became an important market for British manufactured goods, especially cotton textiles.[1]

In America as in India the French had considerable success at the opening of the war. Here the British colonies lay in a long line from Maine to Florida, facing the Atlantic with the Appalachian Mountains standing as a barrier between them and the interior. The French had two main settlements, Canada in the North along the St. Lawrence and Louisiana around the mouth of the Mississippi. From these they pushed up the Ohio River and down through the Great Lakes, attempting by a pincer movement to occupy the land behind the English colonies and prevent any further westward expansion. In this movement the

[1] See page 447 below.

key point was Fort Duquesne, laying at the western end
of the only easy way through the mountains.

Fighting began in earnest with an attack on Fort
Duquesne in 1755, defeated with heavy losses. At this time
the French, though Canada had only about 150,000
inhabitants against two million in the English colonies,
held a considerable advantage because of their centralised,
military organisation. The English colonies were many of
them far removed from the scene of war and were unac-
customed to act together. Later the British naval blockade
prevented reinforcements from reaching Canada while
carrying there a large invading army.

From 1758 to 1760 Wolfe overran Canada in a series of
campaigns culminating in the capture of Quebec. Fort
Duquesne was taken in 1759 and renamed Pittsburg.
Today it is a great railway junction and a centre of
American heavy industry. The conquest of Canada involved also the conquest of the huge unsettled area between
the Appalachians and the Mississippi. During the same years
Senegal in West Africa, Florida and a number of West
Indian islands were seized. At the time, these islands with
their valuable sugar and plantations were regarded as
being more important than Canada. When the prelim-
inaries of the Treaty of Paris were under discussion there
was a serious debate as to whether Canada or Guadeloupe
should be retained. The Duke of Bedford expressed a
widely held opinion when he remarked, "I do not know
whether the neighbourhood of the French to our Northern
Colonies was not the greatest security of their dependence
in the Mother Country who I fear will be slighted by them
when their apprehensions of the French are removed."
That Canada was in the end preferred to Guadeloupe was
due to strategic rather than economic reasons: the danger
from a hostile foreign power in North America was rated
higher than that from any possible rebelliousness on the
part of the Colonists.

When in 1763 the Treaty of Paris ended the Seven Years'
War, England kept her Indian conquests, Canada, Senegal

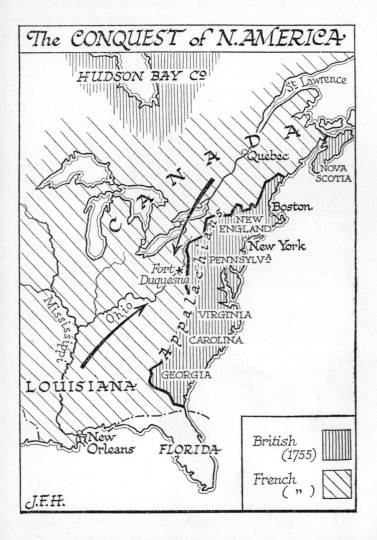

The CONQUEST of N. AMERICA

HUDSON BAY Cᵒ

St Lawrence

CANADA

Quebec

NOVA SCOTIA

Boston

NEW ENGLAND

New York

PENNSYLVᴬ

Fort Duquesne

Appalachians

VIRGINIA

CAROLINA

Mississippi

Ohio

LOUISIANA

GEORGIA

New Orleans

FLORIDA

J.F.H.

British (1755)

French (")

and some but not all of the French West Indian islands. The Empire had now attained its greatest dimensions till the Napoleonic wars brought fresh gains. This treaty was negotiated in strict secrecy and concluded without the knowledge of Frederick of Prussia who was left to make what terms he could on his own, an act of treachery that was to prove very expensive before long.

Meanwhile politics in England had undergone a fresh change. The disintegration of the Whigs and the accession in 1760 of George III who, unlike his predecessors, was more interested in English than in German affairs, gave the Crown one more opportunity to enter politics as an independent force. George did not, as has sometimes been supposed, attempt, like the Stuarts, to free himself from the control of Parliament. The time when that was possible had long passed. Rather he tried to make himself "the first among the borough-mongering, electioneering gentlemen of England".

The King had still considerable powers of choosing his ministers, and once George had selected men sufficiently subservient, notably his Scottish tutor, Lord Bute, he was able to swing on to his side the whole machine of official patronage and corruption. To the great Whig families who had created this machine and monopolised it for half a century, this was shockingly improper and they put up what fight they could. But under Newcastle they had grown soft and demoralised and their followers soon deserted to the side with the longer purse. After a decade of confused groupings in which party distinctions seemed almost to disappear, new parties arose, bearing the old names but standing for different things.

The Tories, free at last from the taint of Jacobitism, were now the 'loyal' party: the Whigs entered into a long period of opposition and weakness. The new Tory Party had gathered to itself, in addition to its old core of country squires, many of the great landowners who had formerly supported the Whigs and a large section of the upper classes of the towns, the bankers and army contractors, all those whose profits flowed from their dependence upon the Government of the day and flowed fast if that Government's policy was one of war. The Whigs kept a handful of the old traditionally Whig families, what became later the Holland House clique, but as time went on they developed more and more into a party of the town middle and lower class and of the industrial capitalists, who, concentrated in the new towns that had not secured borough status, had up to now played no very active part in politics.

Two poles of attraction began to appear: the imperialism of the Court, Government and financiers, drawing to itself all the privileged classes, and a new radicalism, at first aristocratic and slightly cynical but later proletarian and genuinely revolutionary, drawing a mixed following of the dispossessed, the unprivileged, and, in each generation, a host of those who saw in the profession of radicalism a means of entering the ranks of the privileged. The first developments of English radicalism will be best considered in relation to the rebellion of the American Colonies, with which it had the closest connections.

4. THE AMERICAN REVOLUTION

The Seven Years' War ended with vast colonial conquests: it left also a vast National Debt and a burden of taxes so heavy that financiers believed the upward limit of taxation had been reached. As usual the bulk of the new taxation was placed upon articles of general consumption: beer, malt, spirits and an additional 5 per cent. *ad valorem* on all goods paying customs duties. The Government decided, on the pretext that the war had been fought for the benefit of the colonies, and although the American colonies had in fact borne a considerable share in the expenses of the campaigns in Canada, to impose taxes on the colonists intended to cover part of the cost of the Army and Navy still kept in America.

Grenville's Stamp Act of 1765 evoked immediate protests and was repealed in the following year, but a nominal tax was retained and the right of the English Parliament to tax the colonies was specifically insisted upon. The colonists, who had representative bodies of their own, raised the old slogan, "No taxation without representation." It was over this issue that the Revolution was ostensibly made. There were, however, other issues which went far deeper, though they made a less effective platform case and so remained in the background.

The economic organisation of the Empire in the Eighteenth Century, embodied in the Navigation Acts, had as its object the utilisation of the trade and wealth of the colonies for the exclusive benefit of the English ruling class. The most valuable products of the colonies, the tobacco of Virginia, the rice of the Carolinas, the sugar of the West Indies and the tar and timber of New England, priceless material for naval construction, might only be exported to England or Scotland. It must be added, however, that these goods received a preference in the home market. Equally, the colonies were forbidden to import manufactured goods from any foreign country and the development of colonial industry was checked where it might endanger an established home industry. Thus, although the smelting of iron reached some importance in New England early in the Eighteenth Century, the manufacture of iron and steel goods there was prohibited and the raw iron had to be shipped across the Atlantic to England, from which the Americans had to import manufactured iron goods for their own use.

The prohibition of direct trade between the American colonies and Europe was not a very serious matter: far more important was trade with the French and Spanish settlements in America itself. This trade was forbidden by all three countries, all of which subscribed to the mercantilist theories on which the Navigation Laws were based. In practice it was quite impossible for such trade to be stopped and it was carried on on a large scale, smuggling becoming one of the national employments of all the Americas. The Navigation Laws, indeed, were only tolerable because they were not and never had been strictly enforced. But with the Stamp Act and the attempt to tax the colonists went a general tightening up of the Navigation Laws, partly in the interests of home industry and partly for the sake of the additional revenue.

British warships began to hunt down smugglers, and it is probable that taxation was doubly resented because it was intended to maintain armed forces that were no longer needed to protect the colonists from the French but were used only to prevent them from carrying on what they regarded as their lawful occupation. If there had still been any danger from Canada the colonists might have been forced to submit to these innovations, but with the fall of Quebec they no longer felt any need of British protection or any inclination to submit to British dictation. The Home Government could not have chosen a more unsuitable time to make their demands.

A great deal of ingenuity has been wasted by historians on both sides in trying to make out a good legal case. Such a case can easily be made but it is quite futile to pass judgment upon a revolution on legal grounds. The important thing is that the American bourgeoisie were growing up, and like the English bourgeoisie of the Seventeenth Century, were forced by the very fact of their growth to break the barriers standing in their way. Allowing for the complicating addition of a national question, the American Revolution and the English Revolution form an almost exact parallel, both in their objects and in the forces at work. The American Revolution had its upper class leadership and its lower middle class rank and file, its internal class struggle centred mainly around the agrarian question, a struggle not finally decided till the defeat of Andrew Jackson. The war was fought mainly by the small farmers, traders and artisans but its benefits went to the merchants and planters of whom Washington was a typical representative.

Because the American Revolution was also a national war, the support it received in England was of a special character. The defenders of the colonists had to be prepared to be dubbed anti-English and disloyal. The Revolution coincides remarkably with the birth of English Radicalism and helped to create the conditions for the birth of a working class movement. Because the English bourgeoisie, their own Revolution accomplished, had begun to be reactionary, the way was opened for a new class to take the field and for a new revolution to be placed on the order of the day.

One group, indeed, led by Pitt, now Earl of Chatham, opposed the coercion of the Americans as intelligent imperialists on the ground that it must lead to the break-up of the Empire, but a powerful minority openly claimed for them the right to determine their own destiny. John Wilkes began his political life in the 1750's as an imperialist of the Chatham school. At this time he seems to have had no other idea than to play the political game as it was played by all young gentlemen of ability and means. In the early years of the reign of George III, during his famous battles over General Warrants and the freedom of the press, he reached a position far to the left of any then existing political group, and, almost in spite of himself, became the recognised leader of the London masses and the City merchants.

For half a generation "Wilkes and Liberty" was the most popular of slogans; 1768, the year in which he was elected and unseated for the County of Middlesex, was marked by unprecedented demonstrations and strikes. On May 10th soldiers fired into a large crowd, killing six and wounding many more. This 'massacre of St. George's Fields' only raised the agitation to new heights. Weavers, merchant seamen, watermen, tailors, coal heavers and others struck for a mixture of economic and political reasons. Wilkes himself seems to have developed with the development of the mass movement. As Lord Mayor and Sheriff of London he acted as a popular tribune, his actions including the checking of profiteers in flour, a strong resistance to the pressing of Londoners into the armed forces and the improvement of prison conditions. Yet it is typical of his limitations that he always opposed any measure to interfere with the activities of the East India Company. His rich supporters were directly interested in the exploitation of India, while the masses were as yet completely ignorant and indifferent.

Wilkes and his followers took part in the General Election of 1774 as a definite political group with a programme that included shorter parliaments, the exclusion from Parliament of pensioners and placemen, fair and equal representation and the defence of the popular rights in Great Britain, Ireland and America—a programme the same in essentials as that of the Chartists. About twelve seats were won, a remarkable achievement when it is remembered how few constituencies were broad enough to give any reflection of popular feeling.

As early as 1768 Wilkes had been in close contact with the leaders of the revolt in the American colonies, and as the struggle over taxation became more acute he became their principal spokesman inside and outside Parliament. A very large section of the merchants, particularly those who had trading connections with and even partners in America, were at this time strongly opposed to the action of the British Government. After the outbreak of war, when many of his wealthier supporters had deserted him to get Government contracts and many of the politically un-developed workers had been caught up in the inevitable war fever, Wilkes continued and even strengthened his advocacy of what was now an unpopular cause. From 1779, the enthusiasm for the war began to diminish and he once more appeared likely to play an important part in politics.

In 1780, however, his active career was ended by the Gordon 'No Popery' Riots, a curious volcanic eruption of the London slum population, directed against a cause for which Wilkes had always fought and yet to a large extent the product of his earlier agitation. As a city magistrate, Wilkes helped to put down the riot, and in doing so snapped the chain that bound him to the London masses.

His agitation dropped away and had no direct connection with the working-class movement of the next decade[1] or with the 'Left' group of aristocratic Whigs led by Charles James Fox, yet it can only be understood as one of the first heavings of a wave which soon swept over all Europe.

In Ireland the response to the American Revolution was far greater than in England. A force of 80,000 Volunteers was raised in 1778, nominally to protect Ireland from invasion. The overwhelming majority of the Volunteers regarded themselves rather as an army of national liberation, and there is little doubt that at this time, when England's forces were fully occupied elsewhere, Ireland could have secured complete independence. But the aristocratic and middle class leaders of the Volunteers, having used them to obtain free trade and the legislative independence of the corrupt and oligarchic Dublin Parliament, disarmed and betrayed them. Wolfe Tone a few years later bitterly declared that: "The Revolution of 1782 was a Revolution which enabled Irishmen to sell at a much higher price their honour, their integrity, and the interests of their country; it was a Revolution which, while at one stroke it doubled the value of every borough-monger in the kingdom left three-fourths of our countrymen the slaves it found them, and the government of Ireland in the base and wicked, and contemptible hands who had spent their lives in degrading and plundering her. . . . The power remained in the hands of our enemies."

So far as America itself was concerned the Stamp Act was only the beginning of a ten years' dispute which culminated in an American ban on English goods, an attempt to secure their importation by force, the 'Boston Tea Party', the closing of the port of Boston as a reprisal and the outbreak of hostilities at Bunkers Hill in 1774. The first years of the war saw a number of English successes. The colonists suffered from the same defects of discipline and organisation which had handicapped the Puritans of

[1] But Horne Tooke, at one time associated with Wilkes, was later a leader of the Corresponding Society. See page 338 below.

the Seventeenth Century, and these were accentuated by the rivalries and disunity of the separate States. Like the Puritans they had to create the instruments of struggle during the actual conduct of the war. They were helped in this by the brutal methods of the British forces, composed largely of German mercenaries aided by Red Indians. In October 1777 the Americans won their first great victory when General Burgoyne and 5,000 regulars were forced to surrender at Saratoga. This victory brought France, Spain and later Holland into the war against England, which, largely owing to the way in which Prussia had been deserted at the Treaty of Paris,[1] was forced for the first time to fight without a European ally. The Baltic States, on whom the Navy depended more since the revolt in America than ever for its supplies of timber, tar and hemp, formed a pact of armed neutrality directed against England.

For the first time in the century the Navy lost its command of the sea and it was largely the French blockade which led to the surrender of Cornwallis, British commander in America, at Yorktown in 1781. British supremacy in India was seriously threatened and it was only on account of some successes there and the naval victory of Rodney in the West Indies that the war could be brought to an end on reasonably favourable terms in 1783. The independence of America was recognised and Florida and Minorca were surrendered to Spain.

The victory of the American Revolution was a blow to the whole corrupt, borough-mongering, oligarchic system of the Eighteenth Century and was followed by an immediate and powerful reaction against it at home. The first effect of this was to bring the Whigs back to power for a short time, during which they made some efforts to check the political activities of the Crown and even to remove some of the possibilities of parliamentary corruption.

When, in 1783, Chatham's son, William Pitt the younger, became Prime Minister as the leader of the reorganised

[1] See page 302 above.

Tory Party, and strengthened his position in an election won in 1784 by methods that even then were regarded as exceptionally discreditable, he found it convenient to appear as a reformer and an enemy of corruption. Corruption had, however, become too powerful a vested interest for any change to be possible as long as the existing balance of class forces was preserved and within a few years the outbreak of the French Revolution had transformed most of the critics into defenders of the British constitution as a God given and perfect masterpiece.

Any attempt at the slightest alteration of this masterpiece was branded as Jacobinism. This had the effect of reducing the advocates of reform in Parliament to a handful of Whigs sufficiently well connected to be able to ignore such accusations, but it had also the effect of making Parliamentary Reform a matter of passionate interest to the working masses.

5 . WAR AND INDUSTRY

The real history of the period between 1688 and the middle of the Eighteenth Century can be summed up in the three words: accumulation of capital. We have seen in the preceding sections of this chapter some of the ways in which this accumulation was taking place. First, through the growth of the National Debt and consequently of taxation, concentrating great masses of capital in the hands of the small class able to provide the State with finances for war. Second, in the rapid increase of trade, based primarily on the monopoly control of a colonial empire. And, third, in the direct plunder of India. In the next chapter another source of accumulation will be described, the final destruction of the class of yeomen and the establishment of agriculture on a fully capitalist basis.

On the surface the period seems devoid of startling changes. Society was relatively stable, there were no marked alterations in the relations between the various classes, no revolutions and few signs of open discontent among the mass of the people. It was an age of the un-questioned acceptance of recognised authority, of the domination of squire and parson in the countryside, an age in which elegance was more prized than imagination and in which the word enthusiasm carrying the implica-tion of fanaticism, was always used in a disparaging sense. Only, beneath the surface, the streams of gold poured into the City, their level growing higher year by year, till the time when the flood burst out, transformed by some magic into mills and mines and foundries, and covered the face of half England, burying the old life and ways for ever. To this flood men have given the name of the Industrial Revolution, which forms the subject of the next chapter.

In actual fact, of course, it did not happen in quite the sudden and dramatic way in which this description might suggest. What I have tried to convey is that here was a particularly striking example of the transition from a quantitive change—wars becoming *more* costly, the ex-ploitation of the colonies *more* profitable, the capitalists becoming *more* rich—to a qualitative change—a change *from* a country predominantly agricultural *to* a country predominantly industrial, *from* an economy dominated by merchant capital *to* one dominated by industrial capital, *from* a country with class conflicts relatively masked and suppressed *to* one divided into classes violently and inevitably antagonistic.

With each accumulation of capital went increased possi-bilities for its profitable utilisation. The wars of the Eighteenth Century were almost all followed by the acquisi-tion of new colonies: the colonies already established were growing rapidly in wealth and population. The American colonies had about 200,000 inhabitants in 1700 and between one and two million fifty years later. Between 1734 and 1773 the white population of the British West Indies rose from 36,000 to 58,000 and the slave population at least in proportion. The West Indies were, indeed, the most profitable of British possessions. In 1790 it was calculated that £70,000,000 was invested there against

£18,000,000 in the Far East and that their trade with England was almost double the imports and exports of the East India Company. The richest West Indian planters, unlike the inhabitants of the American colonies, formed an integral part of the English bourgeoisie, which was why the American Revolution had no counterpart among them.

Such a continuous increase of colonial wealth and trade provided a constantly rising market for British goods, a market for which the small scale, hand production methods of the home industry was hardly adequate. And the wars of the Eighteenth Century, large scale and long continued wars waged by professional armies, created not only a steady demand for British goods, but for goods of a special kind for standardised goods.

Armies now wore regular uniforms and needed thousands of yards of cloth of a specified colour and quality, needed boots and buttons, needed muskets all capable of firing bullets of a definite calibre and bayonets all made to fix exactly on to these muskets. Not only the British armies had to be fed, clothed and equipped, but many of the armies of Britain's allies, who depended equally upon her subsidies and her industry to keep them in the field.

It was this demand for ever-increasing quantities of standard goods, and not the genius of this or that inventor, which was the basic cause of the Industrial Revolution. In theory the technical inventions of Watt, Arkwright or Roebuck might have been made at any time. In fact, they were made towards the end of the Eighteenth Century just because the conditions of the time were forcing men to use their wits on the problem of the mass production of commodities and because the accumulation of capital had reached a point at which full use could be made of mass production methods.

The wars of this age gave golden opportunities to all those who had the capital or the credit to take up army contracts, and the floating of loans and the remittance of subsidies to Allied Powers was equally profitable. Like

most other things in the Eighteenth Century these contracts were freely jobbed and bankers and army contractors
formed a permanent and not too reputable section of all
Eighteenth Century Parliaments. There was a continuous
interpenetration of the landed aristocracy and the banking
and merchant classes. In every generation scores of City
magnates acquired titles and bought landed estates,
especially in the Home Counties. Often their descendants
could hardly be distinguished from the families who had
done their jobbing in the Seventeenth or even Sixteenth
Centuries. Apart from the growing return to be obtained
from capital invested in land, its possession gave a social
status which could be obtained in no other way. At the
same time the landowners began to invest their profits in
industry and commerce, while the younger sons of great
families still often went into trade.

Such were the general conditions which led in England
to the Industrial Revolution. In France the same series
of events, under different circumstances, had quite different
results. From the War of the Spanish Succession onward,
France had been on the losing side. Even her victory in
the American War brought no tangible benefit to offset
its cost. One by one France was stripped of her colonies.
Yet it was only as the centre of a great colonial Empire
that the complicated and expensive bureaucratic and
military organisations of the French State could justify
themselves. Without colonies the State became top-heavy
and was perpetually on the verge of bankruptcy.

At the same time the French bourgeoisie benefited,
though to a less degree than their English rivals, from the
general expansion of trade that followed the opening of
the world to European exploitation and from the profits
that even an unsuccessful war bring to this class. The result
was a rising and ambitious capitalist class face to face with
a discredited and bankrupt autocracy, an autocracy shored
up with a certain number of institutions surviving from the
age of feudalism. And below the French bourgeoisie were
the overtaxed and exploited peasantry and artisans, of

whom the latter at any rate saw as their main oppressors the aristocratic supporters of the Monarchy.

The same chain of events, in short, differing in their incidence and operation, produced both the French Revolution and the Industrial Revolution in England, and with them, produced the modern world.

CHAPTER XI

THE INDUSTRIAL REVOLUTION

I. AGRICULTURE

Not only was agriculture by far the most important of English industries in the Eighteenth Century, but the changes which took place at this time in agricultural technique and organisation, and in the distribution of classes among the rural population, created conditions without which the Industrial Revolution would have been impossible. It is, therefore, necessary to begin any account of the Industrial Revolution with the series of events that completed the long drawn out transformation of agriculture from a subsistence to a capitalist industry. These events began before the Industrial Revolution and continued throughout it.

From 1685 a bounty of 5s. a quarter was paid on exported wheat when the price did not exceed 48s., that is, in all but years of famine. The last seven years of the Seventeenth Century were wet and sunless and prices rose well above the 48s. level, but from 1700 to 1765 prices were lower and relatively stable, averaging about 35s. and seldom rising much above 40s. or sinking much below 30s. Exports were considerable and increasing in amount:—

1697–1705	1,160,000 qrs. exported	
1706–1725	5,480,000 ,,	,,
1726–1745	7,080,000 ,,	,,
1746–1765	9,515,000 ,,	,,

This steady export market, together with the considerable export of malt and barley and the provisioning of London provided agriculture with an external outlet which was a constant stimulus to improvements in technique.

Having a steady market, the farmer no longer felt the urge to hang himself "on th' expectation of plenty". The results were especially marked in the Eastern and South-eastern counties whose methods were in strong contrast to those of the still unenclosed cornlands of the Eastern Midlands whose produce could not easily be marketed in the absence of any adequate means of land transport. It was not till later, when canals had been built and a new market opened by the industrialisation of the adjacent regions of Yorkshire, the Black Country and Lancashire that the enclosure movement reached its height in the Midlands.

While some progress in agriculture was made during the Seventeenth Century it was not till after the Revolution of 1688 that it became rapid. The Revolution brought England into closer contact with the far more advanced technique of Holland, and such things as turnips and artificial grass crops like clover, which had been known for a century as curiosities, began to be used on a wider scale. The introduction of these crops meant the abandonment of the old rotation of two corn crops and a fallow for a more scientific rotation in which corn, roots and grass were sown in a four years' course. To get the full value from the new crops deep ploughing and hoeing were introduced, breaking up the soil more thoroughly and keeping it free from weeds.

No less striking was the effect on the breeding of sheep and cattle, which, up to this time, had been valued chiefly for their wool and as draught animals. So long as this was the case, and the bulk of the cattle were slaughtered every autumn because of the scarcity of fodder while those that were kept were half-starved throughout the winter, scientific breeding was impossible. Now it was possible, without any decrease in the production of corn, to feed beasts throughout the winter. Sheep, formerly rivals to tillage, became a valuable addition to the normal course of arable farming. Cattle, instead of being allowed to graze haphazard over the fallows, were stall fed. The average weight of sheep and cattle sold at Smithfield in 1710 was 28 lbs. and 370 lbs. In 1795 it was 80 lbs. and 800 lbs.

The new methods of breeding reacted in turn on the growing of corn. For the first time an abundant supply of manure became available both from the systematic folding of sheep over grass and root crops and from the cattle and pigs fattened in the farmyards. Thus each advance in one branch of agriculture created possibilities of further advance in other branches. While the demand for meat grew with the increase of population, oxen were found unsuitable for the deep ploughing coming into vogue and were gradually replaced by horses.

All these changes had one thing in common: they could only be brought about by the application of considerable quantities of capital. They were entirely incompatible with the primitive open field farming still practised over about half the country and almost incompatible with the small-scale yeoman farming that had replaced it in some areas. The pioneers of the new methods were substantial men, mainly rich landowners farming large estates, men like Jethro Tull, Lord (Turnip) Townshend, Coke of Holkham and Bakewell who led the way in improving the breed of sheep. Consequently, the technical revolution led to, and developed alongside of, a social revolution that changed the whole structure of rural England.

While the enclosures of earlier times had been made with the object of turning arable land into sheep pasture,[1] those of the Eighteenth Century transformed the communally cultivated open fields into large, compact farms on which the new and more scientific mixed farming could be profitably carried out. In addition, much common land not then under the plough, land on which the villagers had certain long standing customary rights of pasturage or wood or turf cutting, as well as other land which had previously been mere waste, was now enclosed.

In other parts of England those of the smaller farmers who were tenants were gradually evicted or were ruined

[1] See Chapter VI, Section 3.

by rents four, five and even ten times as high as had been customary. Land farmed on the new methods could be made to pay these increased rents but this was no help to men whose farms and capital were too small to adopt them successfully. Many of the small freeholders were also forced to sell out by the impossibility of competing with the up-to-date methods of their richer neighbours.

The period saw a marked decrease of farms under 100 acres and a marked increase of those over 300 acres, and it has been calculated that between 1740 and 1788 the number of separate farms declined by over 40,000. The process was begun well before the former date and continued at an increased speed after the latter. The number of Enclosure Acts passed through Parliament indicates roughly how the movement developed, except that in the earlier part of the century much land was enclosed without an Act being obtained. From 1717 to 1727 there were 15 such Acts, from 1728 to 1760, 226, from 1761 to 1796, 1,482 while from 1797 to 1820, the period of the Napoleonic Wars, there were 1,727. In all, more than four million acres was enclosed under these Acts.

Beginning in Norfolk and Essex, the enclosures reached their height in the last part of the century when they began seriously to affect the Midlands. From about 1760 the whole situation was transformed. The growth of population changed England from an exporting to an importing country at a time when few countries had any considerable surplus of corn. Prices rose rapidly and began to fluctuate wildly. From 1764 to 1850 wheat was only four times below 40s. a quarter and in a number of years, especially between 1800 and 1813, exceeded 100s. While good profits had been made in the Eighteenth Century, it was now possible to make great fortunes: it was also possible to lose them. When the war cut off the European grain supply prices fluctuated still more wildly and corn growing became a gamble in which only those with ample resources could hope to survive. This both attracted capitalists to invest in landed property and weakened more than ever the position of the small farmers.

Acts of Enclosure were obtainable with the consent of four-fifths in number and value of the occupiers of land in the parish to be enclosed. Where, as was often the case, most of these were tenants of one or two big land-owners this consent could easily be obtained, and, in general, improper pressure and bribery were freely employed. Force and fraud were not less the characteristics of the enclosures of the Eighteenth Century than of those of More's day.

After an Act had been obtained the land was reallotted among the holders. Even when this reallotment was fairly carried out it was usually accompanied by considerable hardship. Tenants at will might, and often did, lose land which their families had cultivated for generations. Copy and lease holders were often persuaded to sell out and the difficulty which they had in finding the considerable sums of money to meet the legal expenses of the enclosure and the cost of fencing their new farms made them more ready to do so. Even freeholders suffered in the same way, so that the enclosures effected a remarkable concentration of both the occupation and ownership of the land. The result of the enclosures is thus summed up by the French historians, G. Renard and G. Weulersse:—

"As soon as Parliament had passed the Act, the work of redistribution was carried out by a powerful commission, which was under the influence of wealthy landowners to such an extent that reallotment amounted practically to confiscation. The lot assigned to each small proprietor was usually worth much less than the one of which he had been despoiled."

The sums received under conditions amounting virtually to a forced sale were usually too small to be employed successfully in any other business even if the farmer had known how to make good use of them. A few, especially in Lancashire and Yorkshire, became successful manufacturers, but the vast majority spent their money quickly and then sank to the position of wage labourers whether on the land or in the new industrial towns.

A third class, the cottagers, found their rights even more ruthlessly violated. Few were able to establish any legal grounds for the customary rights over the village commons and fewer still received any adequate compensation for the loss of these rights. A whole class that had lived by a combination of domestic industry, the keeping of a few beasts or some poultry and regular or occasional work for wages now found itself thrown back entirely on the last of these resources, since the period of enclosures was also the period in which domestic industry was being destroyed by the competition of the new factories. Lord Ernle fills nearly three pages of his *English Farming Past and Present* with a list of local and domestic industries which perished at this time.

From about the middle of the Eighteenth Century the improvement in agricultural technique began to make it possible to economise in labour. Wages fell rapidly in relation to prices: in many parts cottages were destroyed or allowed to become ruinous and there was both a decrease in numbers and a decline in the standards of life of the majority throughout the greater part of rural England. In the later part of the century there was not only an increase in the total population but a marked shifting of population from one part of the country to another. No reliable figures are available, but it is at least probable that the increase was smaller and the shifting greater than was at one time supposed.

The revolution in agriculture had three results which went far beyond the limits of agriculture itself. First it increased the productivity of the land and so made possible the feeding of the great industrial population in the new towns.

Second, it created a reserve army of wage earners, now 'freed' completely from any connection with the soil, men without ties of place or property. It provided a force of free labourers corresponding to the free capital whose accumulation was outlined in the last chapter, and it was the coming together of this labour and this capital, at a time when the large scale production of commodities was at last possible, which was the essence of the Industrial Revolution.

Third, there was the creation of a vastly increased internal market for manufactured goods. The subsistence farmer, with his domestic industry and his isolation from the outside world, might consume a good deal and yet buy very little. The labourer into whom he had now evolved was usually compelled to consume a great deal less but everything he consumed had to be bought. And it was only on the firm basis of a substantial home market that a great exporting industry could be built up.

2. FUEL, IRON AND TRANSPORT

Early in the Eighteenth Century England was faced with the prospect of a fuel famine. For centuries the great forests had been invaded, trees felled and land brought under the plough. Little had been done in the way of replacement. Wood for domestic use began to be scarce and dear while the iron industry was threatened with extinction. All smelting was done with charcoal, and so primitive were the methods employed that many tons of wood were needed to produce one ton of iron. The timber of the Sussex Weald gave out first. That of Shropshire and the Forest of Dean, to which the industry migrated, was already showing signs of exhaustion. Ireland was soon stripped bare.[1] Strenuous and repeated efforts were made to establish iron smelting on a large scale in New England but here the Navigation Laws proved an obstacle to industrial development. In England itself the production of iron fell year by year and the country became increasingly dependent for its supplies upon Sweden and Russia.

Meanwhile experiments were being made with another possible fuel, coal. From quite early in the Middle Ages

[1] See p. 254 above.

coal had been used for domestic purposes and even in some industries, but it was only mined in quantity around Newcastle, where seams lay close to the surface and where easy transport was available by water. Large quantities of this Tyneside 'sea-coal' were shipped to London.

Attempts had been made to use coal for smelting iron even before the Civil War, but it was not till the middle of the Eighteenth Century, when the fuel situation was becoming really desperate, that smelting with coal was established as a commercial possibility. The Darbys of Colebrokedale and Roebuck, who established his famous works at Carron in 1760, made a series of improvements which showed not only that it was practical to use coal for smelting iron but that with a blast sufficiently powerful to get rid of sulphur and other impurities it was a far more economical and effective form of fuel than charcoal. In 1765 the iron industry found a new centre at Merthyr and henceforward the number and size of the blast furnaces increased yearly. The production of pig iron, which was only 17,350 tons in 1740, had risen to 68,300 tons in 1788 and to 125,079 tons in 1796.

Without coal there could have been no modern, scientific metallurgy and modern metallurgy is the technical key to large scale industry. Without it the construction of the elaborate and delicate machinery needed by the textile industry would have been as impossible as that of steam engines strong and exact enough to serve as a source of industrial power. Iron was soon put to a variety of new uses: the first iron bridge was built over the Severn in 1779 and the first iron ship in 1790. Improvements in the quality and purity of the iron went hand in hand with increasing accuracy in tool making, and engineers began to work not to inches but to the minute fractions of an inch which made it possible for elaborate machinery to be constructed to a pattern and with interchangeable parts instead of empirically.

With the exception of some of its lighter branches such as nail making, the iron industry had never been organised on a domestic basis. The iron masters of Sussex and the Midlands had been substantial men working with a large capital and it was therefore possible for the industry to make rapid progress without much structural alteration. By the end of the century England was a considerable exporting country and had even begun to import high quality ore from Sweden and Spain to be smelted with coal mined at home. It was for this reason that the industry took so firm a root, for example, along the coast of South Wales.

Coal mining also developed rapidly. New coalfields were opened up in South Wales, Scotland, Lancashire and Yorkshire, and output increased from 2,600,000 tons in 1700 to 7,600,000 tons in 1790 and over 10,000,000 tons in 1795. This industry, too, was always capitalist and many peers and great landowners were also coal-owners. The Duke of Bridgewater, for example, famous as a builder of canals, was also noted for the truck system by which he robbed the Worsley miners of a large part of their wages while the Lonsdale and Londonderry families shared the Eighteenth Century habit of regarding their colliers as a kind of serf.

Yet coal had one serious drawback as compared with wood: while the latter was fairly evenly distributed throughout the country, coal deposits were concentrated in a few counties. This disadvantage was only partly counterbalanced by the fact that in a number of places, such as South Wales and the Midlands, deposits of coal and iron were found side by side. Consequently coal could never be an effective substitute for wood so long as internal communications remained in the primitive state in which they were at the beginning of the Eighteenth Century. It was the mining of coal and the beginnings of the heavy industry which gave the first impulse to the improvement of transport and above all to the construction of canals.

In 1700 few roads existed along which wheeled traffic was possible at all times of the year. Lighter goods were carried in panniers slung over the backs of horses but for any bulky articles the cost of such transport was prohibitive. The carriage of coal from Manchester to Liverpool cost 40s. a ton. Even when better roads had been built between some of the important centres land transport remained costly.

The Duke of Bridgewater in 1759 employed Brindley to cut an eleven mile canal between his Worsley collieries and Manchester. This was so successful that when it was completed the price of coal in Manchester fell by exactly one half. Two years later the canal was extended to Runcorn, linking Manchester to the sea. The next venture was to connect this canal with the Trent and the Potteries which needed heavy material, such as clay from Devon and Cornwall and flints from East Anglia, and whose products were at once too bulky and too fragile to be suitable for carriage by road. When the Grand Junction Canal was finished the cost of transport was cut to one quarter and both the pottery industry and the working of the Cheshire salt deposits increased enormously.

Very soon a regular fever of canal building, comparable to the great railway boom of the Nineteenth Century, swept over the country which was quickly covered with a network of waterways.

In four years alone (1790–1794) no fewer than eighty-one Acts for the construction of canals were obtained. The whole interior of England, hitherto forced to consume and produce the great bulk of its own necessities, was now laid open to commerce. The wheat, coal, pottery and iron goods of the Midlands found a ready way to the sea and coal in particular could now be carried easily to any part of the country. Even though a general improvement in the roads was effected at the end of the Eighteenth Century and the beginning of the Nineteenth, canals remained the principal means for the distribution of heavy and non-perishable goods till they were deliberately destroyed by the railway companies forty or fifty years later.

Little improvement was made in the roads so long as they were kept in repair by occasional forced labour of the villages through which they passed, labour organised in a haphazard way by parish overseers. Early in the Eighteenth Century this system was supplemented by the erection of toll gates along the main roads: in this way the upkeep of the roads was paid for by the traffic passing along them. After the Jacobite rising of 1745 some roads were constructed for military purposes but the development was still very uneven. In some places where efficient turnpike trusts existed a road would be good. A few miles farther on, if the trust was corrupt and inefficient, as was not unusual in this period, the road would be correspondingly bad. Farther on again it might still be maintained by parish labour and be almost impassable. The minor roads and by-roads had scarcely altered at all since the Middle Ages.

It was not till the early years of the Nineteenth Century, in the age of the stage coach and the scientific road engineering begun by Macadam, that there was a general improvement. Shortly after, the development of the roads, like that of the canals, was checked by the advent of the railway and little more was done till the motor came into general use.

Bad as roads were about 1800 by the standards of today, they had improved greatly in the preceding century, and, though canals were more important for the carriage of goods, the speed and ease with which communication could now be maintained between all parts of Great Britain, and the regular postal system which was established, proved a great stimulus to the progress of industry by bringing manufacturers more closely into touch with their markets.

3. TEXTILES: THE SPEENHAMLAND EXPERIMENT

The development of the wool industry to a semi-capitalist stage in the Fifteenth and Sixteenth Centuries, with the clothier acting as a virtual employer of the handworker, has already been outlined.[1] We have seen that this development was arrested in the later part of the Sixteenth Century, that the absence of machinery, the restricted market and the insufficient accumulation of capital combined to prevent the growth of a real factory system and of mass production methods. From the Sixteenth to the Eighteenth Century the industry remained in a state of suspension, growing in extent but not altering radically in structure and organisation.

In some respects, indeed, there was a tendency to move backwards. The older centres of the industry, East Anglia and the West Country, where the influence of the clothiers was strongest, remained stagnant, and it was in the West Riding of Yorkshire, where the weaving began afresh on a more purely domestic basis, that the most rapid progress was made. The difference between these areas is illustrated by the reception accorded to Kay's flying shuttle towards the middle of the Eighteenth Century. The flying shuttle was not too costly to be within the reach of the independent weavers, but when an attempt was made to introduce it into East Anglia there was violent opposition on the ground that it threw men out of work and that all the profits were reaped by the clothiers. In the West Riding the domestic weavers welcomed it because it added considerably to their earnings.

Nevertheless the steady growth of the industry, and especially of exports, was bound in time to have its effect. J. Massie, writing in 1764, said that the exports of woollen cloth, which under Charles II "did not much exceed the yearly value of one million pounds, amounted in 1699 to almost three millions sterling, from which vast sum, with occasional ebbings and flowings, our annual exports of Woollen Manufactures have gradually risen to full four millions of late years". The West Riding had its due share of this increase. The number of pieces of "Broad woollen cloth" manufactured there rose from 26,671 in 1726 to 60,964 in 1750, and at the same time

[1] See Chapter VI, Section 1.

the length of the piece had almost doubled from thirty-five to about sixty yards.

Striking as the progress in the wool industry was, it was not there, but in the newer, more concentrated, and, from the beginning, more capitalist cotton industry that the decisive advances were made. It was established only with difficulty and after a long struggle with the powerful wool interests which saw in it a dangerous rival. Fine cotton goods were imported from India and became very popular till an Act of Parliament forbade their import in 1700 on the grounds that it "must inevitably be to the great detriment of this Kingdom by exhausting the treasure thereof . . . and taking away the Labour of the People whereby very many of the Manufacturers of the Nation are become excessively burdensom and chargeable to their respective Parishes".

The prohibition of Indian cotton goods gave an impetus to the manufacture of substitutes at home, though it was a long time before cotton yarn could be made sufficiently strong to be woven without a warp of linen or wool. At first the new industry was considerably hampered by restrictions insisted upon by the jealous wool manu-facturers but the cheapness, lightness and novelty of the cotton cloths gave them a ready sale. It was just because the new industry was artificially planted, depended on a raw material imported from abroad and was forced to be adaptable and ready to adopt new methods to defeat attacks and to overcome technical difficulties that it developed on a capitalist basis and was the first to profit by the inventions of the late Eighteenth Century.

It was from the start centred in Lancashire, where there was wool needed for the warp and a damp climate which proved suitable for spinning cotton yarn. Like all textile industries it was sharply divided into two main sections, spinning and weaving. The latter was the better paid and the more prosperous. Spinning was a slow and laborious process and it had always been difficult for the spinners to supply the weavers with sufficient yarn to work upon. Kay's flying shuttle, by doubling the speed at which cloth could be woven, completely upset the balance between the two sections, creating a chronic shortage of yarn and an urgent necessity for an improved method of spinning.

In 1764 a Blackburn weaver named Hargreaves produced his spinning jenny. A few years later Arkwright invented the water frame which not only spun cotton more rapidly but produced a yarn of finer quality so that cotton fabrics could be made with an admixture of wool or linen. Crompton's mule combined the advantages of both these machines. At about the same time Witney's cotton gin simplified the extraction of workable cotton from the plant and so increased the supply of raw material and there was an immense increase in plantation slavery in the cotton States of the U.S.A.

The balance between weaving and spinning was thus again destroyed, this time in favour of spinning. Henceforward, a continuous series of over-compensating technical advances resulted in each section, stimulating progress in the others and so creating a permanent disequilibrium. Cartwright's power loom enabled the weaver once more to outpace the spinner while other typical inventions concerned woolcombing and the printing of calicos.

Unlike the flying shuttle and the spinning jenny, which were only improved forms of the hand loom and the spinning wheel, Arkwright's water frame and the machines that followed it required external power, supplied at first by water. This necessarily placed them beyond the reach of the domestic workers and led at once to the creation of factories where masses, at first of spinners and afterwards of weavers as well, were collected to work for wages paid by employers who not only owned the material that was being worked up but also the instruments that were used and the place where the work was done.

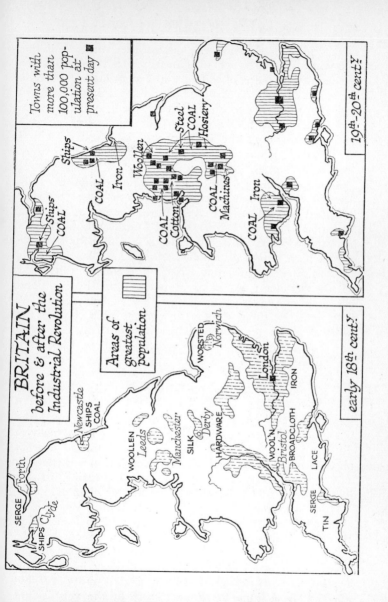

BRITAIN
before & after the
Industrial Revolution

Areas of greatest population

Towns with more than 100,000 population at present day

early 18th cent?

SERGE
SHIPS Clyde
Forth
Newcastle SHIPS COAL
WOOLLEN Leeds
Manchester
SILK
Derby
HARDWARE
WORSTED Norwich
London
WOOL'N Bristol
BROADCLOTH
IRON
SERGE
TIN
LACE

19th-20th cent?

Ships COAL
COAL
Ships
Iron
Woollen
Steel COAL Hosiery
COAL Cotton
COAL Machines
COAL
COAL Iron

L₁

By 1788 there were 143 such water mills and the abundant water power in Lancashire led to a further concentration there of industry and population. In 1785 the steam engine was first used to drive spinning machinery and it rapidly drove out of favour the less manageable and dependable water power. The discovery of large coal deposits kept the industry still in Lancashire and by the end of the century the cotton capitalists were "steam mill mad".

A witness before the Factory Commission of 1833 described the varied recruits drawn into these factories: "A good many from the agricultural parts; a many from Wales; a many from Ireland and from Scotland. People left other occupations and came to spinning for the sake of the high wages. I recollect shoemakers leaving their employ and learning to spin; I recollect tailors; I recollect colliers; but a great many more husbandmen left their employ to learn to spin; very few weavers at that time left their employ to learn to spin, but as the weavers could put their children into mills at an earlier age than they could to the looms, they threw them into the mills as soon as possible."

The main sources of recruitment appear very clearly: it was upon child labour, the labour of handicraftmen who were losing their occupations, of the Irish reduced to starvation level by English rule and above all upon the labour of the new rural proletariat fleeing from the vast distressed area into which enclosures had turned a great part of England that the Industrial Revolution was effected. The conditions and fortunes of the industrial workers in the towns will be dealt with in a later chapter.

Until about 1790 machine production was confined almost entirely to the cotton industry and to Lancashire. Its effects were therefore limited to a small section of the population and it provided employment for many more people than it displaced. When machinery began to be applied to wool textiles hardly a single county was not affected. And since the impact came at the very height ot the enclosures, when the country workers had already been deprived of many of their accustomed sources of income, the effect was disastrous. Prices were rising much faster than wages just when thousands found themselves forced as they had never been before to rely entirely upon these wages. Hand spinners and weavers either found themselves deprived of their occupation or driven into a hopeless contest with the machine which led to untold misery prolonged through more than a generation before domestic industry finally went under.

In 1795, when wheat stood at 75s. a quarter and the wages of agricultural workers averaged, perhaps, 8s. a week, it was clear that a man and his family could not exist upon such a wage unless it were supplemented from some outside source. The labourers themselves were certainly of this opinion and expressed it in bread riots which broke out in almost every county of England. The riots were curiously orderly; there was a little pillaging, and it was far more common for stocks of food to be seized and sold at a reduced price. The riots were, in fact, a crude way of fixing prices at what the people felt to be a reasonable level but they were none the less alarming for that.

Two possible courses lay before the authorities who had no practical means of fixing prices. One was to revive the obsolete legislation of the Sixteenth Century and fix rates of wages based on the cost of living. The other, and obviously the more satisfactory from the point of view of the employers, was to subsidise wages from the rates. This policy had already been adopted in a number of places before the Berkshire magistrates held their famous meeting at Speenhamland on May 6th, 1795. Here they decided that "every poor and industrious man" should have for his support 3s. for himself and 1s. 6d. for each member of his family, "either procured by his own or by his family's labours, or an allowance from the poor-rates" when the gallon loaf cost 1s. This allowance was to increase with the price of bread. The scale was adopted so generally that the decision of the Berkshire magistrates came to be known as the 'Speenhamland Act' and was widely believed to have the force of law.

The effect was soon felt when the cost of the Poor Rate, which had averaged about £700,000 in the middle of the Eighteenth Century and stood at about £2,000,000 in 1790, rose to nearly £4,000,000 by 1800 and later to nearly £7,000,000. Between 1810 and 1834 it only fell below £6,000,000 in six years.

During the Eighteenth Century the Poor Law system had been based on the principle that a person was entitled to relief in the parish where he was born and nowhere else. In practice this meant that all the poor were regarded as potential paupers and were liable to be deported to their place of birth on the suspicion that at some future date they might become chargeable upon the rates. Such a system was in keeping with the static civilisation of the Eighteenth Century: it was wholly out of keeping with the condition of wholesale migration characteristic of the Industrial Revolution. The Speenhamland system, which made paupers expensive to the ratepayers but profitable to the employing classes, gave the old Poor Law its death blow.

About 1720 a quite widespread movement had begun or the erection of workhouses. In many places this resulted in an immediate halving of the rate. The case of Maidstone, given with many more in *An Account of the Work-Houses in Great Britain*, published in 1732, is sufficiently characteristic to stand for the rest. After explaining that many of the poor were still maintained outside the workhouse and that in spite of that the rate had fallen from about £1,000 to £530, the account proceeds: "The advantage of a Workhouse does not only consist in this, that the Poor are maintained at less than half the Expence that their Weekly pay amounted to, but that very great numbers of lazy People, rather than submit to the Confinement and Labour of the Workhouses, are content to throw off the Mask, and maintain themselves by their own Industry. And this was so remarkable here at Maidstone, that when our Workhouse was finished, and publick Notice given that all who came to demand their weekly Pay, should be sent thither, little more than half the Poor upon the List came to the Overseers to receive their Allowance. Were all the Poor in our town obliged to live in the Workhouse, I believe we might very well maintain them for three hundred and fifty pounds a Year at the utmost."

A very large proportion of the inmates of these work-houses, especially the children, were taught spinning, weaving or some such trade. These pauper apprentices were later transported in thousands to the mills of Lancashire, where, being entirely defenceless, they formed the ideal human material for the cotton masters. The scandal of their treatment was eventually the starting point for factory legislation.

Whatever may have been the intention of the Berkshire magistrates, and it is highly improbable that they were the sentimental philanthropists some historians have supposed them to have been, the Speenhamland Act proved to be little more than a subsidy for low wages, led to wholesale pauperisation of the working people, and eventually, by way of reaction, to the Poor Law Bastilles of the Act of 1834.[1] Farmers and other employers everywhere cut down wages, knowing that they would be made up out of the rates. In many areas the whole working population became pauperised and men were sent round from farmer to farmer by the parish authorities till someone could be found to give them work at any price. In other parishes their labour was put up to auction. The system was obviously most profitable to the largest employers, who were able to transfer part of their wages bill onto those ratepayers who employed little or no labour.

It fell most crushingly upon the small farmers who were already faced with great difficulties. Those of them who had survived the enclosures shared few of the advantages

[1] See Chapter XIII, Section 1.

which their richer neighbours derived from the war conditions. The price of cattle and dairy produce, for example, on which they chiefly depended, had risen much less than the price of corn. Now they were asked to pay high rates to supplement the wages of their successful competitors and many of them were ruined by this new burden.

Another effect of the Speenhamland system was to stimulate the growth of population, which increased rapidly in spite of the general distress and the reckless wastage of life in the factories. A peasant population tends to be relatively stable because too large families involve too great a division of the land holdings and because the young men often postpone marriage till they have a farm of their own. The enclosures had removed this restraint. Marriages took place much earlier because the labourer had no possible improvement in his fortune for which it would be reasonable to wait. Now, under the Speenhamland scale, children were actually a source of income, and in some places, one or more illegitimate children came to be looked upon as a kind of dowry which made it easier for a young woman to find a husband.

The growth of factories produced similar results in the industrial areas, where wages were often so low that it was necessary to send the children to work as young as possible. Machinery was soon developed to the point at which few men were needed and widespread unemployment among them was often accompanied by the overworking and intense exploitation of women and especially of children. It was not uncommon for parents to be refused relief unless they sent their children to work in the mills. The period of high wages in spinning which had at first attracted labour from other trades proved of very short duration.

The peculiar misery of the time, due to the revolution in industrial and agricultural production, with its accompaniments of increasing population and high prices, was accentuated by two external factors. First, the years from 1789 to 1802 produced a remarkable and almost uninterrupted series of bad harvests due to weather conditions. And, second, the central period of the Industrial Revolution—1793 to 1815—was occupied by European wars on a scale never before known. It would hardly be too much to say that Britain entered these wars an agricultural and emerged from them an industrial country.

4. THE FRENCH REVOLUTION

Very few people in Europe realised that a new epoch was beginning when the French Estates-General met at Versailles on May 5th, 1789. For nearly a decade France had appeared to be declining into the position of a second Spain. Unbalanced budgets and a bankrupt treasury, an army and a navy incompetently led and irregularly paid, a peasantry permanently overtaxed and suffering from the famine caused by a series of ruinous harvests formed the background to and the reason for the calling of an assembly that had not met since 1614.

Before long the Third Estate found itself in violent conflict with the Crown and the aristocracy and was forced along the path of revolutionary struggle. In this it received strong support from the peasantry and the lower classes in the towns. Châteaux were attacked and burnt and great estates broken up. On July 14th the people of Paris stormed the Bastille. In October they marched out to Versailles and brought the King back as a virtual prisoner to Paris. To foreign observers all these events appeared to confirm their first impression that France was sinking into anarchy and could be neglected as a European Power. Austria, Russia and Prussia, relieved from anxiety in the West, turned to the congenial task of partitioning Poland. Only by degrees did they realise that a new power, and new menace against which the traditional defences were of little avail, was arising out of the chaos.

It was in England that this realisation first found expression. Here the power of the bourgeoisie had been

consolidated in the revolutionary period a century earlier
and here alone, therefore, the dominant sections of the
bourgeoisie had no sympathy with the Revolution in
France. Abroad it might in time set up a commercial
and industrial rival: at home a new revolution could
only raise questions better left alone and rouse classes
which up to now had been successfully kept in subjection.
As the Revolution in France became increasingly violent
and popular their terror increased. 'Jacobinism' meant
an attack on privilege and in England privilege was not
so much aristocratic as bourgeois. While the Revolution
divided every country in Europe into two camps the line
of demarcation was drawn at one point in England and
at another in all the other European countries. In the
first the higher strata of the bourgeoisie were above and
in the second below this line.

On the other hand British interests were not at first
directly threatened for geographical reasons. Britain,
therefore, was one of the last countries actually to join
in the counter-revolutionary war, yet, once involved,
she was the most determined in carrying it through.

Characteristically it was Burke, a former Whig, who
sounded the alarm in his fantastic but eloquent *Reflections
on the French Revolution*. The *Reflections* had an immense
vogue among the ruling class both in England and abroad,
and even in France, where they encouraged the nobility to
an unwise resistance. The powerful "Trade Union of
Crowned Heads" began to rally to the support of the
French monarchy, and in 1791, the Emperor of Austria
and the King of Prussia issued the Declaration of Pillnitz,
in which they invited the powers of Europe to "employ in
conjunction with their said Majesties the most efficacious
means in their power to place the King of France in
a position to establish in perfect freedom the foundations
of a monarchical government equally suited to the rights
of Sovereigns and the prosperity of the French nation."

The Declaration was largely bluff but the French people
had no means of knowing this and they were even more

alarmed at the constant intrigues between the Emperor and the thousands of nobles (including the brothers of Louis XVI) who had left France and were now occupying themselves with counter-revolutionary conspiracy. The willingness of European sovereigns to intervene grew with the spread of revolutionary ideas among their own subjects. In England Tom Paine's *Rights of Man* created an even greater sensation than Burke's *Reflections* to which it was a reply.

Yet it would be a mistake to regard the war of 1792 merely as an attack by the reactionary powers on revolutionary France. 'Liberty, equality, fraternity' was an explosive slogan with a universal appeal that carried it easily across frontiers and the French regarded themselves as the pioneers of a general liberation. The idea of a revolutionary war gained ground rapidly among both the Girondists, the party of the upper middle class, and the Jacobins who represented the lower middle class and the artisans. Both parties were more than prepared to take up the challenge of Austria and Prussia and it was from the Girondists, who hoped to improve their position for their internal struggle against the Jacobins as well as to extend the revolution beyond the boundaries of France, that the actual declaration of war came. There can be little doubt, however, that war was by that time inevitable. It was preceded by a manifesto in which the French Government promised assistance to all nations that should revolt against their oppressors. This was later explained as being meant only to apply "to those peoples who, after having acquired their liberty by conquest should demand the assistance of the republic".

After initial disasters the raw French armies poured into Belgium, which had been prepared to welcome them by a revolt against Austrian rule that had only been suppressed a couple of years before. It was the conquest of Belgium and the denouncing of commercial treaties connected with that country that brought revolutionary France into direct conflict with British interests,

Early in 1793 Britain entered the war, joining with Austria, Prussia, Spain and Piedmont to form the First Coalition.

Before war began the Radical and Republican agitation which arose in England as a reflection of the Revolution in France had been met with a pogrom and severe legal repression. Tory mobs, with the connivance of the magistrates, looted and burned the houses of Radicals and dissenters in Birmingham and elsewhere. Among the sufferers was the scientist Priestly. The Whig Party was soon split, the majority going over to Pitt and the reaction and only a handful under Fox persisting in their demands for reform. Small as it was, this group was of great historical importance because it formed the link between the Whigs of the Eighteenth Century and the Liberals of the Nineteenth Century and the nucleus around which the new forces entering the Liberal Party centred after Waterloo.

Fox and his followers were aristocrats: the period saw also the first definitely working class political organisation, the Corresponding Society. Its official programme was only Universal Suffrage and Annual Parliaments, but most of its members were republicans and disciples of Paine. Paine, who had fought for the Americans in the War of Independence and had helped to formulate both the Declaration of Independence and the Declaration of the Rights of Man, was a passionate advocate of the then novel idea that politics were the business of the whole mass of the common people and not only of a governing oligarchy. Government was only tolerable if it secured to the whole people "Life, Liberty and the pursuit of happiness", and any government which failed by this test ought to be overthrown, if necessary by revolution. His clear and logical exposition of the principles of the French Revolution won a ready hearing among the intelligent working men from whose ranks the Corresponding Society drew its members.

The weakness of the movement lay in its limited character. It was confined mainly to London and to the mechanics and artisans who formed the upper stratum of the working class. It had no roots in the industrial towns of the North. These were full of misery and discontent but the dispossessed peasants and ruined domestic workers who crowded there were not yet capable of political thought or activity. Their protest took the form of desperate acts of violence and destruction, and on more than one occasion the ruling classes were able to direct this violence against the Radicals as at Manchester and Bolton. It was only at the end, when the repression of Pitt was operating to crush the movement, that it began to make contacts with the new industrial proletariat and these contacts came too late to be immediately fruitful.

In 1794 Pitt suspended *Habeas Corpus* and rushed through laws to prohibit the holding of public meetings. The suspension of *Habeas Corpus* lasted for eight years. Even before this *The Rights of Man* was banned and Paine only escaped trial by a flight to France. The rest of his life was spent there and in America. The Corresponding Society and other Radical organisations were declared illegal and Thomas Hardy, a shoemaker, was put on trial for treason along with Horne Tooke and other leaders of the Society. Their acquittal by a London jury, though a defeat for the Government, did not prevent the continuation of the repression or save the Corresponding Society from destruction.

In the years that followed, although the open expression of Radical views was made impossible, frequent strikes, bread riots and machine wrecking riots kept the Government in a state of terror. The whole country was covered with a network of barracks, built so as to prevent contact between the people and the soldiers, who had formerly been billeted in houses and inns. The industrial areas were treated almost as a conquered country in the hands of an army of occupation. Troops were freely used to suppress disorder, but even so were often found to be unreliable because of their sympathy with the crowds they were ordered to attack.

It was for this reason that a new body, the yeomanry, a mounted force drawn from the upper and middle classes, was created at the beginning of the French wars. Quite useless from a military point of view, the yeomanry was, and was intended to be, a class body with the suppression of 'Jacobinism' as its main object. This object they pursued with an enthusiasm and an unfailing brutality which earned them universal hatred.

In Scotland Radicalism developed more strongly and the repression was earlier and more severe. The Society of the Friends of the People included many of the middle class as well as workers and when it assembled a national Convention in Edinburgh in December 1792 160 delegates represented eighty affiliated societies. In August 1793 one of its leaders, Thomas Muir, was brought before a packed jury and the notorious Justice Braxfield on a charge of sedition. The tone of the trial is indicated by Braxfield's remark to one of the jurors, "Come awa', and help us to hang ane o' thae damned scoundrels," and by Pitt's subsequent comment that the judges would be "highly culpable" if they did not use their powers "for the present punishment of such daring delinquents and the suppression of doctrines so dangerous to the country". Muir was sentenced to fourteen years' transportation. Later he was rescued from Botany Bay by an American ship and taken to France where he tried to persuade the Directory to invade Scotland.

After a number of similar trials the movement was forced into more definitely insurrectionary forms, but a body called the United Scotsmen and based on the Irish model remained small and was suppressed in 1799.

The anti-Jacobin fury of the Government and ruling class was all the keener because of the continued success of the French armies. From the middle of 1793 to the middle of 1794—that is to the overthrow of the Jacobins on the '9th Thermidor'—was indeed the heroic age of the Revolution. After Thermidor power was assumed by the Directory, representing all the most disreputable sections of the bourgeoisie, the land speculators, currency crooks and fraudulent army contractors. Yet the Revolution left many permanent gains, above all the division of the great feudal estates and the smashing of all restraints on the development of trade and industry. The way lay open for the *Code Napoleon*, the perfect legal frame for bourgeois development. The settlement of the agrarian question gave a firm basis for any government that was opposed to the return of the Bourbons and the nobility.

Wolfe Tone remarked in 1796, "It is in the armies that the Republic exists." It was certainly the Revolution which created an army that had no equal in Europe. As Captain Liddell Hart says, it "inspired the citizen armies of France, and in compensation for the precise drill which it made impossible, gave rein instead to the tactical sense and initiative of the individual. These new tactics of fluidity had for their simple, yet vital pivot, the fact that the French now marched and fought at a quick step of 120 paces to the minute, while their opponents adhered to the orthodox 70 paces".

Further, the poverty of the young Republic made it impossible to provide the armies with the customary vast baggage trains and cumbersome equipment. The armies were forced to live upon the country they passed through and so to move constantly and rapidly, and to divide themselves into smaller, self-contained units. By adopting strategical methods in keeping with the actual situation they were able to transform a weakness into a source of strength.

The line formation, then employed by all European armies, was found to depend too much on precise drill for its possibility and was abandoned for the column. With the column was developed a tactic of a covering cloud of sharpshooters who moved ahead of it to disorganise the enemy. Artillery also brought up in advance of the main body was used for the same purpose. Against the unwilling conscripts of the European despotism these tactics proved invincible.

It was in the exact recognition of the merits and limitations of the instrument in their hands that the military genius of Carnot and Napoleon lay. Instead of trying to force the French Army into the orthodox mould they took it for what it was and allowed it to attain its own perfection. Napoleon's greatest victories were almost all based on the rapidity of his movements before the actual battle and the weight and decision of the attack thrown at a carefully selected vital spot. It was only as the revolutionary impetus faded that he lost his elasticity and came to depend on mere mass rather than on mass in motion. His methods finally hardened into a dogma as petrifying as the dogmas it originally displaced.

The French Navy never reached any great heights, partly because enthusiasm is no substitute for discipline on board ship and partly because the Norman and Breton fishing ports from which the old navy had drawn most of its best recruits remained clerical and reactionary throughout the Revolution. From Howe's victory of the First of June in 1794 Britain maintained a naval superiority that was rarely challenged. At the beginning of the war Britain had 158 ships of the line to 80 possessed by France. By 1802 the numbers were 202 against 39 and after Trafalgar 250 against 19. At this time the combined fleets of France, Spain and Holland only totalled 92. The marked inferiority of the French Navy was itself a reason for concentrating almost all effort on land operations instead of wasting resources in a futile attempt to make up leeway on the sea.

5. THE NAPOLEONIC WARS

From the formation of the First Coalition in 1793 Britain took first place in the various combinations against France. Other powers changed sides or drifted in and out of the war, but with one short interval after the Treaty of Amiens in 1802 Britain remained continuously at war till the capture of Paris in 1814. The main source of her strength was the modern and capitalist economic organisation which enabled trade and industry to increase even under war conditions and vast sums of money to be raised without bankruptcy.

Pitt's war finance was merely an extension of that practised throughout the Eighteenth Century: heavy and increasing taxation of the necessities of life, a huge National Debt and subsidies totalling £50,000,000 to the European powers who were prepared to raise armies against Napoleon. It has been estimated that a labourer earning 10s. a week paid half of it in indirect taxes. Revenue increased steadily from £18,900,000 in 1792 to £71,900,000 in 1815, and in the same two years the interest on the National Debt was £9,470,000 and £30,458,000. Loans were raised at a heavy discount, and, for the £334,000,000 added to the Debt during Pitt's administration alone, only about £200,000,000 was received in cash by the Government.

The effect of this war finance, besides reducing the real wages of the working masses and forcing up prices, was to reinforce the class of financiers and rentiers and to increase enormously the scope and volume of banking and credit operations. The new finance magnates so created became in due course landowners and pillars of the Tory Party. Peerages multiplied: in seventeen years Pitt created ninety-five English and seventy-seven Irish peers. "The ancient nobility and gentry," wrote Cobbett in 1802, "have with very few exceptions been thrust out of all public employments. . . . A race of merchants and manufacturers and bankers and loan jobbers and contractors have usurped their place," and, in 1804, "There always was among the creature and close adherents of Mr. Pitt a strange mixture of profligacy and cant: jobbers all the morning and Methodists in the afternoon."

Yet the wealth at Pitt's disposal could not prevent his coalitions from going down like ninepins before the armies of France. The First Coalition collapsed in 1795 after Flanders and Holland had been over-run and the Duke of York, possibly the most incompetent general

who ever commanded a British army, trounced at Dunkirk.
The West Indies, always a vital concern of the City
interests, absorbed the greater part of Britain's land
forces. In three years, 80,000 men were lost there with no
result. This expedition was in line with past practice,
except that so large a body of inadequately equipped troops
had not before been sent to a tropical climate. The conquest of Italy in 1797 drove Austria out of the war.

Britain was now as isolated as France had been in
1792. The war could probably have been ended but
for the earliest and most fatal of Napoleon's strategic
miscalculations. This was his decision to strike at Britain
through Egypt and the East instead of through Ireland,
a decision which shows to what an extent revolutionary
realism had given place to grandiose imperial schemes.
Victory at this time, before the French Republic had
finally hardened into a military dictatorship and before
the demands which a prolonged war forced it to make upon
the peoples of the occupied countries had forfeited their
sympathy, might well have transformed the whole subsequent course of European history.

Ireland had been more affected by the French Revolution
than, perhaps, any other country in Europe. Under the
leadership of Wolfe Tone the United Irishmen had combined a demand for Irish independence with the Radical
republicanism of Paine. Tone at least had a profound
understanding of the relation of class to the national
struggle. Rightly distrustful of the aristocracy and middle
class after the betrayal of the Volunteers he made his
appeal to "that large and respectable class of the community—the men of no property". The United Irishmen
quickly took the lead of the whole national movement
and, for a time, they succeeded in breaking down the
hostility between Catholics and Protestants and combining
both against England and its adherents in the Irish ruling
class.

Preparations for revolt were pushed ahead, and in
1796 Tone went to France to persuade the Directory to

send an expedition to Ireland to co-operate with the rebels there. He had to contend with the Eastern preoccupation already stirring in Napoleon's brain and though a force of 15,000 men was prepared, plans for the invasion were only half-hearted. When at the end of the year the fleet left Brest for the Munster coast a combination of bad weather and military blundering prevented a landing at Bantry Bay.

One chance was thus missed but a second presented itself in the summer of 1797. This time Holland was the base selected for an expedition and for more than a month the whole of the British North Sea fleet was paralysed by the Nore Mutiny. Through mismanagement the expedition was not ready till after the mutiny had been crushed[1] and news of it only reached the Continent when it was all over. The cautious Dutch commanders then refused to sail and with the death of Hoche, the only French general who appreciated the importance of Ireland, hopes of effective intervention faded.

For two years the Irish had waited for help, and, now that it was apparent that no help was coming, the policy of the English authorities was to torment the peasants into a hopeless insurrection. Sir Ralph Abercrombie, the English commander in Ireland, himself declared that "every crime, every cruelty that could be committed by Cossacks or Calmucks had been committed here". The alliance between Catholics and Protestants had broken down and when the Catholic peasants rose in May 1798 they rose alone. The rising was suppressed, after some hard fighting, with such brutality that the country was completely cowed and when a small French force did land in August they found that the rebellion was over and were unable to rally any support before they were surrounded and forced to surrender. Tone was captured

[1] The Nore Mutiny was a sequel to the successful mutiny at Spithead earlier in the year. Neither was directly political but both arose from the low wages, irregular payments, bad food and brutal conditions prevailing in the fleet. But many of the sailors who were Irish must have counted on the mutiny assisting their cause.

soon after in a naval engagement and committed suicide in prison. In 1803 a second insurrection led by Robert Emmet was crushed.

While the rebellion in Ireland was still going on Napoleon had sailed for Egypt. The destruction of his fleet at the Battle of the Nile (August 1798) cut his troops off from home and left them in a position from which no victories were likely to extricate them. With Napoleon out of the way Pitt was able to form a Second Coalition with Russia and Austria. A Russian army drove the French out of North Italy and the Bourbon king of Naples was able to effect a counter-revolution in the South with the aid of Nelson's fleet. In the autumn Napoleon slipped back to France, leaving his Army to its fate. By the *coup d'état* of 18th Brumaire (November 9th) he overthrew the Directory and established himself as First Consul. His later decision to declare himself Emperor changed nothing but a name. The war now definitely entered its second phase.

In the beginning the French armies were welcomed as liberators by the middle and lower classes of the countries they conquered. To Italy, Switzerland, the Rhineland and the Low Countries they carried the bourgeois revolution. A recent biography of Marx describes the typical reaction in Trier: "The inhabitants at Trier received the French with enthusiasm. The Revolution released the peasants from the trammels of feudalism, gave the bourgeoisie the administrative and legal apparatus they required for their advancement, freed the intelligensia from the tutelage of the priests. The men of Trier danced round the 'tree of freedom' just like the inhabitants of Mainz. They had their own Jacobin club. Many a respected citizen in the thirties still looked back with pride to his Jacobin past."

Much that was done in these years proved of permanent benefit, but presently the people of the occupied countries found that they were to be allowed, at best, a second class revolution with their interests always subordinated to

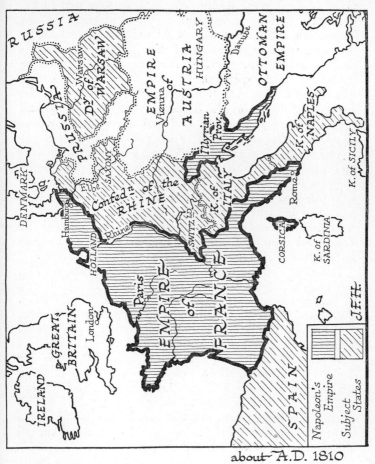

about A.D. 1810

those of France. The price of liberation was heavy taxes and the conscription of their sons to fill the gaps in the ranks of the French Army. War was, or appeared to be, necessary for the continued internal stability of the Napoleonic regime yet war could only be carried on by the progressive exploitation of the 'liberated' territories and the longer war went on the more territory must be 'liberated' and exploited. In this way a contradiction was set up from which there was no escape. Further, the practice of living on the country, which the Army had begun from mere necessity and had turned into a source of military strength, was always a political weakness.

The result was that the very classes which had welcomed and been aroused to political maturity by the French were gradually alienated. Their history is that of Beethoven, who intended to dedicate his *Heroic Symphony* to Napoleon and then thought better of it. By breaking the shell of feudalism and ending the curious torpor that marked the Eighteenth Century Europe the French created a bourgeois nationalism that turned inevitably against its creators.

Napoleon had many years of victory before him in 1799, however, and the reckoning was delayed by the incapacity of the monarchies, through whom the new nationalism was forced, however unwillingly, to express itself. A short and brilliant campaign reconquered Italy and the Second Coalition was smashed at Marengo in the last days of 1800. The years that followed, with Britain alone left in the war and no important land operations, were spent in drawing up the *Code Napoleon* and creating a modern and efficient civil service. The Treaty of Amiens, recognised by all parties as a mere truce, brought hostilities to a close from 1802 to 1803. It left France in control of Holland and all the west bank of the Rhine.

When war was resumed Napoleon had as allies Spain and Holland. The French Army was camped at Boulogne ready for a descent on England if the French and Spanish fleets could be concentrated to cover the crossing. How far this plan was serious has never been certainly determined.

In March 1805 the Toulon fleet slipped past the blockade and sailed for the West Indies with Nelson in pursuit. The Brest fleet failed to escape and the Toulon fleet doubled back to join the Spanish in Cadiz. In October both fleets were destroyed at Trafalgar.

Before Trafalgar was fought, however, the scheme for the invasion of England was abandoned. By the promise of unheard of subsidies Pitt had persuaded Austria and Russia to join in the Third Coalition and the French Army had been marched across Europe to meet the new enemy. It is myth that Trafalgar saved England from invasion: what it did was to place her naval supremacy beyond question for the rest of the war.

On the day before Trafalgar Napoleon defeated an Austrian army at Ulm on the Danube. Soon after he entered Vienna, and on December 2nd overwhelmed both Austrians and Russians at Austerlitz. Pitt died in January, leaving the country to be governed by his jackals, Castlereagh, Sidmouth, Eldon and Perceval.[1] In October the King of Prussia, who had characteristically refused to join the Third Coalition when his intervention might have been effective, was pushed into war by the rising national feeling in Germany and crushingly defeated at Jena. For six years neither Austria nor Prussia counted as European Powers and after another defeat at Friedland in 1807 the Tsar of Russia made his peace. Napoleon now ruled over an Empire which included Northern Italy, the East coast of the Adriatic, all the territory west of the Rhine with Holland and a large area of North Germany from Cologne to Lubeck. Spain, Naples, Poland and all Central and Southern Germany formed vassal states.

It was upon Russia and Spain, the two remotest and least developed of the European Powers, that Napoleon was finally broken. Neither of these countries had a strong middle class such as had made the victory of the French easier elsewhere. For a time Napoleon and the Tsar

[1] For a characterisation of some of these gentlemen, see Shelley's *Mask of Anarchy*, a poem inspired by the Peterloo massacre.

Alexander combined to dominate Europe but Napoleon was not prepared to treat Alexander as an equal and the latter refused to be subordinate. Failing all else Napoleon tried to strike at England by imposing a European ban on her manufactured goods. England replied with a blockade, and though neither ban nor blockade were completely effective, a strain was begun under which the alliance between France and Russia and the other North European countries crumbled away.

Before this happened, however, Portugal, for a century dominated by the British Government, refused to recognise Napoleon's 'Continental System.' A French army was therefore sent to prevent trade between Portugal and Britain. At the same time, Napoleon attempted to change his indirect control over Spain for a direct rule by making his brother Joseph king. This provoked an instantaneous and universal revolt. The Spanish proved to be the worst regular soldiers and the best guerillas in Europe: the armies were defeated wherever they showed themselves but the people's war went on and forced Napoleon to concentrate larger and larger forces in Spain.

In 1808 Sir Arthur Wellesley, later Duke of Wellington, was sent with a small army to defend Portugal and assist and encourage the Spanish insurrection. The French had now some 300,000 men in the Peninsula but were seldom able to concentrate more than about one fifth against Wellington, the rest being engaged in small operations all over the country. Every attempt at a concentration left large areas open to the guerillas, so that the regular and irregular wars set up an interaction before which the French were helpless. The details of the six years' campaign, the advances, retreats and battles, are relatively unimportant. In 1811, when Napoleon had to draw away part of his forces for his Russian venture, Wellington was able to take the offensive and step by step the French were driven out of the Peninsula.

An army of nearly half a million—Poles, Italians and Germans as well as Frenchmen—was massed by Napoleon in 1811 for an attack on Russia. The march of the Grand Army to Moscow and its disastrous retreat set Europe once more ablaze. Germany rose against the defeated Emperor and at last the French found themselves opposed not to the conscript armies of kings but to nations in arms. Although he quickly collected a new army almost as large as the one he had lost, Napoleon was decisively beaten at Leipzig in October 1813. In spite of this he rejected an offer of peace which would have given him the Rhine as a frontier, and in April 1814 the allies entered Paris, the Bourbons were restored and Napoleon banished to Elba.

England, Russia, Austria and Prussia then settled down at the Congress of Vienna to fight over the spoils of victory. Their deliberations were interrupted in 1815 by the sudden return of Napoleon to France and the Hundred Days' Campaign which ended with his defeat at Waterloo.

The main features of the settlement arrived at by the Congress of Vienna was the restoration of despotism and the triumph of what was called the 'principle of legitimacy'. This was only neglected when it happened to run counter to the interests of Austria, Russia or Prussia: thus Poland, Venice, Saxony and other small States were swallowed or dismembered by their more powerful neighbours.

Revolution was felt to be as much the enemy as France and the victory of reaction was sealed by the Holy Alliance in which Austria, Russia and Prussia agreed to give each other mutual support against the horrors of insurgent democracy. The Holy Alliance was used to justify international action against risings in Italy, Germany and elsewhere. Yet neither Metternich nor Alexander could restore Europe to its sacred torpor or do more than delay for a little the process set on foot by the Revolution, and the Holy Alliance did not survive the upheavals of 1830.

In France the restoration of the Bourbons did not mean the restoration of aristocratic privilege in the villages or the supersession of the *Code Napoleon*. In Germany, though Prussia extended its power over the Rhineland, many of the social changes resulting from the French occupation went undisturbed. The patchwork of German States were drawn together into the German Confederation in which Austria and Prussia both participated and which inevitably became the theatre of a battle between them for the hegemony of Central Europe.

England's share in the plunder was taken mainly outside Europe. The foundations for a great extension of the Empire were laid, perhaps unwittingly, by the acquisition of a number of strategic key points: Malta, Mauritius, Ceylon, Heligoland and the Cape, then inhabited only by a few Dutch farmers and valued only as a stopping place on the way to India. The British bourgeoisie came out of the war ready to consolidate a world monopoly for the produce of their factories and to begin a period of hitherto unimagined advance. Yet the first result of the peace was a severe political and economic crisis.

CHAPTER XII

THE TRIUMPH OF INDUSTRIAL
· CAPITALISM ·

I. ENGLAND AFTER WATERLOO

IN THE GENERAL rejoicings that followed the
Treaty of Amiens, Cobbet wrote:

"The alliterative words, peace and plenty, sound well in
a song or make a pretty transparency in the window of an
idiot; but the things which these harmonious words
represent are not always in unison." The optimism with
which the bourgeoisie greeted the Peace of 1815 was even
less well founded. Manufacturers had assumed that the
ending of the war would at once throw open a vast market
for their wares and had piled up stocks accordingly.
Instead, there was an immediate fall in the demand for
manufactured goods.

While it was true that the European market had been
largely closed by Napoleon's Berlin Decrees,[1] and the
American market by the war which had resulted from the
British claim to search and seize neutral ships going to
Europe, huge war contracts had compensated for these
losses. These contracts had ceased abruptly after Waterloo,
while Europe was still too disturbed and too poor to take
any great quantity of British goods. One important new
market had been actually opened by the war, which had
cut Spain off from South America and left its colonies
there virtually independent, but this had only led to
crazy speculation and the flooding of the market with
all kinds of goods for many of which no possible
demand existed. For the rest, there were the West
Indies and the Far East, neither of which could absorb

[1] See page 350 above.

MƐ

more than a limited quantity of rather specialised goods.

The result was that in 1815 exports and imports fell and there was a heavy slump in wholesale prices, a smaller one in retail prices and widespread unemployment. The heavy industries, peculiarly dependent on war demands, were the hardest hit. Iron fell from £20 to £8 a ton. In Shropshire twenty-four out of thirty-four blast furnaces went out of production and thousands of iron-workers and colliers were thrown out of work.

Other causes helped to intensify and prolong the crisis. Three hundred thousand demobilised soldiers and sailors were forced to compete in an already overstocked labour market. Wages fell, but prices were kept artificially high by the policy of inflation which Pitt had begun in 1797 when he allowed the Bank of England to issue paper money without a proper gold backing. Taxation was kept at a high level by the huge Debt charges, amounting in 1820 to £30,000,000 out of a total revenue of £53,000,000. The reckless borrowing by means of which the war had been financed left an unnecessarily heavy burden upon succeeding generations. While not, as Cobbet and many of the Radicals supposed, the real cause of the crisis, inflation and high taxes greatly increased the misery which it produced and prevented the rapid recovery of industry.

The Radical Samuel Bamford describes the sudden outburst of class conflict which marked this post-war crisis:—

". . . a series of disturbances commenced with the introduction of the Corn Bill in 1815 and continued, with short intervals, until the close of the year 1816. In London and Westminster riots ensued and were continued for several days, while the Bill was discussed; at Bridport there were riots on account of the high price of bread; at Bideford there were similar disturbances to prevent the export of grain; at Bury[1] by the unemployed to destroy machinery;

[1] Bury St. Edmunds, not Bury, Lancs.

at Ely, not suppressed without bloodshed; at Newcastle-on-Tyne by colliers and others; at Glasgow, where blood was shed, on account of soup kitchens; at Preston, by unemployed weavers; at Nottingham by Luddites who destroyed 30 frames; at Merthyr Tydvil, on a reduction of wages; at Birmingham by the unemployed; at Walsall by the distressed; and December 7th, 1816, at Dundee, where, owing to the high price of meal, upwards of 100 shops were plundered."

Such rioting was not in itself a new thing. The bread riots of 1795 have been referred to already. In 1812, Byron, in his superb speech against the proposal to make machine wrecking punishable by death, had ridiculed the efforts of the military to suppress the Luddite riots in Nottingham:—

"Such marchings and counter-marchings!—from Nottingham to Bullwell, from Bullwell to Banford, from Banford to Mansfield! And when at length the detachments arrive at their destination in all 'the pride, pomp and circumstance of glorious war', they came just in time to witness the mischief which had been done, and ascertain the escape of the perpetrators, to collect the *spoila optima* in the fragments of broken frames, and return to their quarters amidst the derision of old women and the hooting of children."

The Luddite riots centred in the Nottingham hosiery area, where the introduction of the stocking frame into a semi-domestic industry had cut prices to a point at which the hand stocking knitters found it almost impossible to make a living. Machine wrecking took place also in the West Riding and elsewhere. Strikes, many of them fought out with extreme bitterness, were common both before and after the passing of the Combination Acts of 1799 and 1800.[1]

What distinguished these earlier disturbances from those which followed Waterloo was the consciously political character of the latter. Masses of workers were coming

[1] See Chapter XIV, Section 1.

out in a political general strike that was everywhere expected to be the prelude to an armed rising. The word for such a rising was never given, and the only sequel was a skirmish at Bonnymuir between the 10th Hussars and a little body of weavers led into a trap by Government agents. Neither the conditions nor the leadership for a successful insurrection really existed at this time.

The 'Six Acts' were in fact followed by a temporary suspension of Radical agitation. For this they were perhaps less responsible than the revival of industry that began in 1820 and continued up to the boom year of 1826. Such a revival was inevitable once the effects of the war had passed, because British industry really did have a world monopoly at this time. This is the fundamental difference between the crisis after 1815 and that following the World War with which it has far too often been compared. Manufacturers bent on cutting wages liked to talk about foreign competition but actually no other country had any considerable large scale industry or any surplus of manufactured goods for export. France and the United States were just beginning to develop a cotton textile industry, but even by 1833 their combined output was only two-thirds of that of Britain. In mining and the iron and steel industries British supremacy was equally marked.

Exports increased from £48,000,000 in 1820 to £56,000,000 in 1825 and imports from £32,000,000 to £44,000,000. But this was only one side of the expansion. At home the same period was marked by the steady decline of small scale and domestic industry before the competition of the factories. It was the era of the consolidation of the home market. The decline of the domestic industries was uneven, taking place in the cotton before the linen and woollen industries, in spinning before weaving and in East Anglia and the West Country before the North and Midlands. It was not completed before the 1840s and was the cause of the most widespread and prolonged suffering. But it divided the working classes into sections with differing interests and wrongs, and forced those who were the worst sufferers into futile and objectively reactionary forms of protest.

With the consolidation of the internal and external monopoly of the British industrial capitalists a new period began, with new class groupings and new political tactics. Its advent was marked in August 1822 by a dramatic incident. Castlereagh, universally believed, rightly or wrongly, to be responsible for the Government's social policy, cut his throat. Great crowds lined the London streets as his coffin was carried to Westminster Abbey, cheering as they saw in his passing the passing of the Age of Peterloo.

2. THE WAR IN THE VILLAGES

The working people of England were peculiar among their fellows throughout Europe in that they alone derived no benefit from the French Revolution and the wars which followed it, while at home they were the one class which was poorer and not richer at the end of these wars than at their beginning. This is especially true of the farm labourers, and it would be hard to say if they suffered more from the high prices of the war period or the lower prices which followed it.

From 1793 to 1815 every available scrap of land was ploughed up for wheat: however poor or unsuitable the soil there was still the possibility of profit with prices running up to 100s. a quarter. One result of this was that agriculture became dangerously specialised and that when the slump came farmers on poor land had nothing to fall back upon. Also, the higher the price of wheat the greater the incentive to enclose and the more unjustly the enclosure was likely to be carried out. The barest common and the smallest garden were grasped at by landlords eager to turn them into gold. Farmers prospered as a whole, but the landlords and the tithe owners prospered still more. Only the real wages of the labourers fell continually. When a proposal was made in 1805 to fix a legal minimum wage it was ridiculed on the ground that to fix a wage in relation to the price of bread at the standard of 1780 when the average wage was 9s. would have meant a wage of £1 11s. 6d. The actual wages paid at this time certainly did not average more than one-third of this sum.

The peace brought a rapid change. Wheat cost 109s. a quarter in 1813, 74s. 4d. in 1814, and 65s. 1d. in 1815. In 1816, under the influence of the Corn Law of 1815 and a bad harvest, it rose again to 78s. 6d., though here the bare figures, being averages for the year, do not tell the whole story, since the price was much lower at the beginning of the year and much higher in the autumn. The Corn Laws saved the landlords and some of the farmers: they did nothing to save the labourers from unemployment, lower wages and cuts in Poor Law relief.

In 1816 corn fell and wages fell but rents and food prices remained high. The result was riots which in the East Anglian wheat counties amounted almost to a general revolt. Houses and stacks were fired. At Bury and Norwich the rioters fought the yeomanry in the streets. At Littleport in the Isle of Ely a three-day rising ended in a pitched battle in which two labourers were killed and seventy-five taken prisoners. Five of these were hanged and nine transported. General if temporary increases in wages followed these riots.

The general tendency, however, was for a continued decline in the standard of life. The Speenhamland scale of 1795, conceived as the bare minimum on which existence was possible, had allowed seven and a half gallon loaves for a family of four: the scales prevailing in 1831 allowed only five. In a little over a generation the mass of the rural population passed from a beef, bread and ale standard of living to a potato and tea standard. It was this fact which lay behind Cobbett's hatred of potatoes and his curious-seeming denunciation of tea-drinking as "a destroyer of health, an enfeebler of the frame, an engenderer of effeminacy and laziness, a debaucher of youth and a maker of misery for old age."

Cobbett was not a clear political thinker. A yeoman of genius, looking back, as the dispossessed peasantry whose woes he voiced always will, to a largely imaginary golden age and dreaming of an impossible return, he proposed a great many impracticable remedies for troubles he only partly understood. Yet one thing he did grasp, that the common people, his people, had been robbed, were being robbed and would continue to be robbed until they combined to check and control the property-owning class. This clear, simple conception of politics gave his demand for democracy, for Parliamentary Reform, a directness and an application to the desires of the masses which made him hated and feared by every Government between 1810 and 1830.

His *Political Register*, written in an English prose so clear that no one could ever mistake his meaning, was the first to denounce every act of oppression and was felt by thousands all over England to be an amplification of their own voice. Above all it fought for the country worker, the most exploited, most ignorant and most helpless figure of the age and the one best known to and best loved by Cobbett himself. He was not an even-tempered man, and he raged furiously against the landlords, tithe-owners and bankers, and against "the Thing", the whole conspiracy of the rich against the poor. Without Cobbett there would doubtless have been discontent and revolt in these years, but it would have been ill-directed and aimless.

There were many bankruptcies in 1815 and the years following and much land went out of cultivation. But more still was under-farmed: less labour was used, less manure, less stock kept, fewer repairs carried out. High taxation and the claims of bankers and mortgagees added to the difficulties of the time. Not only the farm labourers but the village craftsmen, the blacksmiths, carpenters and wheelwrights, suffered severely and all these were to be found taking an active part in the movement of revolt that swept over Southern England in the year 1830.

M 1

Quite a part from this revolt and the sporadic rick-burning that followed and preceded it, the class struggle in the countryside took a peculiar form, that of organised poaching. The villagers who had lost their strips of land and their rights over the commons turned inevitably for revenge and compensation upon the landlords' game preserves. For some sixty years a relentless guerilla war went on all over England between gangs of armed poachers and rival gangs of the gentry and their game keepers. From 1770 a series of laws increasing in severity were passed by Parliaments consisting almost entirely of land-owners. In 1800 poachers became liable to hard labour and to two years' imprisonment for a second offence. In 1803 it was enacted that any poacher who pointed a gun or attempted to cut or stab while resisting arrest should be hanged as a felon. In 1817 any person not belonging to the class entitled to pursue game who might be found in any park or wood with a gun or any other weapon became liable to transportation. In practice, transportation was almost always for life, since no passages were paid home and the transported man rarely returned.

These laws did not check poaching, they only increased the size of the gangs and made the poachers increasingly reckless in what they would do to avoid arrest. Spring guns and mantraps were added to the other methods of protecting game allowed by the law, and every captured poacher had the certainty of being tried before a bench of magistrates every one of whom regarded him as their natural enemy. At Bury St. Edmunds commitments for poaching rose from five in 1810 to seventy-five in 1822. In only three years from 1827 more than 8,500 men and boys were convicted of offences against the Game Laws and of these a very high proportion were transported.

Poaching was the most obvious and often the only way of adding to a starvation wage, since game sold easily at high prices, but it was also often a deliberate or half deliberate defiance, an answer to the war of the rich upon the poor and a reflection of the sullen anger of this hungry time. The poacher was rarely a criminal in the ordinary sense: he was more likely to be a man of outstanding intelligence and daring.

In 1830, this anger flared up in what has been called "the last labourers' revolt". Its immediate cause was the introduction of the threshing machine. Threshing was the one remaining rural industry at which a living wage could be earned or at which the villager could supplement his ordinary income. But the threshing floor and the hand flail could not compete with machinery which was not only cheaper and quicker but extracted the grain more thoroughly. Besides this, 1830 was a year of general economic crisis and of exceptional agricultural distress, increased by a terrible epidemic of the rot which, it has been estimated, killed off two million sheep.

The first riots were in Kent, where threshing machines were destroyed in August. Rick burning, too, was common, but the movement was not merely one of destruction. A complete social programme is hinted at in the well-known letter circulated over the signature of "Captain Swing", and which declares:

"We will destroy the corn stacks and the threshing machines this year, next year we will have a turn with the parsons and the third year we will make war upon the statesmen."

Although the outbreak began with machine smashing, the demand for a living wage—2s. 6d. a day in Kent and Sussex, 2s. in Wiltshire and Dorset where conditions were generally worse—was brought more and more to the front. A striking feature was the readiness of farmers in many places to accept these demands, to point out that they could only be granted if tithes and rent were reduced, to take part in the movement and direct it against the landlords and parsons. A number of cases are even on record in which farmers helped in the destruction of their own machinery.

As it spread westward throughout November the rising took on a more violent and desperate character. Rioting and demands for money became more frequent. In Hampshire workhouses were destroyed and there were brushes with the yeomanry. Quickly as it spread and threatening as it appeared to be, the revolt was doomed from the start. A whole generation of starvation and the pauperisation of the Speenhamland system had sapped the strength and destroyed the solidarity of the villagers. The Game Laws had taken away thousands of their natural leaders, the men of the greatest energy and independence. They were capable of a wild outburst, but not of any sustained effort.

With almost pathetic ease the revolt collapsed once the authorities brought their forces into action. In spite of this the ruling class was thoroughly alarmed and correspondingly brutal in its counter measures. Among those who were especially active were the Barings, a great banking family whose prosperity dated from the Pitt era and one of whom distinguished himself by beating with his stick a handcuffed prisoner awaiting his trial.[1]

In all, nine men were hanged, at least 457 transported, and about as many more imprisoned. The transported men came from thirteen counties, but 250 were from Hampshire and Wiltshire. All were from the South and East of England. In the North, where alternative employment was available in the mines and factories, wages were always higher and the Speenhamland system was never so universally applied. It is worth recording, though it is not possible to say how far the fact is connected with this rising, that agricultural wages in the 1830's were on the average about a shilling a week higher than either in 1824 or 1850.

The Government attempted to round off their victory by putting Cobbett on trial for articles written in the *Political Register*. The Crown lawyers who had triumphed over terrified and illiterate labourers soon found themselves on the defensive while Cobbett revealed how one of the imprisoned rioters had been threatened with death and

[1] See page 462 below.

then promised a pardon if he would say that Cobbett had incited him to violence. After this his acquittal was certain and was received with immense enthusiasm. Unfortunately this victory did nothing to help either the hundreds transported nor the thousands who remained in the villages.

The main importance of the rising lies in its being the last great political movement in the country districts. Agriculture had its ups and downs after this, but was always somewhat the poor relation of industry, and the farm workers, the heroes of so many struggles since the great rising of 1381, sank into a torpor only partly broken by the Trade Union agitation of Joseph Arch in and after 1872. Whatever may happen in the future, an *independent* movement is hardly to be expected among the rural proletariat.

3. FACTORY LEGISLATION

This history of factory legislation is in a great measure the history of the development of machinery. In the earliest stages of the Industrial Revolution, when machinery was crude, soon obsolete and worked by the uncertain and irregular power of water, factory owners were determined to get the fullest possible use out of this machinery in the shortest possible time. Hours of work rose to sixteen and even eighteen a day, and where as few hours as twelve were worked a shift system was common so that the machinery was never idle. In this way the greatest output could be obtained with the least outlay of capital- and it is important to remember that many mill owners started with a very small capital indeed, in some cases no more than £100.

The results of this system in human misery, and especially of the terrible wastage of child labour, are common knowledge. When the facts about factory conditions first became generally known they shocked even the tough conscience of the early Nineteenth Century, and humanitarian people, and especially Tory landlords who drew their wealth from the more genteel exploitation of the agricultural workers[1] began to agitate for the prohibition of some of the worst abuses. They would have found their agitation very unfruitful if other forces had not been operating to produce the same results.

As early as 1800–1815, in the years during which he managed the New Lanark Mills, Robert Owen had shown that output was not in direct proportion to the number of hours worked, and that it was possible to work a $10\frac{1}{2}$ hour day, to do without the labour of very young children, and yet to make substantial profits. With the development of faster, more accurate, more powerful, and more costly machines and with the substitution of steam power for water power, the advantages from a very long working day became less. It was always the water power mills where hours and conditions were worst and whose owners put up the most stubborn opposition to any kind of change. More capital was sunk in machinery, the relation between the capital so used and the capital used for the payment of wages gradually changed. The amount of actual manual labour needed to produce a given article decreased, and at the same time the speed at which the new machinery could work became increasingly greater than the speed at which the men and women who tended it could work for a day lasting for sixteen or eighteen hours. It became less economical to work the machine at part speed over a long day than at full speed over a shorter one.

This does not mean that the factory owners welcomed shorter hours or allowed the passing of the Factory Acts without a bitter struggle. The Factory Acts, politically speaking, were the product of two inter-related sides of the class struggle. First, they were extorted by the constant agitation of the working classes themselves, who linked their demands for Parliamentary Reform with demands for shorter hours, higher wages, better factory conditions

---

[1] The *Morning Chronicle* published figures showing that on the estates of the Earl of Shaftesbury labourers earning 7s. to 8s. a week were being charged 1s. 6d. and 2s. for the rent of their cottages.

and the abolition of child labour, and, indeed, regarded Reform largely as a means of securing these things. Secondly, they were a by-product of the savage internal struggle between the two main sections of the ruling class, the industrialists and the landowners.

The industrialists were pressing for the repeal of the Corn Laws, since cheaper food would enable them to reduce wages and so compete more effectively in the world market. In revenge, and to prevent too much attention being concentrated on themselves, the landowners campaigned against the long hours and oppressive conditions in the factories of their rivals. Oastler, the Tory Chartist and leader of the Ten Hours Agitation, curiously illustrates in his own person the point of contact of the two tendencies.[1]

Marx in 1847 commented that:

"The English workers have made the English free traders realise that they are not the dupes of their illusions or of their lies; and if, in spite of this, the workers have made common cause with them against the landlords, it is for the purpose of destroying the last remnants of feudalism and in order to have only one enemy to deal with. The workers have not miscalculated, for the landlords, in order to revenge themselves upon the manufacturers, have made common cause with the workers to carry the Ten Hours' Bill, which the latter have been vainly demanding for thirty years, and which was passed immediately after the repeal of the Corn Laws."

The arguments of the manufacturers were both general and particular. There was an appeal to the sacred principles of *laissez faire*, the prevailing dogma that it was socially desirable that everyone should be free to follow his own "enlightened self-interest" and that thereby, in some mysterious way, the general good of the community would be furthered. On these grounds any State interference with industry was condemned as an infringement of natural law. It is worth notice, in passing, that in the

[1] See Chapter XIII, Section 2 and Chapter XIV, Section 2.

heyday of *laissez faire* two important exceptions were made: one by which workers were legally forbidden to form combinations to improve their wages and the other by which the landlords were able to secure the prohibition of the import of wheat.

Apart from these general principles the menace of foreign competition was urged.[1] It was argued that to restrict hours or to force employers to fence their machinery would make it impossible for them to sell their goods abroad. In this way factory legislation, however well-meaning, would only lead to unemployment and greater misery for the workers. Another favourite argument was that "all profits are made in the last hour" and that therefore to reduce the hours of work by one would automatically destroy all profits. These arguments, as it proved, were so completely at variance with the economic facts that they convinced few people besides those who put them forward.

The first legislation, passed in 1802, was a very mild Act to prevent some of the worst abuses connected with the employment of pauper children. It was followed by the Cotton Factories Regulation Act of 1819 which forbade the employment of children under nine in cotton factories and limited the hours of those between nine and sixteen to 13½. As no machinery was ever provided for the enforcement of this Act it remained a dead letter.

It was not till 1833, after the passing of the Reform Bill and under pressure of a most violent working class agitation throughout the whole of the North of England, that an effective Act was passed. This prohibited the employment of children under nine except in silk factories,[2] limited the hours of older children and provided a number of factory inspectors to see that these restrictions were

[1] Except in the case of the 'climbing boys'. Here there was no question of foreign competition, and defenders of this particular atrocity had to do a little independent thinking.

[2] Silk was the only textile industry faced with serious foreign competition. Engels commented: "The monopoly that the hypocritical free traders repealed with regard to foreign competitors, that monopoly they created anew at the expense of the health and lives of English children.

carried out. Finally in 1847 the Ten Hours' Bill limited the hours of women and young people, and, in practice, secured a ten hour day for most of the men, since it proved unprofitable to keep the factories open for them alone. This result was not achieved for some years, however, during which the employers tried every conceivable evasion and device short of flat defiance of the provisions of the Act.

These Acts applied only to the textile industries. They did not apply, for example, to mining, and the Mines Commission of 1842 disclosed that the conditions had actually become worse since the Act of 1833 had resulted in an increase of child labour in the mines, especially in Lancashire and the West Riding. The fact was that the wages of adult workers were so low that parents were forced to put their children into any occupation that was open for them.

Before each Factory Act was passed, the employers were full of insuperable difficulties, of things that had always been done by child labour and could not be done otherwise. Afterwards it was quickly found that machines could be devised to serve the same ends, usually with a saving of labour and production costs. "The compulsory regulation of the working day as regards its length, pauses, beginning and end, the system of relays of children, the exclusion of children under a certain age, etc., necessitated more machinery and the substitution of steam as a motive power in the place of muscles . . . in one word, the greater concentration of the means of production and a correspondingly greater concourse of work-people." (*Capital*, I, p. 479.)

Thus, for example, the extension of the Factory Acts to the match industry resulted in the invention of a dipping machine, which made the manufacture of matches much more healthy and at the same time, in one factory, enabled thirty-two young workers to do the work which had previously required 230.

Perhaps the most striking example of the way in which capitalists were able to turn the labours of the humanitarian to their advantage is provided by the Davy lamp. Sir Humphrey Davy was so shocked at the prevalence of accidents in the mines that he invented, in 1816, his lamp to prevent explosions. The lamp was quickly and widely adopted, Davy himself refusing to take any royalties for what he regarded as his gift to humanity. The actual result was an increase in the number of accidents, since the owners were able to open up deeper and more dangerous seams, and, in many cases, the existence of the lamp was made an excuse for not providing proper ventilation.

If the Factory Acts led to the use of more and better machinery, this result was not of course uniform. Only the larger and more prosperous concerns were able to carry out the necessary changes in such a way as to increase their profits. The factories that were already the most obsolete, and especially the old water-power mills, were just those which could not be adapted to meet the new conditions. Some went under or were absorbed by richer firms, but their disappearance did not mean that the industries as a whole declined. On the contrary, the Factory Acts led to an increase in industry by providing a stimulus to the adoption of more efficient methods and at the same time led to a concentration in the hands of the largest and most modernised firms, with a corresponding concentration of capital. They actually helped the larger concern to drive the smaller out of the market.

Another result of factory legislation was, as Marx said, "to spread the mass of labour previously employed more, evenly over the whole year; that this regulation was the first rational bridle on the murderous meaningless caprices of fashion, caprices that consort so badly with the system of modern industry; that the development of ocean navigation and of the means of communication generally has swept away the technical basis on which season-work was really supported. . . . But for all that, capital never becomes reconciled to such changes—and this is admitted over and over again by its own representatives—except 'under pressure of a General Act of Parliament' for the compulsory regulation of the hours of labour."

Factory legislation, in short, however much the factory owners may have disliked it, was a part and perhaps a necessary part of that development which included the displacement of water power by steam, the wholesale use of machinery to manufacture not only consumption articles but the means of production themselves and the transfer of the decisive point in production from the small to the large unit which constitutes the final triumph of industrial capitalism in England. The time had come for this triumph to result in an open conflict between the industrial capitalist and the landlord and financier combination for political supremacy.

4. THE ROOTS OF LIBERALISM

From 1793 the Tory Party was able to collect behind it the bulk of all the property-owning classes for the struggle against Jacobinism at home and abroad. The Whig remnant, which was not prepared to join the anti-Jacobin front and was yet incapable of leading a mass movement against a government, which, after all, represented the classes from which its members also came, ceased to be of any practical importance. It was a sect, based upon tradition and sentiment rather than upon any genuine class interest. Parliamentary politics inevitably became more of a struggle between groups within the Tory Party than between parties. For though the Tories united all sections of the upper classes they did not place them all upon an equal footing.

The landowners, with the City merchants and the finance oligarchy, who usually ended by buying landed estates and showed great aptitude for acquiring the character and outlook of the landowners, kept the reins of power in their own hands. The industrial capitalists continued to be regarded as outsiders, against whom the political game, with its jobbery and manipulation of boroughs, was kept rigidly closed. Few of the new factory towns of the North, where their strength lay, sent members to Parliament. Factory owners might and sometimes did buy land and so acquire a political standing, but as a class they had their own special interests, often bluntly opposed to those of the landlords and bankers. Their whole character and outlook was bourgeois and not aristocratic.

The first great cleavage came in 1815, after the external Jacobin danger had been finally laid, over the Corn Laws, which the industrialists regarded as a sacrifice of their interests to those of the landlords. For a time, the internal ferment which culminated in Peterloo prevented an open break, but from about 1820 there were many signs of coming change. One was the revival of the Whigs on a new basis. The eighteenth century Whigs had been aristocratic and commercial: the nineteenth century Whigs, who soon came to call themselves Liberals, were a party of the industrial capitalists and the middle class of the large towns, led, however, at first, by the members of the old Whig aristocracy who had survived from the pre-Revolution age.

Equally striking and more immediately important was the change in character and ultimate break up of the Tory Party which found expression first in a change of policy at home and abroad and finally in the passing over of a large section of the Tories to join the Whigs just before the passing of the Reform Bill. On the death of Castlereagh, which coincided with the revival of trade and the dying down of the agitation for Reform, a new group headed by Canning and including Huskisson, Palmerston, sometimes Peel and other 'moderate' Tories came to the front. They found themselves often in conflict with the High Tories led by Wellington and Lord Eldon.

With the new situation new tactics had become necessary. The 'Six Acts' had staved off one revolutionary crisis, but the more far-seeing members of the ruling class began to understand that such methods were unlikely to be always effective in the future. They were not unwilling to coerce (as the events of 1830 and, later, of the Chartist period were to show) but they preferred to avoid the necessity of coercion where other methods would serve. The result was a whole series of 'liberal' measures, both before and after the Reform Bill, which had as their object the unobtrusive strengthening of the State apparatus, and which, though apparently less repressive than those of the Peterloo era, were in fact much more effective.

Such was the change which took place in the criminal code during the Home Secretaryship of Peel (1823–1830). Under the old code there were some 200 crimes, many of them of the most trivial character, which were punishable by death. Yet crime was widespread, partly because there was no system of police other than the utterly inefficient organisation of night-watchmen, so that the chances of escaping detection were always high, and partly because the very severity of the code led juries to acquit prisoners who were obviously guilty rather than send them to be hanged for some petty theft.

Peel and the other reformers supposed that crime was likely to be decreased, not by making the law more severe but by imposing penalties that really could be enforced and by creating a police force which would be likely to catch a reasonable proportion of the criminals. The re-shaping of the criminal code was therefore followed by the establishment of a new police force (Peelers), first in London and extending gradually to the provinces.

For political purposes the police had the advantage of strengthening the power of the State without the danger of serious internal disorder which the use of the yeomanry or of regular troops always involved. At the same time, the decline of Radical agitation after 1820 made it possible to relax the censorship imposed on the press and to withdraw many of the spies and provocateurs from the Radical and working-class organisations. It was now obviously wise to avoid rather than to provoke disorder. The partial repeal of the Combination Acts in 1824 was similar in effect. So long as Trade Unions were illegal every Union was the ground for a possible conspiracy. Francis Place, to whose astute lobbying the repeal was largely due, had persuaded the Government, and possibly himself, that once legalised Trade Unions would become unnecessary and would decay and disappear.[1]

In somewhat the same spirit Huskisson at the Board of Trade set about revising the tangle of tariffs, some protective and some imposed for revenue purposes, with which the Statute Book was cumbered. Protection, necessary at an earlier stage, was now a nuisance to industries which had no visible rivals and only wished to produce as cheaply and sell their goods as widely as possible. Huskisson abolished some tariffs, reduced more to a nominal figure and opened the way to a general abolition by a system of Imperial Preference, then a halfway-house to Free Trade rather than to Protection. Huskisson had a higher opinion of the commercial value of colonies than had been current since the American War of Independence, and was in a sense the father of the school of Liberal Imperialists. The Navigation Laws were considerably modified, and the general effect of the changes was to promote the import of raw materials at the lowest possible prices.

After 1822, Canning became Foreign Secretary, and here, too, policy developed along 'liberal' lines. During the years following Waterloo Britain had tagged along rather reluctantly behind the Holy Alliance, consenting rather than participating in its activities as the policeman of European reaction. But by 1822 the immediate danger of revolution had passed, and was replaced, from the point of view of the British Government, by the much more real danger of the permanent domination of Europe by Austria, Russia and Prussia. Canning therefore fell back upon the old Balance of Power principle, by inclining towards an understanding with France, now a highly respectable power with a Bourbon monarchy and quite

[1] See p. 413 below.

prepared to engage in repressive activities in Spain when a democratic revolution broke out there in 1822.

Canning did nothing to interfere, but sent an army to see that this intervention did not extend to Portugal and made it quite clear that no interference would be tolerated in South America. Here, British interests were direct and considerable. The Spanish colonies in America had cut themselves loose during Napoleonic Wars when they were isolated from Europe by the British naval blockade. Since 1815 a series of wars had been fought, but Spain had never been able to re-establish an effective control. The British merchant class, for whom South America had become an important market since the war, assisted the rebels with loans. Six thousand British volunteers had fought in their ranks under General Boliver and their navy was commanded by a former officer of the British Navy, Lord Cochrane. Canning's 'Liberalism' was therefore a natural result of the reluctance of the British bourgeoisie to allow a great market, in which they had secured a virtual monopoly, to slip out of their hands.

Finally, the revolt of the Greeks against Turkish rule opened that Eastern Question that runs so tortuously through the history of the Nineteenth Century. Here Austria and Russia were on opposite sides and Canning saw in intervention in Greece a method of splitting the Holy Alliance. He was careful to intervene in such a way as not to strengthen the position of Russia in the Balkans or allow her to advance farther along the shores of the Black Sea towards Constantinople. A British, French and Russian fleet defeated the Turks at Navarino in 1827, but both Britain and France were careful that the new Greek State should not be under Russian control.[1]

The Whigs co-operated to a large extent with the policy of the Government during these years, and there seemed a probability that they would merge into the Canning group, which had much more in common with them than with the High Tories. The death in 1827 of Lord

[1] See Chapter XIII, Section 3.

Liverpool, the Prime Minister, a nonentity who had served to prevent open war between the Canning and Wellington groups, laid bare the disintegration of the Tory Party. Canning formed a Ministry of his own followers, with Whig support and with the High Tories more or less in opposition. Six months later, he too died and after a period of confusion Wellington formed a Government from which Huskisson, who had succeeded to the leadership of the Canning Tories, soon resigned. The state of the Tories can only be compared to that of the Whigs about 1760.[1]

Professor G. M. Trevelyan seizes one aspect of the position very acutely when he writes:—

"The political history of the period is bewildering to the student, and rich in paradoxical happenings, because, while the old parties were breaking up, 'the spirit of the age' and the constant pressure of the unenfranchised from without overwhelm from day to day the policies of the nominal holders of power. The scene has all the confused inconsequence of a great military retreat, when no one knows what anyone else is doing, and positions are taken up only to be abandoned."

The point was precisely that behind the personal squabbles and the "confused inconsequence" of the politicians, and working through them, were vast new class combinations, that the Industrial Revolution had reached the point at which the class it had engendered was becoming strong enough to dictate a new policy even before it had acquired direct political power. As often happens in such times, the Government was driven to actions which were immediately inevitable but certain to be ultimately disastrous to themselves.

Hardly had Wellington taken office than he was faced with the alternative of civil war or agreeing to Catholic Emancipation in Ireland. He chose the latter, though he knew that for the Established Church, the main prop of the High Tories, Catholic Emancipation was the

[1] See page 302 above.

unspeakable thing for which there could be no pardon. By this almost accidental event, accidental, that is, in the sense of having no direct connection with English internal politics, the destruction of the Tory Party was completed. It was left with neither cohesion nor leadership, common principles, nor common policy. And the precise character of the coming change was determined by the fact that the Canning Tories were merged into the Whigs and not, as had at one time appeared probable, the Whigs in the Canning Tories.

When, in the late twenties, the trade revival turned again into a slump, and the Whigs could release against the Tories and against the sinecures and absurd anomalies of the unreformed Parliament the discontent of the hungry masses, there was no force left that could offer any effective resistance.

5. THE REFORM BILL

By 1830 the economic crisis had reached its height. Factories were closing down, unemployment increased rapidly, and the wages of those still employed fell. In the South the movement of revolt already described broke out in the autumn. In the North Trade Unions sprang up like mushrooms and the air was full of wild rumours of workers arming and drilling. The revolution which took place in Paris in July and in Belgium in August helped to increase the tenseness of the atmosphere.

As in 1816, economic distress led quickly to a demand for Parliamentary Reform. There was this important difference, that while from 1816 to 1820 the demand for Reform had come almost entirely from the working class, it was now a middle class demand as well. Having far closer contact with the masses than the Tories had, the factory owners and shopkeepers realised the dangers of mere repression and set to work to turn the discontent of the people into a weapon for securing their own political supremacy.

The agitation for Reform was therefore more widespread and more dangerous than ever before and though Reform meant quite different things to different classes it was possible for a wire-puller as brilliant as Place to gloss over these differences and even to turn them to good account. When Lovett and the Owenites created their National Association of the Working Classes and Others, known popularly as the Rotundists from their usual place of meeting,[1] with a programme of universal suffrage, a secret ballot, and annual parliaments, Place saw at once the danger and the value of such an organisation. It was dangerous because it meant business, and because it regarded Parliamentary Reform as the first step towards social reform and economic equality. It was useful because it could be turned into a weapon with which to blackmail the Tories into acquiescing in a certain measure of Reform (enough for the needs of the middle classes) as an alternative to Revolution, which Place and the Whigs were never tired of painting in lurid colours while claiming that it was only being averted with the greatest difficulty by their own tact and moderation.

Bronterre O'Brien, later a leader of the Chartists, exposed this device bluntly in the *Poor Man's Guardian*, the organ of the Rotundists:—

"Threats of a 'revolution' are employed by the middle class and 'petty masters' as arguments to induce your allowance of their measures . . . a violent revolution is not only beyond the means of those who threaten it, but is to them their greatest object of alarm."

To make the fullest use of the situation, Place created his own National Political Association, a body under middle class control but with a large working class membership which could be stimulated to produce the necessary revolutionary scare within carefully controlled limits. It worked in close harmony with Thomas Attwood's Birmingham Political Union and kindred organisations in all parts of the country. The Rotundists

[1] Now the Blackfriars Ring.

only influenced the most advanced sections of the workers, and the Reform Bill did undoubtedly win the enthusiastic support of the majority, although it gave them few direct benefits. Why this was so can only be understood by considering the character of the unreformed Parliament and of the proposed changes.

The character of Parliament, the classes which dominated it, the methods by which elections were carried out, its unrepresentative nature and the accompanying system of sinecures and jobbery differed in no fundamental respect from that prevailing in the eighteenth century and already described.[1] A few sinecures had been abolished and corruption was forced by the growth of criticism to be a little more discreet, but these gains were more than outweighed by two changes for the worse.

The growth of population since 1760, and the changed distribution of that population, had made the members even less representative. Great new towns had sprung up which returned no members: these included Manchester, Birmingham, Leeds and Sheffield. Many of the old boroughs had remained small or had even declined in population. So that, quite apart from the fact that members did not in any case represent the bulk of the inhabitants of the places for which they sat, the industrial areas were almost disfranchised as compared with the rural areas and small but old market towns dominated by the local gentry. And, second, the class of forty shilling freeholders in whom the county franchise was vested had been almost swept out of existence by the enclosures. With the disappearance of the class of yeomen the electors were mainly the landowners and a heterogeneous collection of individuals who chanced to have smaller holdings of land.

The Reform Bill had really two sides. One regularised the franchise, giving the vote to tenant farmers in the counties (and thereby increasing the influence of the

[1] See Chapter X, Section 2.

landlords in these constituencies) and to the occupiers of houses valued at over £10 per annum in the boroughs, that is, to the town middle class. In a number of boroughs the right to vote was actually taken from a large number of people who previously had exercised it. About this side of the Bill the working class was naturally unenthusiastic, but it was carefully kept in the background while a furious campaign was worked up against the rotten boroughs and the sinecurists.

The really popular part of the Bill was that which swept away the rotten boroughs and transferred their members to the industrial towns and the counties. Fifty-six boroughs lost both their members and thirty more lost one. Forty-two new constituencies were created in London and the large towns and sixty-five new members were given to the counties. The workers were persuaded that once the old system of graft and borough-mongering was swept away they could count on an immediate improvement in their conditions. Most of them believed this: hence the enthusiasm aroused by the Bill and hence their speedy and complete disillusionment afterwards.

The general election of August 1830 was held early in the development of the great Reform agitation, but late enough to give a small majority to the various groups pledged to Reform but not yet amalgamated into the re-constituted Whig Party. In November Wellington was forced to resign and a Whig ministry took office, just in time to incur the odium of the stamping out of the revolt of the village labourers.

In March the new Prime Minister, Grey, and his lieutenant, Lord John Russell, introduced the Reform Bill, whose most striking and unexpected feature was the proposal to abolish all the rotten and pocket boroughs without compensation to their owners. Macaulay has described the scene in the Commons when the Second Reading was carried by a majority of one:—

"And the jaw of Peel fell; and the face of Twiss was as the face of a damned soul; and Herries looked like

Judas taking off his necktie for the last operation. We shook hands, and clapped one another on the back and went out laughing, crying and huzzaing into the lobby." It should be added, to complete the picture, that Macaulay had just made his most famous speech, supporting the Bill as an alternative to "the wreck of laws, the confusion of ranks, the spoliation of property and the dissolution of the social order".

A few days later the Government was defeated in committee and resigned. A new election was held in May amid intense excitement. Almost every seat with any kind of popular franchise, including seventy-four of the eighty county seats, was carried by the Whigs, and this, with about one-third of the rotten boroughs held by them, was enough to give them a majority of 136. The Bill passed through the Commons but was rejected by the Lords in October. It is significant that most of the votes against came from the Bishops and the host of war profiteer peers created by Pitt.

It was at this point that the machinery thoughtfully prepared by Place was really set in motion. With the help of secret Government funds and money provided by wealthy supporters of the Bill widespread riots were staged and reports were circulated of vast insurrectionary movements arising in the industrial towns. To a large extent the popular indignation against the Lords was quite genuine and the general unemployment and hunger gave the masses good reason to riot and demonstrate. Amid this excitement the demands of the Rotundists for universal suffrage appeared academic and remote from the actual political conflict. In this way the Whigs were able to get the better of two sets of enemies at the same time.

The Lords were given some months for the lesson to sink in. Meanwhile a great part of the centre of Bristol was burned down, Wellington and the Bishops had their windows broken, scores of petitions rained in from all over the provinces and London was the scene of huge and stormy demonstrations. In December a new Bill was introduced into the Commons and on April 13th it was passed by a small majority in the House of Lords.

The Tories, however, then tried to emasculate the Bill in committee and in May the Government resigned. Wellington tried to form a new Government but was unable to secure even the support of his own party. Place and the Whigs, perhaps alarmed at the success of their previous manipulation of mass fury, employed the new but equally effective device of a run on the banks. After nine days Wellington gave up his attempt and Grey returned with a promise from William IV to create enough new peers to force the Bill through the Lords. Before this threat they surrendered and the Bill passed into Law on June 7th, 1832.

Meagre as it seems in many ways (it increased the electorate only from about 220,000 to about 670,000 in a population of 14,000,000), its importance can hardly be exaggerated. First, by placing political power in the hands of the industrial capitalists and their middle class followers it created the mass basis for the Liberal Party which dominated politics throughout the middle of the nineteenth century. In the fifty-five years between 1830 and 1885 there were nine Whig and Liberal Governments which held office for a total of roughly forty-one years: in the same period six Tory governments had only fourteen years of office. Striking as this is, it is more remarkable still that the Tories were only able to govern at the cost of carrying through what were really Liberal policies, as in the case of the repeal of the Corn Laws and the Reform Bill of 1867. The Reform Bill created the political institutions necessitated by the economic revolution of the two preceding generations.

Second, it altered the political balance as between Commons, Lords and Crown. The Commons gained at the expense of the Lords because they were now able, however fraudulently, to claim to be the representatives of the people against a clique of aristocrats and because the abolition of the rotten boroughs robbed the peers of much of their power to control the composition of the Lower House. For the same reason the Crown lost the last of its means of direct interference in Parliamentary politics. By ceasing to have at its disposal the patronage and power of corruption it had wielded in the Eighteenth Century it ceased to have a following of its own in the House of Commons. From this time the influence of the Crown, though often considerable, had to be exercised secretly and indirectly, through its private contacts inside the ruling class and with the heads of foreign States. It was for this reason that it remained much more powerful in foreign than in home affairs.

The third consequence of the passing of the Reform Bill, though perhaps the most important, was unintended and indirect. The workers who had done most of the fighting soon realised that they had been excluded from all the benefits, and the Poor Law Act of 1834 convinced them that the Whigs were at least as indifferent to their interests as the Tories had been. It was not accidental that the years immediately after 1832 were marked by a disgusted turning away of the masses from parliamentary politics to revolutionary Trade Unionism, or that, when the limitations of this weapon had been exposed, they proceeded to build up in the Chartist Movement the first independent political party of the working class.

CHAPTER XIII

LIBERAL ASCENDANCY

I. THE NEW POOR LAW AND THE RAILWAY AGE

THE YEARS AFTER 1832 were spent by the Whig bourgeoisie in digging themselves in, in consolidating their position at the expense both of the landowners and of the workers whom they had been forced to accept as allies during the struggle for the Reform Bill. Their first task was to extend the victory of 1832 into the sphere of local government. If the parliamentary system had been antiquated and chaotic, the government of the boroughs was perhaps worse. Towns were controlled by corporations elected anyhow and usually representing some local landowner or a clique of influential individuals within the town. Many of the newer towns, having grown out of villages in the last generation or two, had no real administrative machinery at all. The country districts were governed despotically by the Justices of the Peace, while a great confusion of committees with unco-ordinated functions and conflicting claims had been set up from time to time to deal with special problems. In this confusion corruption and inefficiency naturally flourished.

The Burgh Act in Scotland (1833) and the Municipal Reform Act in England (1835) swept away most of these bodies and replaced them by corporations elected, in the first case, by the ten pound householders and in the second by all ratepayers. In practice this ensured the control of most of the larger towns by the Whig middle class, since it was not till late in the century that the working class began to enter municipal politics as an independent force.

The rural districts were left, as the Whigs had been forced to leave them after 1688, in the hands of the Tory squirearchy. It was only in 1888 that County Councils were set up to provide any form of local self-government for the areas not included in the boroughs. This duality in local administration gave the landlords as a class a continued social basis throughout the whole period of the ascendancy of the industrial capitalists. It enabled them to fight a prolonged battle over the Corn Laws, and made the two-party system of parliamentary government a reflection of the division within the British ruling classes.

Among the other measures of this first post-Reform Whig Government, the Factory Act of 1833 has been dealt with already and the abolition of negro slavery will be dealt with in a later section.[1] The intense class conflicts amid which these changes took place will also be described later, but it is necessary that they should be kept constantly in mind. Nothing aroused more bitter class feelings, or revealed more completely the real character of Whig rule, than the Poor Law of 1834, which applied to the solution of the most vexed of all the problems of local government the principles of the orthodox political scientists of the day.

A revision in the Poor Law was necessary to the ruling class for two reasons. First, because a crisis in national and local finance appeared to be rapidly approaching. In 1815, out of a total budget of £67,500,000, roughly £25,500,000 had been raised by direct taxation, over £14,000,000 coming from the income tax. After the war the bourgeoisie were able to secure the abolition of the income tax, and in 1831 only £11,500,000 out of a total revenue of £47,000,000 was obtained by direct taxation. This amount was no more than two fifths of the sum paid as interest to the holders of the National Debt. The result was a series of unbalanced budgets, together with an altogether disproportionate burden of taxation upon the mass of the people.

[1] See Chapter XV, Section 4.

Locally, the Speenhamland system, growing less and less suited to the needs of an industrial country, had brought many parishes almost to bankruptcy. After dropping almost to four and a half million pounds in the middle twentiest the Poor Rate, under the influence of the economic crisis, had shot up again to over £7,000,000 in the financial year 1831-2.

The Speenham system was not, however, merely expensive. It also prolonged the struggle of small scale against factory industry and dammed the supply of cheap labour which the manufacturers wished to see flowing into the industrial towns. For a generation the hand weavers and petty craftsmen had fought desperately to escape the factories. Year by year their incomes had fallen till a man could not hope to earn more than five or six shillings for a full working week. Even with the help of poor law grants these were starvation wages—but at least the weavers and the unemployed and casually employed farm labourers starved in the open air. In 1834 they were offered a choice between the factory and the workhouse. Thus the Poor Law by abolishing outdoor relief brought fresh sections of the workers into profit-earning employment, much as the hut tax brought the African negroes at the end of the century.

The principle of the new law was simple: every person in need of relief must receive it inside a workhouse. Throughout the Speenhamland period workhouses had survived as places mainly for the reception of the aged, the disabled, of children and of all those too helpless and too defenceless to avoid being imprisoned there. These workhouses were taken as the model on which many more were built, not now by separate parishes but by groups of parishes known as 'unions'.

For the new system to have its full effect it was necessary that the condition of the pauper should be 'less eligible, than that of the least prosperous workers outside. In the sinister language of Poor Law Commission of 1834, the able bodied inmate must be "subjected to such courses of labour and discipline as will repel the indolent and vicious". At a time when millions of people were on the verge of starvation, this object could only be achieved by making the workhouse the home of every imaginable form of meanness and cruelty. Families were broken up, food was poor and scanty and the tasks imposed were degrading and senseless, oakum picking and stone breaking being among the most common.

The administration of the Act was deliberately removed as far as possible from popular control by the appointment of three virtually irresponsible Commissioners, the 'three Kings of Somerset House', who became for a whole decade, together with their Secretary, Edwin Chadwick, the most detested men in England. This action, and the reasons for it, curiously resemble the setting up of the Unemployment Assistance Boards by the National Government in 1934.

Cobbett, in the last year of his life, began the struggle against the 'Poor Law Bastilles' in the House of Commons, but it was left to others to carry it on and to merge it in the great class movement of Chartism. Nothing did so much as the Poor Law to make the Whigs unpopular or to convince the people that they had been cheated over the Reform Bill. Huge and angry demonstrations applauded such speakers as Oastler or the Methodist minister, J. R. Stephens, who declared at Newcastle that: "Sooner than wife and husband and father and son should be sundered and dungeoned and fed on 'skillie'—sooner than wife or daughter should wear the prison dress—sooner than that —Newcastle ought to be, and should be, one blaze of fire with only one way to put it out, and that with the blood of all those who supported this measure."

In some places workhouses were stormed and burnt after fierce clashes between people and troops. In many of the northern towns it was ten years or more before the new law could be regularly enforced. At Todmorden it was thirty years before a workhouse was built. The mass agitation, however, died with the passing of the first phase of Chartist activity about 1839 and the Poor Law was able to achieve its main objects both in the rural and industrial areas. In the late thirties the Poor Rate fell to between four and four and a half million pounds.

For this there were outside reasons, of which the most important was the coming of the Railway Age. In 1823 the Stockton-Darlington Railway had been opened: in 1829 the much more important line connecting Manchester and Liverpool. At first the railway was looked on only as a means of carrying goods, but it was soon discovered that the steam engine was capable of far higher speeds than had been imagined and that it could carry passengers more quickly and more cheaply than the stage coach.

A regular fever of railway building, accompanied by a speculation boom and much gambling in stocks and land values, set in. In the years 1834–6 about £70,000,000 was raised for railway construction. First in the industrial areas, then on the main routes radiating from London and then on the minor branches, thousands of miles of track were laid down. Much of the capital expended on these works brought in no immediate profit, and in 1845 there was a severe crisis extending to many branches of industry and affecting a large proportion of the banks. This crisis was rather the result of speculative optimism than of any real instability of the railway companies and soon passed, to be followed by an even greater outburst of building.

The result was what may almost be called a second Industrial Revolution. The Railway Age marks the beginning of an immense increase in all branches of industry, a strengthening of the monopoly of British manufacturers and the commencement of modern heavy industry. Exports rose from £69,000,000 in 1830 to £197,000,000 in 1850, but more important than this mere quantitative increase was the stimulus given to certain key industries especially coal mining and iron. The output of pig iron was 678,000 tons in 1830: in 1852 it was 2,701,000 tons. Coal output rose from ten million tons in 1800 to one hundred million tons in 1865.

Britain was not only the first country to construct a complete railway system for herself but soon began to build railways, at an immense profit, in countries all over the world, especially in the colonial and semi-colonial countries which had not a sufficiently dense population or sufficient concentration of capital to build for themselves.

In such cases railways were usually not only built by British contractors but financed by loans raised in London. In this way a new phase in British commerce was entered upon. Up to about 1850 exports were mainly of articles for consumption, and above all, of cotton textiles. From that date larger and larger quantities of iron ware, rails, locomotives and trucks and of machinery of all kinds were sent abroad. Britain began to export the means of production and the centre of gravity of British industrial capitalism began to shift from Manchester to Birmingham. It was a most profitable, but, in the long run, a suicidal progress, since in time it created and equipped rival industries in every continent.

The immediate internal effect of the railway boom was to create a large demand for labour, both directly for railway construction and indirectly in the coal mining, iron and steel and other industries. From 1830 thousands of navvies were at work, the number rising constantly till by 1848 there were nearly 200,000. Many were Irish, but the majority were probably English labourers 'released' by the Poor Law of 1834. Others went into the mines, where, being desperate and unorganised, they competed with the men already employed. Thus it was declared that in Stafford in 1843 the butties were "very apt to take men into the pit from the plough or other trades, who will come and work for 3*d*. or 4*d*. a day less than the regular miners".

In the second place, the railways made it much easier for workers to get from place to place, to leave the villages and find a factory town where work was to be had. The Poor Law Commissioners in 1835 and 1836 claimed in their reports to have had much success in assisting migration from the 'distressed areas' of East Anglia and the South to the North and Midlands.

A second kind of emigration was also made possible on a far larger scale than before by the railway and its complementary development the steamship. In 1837 the colonisation of New Zealand began. In 1840 the number of settlers in Australia was so large that its use as a convict station was virtually abandoned. Many emigrants went to Canada, while the building of railways in the United States (2,500 miles by 1840) opened vast new territories beyond the Alleghany Mountains. By 1840 about 70,000 people a year were emigrating, a number nearly doubled in the middle fifties with the discovery of gold in Australia and California.[1]

By 1840 the Whig Government was tottering. Five unbalanced budgets and a prolonged slump destroyed its prestige. The Poor Law was unpopular not only with the workers who had no votes but with a large section of the lower middle class who had. To other sections of the bourgeoisie the intense class struggles centred around the demand of the Charter seemed to demand an end to social experiment and the formation of a strong, reactionary government.

Besides this, the Whigs were unable, because of their peculiar class structure, to tackle the question of the Corn Laws, whose repeal was now becoming inevitable. The industrialists who formed the backbone of the party were set upon repeal, but the old Whig landowning families still occupied many of the leading positions and were unable to bring themselves to introduce a measure which they believed would drastically reduce their incomes as landowners. The shelving of repeal satisfied neither side and was everywhere correctly interpreted as a sign of weakness.

Under these circumstances the elections of 1841 resulted in a Tory victory and the formation of a government headed by Peel. The landowners were intensely relieved, but

[1] See Chapter XV, Section 2.

economic necessity soon pushed the new Government along the road to Free Trade and the repeal of the Corn Laws.

2. THE CORN LAWS

The Corn Laws of 1815 were the last clear-cut victory of the landowners as a class in England, but it was a suicidal victory because it inevitably isolated them from every other class and enabled the industrialists to pose, however hypocritically, as the champions of the whole people against a selfish and monopolising minority. The object of the Corn Laws was frankly to keep the price of wheat at the famine level it had reached during the Napoleonic Wars, when supplies from Poland and France were wholly or partly prevented from reaching England.[1] All wheat imports were forbidden when the price fell below 50s. the quarter.

From the beginning the Corn Laws were hated by everyone except the landowners and farmers, and even the latter found that in practice the fluctuations in wheat prices were ruinously violent and that the market was often manipulated so as to rob them of the profits they might have expected to make. Attempts in 1828 and 1842 to improve the Laws by introducing a sliding scale were not successful. Opposition to the Corn Laws, coupled with demands for Parliamentary Reform, were widespread throughout the Peterloo period, but died down after 1820, to be revived again by the coming of the industrial depression of 1837. This time it was an agitation not so much of the mass of the people as of the industrial bourgeoisie anxious to reduce labour costs.

From 1839, when the Anti-Corn Law League was formed by Cobden and Bright, it contended with the Chartists

---

[1] Even at the height of the war, in 1811, Napoleon was forced by the distress of the peasants of North France to allow corn to be exported to England. In other years the trade was often winked at by the authorities.

for the leadership of the working class. "The people," wrote Marx in 1847, "see in these self-sacrificing gentlemen, in Bowring, Bright and Co., their worst enemies and the most shameless hypocrites. Everyone knows that in England the struggle between Liberals and Democrats takes the name of the struggle between Free Traders and Chartists." Chartists organised counter-demonstrations to those of the League, brought the League speakers face to face with the facts of their condition, and in some industrial towns made it impossible for the League to hold meetings except those of their own supporters admitted by ticket. And C. R. Fay, the latest historian of the Corn Laws, describes how in the summer of 1842, the time of the great Lancashire turn out, "The red-hot orators of the League were transformed into pale policemen. The Delegates left London for the North, to keep there the peace of Her Majesty, whom Peel and Graham (the Tory Home Secretary) served."[1]

Nevertheless the Chartist agitation, which made the quarrel of Leaguers and Tories sound like the chattering of children, was one of the factors which had most to do with securing the repeal of the Corn Laws. Before the menace of revolution the warring sections of the ruling class were forced to sink their differences and, besides the repeal, to pass a Factory Act, a Coal Mines Act and the Ten Hour Act of 1847. It was the working class more than "rotten potatoes" that "put Peel in his damned fright".

It would be a mistake, too, to imagine that the League's agitation was without effect on the workers. Unprecedented in scale and lavishly financed (£100,000 was collected in 1843 and 9,000,000 leaflets distributed) this agitation had all the advantages that the railways, cheap newspapers and the penny post could give. Whenever Cobden or Bright spoke their words were widely reported in scores of papers and the League orators were able to move swiftly and easily all over the country.

[1] See p. 424 below.

They had facilities for spreading the Free Trade gospel that Pym and even Cobbett could never even have imagined.

In the light of this continued outside pressure, combined with the plain fact, which was becoming generally understood, that the growth of population was making it impossible for England to feed herself, the hesitating steps taken by Peel towards Free Trade after 1841 must be traced.

The first of these steps was dictated by the confused finance which he took over from the Whigs. A mass of tariffs and duties were swept away and replaced by an income tax which was both simpler and more productive, and in the long run less burdensome upon industry. These tariffs, being industrial, were not defended by Peel's landowning supporters. But the effect of their disappearance, whether intended or not, was to leave the Corn Laws as an isolated anomaly, increasingly conspicuous and increasingly difficult to defend.

In these years Peel appears to have made a thorough study of the situation and to have realised that the belief common among landowners that vast stores of wheat were lying in the Baltic granaries ready to be poured into England was a pure fantasy. He knew, what few people on either side knew, that the surplus for export in any country was still quite small and that the most the repeal of the Corn Laws would do would be to prevent an otherwise inevitable rise in prices which might have had revolutionary consequences. He was, therefore, quite prepared, when the Irish famine provided him with an excuse, to force through the repeal against the will of the majority of his own supporters.

Before this point was reached, however, there was a political crisis with important results. Faced in the winter of 1845 with a revolt inside the Tory Party, Peel resigned. The Whigs, who had been forced by the pace set by the League to declare for complete repeal, set about forming a government. Suddenly, and on the thinnest of excuses,

N1

Lord John Russell announced that he could not form a government and handed back the responsibility to Peel. For once, an act of unashamed political cowardice was overwhelmingly rewarded. By forcing Peel to destroy the Corn Laws with Whig support, Russell precipitated a break within the Tory Party which left it helpless for twenty years.

The revolt against Peel was led by a young and almost unknown Jewish politician, Benjamin Disraeli, and it was Disraeli who re-created the Tory Party at the beginning of the age of imperialism, no longer primarily as a party of the landowners but as the party of the new power of finance capital.[1] When Peel died in 1850 a number of the Tory Free Traders joined the Whigs. Among them was William Ewart Gladstone, then aged 41.

The Corn Laws were repealed in June 1846, a small, temporary tariff being retained till 1849. The effect was hardly what had been expected. There was no fall in prices, in fact the average for the five years 1851–5 was 56s. against 54s. 9d. in the five years 1841–5. For this there were a number of reasons: increasing population and a greater demand due to the revival of industry, bad harvests in a number of years and the Crimean War in 1853 which interrupted the import of wheat from Poland. New but relatively small sources of supply were opened up in Turkey, the U.S.A. and elsewhere, and it is quite obvious that if the Corn Laws had been in operation prices would have been still higher. Later still, the American Civil War interrupted the export of corn for several years, and it was not till about 1870, when the great wheat belt of the Middle West had been opened up by railways, that really large quantities of corn began to come in.

The manufacturers gained by repeal not through the cheapening of food, which had been their main argument when trying to win popular support, but by a larger flow of imports and a steadily expanding market

[1] See p. 409 below.

for their goods. Thus, as the import of wheat from the Levant increased, so the export of Lancashire cottons rose from £141,000 in 1843 to £1,000,000 in 1854.

In this respect the repeal of the Corn Laws must be regarded as part of the whole Free Trade legislation which helped to make the period between 1845 and 1875 the golden age of the manufacturers. Free Trade in corn was followed by Free Trade in sugar, and, finally, in 1860, in timber. Until the growth of industries abroad, nothing now stood between the British manufacturer and the markets of the world.

Engels sums up the whole period thus:

"The years immediately following the victory of Free Trade in England seemed to verify the most extravagant expectations of prosperity founded upon that event. British commerce rose to a fabulous amount: the industrial monopoly of England on the market of the world seemed more firmly established than ever: new iron works, new textile factories, arose wholesale; new branches of industry grew up on every side. . . . The unparalleled expansion of British manufactures and commerce between 1848 and 1866 was no doubt due, to a great extent, to the removal of protective duties on food and raw materials. But not entirely. Other important changes took place simultaneously and helped it on. The above years comprise the discovery and working of the Californian and Australian goldfields which increased so immensely the circulating medium of the world; they mark the final victory of steam over all other means of transport; on the ocean, steamers now superseded sailing vessels; on land in all civilised countries, the railroad took the first place, the macadamised road the second; transport now became four times quicker and four times cheaper. No wonder that under such favourable circumstances British manufactures based on steam should extend their sway at the expense of foreign domestic industries based upon manual labour."

Times were good for the British capitalists, and they regarded their good fortune as a law of nature and expected it to last for ever.

The effects of Corn Law repeal upon agriculture were much more surprising, unless they are regarded as a parallel to those of the Factory Acts upon industry. Instead of ruin, increased prosperity, instead of the acreage under the plough contracting, an expansion. The mere threat of foreign competition led to a number of improvements in technique. As compensation for their loss of the Corn Laws the landowners in Parliament advanced themselves money for improvements at a very low rate of interest, thus enabling themselves to add to the value of their land and make a handsome profit out of the farmers who were charged for the improvements at a considerably higher rate.

A machine for pipe making, invented in 1845, made land drainage possible on a large scale. This added greatly to the productivity of the heavy wheat-growing land, made it more workable and made the use of artificial manures profitable. Nitrates, guano and bone manure all came into common use at this time. Much new machinery was introduced, so that at the Royal Agricultural Society's Show in 1853 no fewer than 2,000 implements were exhibited.

A more direct stimulus to the use of machinery was given by the increase in the wages of farm workers which took place between 1845 and 1859 as the result of the great demand for labour in the mines, in the construction of railways, etc. In time, this increase in the use of machinery led to a reduction in the number of labourers employed, although the area under cultivation had increased by half a million acres and the total agricultural production had increased far more in proportion.

The greater application of capital to agriculture produced a further increase in the size of farms. Between 1851 and 1871 farms of all sizes below 100 acres decreased in number while farms of 300 acres and over increased from 11,018 to 13,006, the greatest proportional increase being in those of over 500 acres.

This period of prosperity lasted till the end of the short boom which followed the Franco-Prussian War. It then ended abruptly and a long depression set in with the arrival of American wheat and Australian wool in bulk. The improvement in the condition of the labourers ended much earlier when the rise in prices produced by the influx of Californian and Australian gold brought about a steady decline in real wages.

The simultaneous prosperity of industry and agriculture is the explanation of the remarkable absence of open conflict between manufacturers and landowners in the twenty years which followed the repeal of the Corn Laws. No great political issues divided the different sections of the ruling class till the resurgence of the Reform agitation in the sixties. Politics became a pleasant game, as in the Eighteenth Century, with Palmerston, embodiment of all the most conservative aspects of Whiggery, as presiding genius. The Great Exhibition of 1851, intended to usher in an era of universal peace but in fact followed by a new round of European wars, did nevertheless prelude in England a period of extraordinary social stability in which the details of political events became of far less interest than the steadily mounting statistics of exports and imports or the leaping and bounding of the income tax returns. It was, *par excellence*, the Victorian Age.

3. FOREIGN POLITICS: PALMERSTON TO DISRAELI

The principles underlying Liberal foreign policy in the middle third of the Nineteenth Century were extremely simple. They were the principles of the 'inspired bagman', the man with goods to sell. Behind the screen of a navy far larger than that of any rival Power the economic penetration of the British Empire and of the Far East was pushed ahead. In Europe all serious entanglements were avoided as far as possible, British influence being only exerted to prevent any one Power from securing a predominating position. The more powerful States were treated with the utmost circumspection: the smaller ones were bullied when ever bullying seemed likely to be profitable.

The embodiment of this policy was Lord Palmerston, who reigned almost without interruption at the Foreign Office from 1830 to 1865. In home affairs he belonged to the most reactionary section of the Whigs. In foreign affairs he has enjoyed an entirely undeserved reputation for Liberalism. Marx, in 1853, after a careful study of all the information then available declared bluntly that "Palmerston has been sold to Russia for several decades". Whatever the truth of this may be, and it is still impossible to arrive at any certainty, it is at least clear that the policy followed by Palmerston did play into the hands of Russia.

He encouraged the Poles to revolt in the expectation of help from England and then betrayed them, much as he encouraged and betrayed the Danes in 1864. He approved the sending of Russian troops to crush the Hungarian Revolution in 1848. His support of the revolution in Italy may have been the result of an appreciation of the fact that the unification of Italy would weaken Austria and so, indirectly, strengthen Russia. During the revolt of the mountain tribes of Circassia around 1850 Palmerston played a part not unlike that of Sir Samuel Hoare during Mussolini's recent conquest of Abyssinia. It was Palmerston, too, who hastened to recognise Napoleon III after his *coup d'état* in December 1851 and Palmerston who bears the heaviest responsibility for the predatory wars upon China in 1840 and 1860.

Nevertheless it was probably inevitable that England and Russia should clash after 1840. The failure of the revolutionary movement throughout Europe, a failure largely the result of Russian intervention, had left Russia without a rival on the Continent. Austria was decadent and bankrupt. Germany still divided into a patchwork of minor States which had not yet submitted to the primacy of Prussia; France, where the struggle had been most severe, still disturbed. Russia was "the great stronghold, reserve position and reserve army of European reaction".

What was more to the point immediately, the advance of Russia threatened the interests of the British bourgeoisie in two directions. First in Asia, where Turkestan was being devoured in giant bites. Already the Russian advance towards India was causing alarm, since India was now becoming the keystone of the whole structure of British industry and finance.[1]

The direct threat to India was perhaps remote in 1850: the threat through Turkey was more immediate. With the development of the steamship the Mediterranean route to India and the East had once more become important. Steamers still had great difficulty in using the Cape route, and there was still a lack of coaling facilities. From about 1835, therefore, regular steamship lines were running from England to Alexandria and from Suez to India. The Suez Canal was not opened till 1869 but plans for its construction were already well advanced. The growing importance of this corner of the Mediterranean is at least one good reason for the curious interest shown by both Russia and Britain in the Holy Places at Jerusalem round about 1850.

Russian penetration into Turkey would not only have placed her astride of the route to India; it would also have made her predominant in the Eastern Mediterranean where both France and Britain had considerable direct interests, while the presence of Russian troops on the Danube would have turned her already strong position in Central Europe into one of unquestioned mastery. The Turkish Empire at this time extended over the whole of the Balkan Peninsula, but its hold was weakening

[1] On the other hand, British exports to inner Asia grew rapidly from about 1850 at the expense of Russia.

and strong movements of national revolt were growing among the Serb, Bulgar and Roumanian populations. It was part of the policy of Tsarism to capture these movements and use them to weaken both Turkey and Austria.

Entirely selfish as were the motives of Britain and France in waging the Crimean War, a Russian victory would have been a disaster for progress and democracy throughout Europe. It was some realisation of this which made the war extremely popular in England, the only opposition coming from the Bright-Cobden group. It was absurd and hypocritical enough for the exploiters of India and Ireland or the sharks and adventurers who supported Napoleon the Little to inveigh against Tsarist tyranny, but among the masses, in whose minds the fate of Poland and Hungary was fresh, hatred of Tsarism was both genuine and generous.

The pretended reasons for the war, the guardianship of the Holy Places and the treatment of Christian minorities in Turkey, were entirely trivial. It was characteristic of the prolonged discussions that preceded the outbreak of war that the British Government, having agreed to terms with Russia, proceeded to induce the Turkish Government to reject them, by unofficial assurances, made through Lord Stratford de Redcliffe the Ambassador at Constantinople, of naval and military support in the event of war.

The military occupations, centred upon the siege of the naval base and fortress of Sebastopol, were one long series of blunders. Sebastopol could have been taken easily at any time for six weeks after the battle of the Alma (September 20th, 1854), but the French and British commanders decided through over-caution on a formal siege which they had not the forces to make effective. The besiegers soon found themselves caught by the winter, with neither the organisation nor the equipment that was required. Sickness and cold killed thousands and it was later stated by Florence Nightingale that of the

25,000 who died in the British forces, 16,000 were put to death by the inefficiency of the military system.[1]

The war was only successful because the Russian generals and administrators were even more incompetent. Serious weaknesses, which the outside world had not suspected, were revealed, weaknesses which were to become more apparent in the Russo-Japanese War and in 1914. Russia, economically and socially still in the Eighteenth Century, proved less and less capable of waging a large-scale war in exact proportion as the growing mechanisation of war demanded a basis in machine industry. In 1854 this process had only begun, and on both sides the arms, tactics and organisation hardly differed from those that had served in the Napoleonic Wars.

The fall of Sebastopol in September 1855 was followed by a peace treaty in which the real problem of Turkish rule in the Balkans was shelved, the Turkish Empire was patched together again and Russia was forbidden to fortify any harbours on the Black Sea or to keep any warships there.

This treaty had the desired effect of holding up the advance of Russia till 1870, when the victories of Prussia over France altered the whole balance of forces in Europe. The clauses in the treaty neutralising the Black Sea were denounced, and a new forward policy begun, culminating in the Russo-Turkish war of 1876. On this occasion a naval demonstration ordered by Disraeli checked the Russian advance without Britain becoming involved in actual war, and though, by the Treaty of San Stefano in 1878, a number of new States were carved out of the Balkan provinces of Turkey, this area did not become a Russian sphere of influence but a battle-ground between that country and Austria.

---

[1] This was the first and last war in which the home population had accurate information of what was happening. The job of War Correspondent had been created by the electric telegraph and had not yet been destroyed by military censorship. Hence the sensation caused by the despatches of Russell of *The Times*.

The Crimean War was the first of a series of European wars that were the natural result of the failure of the revolutions of 1848, which cast the rising centralised nation States into the form of military despotisms. It was followed by the Schleswig-Holstein War of 1864, the Austro-Prussian War of 1866, the series of wars connected with the unification of Italy and the Franco-Prussian War of 1870. After 1871 a new period opened, a period in which the formation of compact, aggressive States had been completed and these States began to form themselves into rival groups. This was the period of Imperialism, leading to the World War of 1914, and it will be discussed in later sections.[1]

In this series of wars Britain played only a small direct part and their effect on British history in this period was not great. Far more important in many ways was the American Civil War which began in 1861. This was at bottom a war to determine whether the future development of the U.S.A. was to be into an industrial country or one with a plantation economy, an economy in which foodstuffs and raw materials were produced for export by slave labour and which was governed by a slave-owning aristocracy. Beyond a certain point these two economies could not exist side by side and the war was therefore a class struggle between a landed aristocracy on the one side and bourgeois democracy on the other. It was a modified form of the struggle begun in Europe by the French Revolution, just as slavery was in certain respects the specifically American form of feudalism.

It was as a class struggle that it was regarded in England, and support was given to North and South on strictly class lines. Almost the whole ruling class was solid for the Southern slave-owners, the landowners from natural sympathy, the cotton and shipping magnates because the North blockaded the Southern ports and prevented cotton from reaching Lancashire. There was an influential demand for the recognition of the Southern Confederate

[1] See Chapter XVI.

Government, and every opportunity was taken to hamper and irritate the North. The climax was reached when the privateer *Alabama* was allowed to get away from Liverpool and worked havoc among the merchant shipping of the North.

The whole working class was equally solid in support of the North. This was most noteworthy in the case of the Lancashire cotton operatives, who suffered terribly from unemployment but resisted every effort of the employers to swing them into a campaign to force the North to raise the cotton blockade. It was this class conflict arising from the Civil War which first broke through the complete stagnation in which the working class movement had remained since the collapse of Chartism in 1848. It was the beginning of the agitation which led to the Reform Bill of 1867, to the rebirth of Socialism and to the rise of Fenianism in Ireland. These developments will be dealt with in later sections: it is only necessary here to touch on some of the economic effects of the Civil War.

Cotton in 1861 was still the most important British industry and the great bulk of the cotton spun in Lancashire came from the United States. In 1860 1,115 million pounds of cotton had been imported from the United States and 204 million pounds from India. By the autumn of 1863, when the famine reached its height, nearly 60 per cent. of the textile workers were unemployed. Those who were still working had their earnings greatly reduced by the substitution of inferior Indian and Egyptian cotton for that of America. Wages fell to 4s. and 5s. a week in a number of cases. For the workers the famine was an unrelieved tragedy: the employers were able, in the long run, to turn it into a source of additional profits. New cotton fields were established in Egypt and India (imports of Indian cotton had risen to 446 million pounds by 1865), the whole profit of which went to British instead of American capitalists. These cotton fields seriously decreased the area available for growing food in India and Egypt, already barely large enough for the needs of their peoples.

At the same time the famine eliminated a number of the smaller, less profitable mills and led to extensive rationalisation in the rest. By 1868, when the industry had once more returned to the normal, there were fewer factories at work, more spindles, greater output and 50,000 fewer operatives. In the weaving section, there was actually an increased output from fewer looms.

The permanent results were not quite so satisfactory. The victory of the North, once the disorganisation caused by the war had been overcome, led to the growth of a great textile industry, first in New England and later in the Southern States, protected by high tariffs. The increased imports of Indian and Egyptian cotton into Lancashire would probably by themselves have forced the United States to consume an increased proportion of their own raw cotton. In the long run the Civil War did much to destroy the monopoly of Lancashire and to hasten the transference, already referred to, of the centre of gravity of British industry from Manchester to Birmingham, a transfer followed in due course by corresponding political changes.

4. THE SECOND REFORM BILL

Palmerston died in 1865, after having been almost continuously since 1810 a member, first of Tory and then of Whig, ministries. His death completed the evolution of the Whig Party towards Liberalism, the winning free of the industrialists from the equivocal leadership of a group of aristocratic landowners. With Palmerston out of the way and Lord John Russell growing senile, the leadership of the party passed into the hands of Gladstone and the predominance of the industrialists found expression in the increasingly close relations existing between Gladstone and the official party leadership and the Radical group headed by Bright.

The alliance with the Radicals committed Gladstone to an acceptance of their demand for an extension of the parliamentary franchise. It was in this agitation that the renewed militancy of the working class, mentioned in the last section as one of the results of the American Civil War, became apparent. As early as 1861 some of the Trade Unions had taken up the question of Parliamentary Reform. In 1864 the International Working-Men's Association (First International) was founded, and it quickly acquired such a standing that early in 1865 the Cobdenites approached its General Council to secure their co-operation in the Reform agitation. In 1866 the London Trades Council, which had been formed in 1860 to co-ordinate support for a great builders' strike, took up the question and the London Working-Men's Association was formed.

There were thus two parallel agitations, one conducted by Cobden[1] and Bright and the bourgeois Radicals, the other by the Trade Unions, receiving much of their political inspiration from the International. It is important to remember that this was the first time for nearly twenty years that working-class organisations as such had interested themselves in political questions. The agitations sometimes converged and sometimes separated, as the Radicals attempted to water down the demand of the Unions for complete manhood suffrage. In 1866 Gladstone, to the great disappointment of the Left, introduced a Bill which only reduced the £10 property qualifications in the boroughs to £7. Even this was too much for the Whig remnant which had survived Palmerston, and a group known as the 'Adullamites' and led by Robert Lowe, went over to the Tories and brought about the defeat of the Government. The departure of this group had the effect of greatly increasing the weight of the Radicals inside the Liberal Party.

It had a further result no one, perhaps, anticipated. Gladstone's Bill had aroused a very moderate enthusiasm but Lowe had opposed it frankly on the ground that in principle the workers as workers were unfit for the franchise. It was the insolence of this challenge which

[1] Cobden died in 1865.

suddenly made Reform a class question and almost a question of honour. In the autumn of 1866 the ruling class was amazed and alarmed at the outburst they had provoked. In scores of industrial towns huge demonstrations were held in which almost the whole working and lower middle class population seemed to be taking part. In these demonstrations the Trade Unions normally took part as organised bodies with their banners. In London there were huge gatherings at Trafalgar Square and Hyde Park, the latter turning into a vast riot in which half a mile of railings were torn up. This was the immediate sequel to the formation of a Tory Government by Disraeli.

Disraeli had characterised all talk of an extension of the franchise as 'the doctrine of Tom Paine', but he had not counted on this storm. The Reform agitation, the birth of the International, the revival of Trade Unions, underlined by the 'Sheffield outrages' and the activities of the Fenians combined to convince the Tories that they were on the verge of a revolutionary outbreak, and it was as a concession to avert revolution that Disraeli brought forward his Reform Bill in 1867.

This Bill gave the franchise to all householders and certain others in the boroughs: it left voteless the agricultural workers and those industrial workers, including a large proportion of the miners, who did not happen to live in Parliamentary Boroughs. In 1885 the franchise was made uniform for both boroughs and counties. Almost equally important was the Ballot Act of 1872, which abolished open voting at the hustings. Without this Act the extension of the franchise to the agricultural workers would have been little more than a bad joke.

The great importance of the Reform Bill of 1867 was that it provided the basis for the formation of an independent parliamentary party of the working class. The Chartists had been an agitational party of the disfranchised, subject to violent fluctuations of fortune as conditions grew more or less favourable for their agitation. The Labour Party handicapped as it was by its origins in bourgeois Radicalism and by the opportunism of its leaders, grew up with one leg in the Trade Unions and the other in Parliament and so had a solidity which the Chartists never possessed.

A whole generation was required for the birth of this new party, and in the interval the immediate advantage went to the Radicals. At the election of 1868 a substantial Liberal majority was returned. The Whig element had been eliminated, the Radicals strengthened by the return of many of their group in the industrial towns, and when Gladstone formed his Government Bright received for the first time a seat in the Cabinet. The years that followed were marked by a number of important social reforms. The ruling class could afford to make concessions and the temper shown by the masses in 1866 was not quickly forgotten. Under the extended franchise both parties were forced to bid for working class support and there was little practical difference in internal policy whether the Government was Liberal as from 1868 to 1874 or Tory as between 1874 and 1880.

The establishment of a system of universal elementary education, the work of the Act of 1870 associated with the name of W. E. Forster, was one of the most important measures of this period. It was indeed urgently demanded by the requirements of industry in the new age. In the past it had not been important for the working class to be literate, but now, with the fiercer foreign competition that was being experienced and the higher standards of education existing in Germany, the United States and elsewhere, it was an obvious necessity. At the same time, as England became the commercial and financial centre of the world, an increasing number of clerks and supervisory workers were required, and these had to be drawn from the working class. Finally, the workers were showing a disturbing tendency to educate themselves, and there was no guarantee that this self-education would not develop along subversive lines.

The victory of Liberalism was also directly responsible for the reform of the Civil Service. In the past all branches of the Service had been the preserve of the aristocracy and their hangers on. The result was a bureaucracy that was neither capable nor honest. In 1870 all posts were thrown open to be competed for by public examination, and the Civil Service began to be staffed largely by the middle class. In certain branches, however, notably in the Foreign Office and the Diplomatic Corps, social qualifications continued to weigh very heavily and these remain even to-day in the hands of the upper class. A similar effect, with similar limitations, was secured in 1871 by the abolition of the practice of purchasing commissions in the Army.

These reforms, whose point turned rather against the aristocracy and against the Established Church which lost its virtual monopoly of elementary education, were the work of the Liberals. The Tories, as might be expected, concentrated rather upon factory legislation, housing and sanitation. During the Industrial Revolution, towns were allowed to grow up without check or plan, hideously ugly and barbarously unhealthy. It was not till the terrible cholera epidemic of 1831 and the following years had bludgeoned the rich into a realisation that pestilence could not be confined entirely to the slums, that anything at all had been done to secure adequate drainage or a supply of uncontaminated water. Further outbreaks in 1849 and 1854 made the authorities take more steps in the same direction, and the Public Health Act of 1875 co-ordinated and extended what had already been accomplished in sanitation.

In was during the government of Gladstone that attention was forced upon Ireland by the Fenians. Nothing could be more revealing than Gladstone's famous exclamation when he was called on to take office in 1868, "My mission is to pacify Ireland". Here 'pacify' is the operative word. For all sections of the ruling class, Ireland was a conquered province to be governed in their interests, peacefully if possible, but by violence when necessary. It was within the limits set by this conception that the whole struggle between Liberals and Tories over the Irish question was waged during the late Nineteenth Century. Their differences were purely tactical and it was among the working class alone that the belief that Ireland was a nation with the right to determine its own destiny found any support.[1]

One outstanding event of the period, and the one which marks decisively the turn into a new age, must receive more detailed consideration in a later chapter. This was the purchase by the British Government in 1875, on the initiative of Disraeli and with the assistance of the Rothschilds, of the shares in the Suez Canal held by the Khedive of Egypt. It is important both for its place in the development of the British Empire and for the close co-operation it reveals between the Tory Government and the powerful international finance oligarchy.

New figures appear on the scenes, Rothschilds, Goschens, Barings and the like and they exercise an increasing influence upon British policy and turn it into a new direction. As they grew in power, and as the influence of banking over industry extended the Liberal Party became more and more a party of the middle class and its authority diminished[2] while the rise of the Labour Party on the other side ate away its mass basis among the workers. It is entirely characteristic that it was just as the Tory Party ceased to be really representative of the landowners that it adopted a pretentiously self-conscious 'Merrie England' propaganda patter. The peculiar task of Disraeli was to reconcile the English aristocracy to their position of junior partner in the firm of Imperialism Unlimited.

[1] See Chapter XIV, Section 4.
[2] But note as an important counter tendency the growth of an Imperialist wing of the Liberal Party, often curiously touched as the case of Joseph Chamberlain, by Radicalism. This wing was of great importance in 1914. Latterly the interests of Imperialism have found the Tories more serviceable, but the Sir J. Simon group survives as a curiosity.

It was indeed a pressing necesisty for the British bourgeoisie to learn new ways, for in the late seventies a deep
economic and social crisis was upon them, not to be overcome so lightly as the periodic crises of the bounding
years of dominant Liberalism.

CHAPTER XIV

THE ORGANISATION OF THE
WORKING CLASS

I. REVOLUTIONARY TRADE UNIONISM

FROM THE EARLIEST times in which wage earners
have existed as a class, they have formed associations to
defend their interests and rights against their employers.
Such associations, whatever they may have been called,
and whether nation-wide organisations like the Great
Society of the Fourteenth Century or local craft bodies
like the Yeomen Gilds, were in essence Trade Unions.[1]
So it was, when the industrial proletariat came at the close
of the Eighteenth Century to be conscious of its corporate
existence, that the Trade Union was the form of organisation spontaneously adopted, and the early struggles of
this class were inspired by what may almost be called
revolutionary syndicalism.

The weapon lay ready to hand. In spite of the condition
of illegality in which the workers' organisations had to
exist in the Eighteenth Century, we have many glimpses
of their activity. A proclamation against unlawful clubs
in Devon and Somerset in 1718 complains that "great
numbers of wool combers and weavers . . . had illegally
presumed to use a common seal and to Act as Bodies
Corporate by making and unlawfully conspiring to execute
certain By-Laws or Orders, whereby they pretended to
determine who had a right to the Trade, what and how
many Apprentices and Journeymen each man should
keep at once . . . and that when many of the said conspirators wanted work because their Masters would not

[1] These were Gilds formed by journeymen, that is, wage labourers.
See p. 88 above.

submit to such pretended Orders and unreasonable demands, they fed them with Money till they could again get employment, in order to oblige their Masters to employ them again for want of other hands."

Three hundred Norwich wool weavers, again, in 1754, desiring to obtain an increase of wages, retreated to a hill three miles from the town and built huts, where they lived for six weeks supported by contributions from their fellow workers. By 1721 the journeyman tailors of London had a powerful and permanent Union, and early in the Eighteenth Century we hear of combinations and destruction of stocking machines in the Nottingham hosiery industry.

Such organisations were always liable to prosecution under the Common Law for conspiracy or for acts "in restraint of trade", and were expressly declared illegal in the wool industry by Act of Parliament in 1726. But until the advent of the Industrial Revolution and of large-scale factory industry they were of necessity localised and usually quite small bodies of craftsmen, obnoxious to their employers but not felt to be a menace to the State or to social organisation as a whole. These craft bodies were often allowed to exist without molestation except in times of special stress, and the existing law was felt to be strong enough to keep their activities within decorous limits.

The Industrial Revolution changed all this by making wider and more formidable combinations possible. When the industrial discontent was crossed with political Jacobinism the ruling class was terrified into more drastic action, and the result was the Combination Laws of 1799 and 1800. These laws were the work of Pitt and of his sanctimonious friend Wilberforce, whose well-known sympathy for the negro slave never prevented him from being the foremost apologist and champion of every act of tyranny in England, from the employment of Oliver the Spy or the illegal detention of poor prisoners in Cold Bath Fields jail to the Peterloo massacre and the suspension of *Habeas Corpus*.

The Act of 1799, slightly amended in 1800, made all combinations illegal as such, whether conspiracy, restraint of trade or the like could be proved against them or no. In theory, the Act applied to employers as well as to workmen, but though the latter were prosecuted in thousands, there is not a single case of any employer being interfered with. Only too often the magistrates who enforced the law were themselves employers who had been guilty of breaches of it. Prosecutions under the old common law also continued to be numerous.

Against the old-fashioned Craft Unions the Act was not regularly enforced, though there were a number of notorious cases like those of *The Times* compositors in 1810 or the coachmakers in 1819. It was the workers in the textile factories who were most affected. "The sufferings of the persons employed in the cotton manufacture," wrote Place, "were beyond credibility: they were drawn into combinations, betrayed, prosecuted, convicted, sentenced, and monstrously severe punishments inflicted upon them: they were reduced to and kept in the most wretched state of existence."

By 1800 the relatively high wages paid at first in some sections of the textile industries were already a thing of the past, and for twenty years they declined continuously. The severity of the law was not able to prevent the formation of Unions, and indeed there are few more splendid episodes in the history of the working class than the way in which the laws against combinations were defied, but it prevented union organisation from having much chance of success. Strikes were common and were carried through with remarkable tenacity, but the end was always wholesale arrests, broken organisation, defeat and new reductions in wages. Characteristic of the time was the long strike of Tyne and Wear seamen in 1815 against the undermanning of ships, a strike only broken by the calling in of troops and marked by bad faith on the part of the shipowners so flagrant that it scandalised even the Home Office representative sent into the area by Sidmouth.

In 1824 Place and others were able to push through Parliament a Bill repealing the Combination Laws, working so quickly and quietly that the employers were hardly aware of what was being done. The next year the latter were able to get the repeal modified by an Act which, though it left the formal existence of Unions legal, made illegal almost every kind of activity they were likely to undertake.

Even so, this was a great improvement on the status of before 1824, and there was an instant outburst of organising activity and strikes such as had never before been known. In August 1824 the Lancashire weavers met to establish a permanent organisation. The Manchester dyers struck for higher wages. There were strikes of Durham and London shipwrights and of Bradford wool-combers and weavers. The period was one of fiery energy, when Dick Penderyn was leading the ironworkers of Dowlais and Merthyr in a guerilla warfare against the yeomanry and regular troops that was only ended by his capture and execution in 1831. All through 1826 Lancashire was in the grip of almost continuous strikes, accompanied by wholesale destruction of looms and frequent clashes between strikers and soldiery.

It was in Lancashire that the first outstanding Trade Union leader appeared. John Doherty had served his apprenticeship in the days of illegality, when he became a trusted leader of the cotton spinners. Experience of defeat before and after 1824 convinced him of the necessity of uniting local organisations into a solid union, and he was the moving spirit in a conference of English, Scottish and Irish textile workers held in the Isle of Man in 1829, at which a Grand General Union of the United Kingdom was set up. This, in spite of its name, appears to have been a union of cotton spinners only, but in 1830 Doherty became secretary to the National Association for the Protection of Labour.

This was the first Trades Union, or Union of Trades, as distinct from organisations catering for one section of workers only. It aimed at uniting the whole working class, and did actually reach a membership of 100,000, while its weekly journal, although costing 7*d.* because of the high tax, had a circulation of 30,000.

The National Association soon perished for reasons that are still obscure, and the next important development was the Operative Builders' Union which was formed in 1833 out of a number of craft unions and soon reached a membership of about 40,000, mainly around Manchester and Birmingham. Early in 1834 this Union became merged in a new organisation, the Grand National Consolidated Trades Union.

In this the idea of the one big union reached its fullest embodiment. Its objects are stated in one of the rules: "That although the design of the Union is, in the first instance, to raise the wages of the workmen, or prevent any further reduction therein, and to diminish the hours of labour, the great and ultimate object of it must be to establish the paramount rights of Industry and Humanity, by instituting such measures as shall effectually prevent the ignorant, idle and useless parts of Society from having that undue control over the fruits of our toil, which, through the agency of a vicious money system, they at present possess; and that, consequently, the Unionists should lose no opportunity of mutually encouraging and assisting each other in bringing about A DIFFERENT ORDER OF THINGS, in which the really useful and intelligent part of society only shall have the direction of its affairs, and in which a well-directed industry and virtue shall meet their just distinction and reward and vicious idleness its well-merited contempt and destitution."

In this declaration two things are apparent: first an instinctive and revolutionary class consciousness, and second, the confused and moralising opinions of Robert Owen. The two trends proved incompatible, and it was upon this above all that the Grand National destroyed itself. Owen had reached, about 1817, to conceptions of Socialism and Co-operation, but it was a Socialism which took no account of class, which based itself upon abstract ideas of Right and Justice and which dissipated itself into all kinds of projects for currency reform, ideal common-wealths and the almost miraculous establishment of the millennium.

By 1834 Owen was at the height of his fame and he was welcomed as an ally by the working class leaders of the Union movement. The strength of the Grand National lay in the profound disillusionment which spread among the masses after the Reform Bill of 1832 and their conviction that Parliament and political action were useless to them and that their social aims could only be accomplished by industrial organisation and strike action. Owen shared their dislike of Parliament, but wished to subordinate strike action to the establishment of co-operative enterprises which would gradually and peace-fully supplant capitalism.

Before the establishment of the Grand National, Owen's doctrines had involved the Builders in costly attempts to set up productive gilds and in the building of a great Guildhall at Birmingham. He insisted that there must be no harsh criticism of the employers, and though he advocated a general strike for the Eight Hour Day he regarded this rather as an apocalyptic act than as a serious class struggle.

Quarrels which broke out between Owen and Morrison and the other left wing leaders soon weakened the Union at a time when it was already in great difficulties. At first its success had been staggering. In a few weeks its membership grew to half a million. It had taken over a number of strikes from the Builders and other con-stituent bodies, including the Derby Turn Out, where the members had been presented with a demand that they should sign what became known as 'the document' pledging themselves to leave the Union and take no part in its activities, and a strike which paralysed the greater part of Lancashire for sixteen weeks. Once the Grand National had been formed, strikes broke out everywhere, making demands on its resources that it had no means of meeting and at the same time scaring the

Government into a belief that the Revolution was at hand. It was under these circumstances that the arrest of six farm labourers at Tolpuddle in Dorset, on a charge of administering illegal oaths, acquired a national importance. The men were hastily tried and sentenced to transportation, in spite of enormous protests. At least 100,000 people took part in the demonstration at Kings Cross, on the outskirts of London, which was deliberately made into a vast parade of Trade Union solidarity. The agitation was not at once successful, but in 1836 the sentences were remitted and later the men returned home.

Meanwhile the Grand National was becoming less and less able to cope with the organisational difficulties created by its own rapid growth. The Derby Turn Out ended in defeat, but a crop of new strikes took its place. Owen's dispute with the left wing grew so bitter that he closed down the journals of the Union to prevent his rivals from expressing their views. The decline was as rapid as the growth, and in August 1834 a delegate conference decided to dissolve the Union which had already become no more than a shell. Morrison had already left the executive in despair of accomplishing anything, and died a year later in great poverty.

The collapse of the Grand National was not the end, even for a time, of Trade Unionism. Local and sectional unions continued to exist, in most cases with much diminished memberships and with narrower aims, but it was the end both of attempts at organisation on a grandiose scale and of the naïve hopes which such attempts aroused. It had seemed that all that was necessary was to proclaim a general strike and the walls of capitalism would fall of their own accord. The general strike was preached as the end and not as one way of beginning the struggle.

Revolutionary Trade Unionism *alone* had failed: political agitation at the tail of one of the old bourgeois parties had been even more fruitless. The next stage was a political agitation with its roots in the mass organisations of the working class. The workers were far from being disheartened by the defeat of the Grand National, and it was only two years after its dissolution that the first signs of the Chartist movement began to appear. The Chartists in their turn made many serious mistakes but they were mistakes at an altogether higher political level.

2. THE CHARTISTS

The stronghold of Chartism, as of Trade Unionism, lay in the industrial North, but its origin was among the thoughtful, Radical artisans of London. The soil of London, with the proximity of Parliament, the relative prosperity of its artisans, many of whom were employed in the luxury trades, and their habits of political discussion rather than political action, was perhaps the most favourable for the seed to take root. But once transplanted to the richer soil and keener air of the North, it grew strangely into something quite unpromised. The excellent Lovett, who had come once more under the influence of Place, was as disconcerted as anyone at the thorny monster he had helped to raise.

The London Working-men's Association was formed in June 1836 as a political and educational body intended to attract the "intelligent and influential portion of the working classes". It was Radical and Owenite in outlook and might have proceeded quietly and unobtrusively in a course of modest usefulness if the crisis which broke early in 1837 had not revived the demand for Parliamentary Reform. In February the Association drew up a petition to Parliament in which were embodied the six demands that afterwards became known as the People's Charter. They were:

Equal electoral districts;
Abolition of the property qualifications for M.P.s;
Universal manhood suffrage;
Annual Parliaments;

Vote by ballot;

The payment of M.P.s.

These demands, which for Lovett and his friends were ends in themselves, were accepted with enthusiasm by hundred of thousands of industrial workers who saw in them the means to remove their intolerable economic grievances. Engels declared that the Six Points were "sufficient to overthrow the whole English Constitution, Queen and Lords included". "Chartism," he wrote, "is of an essentially social nature, a class movement. The 'Six Points' which for the Radical bourgeoisie are the end of the matter . . . are for the proletariat a mere means to further ends. 'Political power our means, social happiness our end,' is now the clearly formulated war-cry of the Chartists."

In the spring of 1836 the Six Points were drafted into the form of a Parliamentary Bill, and it was this draft Bill which became the actual Charter of history. It was endorsed at gigantic meetings all over the country: 200,000 assembled at Glasgow, 80,000 at Newcastle, 250,000 at Leeds, 300,000 at Manchester. At all these meetings the Charter received emphatic approval and the tactics by which it was proposed to secure its acceptance soon took shape. These were, a campaign of great demonstrations, a mass petition to Parliament,[1] a national Convention (the name was chosen deliberately for its connection with the French Revolution), and, if the petition were rejected, a political general strike or 'sacred month'.

As the movement spread beyond London its character changed and sharp divisions arose among its leaders. The customary distinction between moral force Chartists and physical force Chartists, though partly correct and commonly made at the time, is not entirely satisfactory. More accurately three groups may be distinguished. The right wing was composed of Lovett and his London followers

[1] Political petitions were a long-recognised method of agitation. They had been employed freely by the Wilkesites and on a much larger scale against the Corn Laws in 1815.

and those of Attwood, a Radical banker from Birmingham. They represented the more or less prosperous artisans and petty producers of their respective areas and were mainly concerned with the purely political aspects of the Chartist agitation. As the conflict between the Chartists and the ruling classes grew keener they fell back more and more on methods of education and peaceful persuasion.

Then there was a vast centre, grouped round the dynamic figure of Feargus O'Connor. From the beginning O'Connor had the support of the great majority of the industrial workers, the miners and the ruined and starving hand workers of the North. This support he never lost, in spite of his many blunders and weaknesses. But while he called them to fight for the Charter and a better life, his conception of the better life was that of the independent producer. O'Connor was an Irishman, nephew of one of the leaders of the Rebellion of 1798, nurtured on the Irish revolutionary traditions which were quite different from those of England and not always adaptable to English conditions. He was a strong individualist, a man of fiery energy with a powerful but confused intellect, and his appeal was largely to the instinctive hatred of industrialism prevailing among a working class most of whom were no more than one or two generations removed from the land. He was a strong opponent of Socialism and though he talked freely of insurrection he had no clear idea as to how it was to be carried out or what its objects should be.

Much less definite than the right or centre was the left wing among the Chartists. Very often it did not stand out clearly, being usually driven to support O'Connor against the right wing. Its leaders, Bronterre O'Brien in the early stages and later George Julien Harney and Ernest Jones, never had anything like O'Connor's popularity. They differed from him mainly by their much clearer conception of the class struggle and by their Socialism which, especially in the case of O'Brien, was heavily tinged with Owenite ideas about labour money and co-operation. O'Brien's main social plank was land nationalisation. Harney and Jones were younger men, and Jones only came into the movement when it was already in decline. Harney was an over-emotional man with a strong tendency to indiscriminate hero-worship.[1] His main practical importance was as an internationalist, and he did much useful work in making contacts between Chartism and revolutionary movements abroad. Both Harney and Jones held many views in common with Marx, with whom they were closely associated when the latter came to live in England after 1848.

The confusion and weaknesses of Chartism are apparent. Its strength was that while in Europe the working classes were still dragging at the tail of the industrial bourgeoisie, in England the workers were able by 1838 to appear as an independent force and were already realising that the industrial bourgeoisie were their principal enemy. Even in France this point was not reached till ten years later and then only among the workers of Paris and a few of the largest towns.

Elections for the first Chartist Convention took place in October 1838. During the winter the collection of signatures for the Petition was begun, and in February the Convention met in London, where the right wing was disproportionately represented. When Harney raised the question of what should be done in case the Petition were rejected the majority refused to allow this possibility to be discussed. The proceedings dragged on for some months, marked by repeated quarrels between right and left wing groups, while up and down the country some preparations for an armed rising appear to have been made. In July the Government struck. Meetings were forbidden, many arrests were made, and on July 4th a body of police, specially imported from London, attacked a meeting at the Bull Ring, Birmingham, with exceptional brutality. The workers rallied and drove the police out of

[1] Marx and Engels used to refer to him, in private, as Citizen Hip-Hip-Hurrah!

the Bull Ring and it was not till some days later that order was restored in the town. The news of the Birmingham outrage spread rapidly and there were bloody clashes in Glasgow, Newcastle, Sunderland and a number of Lancashire towns.

On July 5th Lovett was arrested. On July 12th the Petition, which had 1,280,000 signatures[1] was rejected. The Convention was now faced with the alternatives of admitting defeat or coming to a definite decision for action. A half-hearted attempt was made to call a general strike, but when it was found that there was no organisation for making the decision effective, the strike appeals were withdrawn. The Convention dissolved on September 14th.

More arrests followed quickly and a decline began that was only made more rapid by the rising in South Wales. This episode is the most obscure in the whole history of Chartism. It is still uncertain whether it was part of a plan for a widespread insurrection, or a spontaneous local outburst, or even a mere attempt at the forcible rescue of the Chartist leader Henry Vincent from Newport Gaol. It is at least probable that any success would have been followed by similar risings elsewhere.

All that is certain is that some thousands of partly-armed miners led by John Frost marched down on Newport through torrents of rain on the night of Sunday, November 3rd, 1839. Other contingents which should have joined them failed to arrive, and when the drenched and weary column reached Newport they were fired on by troops concealed in the Westgate Hotel. Ten were killed and about fifty wounded. The rest dispersed and Frost and the other leaders were arrested and sentenced to death, the sentence being afterwards commuted to one of trans-portation.

This gave the Government the opportunity they wanted. In a few months about 450 arrests were made, the victims including O'Connor, O'Brien and almost all the outstanding figures. During the first half of 1840 the movement was

[1] The total number of electors at this time was only 839,000.

forced underground and appeared to have been beheaded and destroyed. As the leaders one by one came out of gaol a slow revival began. In this revival the formation of the National Chartist Association in July was the most important event. At this time any national party was illegal, and the movement had consisted only of local organisations with no real central leadership or co-ordinating force. The N.C.A., in spite of its illegality, was thus the first real political party in the modern sense, a party with an elected executive, dues-paying membership and about 400 local sections. By 1842 it had a membership of 40,000 and through it the movement as a whole reached its highest point of influence and activity. The right wing had been discredited by the failure of the first Convention and Lovett soon withdrew from active participation.

The N.C.A. went far to remove one of the main weaknesses of Chartism, and efforts were now made to overcome another, the isolation of the Chartists from the Trade Unions, by building up Chartist groups inside them. This attempt was only partially successful.

O'Connor was released in August 1841, and preparations were made for a second Petition. This was a very different document from the first, the language of which had been respectful and its demands purely political. The second bluntly contrasted the luxury of the rich with the poverty of the masses and included demands for higher wages, shorter hours and factory legislation. The Chartist paper *The Northern Star* reached a circulation of 50,000 and the movement received a valuable political education in its struggle against the Anti-Corn Law League.

The economic crisis, which had eased somewhat after the bad year of 1838, suddenly intensified, bringing unemployment to hundreds of thousands and general wage reductions to the working population. Chartism spread like wildfire and the second Petition was signed by no fewer than 3,315,000 people—well over half the adult male population of Great Britain. Nevertheless it was scornfully rejected by Parliament in May, 1842. Once more the crucial question of the next step arose. The Association was just as hesitant as the Convention had been, but the decision was taken out of their hands by the spontaneous action of the workers.

Strikes against wage reductions broke out all over Lancashire and in August a Trade Union conference in Manchester decided by an overwhelming majority:

"That it is our solemn and conscientious conviction that all the evils that afflict society, and which have prostrated the energies of the great body of the producing classes, arise solely from class legislation; and that the only remedy for the present alarming distress and widespread destitution is the immediate and unmutilated adoption and carrying into law the document known as the people's charter.

"That this meeting recommend the people of all trades and callings to forthwith cease work, until the above document becomes the law of the land."

Taken by surprise the Association could only recognise the strike, which spread swiftly all over Lancashire, Yorkshire, and the Midlands. London and the South, however, failed to respond. Troops were sent into the strike areas and by September a combination of repression and hunger had forced the strikers back to work. There were over 1,500 arrests, and by the end of the year the movement had once again dwindled to small proportions. A revival of trade between 1843 and 1846 came to the rescue of the authorities.

As Chartism declined, O'Connor, who was now without a serious rival, turned his energies to grandiose and crack-brained schemes for the establishment of a chain of land colonies. Thousands of workers and small tradesmen took shares with which two estates were bought and divided among selected colonists, chosen apparently for their political convictions than for their skill as farmers. It was hoped to buy further estates from the profits of the first and so continue to extend the scheme indefinitely. Economically the idea was absurd and doomed to failure from the start, and it took up energy that might have been better spent, but on the other hand it served to hold the movement together at a low level till the crisis of 1846, accompanied by the great famine in Ireland, brought Chartism into its third period of activity. The first sign of this revival was the election of O'Connor as M.P. for Nottingham in 1847.

On the surface this revival had all the vitality of the agitations of 1839 and 1842. There were the same demonstrations, the same enthusiasm and the same terrible background of misery and starvation. But in reality there was a profound difference. The employed had not fully recovered from the defeat of 1842 and had meanwhile been pacified by the passing of the Ten Hour Day Act. The movement was therefore confined mainly to the unemployed. In Glasgow there were severe bread riots in April 1848 and many people were killed and wounded. The Government made the most ostentatious military preparations and raised a large number of special constables from the upper and middle classes.

The mechanical adoption of the old, worn-out tactics of Petition and Convention was in itself a confession of weakness, and when the Convention met it had to discuss the certainty that the Petition would be rejected. The younger leaders, Jones and Reynolds, pressed for an immediate insurrection. The older hands, including O'Connor and O'Brien, who had more means for comparing the situation with that of previous years, judged and judged rightly, that an insurrection would not receive sufficient support to have any chance of success. Not even the stimulus of the revolutions taking place all over Europe could bring the movement back to anything like the levels previously reached.

The Petition, when presented, was found to have only 1,975,000 signatures against the five million O'Connor had claimed, and of these many were fraudulent. The great meeting which was to have accompanied the presentation of the Petition on April 10th was dwarfed by the forces which the Government had called out to deal with a "revolution" they knew would not take place. Some 30,000 people assembled at Kennington Green and O'Connor decided to abandon his plans for a march to Westminster.

Hereafter the story is one of unbroken decline. O'Connor's Land Company became insolvent and had to be wound up, and in 1852 he became insane. After 1853 the Association's death was formally recognised by a decision to discontinue the election of an Executive Committee.

The failure of Chartism was partly a result of the weaknesses of its leadership and tactics. But these weaknesses were themselves only a reflection on the newness and immaturity of the working class. In the forties of the last century the bourgeoisie were still a rising class, had still a positive contribution to make to social progress and could still afford to make substantial concessions to stave off revolt. The distress of the time was more in the nature of growing pains than the sign of irresistible decay.

In 1848, though few people were probably aware of it, Britain was just on the verge of a long spell of trade expansion and prosperity, and even if little of this prosperity reached the workers there was still improvement enough to turn them from thoughts of revolution. Politically, the next twenty years are almost a blank in the history of the working class.

It was with something very like despair that Marx wrote in 1858 that "the English proletariat is becoming more and more bourgeois, so that this most bourgeois of all nations is apparently aiming at the possession of a bourgeois aristocracy and a bourgeois proletariat *as well as* a bourgeoisie. For a nation which exploits the whole world this is of course to a certain extent justifiable". The positive contribution of these middle years, and it was a real contribution whose value has sometimes been underestimated, was made in other fields, those of Trade Unionism and Co-operation.

3. THE NEW MODEL

Even before the old revolutionary Trade Unionism
had passed in the splendour of the Grand National and
the 'Sacred Month' of 1842, the first stirrings of a new
kind of organisation can be discerned. After 1848, when
the hopes of striking political victories vanished, the
'New Model' Unionism grew apace. It built upon a
narrower but more solid foundation. Attempts to form a
Trades Union were abandoned after one more abortive
effort in the National Association of United Trades
(1845–50) had failed. Even here there was a notable
difference. The National Association was more in the nature
of a federal body to which small local unions became
affiliated, and its policy was always cautious, strikes being
avoided whenever possible.

The New Model, however, was not a Trades Union
but a Trade Union. It was a national organisation of
workers employed in a single craft. Nearly always it was
composed of skilled workers. In policy and outlook these
Unions expressed the point of view of the skilled artisans
who had long had their local unions and clubs and from
whom Lovett and the moral force Chartists had drawn
their following.

Their attitude was that expressed by the committee
of the London Compositors as early as 1835:

"Unfortunately almost all the Trade Unions hitherto
formed have relied for their success upon extorted oaths
and violence. . . . Let the Compositors of London show
the Artisans of England a brighter and better example;
and casting away the aid to be derived from cunning and
brute strength, let us, when we contend with our opponents, employ only the irresistible weapons of truth and
reason."

Wages, the price of labour power, were thought of as
being governed solely by the laws of supply and demand.
The Flint Glass Makers declared in 1849 that "the scarcity
of labour was one of the fundamental principles. . . . It

was simply a question of supply and demand." The same idea was more forcibly expressed in the favourite gospel of Tommy Ramsey, a pioneer of Trade Unionism among the Durham miners:

> "Lads unite and better your condition.
> When eggs are scarce, eggs are dear;
> When men are scarce, men are dear."

The result was a tendency to discountenance strikes and to rely instead upon keeping down the supply of labour by restricting the number of apprentices, discouraging overtime, and, in extreme cases, subsidising emigration. "Look to the rule and keep the boys back" was the characteristic slogan of the time.

Such were the principles on which the national Unions grew up about 1850. Rigidly exclusive and often hereditary they catered for a labour aristocracy which had little concern for the masses outside their ranks, but within their limits they developed a solidarity which enabled the Unions to survive the heaviest defeats with an almost unimpaired membership. They brought into the British working class movement business methods and a care for the tedious details of organisation without which little of permanent value could be accomplished. They made Trade Unionism for the first time a normal and regular part of the daily lives of thousands of working men.

These new Unions had high contributions, often a shilling a week or over, and carried out all kinds of functions besides that of conduction trade disputes. Sick benefits, funeral benefits and unemployment benefits were usually paid and the greatest danger was always that of the Union becoming a mere friendly society whose real purpose was completely submerged and whose policy was cautious to the point of being cowardly. This was indeed the fate which overtook many of the New Model Unions and led to the rise of a quite different kind of Trade Unionism in the eighties and nineties. Another and less dangerous side activity was that of helping in the self-education of the members, and this, beginning as early as 1840, has led the way to an important and valuable movement for independent working class education.

Most of the organisational work in the early days had been done by enthusiastic volunteers in their spare time or by middle-class sympathisers like Owen. Now it was necessary to have full-time officials who specialised in such work. This, too, had its dangers, but no permanent organisation on a national scale would have been possible without it.

The first of the New Model Unions was the Amalgamated Society of Engineers, founded in 1850 by the merging of a number of craft Unions, of which the Journeymen Steam Engine and Machine Makers' Society was the most powerful. It was the A.S.E. which formed the pattern for other craft Unions. Its membership of 11,000 seems small compared with the half million of the Grand National or the tens of thousands who flocked into the various ephemeral organisations of the cotton operatives and miners. But it was a permanent membership, paying dues which gave the Society the unprecedented income of £500 a week. The strongest of the other Unions at this time were the Ironfounders and the Stonemasons, each with a membership of four to five thousand.

The difference between the old and the new Unions was quickly shown by the three months' struggle which began in January 1852 over the question of overtime. The employers tried to smash the Society by the old method of refusing employment to all workers who would not sign 'the document' undertaking to give up Union membership. Such methods had been successful in the Derby Turn Out and on many other occasions. Now, however, they failed, and in spite of the complete defeat of the strike the Society ended it with only 2,000 fewer members than at the beginning and within three years all the lost ground had been more than recovered.

In the next ten years the example of the engineers was widely followed. The Lancashire cotton operatives formed a permanent organisation in 1853, the Stonemasons and Ironfounders doubled their membership while the Amalgamated Society of Carpenters, founded in 1860, soon became second only to the A.S.E. in numbers and influence. The Carpenters' Union was the direct result of a stubborn strike in London in 1859 which convinced the men of the need for a more powerful type of organisation.

About 1860 these Unions developed an unofficial central leadership, often known as the Junta. It was composed of officials who were active at the London headquarters whose work put them constantly into touch with one another and who shared a common outlook on Trade Union and political questions. The inner circle consisted of Allen and Applegarth of the Engineers and Carpenters, Guile of the Ironfounders, and Coulson of the Bricklayers. A fifth member, George Odger, was of a different kind. Belonging only to a small Union of skilled bootmakers, he was important as the secretary of the London Trades Council and for his influence in Radical circles. He was the politician of the group, and its mouthpiece when it wished to address a wider public.

From the start the Junta interested itself in politics, but not in the sense in which politics had been understood by the Chartists. They had no idea of leading an independent class movement but used their influence in Union circles to exert pressure on the existing parties. They participated in the Reform agitation of 1866-7 and did useful work in campaigning against such abuses as the Master and Servant Law. They stood just to the left of the Liberal Party and feel often enough into the most glaring opportunism because of their lack of any clearly formulated political philosophy. It was thus possible for them to collaborate at one moment with European revolutionaries on the Executive of the First International and at another with Bright and the Liberals. Their industrial policy was, as S. and B. Webb say, "restricted to securing for every workman those terms which the best employers were willing voluntarily to grant".

But in spite of this, and although they were "possessed with a mania for compromise and a thirst for respectability," they were in the main honest and capable men with a real talent for organisation. The Trade Union movement would never have reached the dimensions it did reach without their unspectacular labours any more than it would have done if their methods had not later been transcended and their doctrines repudiated.

They were in fact a kind of informal T.U.C. General Council, and their final achievement was the calling in 1871 of the first regular and representative Trade Union Congress. It came together mainly to organise the resistance to an application of the conspiracy laws which threatened to put an end altogether to legal Trade Union activities and which led to an agitation which ended with the placing of the Unions upon a secure legal basis. In the General Election of 1874 Trade Union leaders came forward as candidates for the first time independently of the Liberal and Tory Parties, though as individuals they were still only Radicals. This brings us, however, to a new phase: the New Model was now becoming itself antiquated and a new 'new unionism' was needed to replace it. The age of monopoly in which the respectable Craft Unions had grown up was nearing its close and the increasing misery of the millions for whom they did not cater was pressing for attention. The result of these changes will be the subject of the next section, but first something must be said of the development corresponding to the rise of the New Model in another section of the movement, that of the Co-operative Societies.

The earliest Co-operatives were mainly attempts by groups of workers to break the monopoly of the millers and to provide cheap flour for their members. Such were the Hull Anti-Mill Society of 1795 and the Devonport Union Mill of 1817. Then came the floodtide of Owenite revolutionary Utopianism and the Co-operatives were hailed as the key to the peaceful supersession of capitalism. The objects of the Brighton Society in 1829 were thus described: "They purchased at wholesale prices such articles as they were in the daily habit of consuming . . . adding the difference or profit to the common stock (for it is a fundamental rule of these societies never to divide any portion of the funds but to suffer it to accumulate till it becomes sufficient to employ all the members thereon)."

Usually the Societies hoped to established co-operative communities like that of Owen at Orbiston in Scotland. Scores of such societies came into being and disappeared again during the thirties.

The 'New Model' Co-operative was that of the Rochdale Pioneers who began in 1844 to pay a dividend on purchases. The Co-operative movement gradually shed its Utopianism (though vestiges of it still remain in the confused language which some Co-operators still use about the "Co-operative Commonwealth") and the Co-operative Societies began to establish themselves successfully as strictly business concerns, selling goods to their members at current prices and distributing the profit as dividend. In the sixties the Co-operative Wholesale Society came into being to supply goods to the retail Societies and in the next decade it began actually to produce goods in its own factories. Since that time the progress of the movement on the trading side has been rapid and almost uninterrupted. In it thousands of workers have learnt how to organise and administer large scale business enterprise and have demonstrated conclusively that ability to do so is not confined to the capitalist class.

4. SOCIALISM AND THE ORGANISATION OF THE UNSKILLED

Changes in the position of British capitalism and the influence of developments in other countries combined to produce the revival of Socialism and Trade Union militancy in the eighties. The movement in England had always been sensitive to events abroad and had often showed a generous internationalism. To say nothing of the reaction caused by the French Revolution, the Chartists had taken the initiative in the formation of the body known as the Fraternal Democrats, a forerunner of the First International. Founded in 1846, mainly through the efforts of Harney, it lasted till about 1854 and played an honourable part in keeping the movement in Britain in touch with revolutionary happenings elsewhere during one of the great epochs of the European revolution.

Then in 1861 came the American Civil War, followed in 1864 by the formation of the First International. Under the leadership of Marx and Engels it was for ten years the directing force of all the advanced sections of the working class throughout Europe. In England it was supported, for mixed reasons, by leading Trade Unionists, including the members of the Junta, but it was not able to wean them from their respectability and insular craft prejudices. In England the International perished and left no immediate fruits so far as organisation was concerned. In France and Germany, however, it left behind it young and healthy Socialist Parties. By 1880 these parties had already reached respectable dimensions.

The Franco-Prussian War was followed by a short replacement boom, particularly marked in the coal and iron industries. Hundreds of new pits were sunk, and there was a sudden (and temporary) rise in miners' wages. The conclusion of the war stimulated an intense industrial development both in France and Germany and it was just at this time, also, that the U.S.A. recovered from the effects of the Civil War. For these reasons the attack on British manufacturing monopoly developed at a great pace. The boom passed into a profound crisis in 1875, followed by others in 1880 and 1884. And, what was most significant, the recovery after these slumps was less rapid and less complete than in the mid-century period. British industry still continued to make progress, but with greater difficulty and at a slower rate.[1]

[1]See Chapter XVI, Section 1.

The effects of this crisis were felt especially in London. Here the migration of the shipbuilding industry to the Clyde about 1866 had caused widespread destitution, while the gradual decline of small-scale industry was ruinous to a region where, paradoxically, it had survived to a greater extent than elsewhere. The East End contained hundreds of thousands of dockers, unskilled and casual workers among whom unemployment spread to an alarming extent, while their wages when they were employed were extremely meagre. Consequently, it was in London, and not as earlier in the industrial North, that the new movement had its centre and main support.

The first reactions to the change were to be seen among the intellectuals and a minority of the more thoughtful workers. Henry George's *Progress and Poverty* had a wide sale about 1880, focusing attention explicitly upon the private ownership of land but indirectly upon private ownership as an institution. In 1881 Engels wrote a series of leading articles in the *Labour Standard*, the newly-founded journal of the London Trades Council, in which the fundamental questions of the relation of Trade Unionism and working class politics were trenchantly discussed. In all the events that followed the value of the part played by Engels, working quietly in the background, can hardly be over-estimated. It would hardly be too much to say that he was one of the founders of the British labour movement in its modern form, though he must not be made responsible for its weaknesses.

In 1884 the Democratic Federation, founded three years earlier by H. M. Hyndman, a well-to-do adventurer in search of a Party, changed its name to the Social-Democratic Federation and announced a programme in which ill-digested Marxism was combined with a good deal of pretentious nonsense. In the same way, the S.D.F. was a strange mixture of sensible and honest workers and intellectuals like Tom Mann, John Burns, William Morris and Eleanor and Edward Aveling with nondescript adherents of Hyndman.

Hyndman's dictatorial and unscrupulous methods, culminating in the scandal of the General Election of 1885 when three Socialist candidates were run on money secretly obtained from the Tories, soon discredited the S.D.F. Morris and others left to form the Socialist League, but this came under the influence of an Anarchist clique and fell to pieces after bitter internal squabbles.

Eighteen Eighty-four also saw the birth of the Fabian Society, a body which put forward an "improved" and "English" Socialism, substituting for the class struggle the peaceful and gradual permeation of the ruling class and its organs. The Fabian Society itself always remained small, but its ideas were eagerly seized upon by the right-wing leaders of the Labour Party, anxious to find a theoretical justification for their opportunism.

All these early Socialist bodies were still isolated sects, and without the awakening of a mass movement they would have counted for very little. This movement began among the unemployed in East London during the winter of 1886 and 1887, though its progress was retarded by the tactics of the S.D.F. who exploited it as a stunt for purposes of self-advertisement. On November 13th, 1887, the famous 'Bloody Sunday', the police broke up a demonstration with extreme brutality. The result was a concentration of all Socialist and Radical forces in a great free speech campaign, which was accompanied by numerous clashes with the police.[1] At the same time, persistent and fruitful propaganda was carried on in the many Radical clubs to which the majority of the politically conscious workers then belonged.

By 1887 things were moving also in the provinces. In Yorkshire the Bradford Labour Union was being formed. Keir Hardie was beginning to work in what became the Scottish Labour Party, while a Labour Electoral Organisation won some successes on the Tyneside. But the *annus*

---

[1] A reflection of these events, in which Morris played an active part, is to be seen in Chapter XVII, 'How the Change Came', of *News from Nowhere.*

mirabilis, the moment of the breaking through of the latent volcanic forces, was 1888, and the place of this break through was the East End of London, the home of thousands of workers who had never been organised and were regarded as unorganisable.

In May the girls at Bryant and May's match factory were led by Socialists in a successful strike. This was followed by the organisation of a Union among the gas-workers by Will Thorne with the help of Burns, Mann and the Avelings. In a few months the Union had become so strong that the Gas Companies were forced to reduce the hours of work from twelve to eight and raise wages by 6*d.* a day. The Gas-workers and General Labourers' Union, firmly established as a result of this victory, was the first of the 'new' unions which absorbed all the best lessons that craft unionism had to teach but avoided its narrowness and compromising attitude.

When the victory of the gas-workers was followed by the great dock strike of 1889 led by Burns and Mann (themselves actually members of the A.S.E.) the unskilled workers began to pour into the Unions. Within a year 200,000 had been organised. In 1888, too, the Miners' Federation was formed, linking up the older local Unions which had latterly been making considerable progress. By 1893 the Federation, with its policy of a minimum wage and a legal limitation of hours, had grown from 36,000 to over 200,000 members.

All this happened rather in spite of than because of the S.D.F., which remained outside the mass movement and even looked on it with some contempt because it was not avowedly Socialist. Members of the Federation like Burns and Mann who worked actively in the Unions did so as individuals and were often attacked for abandoning their Socialist principles. For the time this attitude did not hold back the masses, but in the long run it was a disaster. The 'Socialists', the theoretically advanced minority, remained a sect, the mass movement was abandoned to the leadership of all kinds of careerists. Moreover, some of the most militant Trade Union Leaders, Burns and Thorne for example, soon became infected with the opportunism prevailing among the older officials with whom they came into contact. Burns had the distinction of being the first Trade Union leader to sit in a Liberal Cabinet. There was never in England that fusion of theory and practice out of which alone right action can grow, and both sides of the movement had to pay dearly for its absence.

Nevertheless the new Unionism did mark a great advance in spite of its lack of political clarity. Engels in 1889 hailed with delight the advance from the 'fossilised brothers' of the Craft Unions:

"The people only regard the immediate demands as provisional, although they themselves do not know as yet what final aims they are working for. But this dim idea is firmly rooted enough to make them choose *only* openly declared Socialists as their leaders." The difference was clearly shown when the General Railway Workers' Union, upon its foundation in 1890, declared, "That this Union shall be a fighting one and shall not be encumbered with any sick or benefit funds." From the start the new Unions adapted a policy of low dues and wide recruitment instead of one of high dues and exclusiveness. For the first time, women were catered for, and the Gas-workers extended their organisation to Ireland.

When Engels in 1892 issued a new edition of his *Condition of the Working Class in England in 1844*, he picked out this mass movement as the most important sign of the times: "That immense haunt of human misery (the East End) is no longer the stagnant pool it was six years ago. It has shaken off its torpid despair, it has returned to life, and has become the home of what is called the 'New Unionism', that is to say, of the organisation of the great mass of 'unskilled' workers. This organisation may to a great extent adopt the forms of the old Unions of 'skilled' workers, but it is essentially different in character. The Old Unions preserve the tradition of the times when they were founded, and look upon the wages system as a once for all established, final fact, which they can at best modify in the interests of their members. The New Unions were founded at a time when the faith in the eternity of the wages system was severely shaken; their founders and promoters were Socialists either consciously or by feeling; the masses, whose adhesion gave them strength, were rough, neglected, looked down on by the working-class aristocracy; but they had this immense advantage, that *their minds were virgin soil*, entirely free from the inherited 'respectable' bourgeois prejudices which hampered the brains of the better situated 'old' Unionists. And thus we see these new Unions taking the lead of the working-class movement generally and more and more taking in tow the rich and proud 'old' Unions."

The new Unionism soon made itself felt and a keen struggle ended in an important victory at the Liverpool T.U.C. of 1890 when the demand to have the enactment of a legal Eight Hour Day placed on the programme was adopted by 193 votes to 155 after a curious debate in which the leaders of the old Unions used the most appparently revolutionary arguments. The importance of the vote was precisely that the Trade Union movement was being forced once more into the field of political action. Early in 1893 a conference of Socialist and working-class bodies was held at which the Independent Labour Party was formed. The S.D.F., with its usual obstinacy, refused to co-operate and the result was that the leadership of the new Party, by far the largest Socialist Party then in existence, passed first into the hands of Keir Hardie and then into those of the most dangerous Fabians and disguised Liberals, like Snowden and Ramsay MacDonald.

The S.D.F. repeated their mistake even more disastrously in 1900 when the Labour Party (first known as the Labour Representation Committee) was formed as a federation of the I.L.P., the Fabian Society and the Trade Unions. At first the new body did not receive very much support. All the candidates it put up in the 1900 General Election failed, and in 1901 the membership of its affiliated bodies was only 469,000. Then came the celebrated Taff Vale case and a fierce newspaper campaign against Trade Unionism. Membership rose to nearly a million and there were several sensational by-election victories. After the Election of 1906 a group of twenty-nine Labour members was returned to the House of Commons.[1]

The independent mass political party of the workers, towards the formation of which a century of effort and sacrifice had gone, was now indeed in existence, but under the leadership of men who were content to follow the lead of the Liberals on almost all questions. Yet such as it was, the Labour Party was in fact the expression of the mass movement of the workers and its rank and file never succumbed entirely to the bourgeois infection which prostrated the leadership. Inside the Party a constant war was going on against this infection. Lenin, supporting the application of the Labour Party for affiliation to the Second International in 1908, declared that "it represents the first step on the part of the really proletarian organisations of England towards a conscious class party and towards a *Socialist* Labour Party". And, in an article discussing the International's decision to accept the Labour Party, he comments that the English Unions are "*approaching* Socialism, awkwardly, hesitatingly, in a zig-zag fashion, but are approaching it nevertheless. Only the blind can fail to see that Socialism is now growing rapidly among the working class in England".

From about 1900, and under the pressure of the tumultuous growth of militancy among the workers, this Socialist opposition made rapid headway inside the Labour Party. In 1914 the outbreak of war interrupted this development and left the reactionaries, for the moment, more firmly established than ever.

[1] See page 490 below.

5. THE WAR FOR THE LAND AND THE NATIONAL STRUGGLE IN IRELAND

The Act of Union of 1801 came as the natural consequence of the suppression of the revolt of the United Irishmen.[1] Corrupted and unrepresentative as it was, an Irish Parliament sitting in Dublin was still a potential centre around which revolutionary nationalism might gather, and therefore it had to be destroyed. Pitt delegated the congenial task to Castlereagh, and by a campaign of bribery in which a million pounds were spent in buying a majority, the Protestant gentlemen who constituted the Irish Parliament at this time were persuaded to vote themselves out of existence. The promise that the Act of Union would be followed by the removal of the legal disabilities imposed on the Catholics was not kept.

Instead, the Act of Union was followed by a series of Coercion Acts intended to crush the continued revolt of the peasants against the crushing burden of rent, tithes and taxes. Banded into such secret organisations as the Whiteboys and the Ribbonmen, the peasants conducted an irregular warfare, and tithes especially could only be collected at the point of the bayonet. Battles like that at Rathcormack where twelve people were killed were frequent. No repression could destroy this revolt, which sprang from the profound misery of the people, but what English bayonets failed to do was done by the Irish native upper class under the guidance of Daniel O'Connell.

John Mitchell said of O'Connell that "next to the British Government he was the greatest enemy Ireland ever had". The spontaneous agrarian revolt was seized upon by him, given a central leadership and distorted into a weapon to increase the political power of the bourgeoisie. With the help of the priests he formed the Catholic Association, which soon gained an undisputed ascendancy

[1] See page 345 above.

over the peasants. The whole strength of the Association was turned to securing 'Catholic Emancipation', by which O'Connell meant the right of the Catholic gentry to become members of the Westminster Parliament.

In 1829 he achieved this object, but at the same time the 40s. franchise was abolished and the Irish electorate reduced from 200,000 to 26,000. This disfranchisement of the small holders removed one of the main barriers to eviction, since up to then the political influence of any landowner depended upon the number of voters who were his tenants and could be trusted to use their votes at his direction. After this victory O'Connell began an agitation for the repeal of the Union, but was careful to confine it within limits that prevented any effective action of the masses.

Ireland was important to the English ruling classes only as a source of cheap food: for the last hundred and fifty years, no matter what form the exploitation has taken, this has been its essence. With the development of manufactures in England, Ireland was turned into a corn growing country. During the high prices of the Napoleonic Wars, rents rose amazingly and there was an extreme subdivision of holdings. After the war, Ireland was the only place from which corn could be freely exported to England under the Corn Laws, and, though prices fell, the profits of the landlords were hardly affected because the fall in prices only meant that the peasants had to produce more wheat to pay their rent. Evictions were frequent and the steady growth of the population always made it easy to find new tenants however extortionate the rent.

In 1835 figures published in the report of the Irish Poor Law Commission revealed that the total value of Irish Agricultural produce was £36,000,000. Of this £10,000,000 went in rent, £20,000,000 in taxes, tithe, and the profits of middlemen and merchants, and less than £6,000,000 to the actual producers, the small holders and labourers. The peasant grew wheat to pay the rent and potatoes to feed himself and his family. These are the facts

which provide the essential background to the Great
Famine which raged from 1845 to 1850.

The facts about the Famine have been grossly distorted
by all orthodox historians. There was really no famine
in any ordinary sense of the word, but only the failure of
one crop, the potatoes. "Providence sent the potato blight,
but England made the famine" was a saying current at
the time. In 1847, when hundreds of thousands of people
died of starvation and hunger typhus, food to the value
of £17,000,000 was actually exported from the country
under the protection of English troops. The million and
a half people who died in these years did not die of famine
but were killed by rent and profit.

The best leaders of the Young Ireland Movement, which
had taken the place of O'Connell's Association, advocated
the forcible seizure of the land and the refusal of all rent
and tithes. Just as Tone had looked to revolutionary France
for an ally, John Mitchel and James Fintan Lalor planned
for an insurrection in conjunction with the English Chartists. The rising was forestalled by the arrest of Mitchel
and Lalor, and the landlord Smith O'Brien into whose
hands the leadership passed was not the man to lead an
agrarian rising against his own class. He and his friends
were unable to prevent a rising, but strong enough to
make it localised and hopeless. The state of physical
weakness to which the famine had reduced the people
was perhaps also partly responsible for this failure in
1848.

The next generation was a time of great misery, of
wholesale evictions and emigrations to the U.S.A., and to
Canada. After the repeal of the Corn Laws Irish wheat
lost its monopoly in the English market and wheat growing
gave way steadily to cattle grazing. The population fell
from 8,170,000 in 1841 to 4,700,000 in 1891, but at the
same time the area under corn fell from 3,000,000 acres
to 1,500,000 acres. Small holdings were 'cleared' of their
occupiers and flung together into large grazing farms,
so that in spite of the decline in the population the pressure

of the peasants on the land available for them did not decrease.

The same period saw the driving out of the hand spinners and weavers by the machine-made goods of Lancashire, a process that in England had been completed a generation earlier. Between 1841 and 1881, the number of workers in the textile industries decreased from 696,000 to 130,000. Irish industry remained backward except round Belfast, where shipbuilding and linen-weaving were carried on almost entirely with English capital. It was for this reason that a powerful section of the English ruling class has always been so determined to prevent Home Rule from being applied to this area.

It was against the evictions that the next big movements, those of the Fenians and the Land League, were directed. The Fenian Brotherhood was formed in Paris by a group of revolutionary exiles in 1852, on the model of the secret Party of Blanqui. It remained unimportant till after the American Civil War, in which thousands of Irish emigrants served with distinction. After the war many of these old soldiers were ready to put their military skill at the service of Ireland. The Fenians soon gained strength, and their leaders established close contact with the First International, of which some of them may have been members.[1] Once more, plans for a rising were betrayed to the English Government and the leaders were arrested. Without them the rising proved abortive and was quickly crushed when it came to a head in 1867.

The Fenians were a political organisation drawing their strength from agrarian discontent: the Land League was founded in 1879 to defend the economic interests of the peasants and only gradually became drawn into political action. Its tactics were to fight eviction by means of the boycott, and members pledged themselves:

"Never to bid for, take or hold the farm from which our neighbour has been evicted for the non-payment of

[1] Engels, at this time living in Manchester, a great centre of Irish emigration, was always in close touch with the Fenian movement.

an unjust rent, and never to take any hand, act or part in sowing or saving the crops thereon and to hold the man who will do so as a public enemy". It soon developed into a nation-wide resistance to the landlords and the Government.

The landowner Parnell, like the landowners O'Connell and O'Brien, found a great popular movement and set to work to divert it into more profitable channels. At first he proposed to combine legal and illegal methods and to make use of the Irish Republican Brotherhood, the direct successors of the Fenians. By this time (1881) the Government was thoroughly alarmed and Gladstone introduced his Coercion Act which made it possible for anyone suspected of supporting the Land League to be imprisoned and held without trial. Parnell was arrested, and while in Kilmainham Gaol he came to an agreement with the Government to put an end to all violent and illegal methods if they would legislate against evictions.

Parnell was released in May 1882. A few days later the new Irish Secretary, Lord Frederick Cavendish, who had come to Dublin to implement the Kilmainham Treaty, was assassinated in Phœnix Park. Parnell denounced the extremists and forthwith turned his energies into a campaign for Home Rule, that is, for local self-government within the Empire. A supreme master of parliamentary tactics, he succeeded in bringing into being a perfectly disciplined body of Nationalist M.Ps. He worked on the belief that such a body would have a sufficient nuisance value to command attention and at times, when the Liberals and Tories were evenly divided, would be able to hold the balance and extort large concessions as the price for their support. These tactics did win concessions, but they led the Irish Nationalist Party into ever greater depths of opportunism until the day in 1914 when their leader William Redmond stood up in the House of Commons to assure the English Government of the support of Ireland in the event of war. That pledge was the death sentence of Parnell's Party.

The first result of the Kilmainham Treaty was the Land Act of 1881. It set up tribunals to fix rents for a period of fifteen years, during which time the tenants were not to be evicted. The object of the Act was to save the landlords from the ruin with which the Land War was threatening them and to cut away the basis for the agitation of the League. In this it was largely successful, for the peasants, bewildered at the desertion of Parnell and other leaders, were ready to snatch at any hope of escaping eviction.

This Act was followed by a series of Land Purchase Acts by which tenants could buy their farms by a series of annual payments. In this way the landowners received a smaller but safe income raised by a State loan and the peasants paid the interest on this loan instead of rent which, if the Land League had been able to continue its activity, they might well have been able to escape altogether. T. P. O'Connor, then quite a young revolutionary, summed up the object of this legislation by saying that "Gladstone's policy was to fix a relation between landlord and tenant; the policy of the League was to abolish the relation and trample landlordism beneath its heels."

Finally, Gladstone attempted by the Home Rule Bill of 1886 to end the Nationalist agitation. He was defeated by the revolt of the openly Imperialist section of the Liberal Party, headed by the Birmingham politician Joseph Chamberlain, and there was a renewed period of coercion under the Tory philosopher Balfour. A second Home Rule Bill was thrown out by the House of Lords in 1893.

The whole history of Ireland from the raising of the Volunteers in 1778 to the present day has followed a tragic pattern of continuous struggle by the peasants and workers to free themselves from English exploitation and the regular betrayal of that struggle by upper and middle-class leaders because such a struggle could not but be directed in time against native as well as foreign exploiters. The Irish landlords in particular, drawing huge rents from the peasants which they spent and invested largely in England, have always been more hostile to their own tenants than to the English.

The key to the whole situation, today no less than when the United Irishmen declared in their manifesto of 1751: "When the aristocracy come forward the people fall backward; when the people come forward the aristocracy, fearful of being left behind, insinuate themselves into our ranks and rise into timid leaders or treacherous auxiliaries," lies in the answer to the question, '*What class* is to lead the struggle for national liberation?'

CHAPTER XV

COLONIAL EXPANSION

1. INDIA

THE ABOLITION OF the trading monopoly of the East India Company in 1813 marked a new stage in the economic exploitation of India. The Company was a trading company, drawing most of its revenue from the profits derived from the sale in England of the exotic products of the East. It was also a London company and London was the traditional centre of British merchant capital. It was not, by 1813, the centre of British industry. From this time can be dated the opening of the Indian market to English factory-made goods, above all to Lancashire-made cotton cloths. In a little over a decade the value of exports to India practically doubled, and the export of cotton goods, trifling in 1813, reached nearly £2,000,000 a year in the twenties.

After 1813 the main trading revenue of the East India Company came from its monopoly of the China tea trade, which it kept for another twenty years. As something like £4,000,000 worth of tea was sold by the Company each year at prices roughly double those paid in Canton, these profits were very considerable. The First Opium War (1839–1841) was fought just at the time when Lancashire was ready to flood China with cheap cottons as it had already flooded India. Hence the war, ostensibly fought to force the Chinese to buy Indian opium against their will had also the more general object of breaking

[1] A certain Sir George Campbell remarked in the House of Commons: "If the Chinese are to be poisoned by opium, I would rather they were poisoned for the benefit of our Indian subjects [!] than for the benefit of any other Exchequer."

down the barriers which prevented the free export of British goods to China. After the war, Hong Kong was annexed and five "treaty ports" opened to British traders. A second war (1856–1858) opened the way for the penetration of the Yangste basin.

Lancashire goods destroyed the hand-loom industry of India with astonishing rapidity. Dr. Bowring, the prominent Free Trade advocate, in a speech made in Parliament, in 1835, declared:

"Some years ago the East India Company annually received of the produce of the looms of India to the amount of from six million to eight million pieces of cloth. The demand gradually fell off to somewhat more than one million pieces and has now nearly ceased altogether. . . . Terrible are the accounts of the wretchedness of the poor Indian weavers, reduced to absolute starvation. And what was the sole cause? The presence of the cheaper English manufacture. . . . Numbers of them died of hunger; the remainder were, for the most part, transferred to other occupations, principally agricultural . . . The Dacca muslins, celebrated over the whole world for their beauty and fineness, are almost annihilated from the same cause."

The population of Dacca, the main centre of the Indian textile industry, decreased between 1815 and 1837 from 150,000 to 20,000.

Less spectacular but more important than the depopulation of Dacca was the gradual destruction of the self-supporting communities which formed the ground pattern of Indian social life. Marx, speaking of both India and China, wrote:

"The broad basis of the mode of production is here formed by the unity of small agriculture and domestic industry, to which is added in India the form of communes resting upon the common ownership of the land. . . . The English commerce exerts a revolutionary influence on these organisations and tears them apart only to the extent that it destroys by the lower price of its goods the spinning and weaving industries, which are an integral part of this unity.''

By the destruction of the village handicraft industry the peasants were thust back on to exclusive dependence on agriculture. India, like Ireland, became a purely agricultural colony, supplying Britain with food and raw materials. The destruction of hand industry meant not only that Lancashire goods secured a monopoly market but that Indian cotton and jute were exported to England instead of being made up at home. This process was assisted by the heavy taxation which was part of the price that had to be paid for the benefit of British rule. Faced with a demand for payments in cash the peasants were forced to sell their surplus produce at prices which had no relation to the cost of its production. In many parts of India the tax collector quickly developed into a species of landlord.

The result has been, throughout the whole of the Nine-teenth Century and up to the present time, a progressive impoverishment of the people, a continuous decline in the average size of the holdings as the proportion of the total population dependent upon agriculture rose, and a growing indebtedness of the peasantry to the village money-lenders. An official investigation showed that in a village in Poona the average holding was 40 acres in 1771, 17½ acres in 1818, and only 7 acres in 1915. In Bengal and elsewhere the holdings are much smaller, averaging about 2·2 acres. Recent figures—the increase between 1921 and 1931 of landless labourers from 291 to 407 per thousand of the population and of the estimated agricultural indebtedness between the same dates from £400,000,000 to £675,000,000—seems to show that this impoverishment not only continues but is developing at an increasing rate.

The abolition of the East India Company's trading monopoly in 1813 coincided with a period of conquest and aggression. Early in the century the Marquis of Wellesley fought a series of wars against the Marathas of

Central India. Under Lord Hastings, Governor-General from 1813 to 1823, large areas of Central India were brought under direct British rule and the native princes who escaped conquest acknowledged British supremacy. From this time the effective control of Britain over the whole country east of the Indus was a recognised fact. In 1824 the first expedition was made into Burma, outside the boundary of India proper, and its coastal area occupied. The seizure of Singapore in the same year gave Britain one of the main strategical keys to the Indian Ocean and the Far East.

From the end of the war in Burma (1826) to 1838 there was a period of peace and of a rapid expansion of British trade in India. This period ended with an attempt to conquer Afghanistan, where the first rumours of the Russian penetration of Central Asia were making themselves heard. The Amir of Afghanistan was dethroned and replaced by a puppet prince supported by an army of occupation 15,000 strong. In 1842 a rising of the tribes forced the Army to withdraw from Kabul and in its retreat across the mountains it was surrounded and completely destroyed. The effect was far-reaching: for the first time a large British force had been defeated and the belief in the invincibility of the white conquerors was shattered. The wars against the Sikhs of the Punjab (1845–1849) did nothing to restore this belief. The Punjab was conquered, but only after desperately close fighting, culminating in the battle of Chillianwallah, in which the Sikhs came very close indeed to victory. The Afghan and Sikh wars must be reckoned as among the main causes of the Mutiny.

British rule in India was based, politically, on the highly trained and disciplined army of sepoys and on the support of the native princes and landowners, who, in their turn, owed their own privileges to British authority. While destroying the village community, the social base of the life of the masses, British rule preserved a kind of petrifying feudalism, a corrupt and artificial oppression of princes and nobles. The masses were thus subjected to a double and, and, in a sense, parallel exploitation. So long as the two sets of exploiters worked in harmony, there was no danger of any effective revolt in an age when India was still entirely agricultural and composed of isolated fragments.

But in the middle of the Nineteenth Century the aggressive policy of the British brought them into conflict with the native feudal upper class. The newly devised 'doctrine of lapse', by which Native States whose rulers died without heirs passed under British rule, cut right across the Oriental custom by which such native princes used to adopt an heir. Between 1848 and 1856 a number of Native States, including Satara, Jhansi, Nagpur and Oudh were annexed. It seemed only a matter of time before the whole country was brought under direct British rule.

At the same time Indian culture and religions were being steadily undermined, and this was especially resented by the high caste sepoys who formed the bulk of the Army. It was as the culminating point of this process that the famous incident of the cartridges greased with animal fat, which actually precipitated the Mutiny, became important. The building of railways, though only 273 miles of track had been laid by 1857, and of the telegraph, were also regarded as signs of the increasing concentration of power in European hands.

The Mutiny, when it broke out, was thus not primarily either a national or an agrarian revolt, but a revolt of the professional army led by reactionary feudal rulers whose power was being threatened by annexations and European innovations. Only in Oudh did it become a general movement against the British and only in a few areas, notably around Benares, did it become a class movement of the peasants against the landlords and tax-collectors. Here lay its main weakness and the secret of its speedy defeat.

From the start the decadent princes who took the lead showed a complete incapacity for decisive or combined action. The revolt was localised and small bodies of white troops were allowed to move about without interference. The decision to restore the authority of the Moslem Mogul deprived the Mutiny of the support of many Hindus and especially of the military and recently conquered Sikhs. The main forces of the sepoys allowed themselves to be shut up in Delhi by a very small British Army, when a bold march into Bengal would probably have roused the whole country.

The Mutiny began at Meerut in May 1857. In a few weeks Delhi had been taken and British garrisons besieged at Lucknow and Cawnpore. The whole of Central India was ablaze, but elsewhere there were only isolated outbreaks. In the Punjab, attempts at mutiny were quickly put down and the absence of any popular rising here left the mutineers isolated in country strange and often hostile. The result was that the Punjab actually became the base from which the movement in Central India was crushed. The smallness of the British forces was compensated for by their cohesion, greatly increased by the telegraph, and by their control of the artillery. By September Delhi had been re-captured and the tide had definitely turned against the Mutiny.

The suppression was carried out with an extreme ferocity born of fear. Kaye and Malleson, in their standard *History of the Indian Mutiny*, record among many other incidents how:

"Volunteer hanging parties went into the districts, and amateur executioners were not wanting to the occasion. One gentleman boasted of the number he had finished off quite 'in an artistic manner' with mango-trees for gibbets and elephants for drops, the victims of this wild justice being strung up as though for pastime, in 'the form of a figure of eight'."

This was at Benares. The same authorities admit that six thousand people "regardless of sex or age" were slaughtered in and around Allahabad alone. Similar events occurred everywhere, and many of these atrocities were committed long before the famous 'Cawnpore massacre' which has been used ever since to excuse them.

After the suppression there was a general reorganisation of the British forces in India. The East India Company had plainly outlived its usefulness and was dissolved, its functions being taken over directly by the Government. The number of British soldiers was increased to 65,000 and the number of Indian soldiers reduced. Most important of all, the native princes were conciliated. As Professor Trevelyan says, "Dalhousie's 'doctrine of lapse' was abandoned after the Mutiny, and the Native States were thenceforth regarded as essential buttresses of the structure of British India." The princes, though their real powers steadily declined, were from this time kept loyal with titles and subsidies and by the tacit understanding that, within reason, they could torment and plunder their subjects as they pleased under the protection of British bayonets.

The building of railways and roads went on apace. The object of these was partly military, partly commercial. They made it possible for troops to be rushed to any corner of the country and they made it possible for English goods to penetrate everywhere and for Indian corn, cotton, tea and other raw materials to be carried cheaply in bulk to the ports. They had an additional and unintended consequence. However much the British bourgeoisie were determined to keep India as an agricultural colony and a market for their industrial products, the necessity of creating a network of railways defeated this aim. Inevitably, and in spite of every obstacle, there grew up around the railways a coal and iron industry. As early as 1853 Marx had predicted this outcome: "When once you have introduced machinery into the locomotion of a country possessing coal and iron, you are unable to withhold it from its fabrication. You cannot maintain a network of railways over an immense country without introducing all those processes necessary to meet the immediate and current wants of railway locomotion, and out of which there must grow the application of machinery, to those branches of industry not immediately connected with railways. The railway system will therefore become, in India, truly the forerunner of modern industry."

The railway not only transformed things, it transformed people. It created an industrial middle class and an industrial working class. It bound the whole country into an economic unity it had never before possessed and gave it the beginnings of a political unity. It made possible for the first time a real struggle for national independence.

And while it did this, it made the retention of India ever more necessary for British Imperialism. Besides being a great market for articles of consumption India became a market for the products of heavy industry, for the means of production, and a field for the export of capital. Hundreds of millions of pounds were poured into the railways, mines, roads and other works and tens of millions were drawn out every year as interest upon these loans. India became the centre and keystone of the whole economic and financial fabric of the Empire.

2. CANADA AND AUSTRALIA

The character of the development of both Canada and Australia has been determined mainly by their geographical situation and features. Canada can hardly be said to exist at all as a geographical entity. It is a northward extension of the U.S.A., a fringe of fertile land sharing the qualities of the United States territory to the south of it, and shading off gradually into the cold Arctic wastes. With one exception all its natural outlets are to the south towards the U.S.A. rather than east or west towards the sea.

The one exception, the St. Lawrence River, was, however, of decisive importance because at the time when the American colonies won their independence the St. Lawrence basin was the only settled area, the west and centre of the continent being occupied only by nomadic Indians. Canada was at this time inhabited by French settlers whose only contacts with their southern neighbours were those of war. Consequently, when the United States revolted, Canada remained an English colony and the two countries expanded westward along parallel and independent lines.

After the War of American Independence, some 40,000 people, the United Empire loyalists, who had supported England and wished to remain under English rule, crossed the frontier into Canada. Some went to the coast provinces, Nova Scotia and New Brunswick, and others to Ontario north of the Great Lakes. The French, though still in a majority, were thus surrounded. For administrative purposes, Canada was divided into two provinces, Upper Canada, mainly English, and Lower Canada, or Quebec, mainly French.

During the next thirty years there was a steady flow of immigrants from England and the population increased rapidly. But the administration was carried out by the distant, bureaucratic and inefficient Colonial Office in Downing Street, and Lord Durham in his report of 1839, had to draw a striking picture of the contrast between the development of Canada and the U.S.A.:

"On the British side of the line, with the exception of a few favoured spots where some approach to American prosperity is apparent, all seems waste and desolate. . . . The ancient city of Montreal, which is naturally the commercial capital of the Canadas, will not bear comparison in any respect with Buffalo, which is a creation of yesterday. . . . A widely scattered population, poor, and apparently unenterprising, though hardy and industrious . . . drawing little more than a rude subsistence from ill-cultivated land, and seemingly incapable of improving their condition, present the most instructive contrast to their enterprising and thriving neighbours on the American side."

In 1837 there were rebellions among both French and English colonists. The two rebellions were quite independent, but both were the result of misgovernment from Downing Street. That in Upper Canada was in part anti-clerical, one of the main grievances being the setting aside of much of the best land for the endowment of a church which had no active existence and to which few of the settlers belonged. Both risings were soon crushed, but they caused much alarm to the British Government, which feared Canada was about to go the same way as the United States. The result was the Durham Commission and a report which advised the granting of Dominion Home Rule to Canada. At the same time, political power was placed in the hands of the English settlers by uniting the provinces of Upper and Lower Canada, thus putting the French, who were in a majority in Lower Canada, in a minority for the composite province.

As the century went on, wheat became more and more the most important Canadian product. The wheat-lands lay far in the centre of the country where they could only be properly developed either as a minor part of the great American wheat belt of which they formed the northern extremity or by the construction of an east-west railway linking the central provinces to the Atlantic. The first of these alternatives would have meant linking Canada dangerously closely to the United States. In 1871, too, the new province of British Columbia agreed to join the Dominion only on condition that such a line was built within ten years. The Canadian Pacific Railway was thus at least as much a political as an economic undertaking. It was the only means of giving the strung-out settlements an artificial unity and preventing their absorption into the United States.

For some years the building of the railway was delayed by scandals of graft and inefficiency which involved the resignation of two governments. It has to a large extent served its political purpose, but it has required constant subsidies to make up losses on working. The opening of the Panama Canal lessened the economic importance of the C.P.R. because it has now become more profitable to send many classes of goods by sea from Columbia to England rather than overland by way of the East coast. In recent years the most striking fact of Canadian history has been the steady penetration of the country by American capital, which now greatly exceeds that of Britain. On the other hand, Britain remains the most important market for Canadian products, which, besides wheat, now include fish, furs, timber and timber pulp, the latter having become of great importance with the growth of the newspaper industry.

Unlike Canada, Australia is at the end of the world, right off all the main trade routes. Consequently it was the last continent to be discovered and developed, and its development was very slow until it had become of sufficient importance in itself to be the terminus of regular trade routes to and from the old world. This isolation was no disadvantage for the first use to which Australia was put, that of a convict settlement. Between 1786 and 1840, thousands of the worst and the best English people were transported there.[1] In spite of the brutal treatment they received, many of them became self-supporting farmers and artisans when their sentences expired. Others escaped into the interior to become bandits and bushrangers.

The next stage was the formation of huge sheep ranches. These were planned deliberately on a large scale during and after the Napoleonic Wars when the West Riding factories had great difficulty in obtaining sufficient supplies of wool. Vast tracts of land were made over to rich capitalists who owned tens and hundreds of thousands of sheep. These "squatters", drawn from the same class as the Government officials, soon became a powerful native aristocracy, and bitter conflicts grew up between them and the poorer settlers who found much of the best land appropriated by the squatters who often owned more than they were able to use.

[1] See page 362 above.

The problem for the ruling class was to find labourers enough in a country where land was to be had for nothing. E. G. Wakefield, the apostle of 'systematic colonisation' and of the doctrine that poverty in England was best cured by the wholesale shipment of the wealth-producing class to the ends of the earth, complained bitterly that:

"Where land is very cheap and all men are free, where everyone who so pleases can easily obtain a piece of land for himself, not only is labour very dear, as respects the labourer's share of the produce, but the difficulty is to obtain combined labour at any price."

This unhappy state of affairs, where, as Marx put it:

"The wage labourer of today is tomorrow an independent peasant or artisan, working for himself. He vanishes from the labour market but not into the workhouse. . . . The labourer loses along with the relation of dependence, also the sentiment of dependence on the abstemious capitalist," had the effect of retarding the accumulation of capital and of preventing it from flowing freely into the new colony.

Wakefield and his friends devised an ingenious scheme to counter this. The idea was to put an end to the free grants of land to the colonists and, instead, to sell it at as high a price as possible. In this way settlers without capital would have to work for some years before they could hope to own any land. The product of the sales was to be used to subsidise more emigration, and so a continuous stream of labourers would pour in to replace those who became independent. In time the price of land would rise and the price of labour would fall till the colony became a genuinely civilised country with a fully established capitalism. He was so far successful that the free grant of land was restricted in 1831 and abolished in 1840, but one of the effects of this was to divert a large part of the stream of emigrants from the British colonies to the U.S.A. The Wakefield System was most fully applied to New Zealand, where the first settlements were made about 1837 by his New Zealand Association.

The struggle of the mass of the Australian colonists against the squatters and the Government came to a head in 1854 with what may be regarded as the last act of the drama of Chartism and of the European revolutions of 1848. The discovery of gold at Ballarat in 1851 attracted thousands of diggers from all over Europe, and among them were many old revolutionaries from England, Ireland, Germany, France and Italy. The squatters who saw in these immigrants a menace to their vast holdings of land, and found that the rush to the goldfields made it hard to obtain shepherds and sheep shearers used their influence with the Government to have heavy taxes and all kinds of irksome police restrictions placed upon them. A Gold Diggers' Union was formed which put forward, along with economic demands, a democratic political programme almost identical with that of the Chartists.

The Government was forced to reduce taxation, which took the form of heavy payments for a licence without which no one was allowed to dig for gold, but accompanied this reduction with an intensified police repression which soon drove the miners to armed revolt. They proclaimed an Australian Republic and fortified themselves behind the Eureka Stockade. On Sunday, December 3rd, 1852, they were surprised by a military force and routed, between thirty and forty being killed. The struggle of the miners aroused so much enthusiasm throughout the country that the Government were unable to carry out their plans for a wholesale repression. Instead, they were forced to reduce the taxation to a nominal sum and to abandon the police restrictions upon the miners. In 1858 a new constitution with universal manhood franchise was conceded, and in the election which followed, Peter Lalor, who had been the leader of the revolt and was wounded at the storming of the Eureka Stockade, was elected with a huge vote.

The gold deposits gave out after a few years, but the population continued to increase from about 200,000 in

1840 to 2,300,000 in 1881. Sheep farming and mining continued to be important, but with the growth of railways considerable industries developed, so that today more than half the 6,500,000 inhabitants are concentrated in the five largest towns. The main lines of conflict are between British and American capital and between the Australian masses and the foreign bankers and bond-holders with whose capital Australian development was financed and who take a heavy yearly toll of interest.

3. EGYPT

The story of British dealings in Egypt is worth telling in some detail, not only because of its intrinsic importance but because it contains in the most concentrated form the whole essence of imperialist method. What took centuries in India was here crowded into little more than a generation, while the compact and unified character of the country the valley of a single great river, enables the whole scene to be realised at a glance.

From the time of the Mohammedan conquest in the Seventh Century to the beginning of the Nineteenth, there were few fundamental changes in Egypt. New dynasties arose, trade routes came into being and declined, but the unchanging basis of peasant cultivation dependent upon the annual cycle of the Nile remained unaltered. Napoleon came and departed, the Turkish Empire crumbled away, leaving Egypt virtually independent under its Khedive. Almost as shadowy as the authority of the Turkish Sultan in Egypt was that exercised by the Khedive over the vast territory of the Sudan and the even remoter Somali coast.

In the fifties came the project of the Suez Canal, and European capitalists began to turn their attention to the Nile valley. The Canal was opened in 1869. Much of the capital was French, but the Khedive Ismail had subscribed nearly half of the shares. At once Egypt became the key to the most important waterway in the world.

More vitally concerned with the control of the Suez than France was Britain, because the canal was on the main route to India. At the same time, the development of important cotton plantations in Egypt, to which a powerful impetus had been given by the American Civil War, was another reason for British interest in this region, since Britain was the chief importer of cotton and the plantations had been developed largely with British capital.

Naturally, therefore, when Ismail began, in the sixties and seventies, to introduce Western improvements, it was to London that he turned for the capital that did not exist in his own country. These were merry years. In little more than a decade 900 miles of railways, hundreds of bridges, thousands of miles of canals and telegraphs, costly docks at Suez and Alexandria were built.

The operations proved almost boundlessly profitable to British bankers and industrialists. First of all loans had to be raised. Between 1864 and 1873 four great loans amounted to over £52,500,000, raised at heavy rates of interest. But Egypt received only £35,400,000 of this sum, the rest going to the London financiers as commission and expenses. This was only the beginning since almost all the money raised was at once paid over to British contractors, who in their turn made vast profits. Thus, the harbour works at Alexandria, for which the Egyptian Government paid £2,500,000, realised a profit of £1,100,000 for the con- tractors. By 1876 the indebtedness of Egypt was about £80,000,000, and the interest on this sum was £6,000,000 a year out of a total State revenue of £10,000,000, all of which had to be screwed out of a peasant population of about eight million, cultivating less than five and a half million acres of land. In 1875, the Khedive was forced to sell his shares in the Suez Canal, which were bought by the British Government through the Rothschilds.

Year by year, as loan was piled upon loan, the country became more and more bankrupt. The peasants, who benefited least by the new railways and docks, were bled white to pay the foreign bond-holders. In 1878 there was cattle plague and famine and it was clear that a crisis was at hand. The Egyptian State machine was breaking down and it was time for Britain, as the representative of the financiers, to step in and protect their interests. A strong agitation compelled the Khedive Ismail to grant a constitution, and a Nationalist Party, openly anti-foreign, began to gain support. This was too much for the British, who had Ismail deposed and replaced by the more subservient Tewfik. The Nationalist movement continued to grow, led by Arabi and other army officers. In 1881 they seized power and established a Government determined to resist foreign encroachments.

Britain and France sent warships to Alexandria, where they organised a "massacre" of Christians, mostly Greeks and Armenians, by hired Bedouin assassins, as a pretext for intervention. But the antagonisms between the different European Powers made immediate action impossible. A conference was held in June 1882, at which Britain, France, Italy, Germany, Russia and Austria agreed not to seek any "territorial advantage, nor any concession of any exclusive privilege", except, according to British addendum, "in case of special emergency".

On July 11th the British created their "special emergency" by bombarding the forts of Alexandria on the excuse that they were being repaired by the Egyptians. An army was landed which defeated Arabi's forces at Tel-el-Kebir, and by the end of September the British were in full military control of the whole country. The most solemn assurances were of course given that the occupation was only temporary and would end when order was restored. For the next twenty-five years the real ruler of Egypt was Sir Evelyn Baring (of Baring Brothers the bankers, later Lord Cromer) whose official post was that of Consul-General. Before describing the policy on which Baring re-organised Egypt in the interests of high finance, it is necessary to outline the events by which British rule was extended to the Sudan.

The Sudan, stretching south from Egypt almost to the Equator, was important not only for its fertility and natural riches but because the upper reaches of the Nile pass through it and whoever controls the Sudan also controls Egypt. Towards the end of the century it became of special value to Britain as a link in the chain of territory which it was hoped would extend right across Africa from Egypt to the Cape.[1]

About 1880 a religious nationalist movement under Mahommed Ahmed, better known as the Mahdi, spread over the whole country. From Dafur in the West to Suakim on the Red Sea and south to the Great Lakes, the Egyptian garrisons were swept away. In 1883 an Egyptian army which had been sent up the Nile against the Mahdi under Colonel Hicks was completely destroyed. Only Khartoum remained in Egyptian hands, and the large garrison there was threatened.

Sir Evelyn Baring and the majority of the British Cabinet, including Gladstone who was Prime Minister at the time, decided that the Sudan must be abandoned for the moment. A powerful minority, working in close harmony with Lord Wolseley and other leading army officers, thought otherwise. Making use of a stunt journalist, W. T. Stead, they whipped up an intense and apparently spontaneous agitation to have General Gordon sent to Khartoum to organise the withdrawal of the garrison, though he had publicly declared his opposition to this policy. Baring's protests were overruled and Gordon arrived at Khartoum in February 1884.

Instead of proceeding with the evacuation as he had been instructed to do, he allowed himself to be besieged, apparently with the idea of blackmailing the Government into sending a relief force, defeating the Mahdi and re-conquering the Sudan. A relief force was sent, after much delay, but it did not arrive till January 28th, 1885, two

[1] See page 469 below.

days after Khartoum had fallen and Gordon had been killed. The expedition then returned, since the re-conquest of the Sudan was impracticable till after the reorganisation of Egypt had been completed. But British Imperialism gained something more immediately useful than a new province, it gained a saint and martyr. The very peculiarities which had made Gordon an imperfect instrument when alive, his naïve piety, his indiscipline and his contempt for convention, made him all the more suitable for canonisation, since the vein of sentimentality running through the British ruling class would have prevented their accepting a saint who was not also something of a simpleton.

For twelve years the Sudan was abandoned. During this time much happened: the position in Egypt had been consolidated, Britain, France and Italy were penetrating the Somali Coast, Abyssinia and Uganda, the vision of Rhodes of a British Empire running unbroken from north to south was being embodied in the settlement of Rhodesia. And, in opposition to this, the French were planning an east to west block which would cut across the British somewhere on the upper Nile.

Then, on March 1st, 1896, the first Italian attempt to conquer Abyssinia was shattered at Adowa. Adowa was more than a defeat for Italy. Indirectly it was a defeat for Britain, Italy's ally in East Africa, and a victory for France which had been supplying Abyssinia with arms and posing as its only genuine friend, with the object of using that country as a base from which to conquer the Sudan and turn the flank of the British. Adowa meant that the way was now clear for such an attempt.

Within a week the British Government had decided to begin the invasion of the Sudan. General Kitchener, with a powerful Anglo-Egyptian army, moved slowly up the Nile, consolidating every step and building a railway as he advanced. In September 1898 Khartoum was re-taken and in November the Sudanese were routed in a bloody battle at Omdurman. Soon after, the victorious Army encountered a handful of French soldiers who had occupied Fashoda, still higher up the river. For a short time, war between France and Britain seemed likely, but the French gave way, partly because their rivals were in effective military occupation of the Sudan but more because they dared not risk a war of which a hostile Germany might take advantage.

The finance of the conquest was somewhat peculiar. Egypt had to pay two-thirds of the £2,500,000 bill, and for years after paid the heaviest part of the cost of administration. But the profits from the exploitation of the new province went entirely to British capitalism. Railways and other works were constructed on the same terms as those in Egypt, and the Sudan soon became a producer of fine quality cotton. The highest point of co-operation between the British Government and the cotton planters was reached in the case of the Sudan Plantations Syndicate, of which the ex-Prime Minister Asquith was one of the directors. Over a large area in which an irrigation scheme was carried out all the land was forcibly rented by the Government from its Sudanese owners at 2s. an acre, and then re-allotted to the original peasant occupiers on condition that one-third of each holding of thirty acres was used for cotton growing. The cultivator was allowed 40 per cent of the proceeds of the cotton crop and the remaining 60 per cent was divided between the Syndicate and the Government. It is not, perhaps, surprising that for the first eight years of its working the Syndicate made an average profit of 25 per cent. Besides being a cotton-growing area, the Sudan is an important and steady market for the products of British heavy industry.

The principle on which Baring ruled Egypt during the twenty-five years of his consulship was that "the interests of the bond-holders and those of the Egyptian people were identical". In practice this meant that the surplus for export must be increased so that the charges on loans could be regularly met. By 1907 cotton exports had increased from £8,000,000 a year to about £30,000,000. As the proportion of land under cotton rose, food had to be imported for a population previously self-supporting. Thus the peasants provided two new sets of profits, one for the exporters of cotton and one for the importers of wheat. While the total productivity of the country rose, they received a steadily diminishing proportion of the value of their crops.

Egypt was governed by a bureacracy entirely under British control, and for a long time organised opposition was impossible. In 1906, however, a particularly gross example of misrule in the judicial massacre at Denshawai provided the spark to set ablaze the smouldering discontent and a new Nationalist movement began to develop. Under pressure of this movement some small concessions had to be made but the World War, during which Egypt became a point of first-class strategic importance, provided an opportunity for even stricter control Egypt was placed under martial law, her nominal connection with the Turkish Empire was at last broken, a rigid censorship was imposed and nearly a million peasants and workers were conscripted for war service in spite of the most specific pledges that this would not be done.

After the War the Nationalist agitation was resumed. In 1919 there were widespread riots and strikes in course of which over one thousand Egyptians were killed. After a struggle lasting for more than a decade Britain was forced to grant Egypt a nominal independence, in which the reality of British rule was preserved, first by a strong military occupation of the Suez Canal zone and secondly by the continued occupation of the Sudan. The great irrigation works which have been constructed on the upper Nile make it possible for Egypt's vital water supply to be interrupted at any time, and it has therefore always been a prime demand of the Egyptian Nationalists that the whole Nile valley should be united under a single independent régime. No British Government has ever been prepared to consider this demand, without which any form of Egyptian independence must remain a mere pretence.

4. TROPICAL AND SOUTH AFRICA

Profitable as the slave trade proved during the Eighteenth Century, its suppression in the Nineteenth Century was even more profitable. While slaves were the only important export from West Africa, no attempts were made to penetrate the interior. Instead, the coast tribes were armed and encouraged to raid inland and bring their captives to some half a dozen trading ports for sale and shipment. The result was a never-ending series of tribal wars and the devastation of immense areas.[1] While some eight million Africans were sold into America during the period of the slave trade, it has been estimated that at least forty million more were killed in the wars and raids or died on the voyage.

The British Government prohibited the slave trade in 1807, but it was not till 1834 that slavery was abolished in the Empire. The area chiefly affected was the West Indies, where the sugar plantations employed great quantities of slave labour. The planters received £20,000,000 in compensation for the loss of their slaves, but the production of sugar declined considerably. By a curious irony, the abolition of slavery here stimulated the African slave trade, because the production of sugar in Cuba and Brazil, where slavery still continued, developed rapidly and created a new demand for labour.

For more than a generation the British Navy was actively employed on the African coast, hunting down slavers of the smaller nationalities, and it was in the course of these activities that the foundation of British power in West Africa was laid. It was soon discovered that this area could produce palm oil, cocoa and other valuable foodstuffs and raw materials and an extensive trade grew up, spirits and firearms being among the main articles of barter. The Ashanti country, forming the hinterland to the Gold Coast Colony, was found to be rich in gold and was accordingly

---

[1] It is probably to these wars that the elements of brutality, fear and superstition in African culture, of which so much has been heard, are mainly attributable.

conquered in a long series of wars which only ended in 1900.

A little to the East, the much more important colony of Nigeria was extended from the settlement at Lagos, founded in 1862 for the suppression of the slave trade. The exploitation of the country was left to the Royal Niger Company, one of those later-day chartered companies which became the favourite instrument for British expansion in Africa during the last twenty years of the Nineteenth Century. Acting with Government support, and usually including in their directorate members of governing circles, these companies were able to work quietly without involving the home authorities officially and to do many things a government could not have done without much opposition. The usual procedure was for them to consolidate their hold over their selected area till the point was reached at which the Government could buy them out and assume direct control. So the territory of the Royal Niger Company was taken over in 1900 and its representative Lord Lugard became the first Governor. The most important of the other Companies were the British East Africa Company and the British South Africa Company.

Because of its climate West Africa was unsuitable for the establishment of plantations under direct European control. A peculiar system of indirect exploitation was therefore evolved by which the native peasant cultivators sell their products to British merchants: as the trade is almost a monopoly of the great Lever Combine (palm oil is used among other things for the manufacture of soap and margarine) the price paid to the cultivators is only a fraction, at one time during the War no more than one eighth, of what their produce would fetch in England. In return, very high prices are charged for the cotton cloth and other articles which are sold to the natives. Recently the advance of tropical medicine has made West Africa safer for European settlers and there are signs that this system is giving way to a more direct exploitation, plantations and factories beginning to be established.

The abolition of slavery had important results also in South Africa, where the close of the Napoleonic Wars left Britain as the ruler of a community of Dutch farmers, the Boers. For Britain the Cape Colony was only important as a point of call on the way to India, and the Boers soon complained bitterly of official neglect and misgovernment. When slavery was abolished in 1834 they believed that they had been cheated out of a large part of the compensation due to them, and two years later thousands of them began the "Great Trek" northwards to form independent republics outside the regions claimed by the British.

The situation was complicated by a great southward movement of the exceptionally well organised and war-like Kaffir tribes, the Zulus and others, who drove out the more peaceful Hottentots and for a number of years contended on almost equal terms with Boers and British. The result was, on the one side, that in their conflicts with the Kaffirs the British were drawn into the interior, outflanking and surrounding the Boers. The latter were kept by the Kaffir wars in the constant exercise of arms, and the final destruction of the Zulu State by the British in 1879 made a further conflict between Boers and British almost inevitable. The Zulu War had been made the occasion for the annexation of the Boer Transvaal Republic, which remained under British rule till the Boers regained their independence by the victory of Majuba Hill in 1881.

Then came the era of Cecil Rhodes and the great plan for an "all red" block stretching from Cairo to the Cape. The British South Africa Company was formed in 1889 for the development of Rhodesia, and in a few years British Africa had been extended as far north as Nyasaland and the shores of Lake Tanganyika. At the same time Kitchener was pressing south through the Sudan, and the Cape-Cairo scheme, which Rhodes proposed to complete with a railway, seemed within measurable distance of accomplishment. But such a line could never be regarded as secure so long as the two armed and hostile Boer Republics, the Transvaal and the Orange Free State, remained in being on its flank. Nor could the British hold on Rhodesia and Nyasaland, for these areas were only easily to be reached from the South.

This is one half, the political and strategical half, of the reason for the Boer War. The other half was the discovery of deposits of diamonds and gold, far greater than any others in the world, at Kimberley and Johannesburg. Kimberley lay just outside the frontier of the Orange Free State, Johannesburg lay well within the Transvaal. Rhodes interested himself in both diamonds and gold from the beginning. By 1887 he was the head of the De Beers Mining Company, and in 1890 he combined with Barney Barnato and Alfred Beit to monopolise the whole South African diamond output. Within a few years his Goldfields of South Africa Limited had secured almost as complete a grip on the great Witwatersrand gold reef. When Rhodes became Prime Minister of the Cape Colony his power seemed almost unbounded.

Thousands of miners, speculators and adventurers of all kinds poured into Johannesburg, forming a cosmopolitan community alien and highly distasteful to the conservative Boer farmers. They found the patriarchal Boer state quite unsuited for the free growth of capitalist enterprise, while the Boers regarded these Uitlanders as fit only to be taxed and obstinately kept political power entirely in their own hands. It was intolerable to Rhodes and his supporters, who included Joseph Chamberlain, now recognised as the leader of the imperialist section of the British bourgeoisie, that the world's richest gold deposits should be left in the possession of a handful of Boer farmers.

Events moved rapidly. In 1895 Rhodes prepared for a rising of Uitlanders in Johannesburg, supported by an invasion of the Transvaal led by his henchman Dr. Jameson. The preparations were badly bungled and Jameson started on his raid before the conspirators in Johannesburg were ready to act. He was rounded up and surrendered ingloriously with his whole force. When he was handed over to the British authorities to be dealt with, he received an almost nominal punishment, and Rhodes, whom everyone knew to be behind the raid, got off altogether. The Boers, realising that war was only a question of time, began to arm as rapidly as possible.

In 1899 the refusal of the Uitlanders' demand for the franchise was seized upon by the British Government as a pretext for interference in the Transvaal, and war began in October. The Boers soon proved to be excellent if undisciplined soldiers. Trained sharpshooters, who used cavalry as a means to increase the mobility of their forces and not, as the British still did, for charges upon prepared positions, in which a mounted man was merely a larger target, their strength lay in defence and in guerilla raids. In attack they were weak, and this weakness involved them in sieges of Ladysmith, Kimberley and Mafeking which they were incapable of pushing to a conclusion. In these sieges and in beating off relieving columns, their whole force was pinned down and they lost the natural advantage which their superior mobility gave them.

The British, badly led, badly equipped and entirely unprepared for the kind of fighting that had to be done, suffered heavy losses in a series of unsuccessful frontal attacks. But the Boers failed to advance into the Cape Colony, where many farmers of Dutch origin were prepared to join them, and in February 1900, by the one really well-executed movement of the war, the British were able to turn the flank of the Boer Army covering Kimberley and to surround and capture it at Paardeberg. Blomfontein and Pretoria were occupied with little difficulty, and the first phase of the war was over.

There followed two years of irregular warfare on the grand scale, in which the Boer leaders, Botha, De Wet and Delarey, repeatedly outwitted the slow-moving, heavily-loaded British regulars. Only by the wholesale destruction of the Boer farm-houses and the herding of the women and children into concentration camps where thousands died of disease, was the resistance worn down. Even so, the Boers were able to make peace in May 1902 on terms which Lord Milner, British High Commissioner at the Cape, who had done everything possible to make war inevitable in the beginning, had refused to consider a year earlier.

Boers and British together were only a small white minority in the middle of a negro population, and for this reason, once the supremacy of British Imperialism had been established, it was necessary to do all that was possible to conciliate the defeated. The Boers received Dominion Home Rule in 1906 and in 1909 the Union of South Africa was constituted. Wherever differences might exist, and they continued to be considerable, the great bulk of the white population was united on the fundamental point of preserving their position as a ruling race exploiting a subject coloured population. So far as the treatment of the Africans was concerned there was little to choose between Boers and British and the natives remain today over-taxed, underpaid, herded into reserves and compounds and kept in a state not far remoted from actual slavery.

The suppression of the slave trade played a big part in the conquest of the third area to be considered in this section the group of colonies and protectorates which make up British East Africa. Here in the eighties of the last century the coast was occupied by a number of small Arab States, carrying on an extensive trade with the fertile and well-populated negro hinterland.

In 1886 Britain and Germany came to an agreement for the partitioning of the whole area, and, as usual, the actual pioneering was handed out to the British East Africa Company. On the excuse that the Arabs were carrying on a trade in slaves, which was certainly the case, troops were sent to East Africa and in a few years, and apparently by accident, the whole coast area had been conquered. The next step was to invade Uganda, the richest and most civilised part of the interior and one in which missionaries had been very busy for some years. When the Government showed some reluctance to pay for the building of a railway from the coast into Uganda the Company raised a great agitation in which the Press and the Churches co-operated enthusiastically. The Government gave way and within a couple of years had taken over the administration of both Uganda and Kenya from the Company.

The conquest of East Africa was linked with the operations of Rhodes and his South Africa Company to the south, and with the opening up of the Sudan to the north. The last stage in this conquest was not reached till after the World War when Britain secured the mandate for German East Africa, now known as Tanganyika Territory. In this way the scheme of Rhodes for a continuous British belt from north to south was at last carried out, but the construction of the Cape-Cairo railway is still far from complete.

Much of the higher land in East Africa, and especially in Kenya, is well suited for white settlement, and the British conquest was followed by the wholesale appropriation of the land from its African owners. In Kenya all the land was declared forfeit as early as 1898. The best land was given or sold to European planters and the natives confined to small and overcrowded reserves with inferior soil. Only in Uganda are they allowed to retain the legal ownership of any portion of the land. Not only were the natives herded into reserves, but in some cases these reserves were later taken from them when, because of the discovery of minerals or for any other reason, they became of value to the Europeans.

Since plantations are useless without a supply of labour, the next step was to force the natives out of their reserves to become wage earners. This is done by imposing direct taxes which have to be paid in cash and are too heavy to be paid by the sale of surplus produce from the overcrowded reserves. In many cases these taxes amount to as much as one sixth of what a man can earn for a full year's work. It was openly admitted by the Governor of Kenya in 1913 that taxation was regarded by the Government as the only possible method of compelling the natives to leave their reserves for the purpose of seeking work. When this method has failed to produce enough labourers, it has been supplemented from time to time by actual forced labour.

East Africa now exports considerable quantities of coffee, cotton, wheat, maize and rubber, and, like most of the other colonial possessions which have been referred to in this chapter, provides a good market for the products of British heavy industry.

CHAPTER XVI

ORIGINS OF THE WORLD WAR

I. IMPERIALISM

THE LAST CHAPTER traced the growth of British power in a number of different parts of the world: it is now possible to draw together the threads and present a picture of the process as a whole, to show how colonial expansion was part only of a development that was transforming the economic structure of British capitalism. First something should be said of the extent of this expansion. In the earlier part of the Nineteenth Century, attention was confined mainly to India. Then came the drive into the hinterland of Canada and Australia and the settlement of New Zealand, and lastly the division of Africa and the Pacific islands among the European Powers. In 1860 the colonial possessions of Britain covered about 2,500,000 square miles with 145,000,000 inhabitants; in 1880 the area was 7,700,000 square miles with 268,000,000 inhabitants and in 1899 11,600,000 with 345,000,000. By this last date the division of the world among the great colonising Powers was almost completed.

The age of Imperialism had begun, and British economy had acquired a new basis. Instead of the old and now vanishing industrial monopoly by which Britain had enjoyed the position of workshop of the world, there was a narrower but more complete colonial monopoly, an extension of British State power over vast 'backward' regions of the earth and the deliberate use of this State power to secure exclusive rights not so much for the export of articles of consumption as of the means of production and of capital. We have traced this development in India, Egypt and elsewhere, and it is because of its importance that the connection between the colonies and British heavy industry has been stressed perhaps to the point of monotony.

The word Imperialism has so often been used loosely that Lenin's very exact definition may be profitably recalled. Imperialism, in his view, is a stage of capitalist development which has the five following essential features:

"1. The concentration of production and capital, developed to such a high stage that it has created monopolies which play a decisive role in economic life.

"2. The merging of bank capital with industrial capital and the creation, on the basis of this 'finance capital' of a financial oligarchy.

"3. The export of capital as distinguished from the export of commodities, becomes of particularly great importance.

"4. International monopoly combines of capitalists are formed which divide up the world.

"5. The territorial division of the world by the greatest capitalist Powers is completed."

It should be added that Lenin dated the arrival of Imperialism as a world-wide phenomenon at about 1900.

The key feature of Imperialism is monopoly, and in Britain monoply developed strongly from the closing years of the Nineteenth Century. This was especially the case in the iron and steel industries, in shipping and ship building, in some new industries like the manufacture of chemicals, soap and margarine and in the case of the railways and banks. Thus, such firms as Armstrong Whitworth, Dorman, Long and Co. and Vickers occupied a dominating position in the heavy industries. The Anglo-American Atlantic Shipping Trust was formed by banker Morgan with a capital of £34,000,000. Levers and Brunner Mond held the germs of the great Unilever Combine and of I.C.I.

By about 1900 the scores of competing railway companies which had sprung up chaotically during he great period of rail construction had been reduced to about a dozen, and between these working agreements existed which paved the way for the further amalgamation into the present four companies. In the same way, private banks were being absorbed into vast joint stock concerns with hundreds of branches all over the country. Barclays Bank was founded in this way in 1896 and soon a small number of such banks controlled all but an infinitesimal proportion of the business of the country. This was of the greatest importance at a time transactions were more and more carried out on a credit basis.

The movement towards monopoly was less marked in the older export industries, expecially textiles, and in coal mining except in South Wales. These industries remained relatively backward, with many small enterprises working with insufficient capital, out-of-date plant and methods which made it difficult for them to compete in mass production with the rival industries of Germany and the U.S.A.

Almost as important a feature of Imperialism as monopoly, and one which in Britain came earlier, was the export of capital, in the form both of loans and investments. We have seen how this export worked out in practice in Egypt in the eighties, and at the same time similar developments were taking place in India, China, South America and in all the less industrialised parts of the world. The export of capital was linked with territorial expansion both as cause and effect. British investments provided excuses for annexation, and when a territory had been annexed British State power was used as a means of furthering the monopoly interests of the London bondlords.

Thus it was after 1900, when the division of the earth among the principal Powers was virtually complete, that the export of capital became most rapid. By 1900 the total amount of British investments abroad was about £2,000,000,000 from which a yearly income of £100,000,000 was drawn. By 1914 both capital and income were approximately doubled. An enormous proportion of this sum was invested in railways. The economist Sir George Paish estimated that in 1909 British investments in foreign railways totalled not less than £1,700,000,000 and that the income from these investments was about £83,000,000. Roughly, British investments were divided in the proportion of six to five between the Empire (including Egypt) and the rest of the world. Outside the Empire, the largest investments were in South America and especially in the Argentine.

The interest on these investments, paid mainly in foodstuffs and raw materials, now far exceeded the profit derived from Britain's foreign trade. Britain became to an ever-increasing extent a parasitic usurer State and the interests of the bondholders became the determining factor in her foreign politics. There was a relative decline of industry, illustrated, for example, by the decrease in the proportion of the population employed in the basic industries from 25 per cent in 1851 to 15 per cent in 1901, with a corresponding increase in the proportion employed in distribution, commerce, domestic service and the luxury trades. Large scale unemployment became a regular feature, and in the years before the War the number of unemployed was seldom much below a million. Another striking sign of decay was the growing frequency of cyclical crises. One such crisis occurred in 1902-4, a second in 1908-9, while a third was developing rapidly in 1914 and was only cut short by the outbreak of war.

The concentration of capital meant not only an increase in the size of enterprises but a vast increase in the number of purely passive shareholders. The typical capitalist was now no longer a factory owner running his own business and making a definite contribution of his own knowledge and energy to industry, but a shareholder drawing dividends and contributing nothing but his capital. In this way, the effective control of huge masses of capital came into the hands of a very small number of individuals whose actual holdings were relatively small. A network, of interlocking directorships linked up all sorts of ostensibly independent concerns, and what was perhaps more important, led to an interpenetration of finance capital with industrial

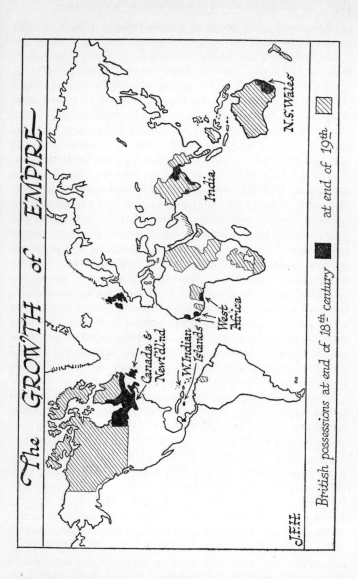

The GROWTH of EMPIRE

J.F.H.

Canada & New'f'l'nd

W. Indian Islands

West Africa

India

N.S. Wales

British possessions at end of 18th century ▪ at end of 19th ▨

capital which concentrated an increasing power in the hands of the bankers.

Another symptom of the parasitism of British capitalism in these years was the slow progress of British industry as compared with that of its principal rivals, Germany and the U.S.A. These three countries took different paths to Imperialism, though the final effect was similar in all cases. While Britain began with territorial expansion and the export of capital and only passed on to the monopoly stage late and unevenly, the U.S.A. with a vast and fairly uniform hinterland in which to expand, began with the establishment of an internal monopoly (the Standard Oil Trust was organised as early as 1882) and only began to appear as a colonial power and an exporter of capital after the Spanish-American war of 1898. Germany, with neither colonies nor hinterland, set out on an attack on the world market on the basis of a deliberate regimentation of home industry, and developed monopoly production to a considerable extent in the form of State Capitalism. Again, while in Britain, depending traditionally upon her export trade and needing to import quantities of food and raw materials, monopoly production developed out of free trade and competition leading to the gradual elimination of small and inefficient enterprises, in Germany and the U.S.A. it developed behind an elaborate screen of protective tariffs.

Britain was first on the scene but soon found herself outdistanced. The following tables show clearly what happened in the key industries of coal and iron.[1]

COAL PRODUCTION

	1860	1880	1900	1913	
Britain	83·3	149·5	228·8	292·0	million tons
Germany	17·0	60·0	149·8	277·3	
U.S.A.	15·4	71.6	244·6	517·0	

[1] The invention of the internal combustion engine made oil a new centre for Imperialist conflict. Oil production was from the start a monopoly affair, and the U.S.A. took and never lost, the lead. Oil not only helped to lead to war, but, with the motor, the tank and the aeroplane, has revolutionised its technique.

IRON AND STEEL PRODUCTION

	1870–4 average.	1900–4 average.	1913	
Britain	6·9	13·5	17·9	} million tons
Germany	2·1	16·2	27·4	
U.S.A.	2·3	29·8	30·0	

The main reason for this relative decline was the existence of the British Empire and the opportunities it afforded the investment of capital at an unusually high rate of profit. British industry was old-established and old-fashioned in many respects, and could only have beaten off its challengers by a thorough reconstruction. But while foreign investment offered its super-profits, there was no possibility of this reconstruction being undertaken. While the loss of the old Nineteenth Century industrial monopoly was inevitable, it is also true that the capital that might have been spent in developing British industry to meet the new conditions was used to a considerable extent in equipping potential rivals.

During the age of colonial expansion, that is, roughly up to 1900, Britain had been most frequently in conflict with France, the next most active colonising Power. From that date the main rival became Germany, which, left well behind in the race for colonies, began to penetrate what the British bourgeoisie had long been accustomed to regard as their own markets. The United States, which had the making of an even more dangerous rival, did not fully enter world politics till the War of 1914–18, though from about 1900 they began to make progress at the expense of British traders in South America. The reason for their late appearance was that they had not yet exhausted the possibilities of the exploitation of their own internal resources and those of Mexico, Central America and the West Indies which had fallen within their sphere of influence.

The partitioning of the world had been completed, not without conflicts and the threat of more which failed to materialise, by 1900. Britain and France had secured the richest booty, both in Africa, Asia and Australasia. Germany and Italy, late comers, had to be content with small and less desirable pickings. In the Far East Russia and Japan eyed one another, preparing to do battle for Korea and Manchuria.

It was becoming clear that the existing division of spoils could not be permanent: it had been made on the basis of the relative strength of the European Powers far back in the Nineteenth Century and no longer corresponded to realities. This was true above all of the division as between Britain and Germany. In the period before the War, it was around certain backward but not strictly colonial areas that Anglo-German rivalry centred. Such were the Balkans, where the German share of trade increased from 18.1 per cent to 29.2 per cent while that of Britain fell from 24 per cent to 14.9 per cent, South America, where German trade rose from 16 per cent to 19 per cent while British trade fell from 31 per cent to 28 per cent, and the slowly decaying Turkish Empire. Even within the British Empire, Germany was gaining ground at the expense of Britain.

Since there were no longer any unappropriated territories of any importance left, the redivision of the world could only be effected by war, and war on a gigantic scale since this was a question in which all of the Great Powers were deeply concerned. It is in the zig-zag path by which this war was reached that the main interest of the history of the years between 1900 and 1914 lies.

2. TRIPLE ALLIANCE, TRIPLE ENTENTE

British foreign policy during the greater part of the Nineteenth Century was, as we have seen,[1] dictated largely by a desire to avoid any over-close relations with other European Powers and to concentrate upon colonial aggression. We have now to trace the abandonment of this policy and the linking up of Britain with one of the two

[1] Chapter XIII, Section 3.

great groups into which Europe was divided by 1914. The story of the formation of these groups goes back at least to 1870, when France was defeated by Prussia. It is a story of complicated and shameless intrigues, of alliances made and repudiated or undermined by other conflicting alliances, a tangle of secret treaties of which possibly all have not come to light even now. It cannot be told here in detail, but a few leading lines can be traced with a fair confidence.

The field was occupied by four main Powers—Germany, Russia, France and Austria-Hungary—with Italy as a much less considerable fifth. After the Franco-Prussian War in which Germany annexed Alsace and Lorraine and exacted a heavy war indemnity, relations between these two Powers were almost uniformly hostile. The French Government was determined, at the first favourable opportunity, upon a war of revenge. German policy, consequently, was directed towards keeping France isolated, since it was clear that she was no match for Germany without allies. The relations of the other Powers were much less straightforward.

The German Chancellor, Bismarck, wished to maintain an alliance with both Austria and Russia, and for a number of years did manage this feat. Even after the 'Three Emperors' Alliance' lapsed in 1887, the connection between Germany and Russia was kept up for three years longer by a secret treaty of whose existence Bismarck's Austrian allies were unaware. The Dual Alliance between Germany and Austria was expanded into a Triple Alliance by the adhesion of Italy in 1882.

In the long run, however, it was not possible for Germany to preserve the alliance with both Austria and Russia, since these Powers were deeply committed to fundamentally opposed policies in South-eastern Europe. Even Bismarck would probably have found the task beyond him, and his fall was followed almost at once by a military alliance between France and Russia. The twenty years' isolation of France was thus ended, while Germany found in Austria

an ally more reliable and less independent than Russia
was ever likely to be. The two Central Powers were drawn
closer together by the menace of Russia, which they
imagined, as everyone did before 1914, was more formidable than was really the case, giving too much weight to
the vast man power and too little to the corruption and
inefficiency of the Russian State.

So far, Britain had remained outside either grouping,
though some tentative efforts were made towards an Anglo-
German agreement by both governments from about
1890. It is worth noting that the Tories were more disposed to consider an alliance with Germany than were the
Liberals, probably because they were the party most
directly connected with colonial enterprises and in this
field had frequently encountered French opposition.

It was the last and most acute of these colonial conflicts
which was indirectly responsible for the beginnings of the
Anglo-French entente. Their humiliation at Fashoda in
1899 convinced the French Government that they were
doomed to impotence so long as they were working in
opposition to both Britain and Germany. They were forced
to choose which they would have for an enemy, just as
Germany had been forced to choose between Austria and
Russia as allies. Then came the Boer War, revealing to the
British Government its dangerous isolation and setting it
to look around for an ally in Europe. The first approach
was made to Germany, but Germany put too high a price
upon her friendship. Negotiations broke off in a torrent of
abuse from the press and politicians of both countries and
the way was now clear for an alliance with France.

Characteristically, this was concluded over the body of a
colonial victim. Morocco, in which prospectors were
beginning to find indications of valuable minerals, was
obviously ripe for conquest by some European Power. It
was also a plum which no power would willingly see go to
another without some adequate compensation. So in 1904
France recognised the 'special interests' of Britain in
Egypt, while Britain, in rather guarded but perfectly well

understood language, promised France a free hand in Morocco.[1] So much was stated: what was implied was that either country would give the other the fullest support against any third power which attempted to put in a claim to Egypt or Morocco.

This understanding came into play in 1911, when France having discovered or created the amount of disorder in Morocco necessary as an excuse, marched in and seized the capital, Fez. Germany then demanded compensation in French Congo and backed her demand by sending gunboats to the Moroccan port of Agadir. The British Government made it clear, through the mouth of the one-time pacifist, Lloyd George, that France would be supported, to the point of war if necessary. War was indeed very close, but neither side was quite ready and a compromise was reached by which the French kept Morocco and Germany was allotted a much smaller slice of the Congo than had originally been claimed.

Even before the new Anglo-French entente had developed fully, relations with Germany had become more definitely hostile and this hostility found expression in a suicidal naval race.[2] German naval construction began in earnest in 1895, and the challenge was instantly taken up. In 1904 the extreme jingo, Lord Fisher, was appointed First Sea Lord, and he commenced a complete rearrangement of naval forces aimed ostentatiously against Germany. The main fighting fleet was withdrawn from the Mediterranean and concentrated in the North Sea. In private conversations, Fisher was actually urging that the German Navy should be surprised and destroyed ('Copenhagened' was the phrase used) in its home ports without even a declaration of war. When reports of this leaked out, they did little to convince Germany of the peaceful intentions of Britain.

[1] The Treaty stated that France had "no intention of altering the political status of Morocco", a formula which in the dealings of civilised with barbarous states is the invariable prelude to annexation. See page 462 above and page 488 below.

[2] It is significant that the first conflict between Britain and Germany arose over concessions for building a Turkish railway in 1892.

Two years later, in 1906, the launching of the *Dreadnought*, carrying a dozen twelve-inch guns instead of the customary four, made all existing battleships so much scrap iron. The Government proposed to build four of these monsters each year, but for various reasons construction fell short of this number in three successive years. In 1909 an extraordinary agitation with the slogan, "We want eight and we won't wait," was successful in sweeping the Government off its feet. There were startling 'revelations' containing horrifying details about German naval construction which later proved to be quite unfounded and to have been deliberately circulated by agents of certain armament firms. The gutter press, with Northcliffe's *Daily Mail* in the van, worked up an invasion scare that was none the less effective because it flew in the face of every political and military possibility. The result of the scare was a greatly increased naval budget and a notable advance in the psychological preparation of the peoples on both sides of the North Sea for war.

While this naval race was going on, Lord Haldane initiated a thorough overhaul of the British Army. Territorials were substituted as a mass reserve force in place of the much less efficient Volunteers, but the main purpose of the reforms was to create an army of 100,000 that could be mobilised instantly for service in France. The British Government refused to conclude any definite military alliance, but the British and French General Staffs held a series of discussions in which a joint plan of campaign was elaborated. As early as 1905 arrangements had been made for the sending of an expeditionary force to France. These staff talks, by which Britain was in fact committed to give military support to France, were carried on in such secrecy that they were unknown even to the majority of the Cabinet,[1] a striking example of the

---

[1] At least three members of the Cabinet, Asquith, Grey and Haldane appear to have been aware of these talks. On the technical side, Sir Henry Wilson, Chief of General Staff, bears the heaviest responsibility. Captain Liddell Hart speaks of the talks as "a rope round the neck of British policy".

way in which the bureaucratic machine in a modern capitalist State becomes independent of the democratic institutions which are supposed to control it.

The tie-up was completed by the equally secret and even more binding Naval Agreement. By this, the French fleet was concentrated in the Mediterranean and the British in the North Sea, both powers undertaking to look after the other's interests in the areas dominated by their respective fleets. This agreement obviously made it impossible for Britain not to take part in any war between Germany and France.

An understanding between Britain and Russia, though it was the inevitable result of the changed relations with France and Germany, took longer to achieve. A deep and traditional antagonism existed in Central Asia and the Near East, and in 1902 Britain had concluded an alliance with Japan. During the Russo-Japanese war relations became very strained and there seemed a possibility that Russia might drift back into the German camp. Yet the British alliance with Japan had the curious effect of making it easier for Britain to come to terms with Russia because it reinsured her position in Asia. Similarly, the weakness of Russia after the war with Japan and the 1905 Revolution made her less feared and more anxious to find allies. The French Government was only too anxious to play the part of go-between, and the first sign of the new relationship was the floating of a loan in London by the Tsarist Government, a loan which gave it the means to stamp out the Revolution. An Anglo-Russian entente was concluded in 1907, and in the next year Edward VII and the Tsar Nicholas met at Revel to cement the alliance.

Edward deserves some attention as a symbolic figure, the perfectly typical monarch of the new era of monopoly capitalism. It would be hard to say whether his strongly French sympathies were derived from his appreciation of Paris as a centre of pleasure or a centre of moneylending: at any rate, his prejudices have historical importance because they happened to run strongly in the same direction as the current of the times. His most intimate friends were jingos like Fisher and Lord Esher and the most vulgar and disreputable finance magnates. Of one of these, E. Wingfield-Stratford, in his book *The Victorian Aftermath* remarks: "It would be difficult to compute what Edward owed to the friendship of Sir Ernest Cassel, but such a computation if made would be most suitably recorded on cash-ruled paper." In return, Edward made use of the Revel visit to exert his influence in the matter of a loan which Sir Ernest was floating in Russia behind the backs of the British Government.

The entente needed only one thing more, a sacrificial victim, and this was readily forthcoming in Persia. By a treaty signed in 1907 Britain and Russia guaranteed the independence and integrity of Persia and divided it into three zones, the South-east falling to Britain, the North to Russia and the rest being left as a kind of neutral territory. In 1909 a democratic revolution took place in Persia, the Shah was deposed, and a real effort was made to introduce a measure of order and good government. This was not at all to the liking of Persia's overlords, and a Russian army proceeded, with some assistance from Britain in the South, to restore order, the Shah and the blessings of European domination.

As in the case of Morocco, the partitioning of Persia was intended not only to let Russia and Britain in but to keep Germany out. Up to this time, neither Britain nor Russia had had a point of direct territorial conflict with Germany, but now this, the one thing needed to make a world war absolutely certain, was added to the existing economic and naval rivalry. Germany, having failed in the earlier colonial race was attempting to stake out a claim in the Near East, which the decay of the Turkish Empire made into one vast danger zone stretching from Bosnia to Bagdad. The assassination at Sarajevo was in a sense an accident, but it was not an accident that the whole train of events from 1908 to 1914 had its seat in this area. Here all the great powers except France had direct interests of one sort or another, and the savage little States which had arisen on the fringe of the Turkish Empire proved to be excellent instruments of imperialist policy.

3. INTERNAL CRISIS, 1906–1914

In the General Election of 1906 the Tories, who had been in office, except for one short interval, since 1886, were swept out by an overwhelming popular vote. During their period of power the Sudan and East Africa had been overrun and the Boer Republics defeated. But the exhausting and inglorious anti-climax to the Boer War had robbed them of any credit that they might have claimed for this achievement. A reaction set in as the people discovered how little they gained from these much advertised colonial triumphs. At home the organised working class had been thoroughly roused by the threat to Trade Unionism in the Taff Vale Judgment. Internally, the Tory Party was split on the question of tariffs. Chamberlain and the other advanced Imperialists saw that the logical development of the Empire was towards a tariff-protected unit: another section of the Party clung to free trade, while its leader Balfour was afraid to commit himself too far in either direction.

The result was that while the Liberals were able to raise the bogey of dear food, the Tories were not in a position to put forward a consistent and determined protectionist case. In any case, the widespread and carefully fostered belief that the long period of prosperity that followed the repeal of the Corn Laws was the result of free trade was still so strong as to make the idea of tariffs unpopular. From a combination of all these causes the Liberals secured a record majority, capturing all the industrial areas with the exception of Chamberlain's stronghold of the Birmingham district. Chamberlain's success here, in strong contrast to the debacle elsewhere, ensured the dominance of the Protectionist group within the Tory Party.

Q I

Alongside the Liberals there was for the first time a compact body of twenty-nine members of the new Labour Party. Besides these, a number of Trade Union candidates had returned as Liberals and many of the Liberal and Radical M.P.s from the industrial areas were uneasily aware of the pledges they had made to their constituents, in particular to secure legislation to reverse the Taff Vale Judgment. One of the first actions of the new Parliament was to pass a Trade Disputes Act far more favourable to the workers than the Government had originally intended. It is the one and only indisputable victory to the credit of the Labour Party in these years.

Nevertheless, the Liberals were faced with something quite new, a political opposition party on its left. True this party was as yet small and moderate in its demands, but the more intelligent Liberal tacticians saw in it a menace that could only be held in check by the most careful demagogy. It was the existence of this Labour group, and still more of the changed feeling in the country which lay behind it, that was the true reason for the series of social reforms associated with the name of Lloyd George.

Lloyd George, a Welsh solicitor with the authentic chapel eloquence and a complete absence of scruples, had earned a reputation as a Radical by his opposition to the Boer War. His main asset between 1906 and 1914 seems to have been his capacity for starting hares, for diverting attention towards all sorts of minor issues and minor enemies—the Lords, the landowners, the Church or the brewers—and away from the questions of prices and wages with which the masses were more profoundly concerned. Certainly the social reforms of the pre-war years, some of them not without their own value, dealt with almost everything except these questions.

The first was an Old Age Pension scheme, providing a pension of 5s. a week for people over seventy whose income did not exceed £21 a year. This was followed by a Town Planning Act sponsored by John Burns, Health and Unemployment Insurance Acts and finally an Agricultural

Charter, launched with unlimited thunder against the landlords, but in fact completely ineffective.

Whatever the other effects of these reforms may have been they succeeded in one of their main aims, that of taking the sting out of the Parliamentary Labour Party. From 1906 to 1914, in a time of great and increasing class conflicts, the Labour Party was content to form a mere radical appendage to Liberalism, mildly critical of details but never venturing upon an independent policy or dreaming of taking any action which might endanger the life of the Government. One occasion on which they did become really angry was when Edward VII neglected to invite some of their leading members to an official reception at Buckingham Palace.

Lloyd Georgism, being in essence an effort to buy off the working class, was naturally somewhat expensive. The vast programme of armaments on which the Liberal Government speedily embarked was even more so. The figures in the following table speak eloquently of the rapid growth of the state apparatus in the epoch of Imperialism:

Average

	1873–5	1905–7	1911–13
Total Budget	£68,700,000	£134,000,000	£163,000,000
Army and Navy	£25,300,000	£59,800,000	£73,300,000

In the beginning of 1909 Lloyd George, newly promoted to the post of Chancellor of the Exchequer, had to find the then huge sum of £16,000,000 in new taxation. Out of this dilemma he forged a subtle offensive weapon to score off the Tory House of Lords and to revive the waning popularity of the Liberal Government as the defender of the people against aristocratic privilege.

In the earlier sessions of Parliament the Lords had rejected or mutilated a series of Liberal measures, in themselves of no great importance and of doubtful popularity. Now Lloyd George introduced a Budget which deliberately included taxes calculated to enrage every section of the Lords from the landowners to the brewers. The House of Lords walked straight into the trap by rejecting the Budget, an act for which there was no historic precedent. Having been presented with what appeared to be a first class election issue, the Liberals went to the country in January 1910 on the slogan of "Peers versus People".

The result, from their point of view, was somewhat disappointing. The Tories gained a large number of seats and when Parliament reassembled they and the Liberals were in roughly equal numbers, the balance being held by the Labour and Irish Nationalist groups. A second election later in the year left the distribution of parties almost unchanged. The Liberals were able to force their Budget through the House of Lords, but only by securing the support of the Irish with a promise to introduce a Home Rule Bill.

The conflict with the Lords ended with a Parliament Act which deprived the Upper House of its power to veto money Bills and restricted their veto on other Bills by a provision that a measure passed through the House of Commons in three successive sessions should become law in spite of having been rejected by the House of Lords. The more intelligent Tories were not dissatisfied by this compromise which regularised the powers of the House of Lords at the same time as it limited them.

The elections of 1910 were fought amid what seemed to the Liberal politicians an extraordinary indifference on the part of the people as a whole. Neither the Lloyd George reforms nor the struggle against the Lords appeared to arouse the expected enthusiasm. The main reason was that by 1910 the conditions of the workers had become appreciably worse than they were in 1900 and Liberalism had entirely failed to provide a remedy.

From the middle of the Nineteenth Century to the nineties, prices had tended to fall, with the development of machine production and especially since the application of machinery to agriculture in America and elsewhere.

Then the tide turned. There was a rapid rise in prices between 1895 and 1900 which continued somewhat more slowly from 1900 to 1906 and very rapidly after 1906. It has been estimated that "the purchasing power of 20s. in the hands of a working-class housewife in 1895 went down to 18s. 5d. in 1900, to 17s. 11d. in 1905, to 16s. 11d. in 1910 and to 14s. 7d. in 1914."

For this rise in prices there were several reasons, of which the chief was probably the gigantic increase in the output of gold which followed the discovery of the Rand gold reef. It will be noted that the two periods of sharpest increase were that following upon the first discovery of the reef and that after 1905 when the conquest of the Transvaal had had time to take effect. The expenditure of all great Powers upon arms, the increase of tariffs and the general development of monopoly were all contributing causes. The rise took place in a period of prosperity, that is, in a period of increasing profits. Between 1893 and 1908, according to the calculation of Chiozza Money, profits increased by 29·5 per cent but nominal wages only by 12 per cent. Thus while profits were rising faster than prices, real wages were decreasing by roughly the same proportion and it was the slow perception of this fact, the realisation of the workers that they were growing poorer just at the time their employers were growing richer, which accounts for the bitterness of the great strike struggles of the early years of the present century. No such open class antagonism had been seen in Britain since the time of the Chartists.

The strike movement had both its origin and its strength in the rank and file. The Parliamentary Labour Party was left far behind, and the Trade Union leaders were either driven into action or found themselves without followers or authority. Local and spontaneous outbursts led to the formulation of national programmes, demands for a minimum wage or for reduced hours. Strikes for Union recognition were common. In the last years before the War the movement began to evolve a political programme, as for example in the demand of the miners for nationalisation,

crude in some of its details but far in advance of that of the
Labour Party. The movement was cut short by the outbreak of war before it had time to reach its full height, but
there are indications at least that it was developing towards
a conscious struggle for power. It is probable that only the
War prevented a General Strike which would have raised
directly the question of revolution.

As early as 1905 there was an important strike among the
miners of South Wales, always an area marked by a peculiar
militancy, and, most significantly, the coalfield where
monopoly organisation had made the greatest strides.
This was followed by strikes among railwaymen, cotton
spinners, engineers and the miners of Northumberland and
Durham.

By 1910 the struggle was in full swing. A strike of the miners
in the Cambrian Combine which lasted from November
into August, 1911, was marked by furious skirmishing in
Tonypandy and Penycraig and was only defeated because
of the weakness of the Federation Leadership. It brought to
the front a new group of militants in South Wales and gave
the inspiration for the national coal strike of 1912.

The next section to move into action were the dockers and
seamen. In June there were strikes at Southampton and
at Hull, where there was considerable rioting. A month
later the Manchester dockers and carters came out, and
almost immediately this dispute was settled, the great
London dock strike began, tying up the whole Thames
from Brentford to the Medway. Thousands of tons of goods
rotted on the wharves and not a load could be moved
without a permit from the strike committee. The determination of the dockers quickly made the Government
abandon their idea of clearing the docks by military force
and the strike ended with the concession of most of the
demands, including a wage of 8d. an hour.

While London was in the grip of the dock strike, Tom
Mann was in Liverpool and Manchester helping to
organise an unofficial strike that soon broadened into a
national rail strike for the recognition of the Union and

the abandonment of compulsory arbitration. Government intervention imposed a compromise settlement which did not prevent further outbreaks in 1912.

Nineteen-twelve saw the first national miners' strike and a further London dock strike against the victimisation of Trade Unionists. The struggle took a somewhat different turn in 1913. There were few large strikes, that in Dublin being by far the most important, but a record number of small, local disputes. It was a year of pause and of the gathering of forces. In 1914 the upward movement was resumed and was accompanied by two significant organisational advances. First was the formation of a Triple Alliance of miners, railwaymen and transport workers, each pledged to turn out in support of the others' demands. In the existing state of feeling this made a General Strike in the near future a virtual certainty. The second was the growth of the Shop Stewards movement among the engineers, a movement reflecting most closely the mood of the rank and file and one which took a leading position during the war years when the official Trade Union machine had been handed over to the Government.

The struggles of 1910 to 1914 ended the fall in real wages and brought a flood of recruits into the Unions. In four years the membership rose from 2,369,067 to 3,918,809.

This movement of the working class was not the only awkward problem facing the Liberal Government. Another was the extraordinary campaign led by the Pankhursts for the extension of the franchise to women. It was carried on by methods of terrorism and met with equally merciless police violence, culminating in the torture of forcible feeding in prison and the notorious Cat and Mouse Act. In June 1914 the Government promised to introduce a Women's Suffrage Bill, but the campaign was continued with unabated fury right up to the outbreak of war, when Mrs. Pankhurst and her daughter Christabel were transformed overnight into equally uncompromising jingos.

Much more serious was the question of Ireland. In return for the support of the Irish Nationalists the Government introduced in 1912 a Home Rule Bill which gave Ireland a measure of independence considerably less than that enjoyed by the Dominions. The Bill was rejected by the House of Lords, and the two years that had to elapse before it could become law were used by the Tories in open preparations for civil war. The key point in the dispute was the future of Ulster, the north-west portion of Ireland which had a fanatically Protestant population largely Scottish in origin. More important, Belfast, with its shipbuilding and flax industries, was the principal stronghold of British Imperialism in Ireland.

Irish nationalists claimed that Ireland was a nation, single and indivisible, and that no English Parliament had the right to partition it. The Ulster Protestants, professing a passionate loyalty that did not prevent them from contemplating the securing of aid from Germany, claimed that no English Parliament had the right to place them under the rule of the Catholics of the South. The dispute at last narrowed down to the two border counties of Fermanagh and Tyrone, but the Tories continued a reckless treason-mongering which grew bolder at each indication of the cowardice of the Liberals. A Solemn Covenant, a warmed-up version of the Seventeenth Century original,[1] was signed by thousands of Ulstermen, who undertook to use "all means which may be found necessary to defeat the present conspiracy to set up a Home Rule Parliament in Ireland". A large body of Volunteers was raised, and the movement was led by Sir Edward Carson and an English barrister, F. E. Smith, both of whom were later appointed to seats in the Cabinet. In England Bonar Law and the Tory leaders openly pledged their support to the rebels and incited the Army to acts of disobedience and mutiny. The speeches made by responsible Tories at this time provide the material for a whole handbook of sedition.

The climax was reached when the Army officers stationed at the Curragh threatened to resign in a body before they would carry out orders to move against the Volunteers.

[1] See page 216 above.

In this action they were encouraged by the very highest military authorities including Sir Henry Wilson who was himself an Ulsterman. This was on March 19th, 1914. A month later a cargo of 35,000 German rifles and 3,000,000 rounds of ammunition was run into Larne under the nose of the British Navy in a ship whose name, with the historical romanticism so typical of the Orangeman, had been changed for the occasion from *Fanny* to *Mountjoy*.[1] Of the Curragh mutiny, and the Tory rebellion generally, Lenin wrote at the time:

"The Liberal Government was completely overwhelmed by the rebellion of the landlords, who stood at the head of the Army. The Liberals were accustomed to console themselves with constitutional illusions and phrases about the law, and closed their eyes to the real relation of forces, to the class struggle. And this real relation of forces was and remains such that, owing to the cowardice of the bourgeoisie, a number of *pre-bourgeois*, medieval, landlord institutions and privileges have been preserved.

"In order to suppress the rebellion of the aristocratic officers, the Liberal Government ought to have appealed to the people, to the masses, to the proletariat, but this is exactly what the 'enlightened' Liberal bourgeoisie were more afraid of than anything else in the world. And so *in fact* the Government made *concessions* to the mutinous officers, persuaded them to withdraw their resignations and gave them *written guarantees* that troops would not be used against Ulster. . . .

"March 21st, 1914, will mark a world-historical turning point, when the noble landlords of England, smashing the English constitution and the English law to atoms, gave an excellent lesson in the class struggle."

In the South of Ireland the challenge from Ulster had been taken up by the formation in 1913 of the Irish Volunteers. Events received a new turn from the Dublin dock

[1] The original *Mountjoy* was the ship which broke through the boom across the harbour at Derry when the Protestants were besieged there by the Catholic Jacobites in 1689.

strike of this year, when the Dublin employers embarked upon a deliberate attempt to smash the militant Irish Transport Workers' Union. In this struggle the police reached new heights of savagery, two workers being beaten to death and hundreds injured. In spite of the enthusiastic support they received from English Trade Unionists the strikers were defeated, but the defeat left an invaluable legacy in Connolly's Citizen Army.

Created as a workers' defence force at a time when the police were acting as a private army of the employers, it remained in being afterwards and drew gradually closer to the left wing of the nationalist Volunteers. Connolly understood what few Socialists except Lenin understood at this time, the relation of the class struggle to the national struggle of a colonial people. He saw in the Irish workers and peasants the true heirs of the tradition of Wolfe Tone· and the Fenians, and that only in a Workers' and Peasants' Republic would the people of Ireland be really free. By his arguments and his practice he communicated this belief to the best elements in the Irish Republican Brotherhood, men like Pearse and Tom Clarke. But while the Brotherhood had taken the initiative in the formation of the Volunteers, the success of the movement attracted the notice of Redmond and his followers who saw nothing more in it than a useful bargaining counter in the parliamentary game. The conflict which resulted led inevitably to a complete split on the outbreak of the War.

Like the Ulster Volunteers, the Nationalists set about obtaining arms, but in striking contrast to the immunity which the former enjoyed was the attempt of the police and troops to intercept a cargo landed at Howth on July 26th. The attempt failed, but later in the day the troops fired on an unarmed crowd at Bachelor's Walk, killing three and wounding thirty-eight. This incident set all Southern Ireland ablaze, and since the negotiations about Ulster had finally broken down, there seemed no alternative to civil war.

Civil war in Ireland, and, less close but more ominous,

the rising tide of labour unrest with the possibility of a General Strike, set the bourgeoisie a problem to which no solution was apparent. Further, the support given to the Dublin strikers, which only the most strenuous efforts of the Trade Union officials had prevented from issuing in sympathetic strike action, suggested the even more terrifying prospect of a merging of the two dangers, of a struggle for the liberation of Ireland, supported by a General Strike in England.

Nor was such a situation peculiar to Britain. In India and Egypt the national movements were making rapid progress. The Russian people were recovering from the defeats of 1905 and 1906 and a revolutionary crisis seemed to be approaching. The Caillaux scandal in France threatened to have even graver consequences than the Dreyfus case, while the terrible burden of armaments had brought that country within measurable distance of bankruptcy. In Germany the Social Democrats were gaining hundreds of thousands of new adherents every year.

There was, in fact, hardly an important country to which a foreign war did not promise an easy if ultimately costly way out of internal difficulties which seemed to have no other solution. The War of 1914 was no doubt the inevitable result of the general situation created by world imperialism, but these internal difficulties must after all be reckoned among its symptoms and dictated to a very considerable extent the precise moment for the outbreak of war.

4. THE ROAD TO SARAJEVO

A great deal of time and energy has been wasted in attempts to fix the responsibility for the World War upon this or that State or politician. Arguments about the Austrian ultimatum to Serbia; the exact date of mobilisation of the respective armies and so forth have a certain academic interest, but they cannot affect the main fact, which was that for more than a decade Europe had been divided into two rival imperialist groups, each heavily armed and seeking to expand at the expense of the other. It may even be true that none of the States concerned 'wanted' war: it is certainly true that none of them wanted war if they could achieve their objects without. What is more important is that without exception they were pursuing policies of which war was the inevitable outcome.

War was the result of the imperialist monopoly stage of capitalist development, but it is possible to single out more precisely points of conflict around which the general politics of the imperialist epoch turned. One, as we have seen, was the trade rivalry between Britain and Germany, which took the form of British attempts to shut Germany out of the colonial and semi-colonial areas and a counter attempt by Germany to break through the British ring by a thrust to the South-east through the Balkans and Turkey.

A second was the Franco-German economic struggle, based on the fact that in Eastern France there were large deposits of iron but little coal, and in Western Germany much coal but little iron. The industrialists of both Powers hoped to unite the whole area under their own control as the result of a victorious war. Third, the ambition of Russia to control the Straits connecting the Black Sea and the Mediterranean was in direct conflict with Germany's eastward drive while Russian influence in the Balkans was constantly exerted to disrupt the Austrian Empire with its large Slav and Roumanian populations.

The situation was embittered by the pace at which preparations for war were pushed ahead, every increase by one group leading to corresponding or greater increases by the other. The German-British naval race has already been mentioned. On land, the competition was no less keen. France and Russia increased the peace strength of their armies from 1,470,000 in 1899 to 1,813,000 in 1907 and to 2,239,000 in 1914. The corresponding figures for

Austria and Germany were 950,000, 1,011,000 and 1,239,000. In the last ten years before the war the cost of the French and Russian armies was £842,000,000 and that of the German and Austrian £682,000,000. It will be noted that these figures give no support to the myth that the Central Powers made a long-prepared attack upon peaceful and unarmed neighbours.

In the last years the pace became killing. Germany raised a capital levy of £50,000,000 in 1913 for special military expenditure. At the same time France raised the period of military service from two to three years and Russia raised hers by six months. Both Britain and Germany speeded up their naval programmes. It was clear that war was very close, if only because the financial experts of all countries were of the opinion that the current expenditure on armaments could not be maintained without serious risk of bankruptcy.

It is not surprising, therefore, that the years before 1914 were punctuated by a series of crises any one of which might have led to a general war. Such were the disputes over Morocco in 1905-6 and in 1911, over Bosnia in 1908, over Tripoli in 1911 and over the Balkan Wars of 1912. In each of these crises the difficulties were overcome, but only at the cost of creating new stresses and less easily resolved conflicts.

It will be observed that two of the three major points at issue turned upon the Balkans, and, while it is not true that the Balkan question was the main cause of the War, it was here that the greatest possibilities of diplomatic aggravation existed, and it is to this area that we must turn for the War's immediate causes. And, increasingly, Serbia became the focus of all disturbance till this barbarous little State acquired an eminence in European politics out of all proportion to its population or importance.

For this there were two reasons. First the spinal cord of Germany's eastern design, vital to her development as an imperialist Power, was the railway to Constantinople, part of a projected Berlin to Baghdad route that would ensure the vassalage of Turkey and ultimately threaten the British and Russian positions in Persia and India. This route passed through Serbia, and so long as Serbia was under Russian control an essential link was missing. In the second place, Serbia became the weapon with which Russia was working for the disruption of the Austrian Empire. The conflict developed slowly in the early years of the century and was precipitated by the murder of the pro-Austrian King Alexander by supporters of the Russian Party. This was followed in 1905 by an economic war between Austrian and Serbia. In 1908 Austria annexed the nominally Turkish province of Bosnia which she had administered since 1879 but which had a population predominantly Serbian. Russia was forced to acquiesce by a threat of war in which Austria had the backing of Germany. The seizure of Tripoli by Italy in 1911, by revealing the full weakness of Turkey, made it easy for Russia to organise an alliance of the Balkan States, whose first object was the reconquest of the remaining provinces of Turkey in Europe but which it was hoped later to turn against Austria.

After a short war the Balkan allies were victorious and Serbia proposed to take as her share the northern part of Albania, while most of Macedonia was allotted to Bulgaria. Austria then intervened and insisted on the formation of an independent Albanian State. Serbia demanded compensation in Macedonia, a demand which Austria privately encouraged Bulgaria to resist. In the Second Balkan War the Bulgarians were defeated and lost a large part of their conquests.

The result was a new Balkan grouping, in which Serbia remained as the instrument of Russia while Bulgaria and Turkey entered into a loose alliance with the Central Powers. Germany in particular emerged as the 'protector' of Islam, a role extremely embarrassing to Britain with her millions of Moslem subjects in India and Africa. In 1913 the reorganisation of the Turkish Army was undertaken by German military experts. Serbia, with Russian support, began to prepare for the seizure of Bosnia by means of an armed rising to be supported by an invasion. Pashitch, the Serbian Prime Minister, is reported on good authority to have declared at the Bucharest Conference which followed the Second Balkan War, "The first game is won; now we must prepare for the second, against Austria."

An intensified campaign of terrorism was launched, in which a number of Austrian officials were murdered, and the shooting of the Archduke Francis Ferdinand, heir to the Austrian throne, at Sarejevo on June 28th, 1914, was not an isolated incident but only the climax of a series of outrages. There can be little doubt that the assassination was prepared with the knowledge of the Serbian authorities or that it was welcomed by the Austrian Government as an opportunity to settle accounts with Serbia. It is only when the Serajevo incident is seen in its place in the whole series of Balkan events that the severity of the Austrian ultimatum and the stubborn refusal of Austria to accept any compromise terms becomes understandable. We have also seen what reasons Germany had to make the fullest use of the case with which the Serbian terrorists had presented her.

The position of Russia was equally simple: to allow Serbia to be crushed was to allow Germany a free road to Constantinople, to give up all her hopes of securing the Straits and all her plans for the disruption of Austria. There was no alternative between war and the abandonment of her struggle with the Central Powers for the domination of Eastern Europe. France had no direct interest in the question at issue in the Balkans, but was completely tied to Russia. To allow Russia to fight alone meant complete isolation in Europe whatever the result of the war, a possibility which the French Government was not prepared to risk on any account. So the train ran from point to point, till the European powder magazine, so zealously crammed with explosives by the labour of a generation, went up in one vast roar.

In England the Serajevo murder attracted little attention at first. To the ordinary man it was only another example of Balkan savagery, while even the Government appears to have been too preoccupied with the crisis in Ireland to appreciate its full significance. As the days passed and the threat of a European war grew louder the overwhelming mass of the British people remained indifferent: Serbia was not popular and it was extremely difficult to persuade anyone that it was necessary to go to war on her behalf.

Difficult or not, it had to be done once it became clear that France was going to be involved, if only because the Anglo-French military and naval arrangements, of which the people knew nothing, were in fact as binding as any formal treaty. They were kept in the dark right up to the end. Sir Edward Grey, the Foreign Secretary, solemnly announced in the House of Commons on June 11th:

"If war arose between European Powers, there were no unpublished agreements which would restrict or hamper the freedom of the Government or of Parliament to decide whether or not Great Britain should participate in a war. That remains as true to-day as it was a year ago. No such negotiations are in progress and none are likely to be entered upon so far as I can judge."

It was a statement outstandingly untruthful and misleading even by the standards of British Liberalism, since Sir Edward knew, what was concealed even from the House of Commons, that Britain was pledged to protect the North Coast of France from naval attack in the event of war.

The attitude of the Government in the days before the War could hardly have been more calculated to make its outbreak certain. France and Russia knew that Britain would intervene on their behalf. Germany was allowed to believe that there was at least a good chance of Britain remaining neutral. Whatever may have been the intention behind this attitude, its result was to encourage both sides to stand out stubbornly for terms that could not possibly be conceded.

In the last few days events moved with extraordinary speed. Just at one moment it appeared that Germany was becoming alarmed at the prospect of war. Italy and Roumania were clearly not going to carry out their treaty obligations and even their neutrality might have to be bought with territorial concessions. But the chance passed, since the rulers of Austria and Russia were now set upon war. Russia mobilised on July 31st, Germany and France on August 1st, and, under modern conditions, mobilisation was equivalent to a declaration of war.

In Britain, in spite of an intense war campaign in the jingo press, the great mass of working class and liberal opinion was in favour of peace. The Government, however, had already made its choice. As early as July 29th the British Grand Fleet had sailed for its war stations in the North Sea. On August 2nd Grey informed the French Ambassador:

"I am instructed to give an assurance that, if the German Fleet comes into the Channel or through the North Sea, to undertake hostile operations against the French coasts or shipping, the British Fleet will give all the protection in its power."

Under these circumstances the invasion of Belgium came as a veritable godsend, enabling the Government to disguise a war of imperialist robbery as a war for the upholding of treaty rights and the defence of small nations. It was even possible to extend to Serbia a little of the heroic glow with which Belgium was speedily invested. In fact, the treaty guaranteeing Belgian neutrality had long been obsolete, Belgium had been drawn into the Franco-British orbit and for years the French, British and Belgian general staffs had been drawing up plans in the certainty that France and Belgium would form a single battlefield. Further, plans had been made for the landing of British troops on the Belgian coast, and it is as certain as anything can be that even if German troops had not entered Belgian territory at the beginning of August, Allied troops would have done so before its end.

All this was carefully hidden from the British people in 1914, when on August 4th an ultimatum was sent to Germany demanding the withdrawal of her troops from Belgian soil. At midnight, no reply having been received, the two countries entered upon a formal state of war.

CHAPTER XVII

WORLD WAR: WORLD CRISIS

1. THE WORLD WAR

YEARS BEFORE HOSTILITIES began, the rival military experts had prepared their plans of campaign. The Germans proposed to concentrate all their forces for a flanking march through Belgium, along and beyond the Meuse, and so to avoid the strong line of forts with which the Alsace-Lorraine border was defended. On this part of their front they decided to stand on the defensive, and, as the plan was originally drafted, even thought of retiring towards the Rhine. In the East, too, they were to be on the defensive, counting on the slowness of Russian mobilisation and allowing the Austrians to bear the brunt of the first encounters. The main army, after passing through Belgium, was to sweep round in a vast semi-circle, moving to the west and south of Paris and eventually coming into the rear of the French armies massed along the fortress line from Verdun to Belfort.

The French plan, viewed in retrospect, might seem to have been designed with the purpose of ensuring a German victory. Their General Staff had full warning of the German scheme, but a curious psychological blindness made them ignore it, because to admit it would have meant to revise their own plan, and this was based rather on political and sentimental than upon military considerations. The frontier north of the Ardennes was left virtually unguarded, while a fierce, and it was hoped, decisive offensive was to be launched into Lorraine. The basis of this hope was an intense and almost mystical belief in the virtue of attack, and above all of French troops in attack, which permeated their military circles in the decade before 1914.

The French plan was tried in August 1914 with disastrous results: the German plan only failed because it was weakened before the outbreak of war and not persisted in after it. By degrees the southern wing of the German Army was strengthened at the expense of the northern offensive wing. When the War began, the advance through Belgium was carried through according to time-table up to a point. Then Moltke, the German commander, attempted a sudden change of plan, abandoning the sweep round Paris for an attempt to surround the French centre, pushed up into a salient at Verdun. To do this the direction of the advance had to be changed over a wide front, and it was this change, and the confusion resulting, which gave the opportunity for the successful counter-attack known as the Battle of the Marne. At the same time, the offensive had been weakened by the detachment of several divisions to the Russian front, where they arrived just too late to play any effective part in the victory of Tannenburg.

The Battle of the Marne, little more than a skirmish by the standards of slaughter set by later battles, was nevertheless the turning point of the whole war. It made a quick German victory impossible and gave time for the great but slowly mobilised material resources of the British Empire to have their effect, and for the naval blockade to cut off the supply of necessary imports. After the Marne, the Western Front settled down to a vast and prolonged siege warfare, after a preliminary stage in which a series of attempted outflanking movements carried the line of battle up to the coast. For three years both sides made repeated and costly, but quite unsuccessful, efforts to break through this trench barrier by frontal attacks. New weapons, such as tanks and poison gas were used, but not on a large enough scale to be really effective. Such attempts were the Battles of Loos and Arras and in Champagne in 1915, of Verdun and the Somme in 1916 and of Ypres in 1917.

The Western Front was, however, only one of many theatres of war. In the East the Russians had some successes against Austrian armies, but their badly armed and led troops proved quite incapable of holding their own against the superior weapons and organisation of the Germans and they suffered immense losses. The closing of the Baltic and Black Seas made it impossible for the British to supply any significant quantities of war materials and Russian heavy industry was unable to meet the strain of a large scale modern war. The key to the situation lay, therefore, in the Dardanelles. If they were forced Turkey would be driven out of the war, arms could be sent to Russia in exchange for the wheat of the Ukraine, and, in all probability, Bulgaria, Greece and Roumania would have entered the war immediately on what would have been apparently the winning side. Incidentally, there would probably have been no Russian Revolution in 1917.

Until February or March, 1915, the Dardanelles lay wide open, but both British and French High Commands were so obsessed with the belief that they could break through in the West that they would not release the forces needed. When the decision was at last taken for an attack, the Turks were given full warning by a naval bombardment followed by a long pause. The landings that were made on the Gallipoli peninsular on April 25th found the defenders just too strong, and, though points on the peninsular were held till December, repeated attempts to break through were driven back with heavy losses. By one of the strangest ironies of history, the Tsarist Government refused to co-operate, for the political reason that they wanted to take Constantinople for themselves and did not wish to see it captured if the British were to have a hand in the operation. No doubt they remembered the remarkable British tendency not to relinquish any territory once occupied, but by their passivity they sealed their own fate.

While these attempts were being made to open the way into the Black Sea, the Russian armies were being relentlessly pounded in Poland and Galicia, losing 750,000 prisoners and countless dead and wounded. In September, when the effects of these defeats had become clear and it was obvious that the attack on the Dardanelles had failed, Bulgaria joined the Central Powers and Serbia was overrun by a joint attack which opened direct communications between Germany and Turkey. Nineteen-fifteen closed with the balance considerably in Germany's favour: against a series of military successes there was little to be placed but the effects of the naval blockade, intensified by an unusually bad harvest.

It was as a counter to this blockade that Germany began the first submarine campaign towards the end of 1915. This was abandoned in April 1916 after protests from the U.S.A., but it had the unintended effect of making the American Government less inclined to object to the high-handed way in which the British blockade was enforced. It was the tightening of this blockade in 1916 that led to a renewed and much more successful submarine offensive in June, after the indecisive Battle of Jutland. In January 1917, 368,000 tons of shipping were sunk and in February it was announced that all ships, neutral or otherwise, might be attacked without warning.

This declaration provided the official ground for the entry of the U.S.A. into the War. A much more weighty reason was the fact that the Allies had been supplied with vast quantities of munitions and war materials of all kinds on credit and that it had become clear that if Germany were victorious, as seemed likely, these debts could never be collected. War was declared on April 2nd, but it was over a year before an American army was ready to take any active part. Nevertheless it was obvious that more than ever it was essential for Germany to seek a quick decision. The effects of the blockade, however, had been somewhat lessened by the conquest of the wheatlands and oil wells of Roumania in the autumn of 1916.

Almost at the same time at which America was entering the war, revolution began in Russia. The March Revolution was the work of two opposed forces temporarily combined: the masses who were tired of the pointless slaughter of the war and the bourgeoisie who wished to carry it on more efficiently than the corrupt Tsarist bureaucracy was able to do. The Revolutionary Government tried to drive the Army into another doomed offensive, but meanwhile the soldiers were streaming home and in November the Bolsheviks, with their simple and popular programme of "Peace, Land and Bread" were able to seize power and set up a government of revolutionary Socialists.

The first action of the new Government was to issue an appeal to all the Powers at war for the conclusion of a negotiated peace without annexations or indemnities. The appeal was coldly ignored, and, as far as possible, kept from the knowledge of the peoples. The Bolsheviks then signed an armistice and began negotiations for a separate peace which was finally signed at Brest-Litovsk on March 3rd, 1918.

The governments were not prepared for peace, but the Russian Revolution began at once to work on the minds and affections of the soldiers and workers all over Europe. Its repercussions in England will be dealt with in the next section. In France there was a widespread demand for peace and there were mutinies in the Army which at one time involved no fewer than sixteen Army Corps. Desertions rose to the alarming figure of 21,000 in the year 1917. In Germany there was a serious naval mutiny led by revolutionary Socialists and a series of strikes. Over a million workers took part in a General Strike in January.

In 1918, therefore, the problem before all the governments was whether the war could be won in the field before the wrath of the people at home had overwhelmed both war and governments. For Germany, where opposition was growing most rapidly and the people were suffering from famine because of the blockade, the urgency was increased by the appearance of the first contingents of American troops in France. The ending of war with Russia released a number of divisions for the Western

Front and the British Army had been almost destroyed in the crazy offensive of the autumn of 1917, when 400,000 men were sacrificed in an attempt to break through in the swamps around Ypres. For a few months the Germans could count on a numerical superiortiy in the West, though it was less pronounced than that previously enjoyed by the Allies.

In March a surprise attack broke through the weakly held line of the British Fifth Army between Arras and the Oise and the gap was only closed with the greatest difficulty. A second attack in April between Ypres and La Bassée and a third in May on the Aisne, while meeting with considerable success, failed to achieve decisive results. The attacks dwindled away and there were no more reserves left to replace the wastage of men and materials. On the other side of the line, American troops were now arriving at the rate of 300,000 a month. On August 8th a series of counter-attacks in force began which gained ground rapidly, driving the German armies from position after position and inflicting heavy losses, though they were able to maintain an unbroken front. Elsewhere the collapse was even more startling. Turkey, Bulgaria and Austria were driven to conclude an armistice and Germany was threatened with an invasion from the South which there were no forces available to meet.

Early in November revolution broke out in Germany. The sailors at Kiel, when ordered to put out into the North Sea, refused to sail and set up Soviets in the ports. Their envoys scattered widely over the country and everywhere the news of their success was the signal for revolt. In Berlin Liebknecht's powerful influence was already stirring the people to action. On November 6th German delegates left Berlin to ask for an armistice: on the the 9th the Kaiser abdicated and a Republic was set up with the right wing Social Democrat Ebert as President.

The terms of the Armistice were little better than an unconditional surrender, but the majority of the German people undoubtedly believed that the peace would finally be made on the basis of President Wilson's famous 'Fourteen Points', a draft settlement which he had published in January as being in his opinion fair and reasonable. These 'Points' included the freedom of the seas, general disarmament, "an impartial adjustment of all colonial claims" and, by omission, they appeared to imply that there were to be no annexations or indemnities.

The enunciation of this programme, together with other statements of a similar character made since America's entry into the war, had had a great effect upon the peoples of the Allied nations. They did not know of the network of secret treaties and understandings—many of them mutually contradictory—by which their governments had in anticipation divided the spoils. At a time when the fine phrases that had served to glorify the commencement of the war were wearing thin, Wilson's programme had come to invest the struggle with a new halo of idealism and had helped to revive the belief that the war was being fought in defence of justice and democracy. The ruling classes were quite prepared to encourage this belief. It received its death blow when the wrangling at the Versailles Peace Conference brought into the light the real objectives, the openly imperialist aims of the bourgeoisie of the conquering Powers.

2. THE HOME FRONT

Like its fellow members of the Second International the British Labour Party surrendered completely to the Government and the ruling class upon the outbreak of war. In 1910, when the danger of a war of the kind which broke out in 1914 was already apparent, the International at its Basle Congress had passed a resolution in which all the Socialist Parties affirmed that in the case of war it was "their duty to intervene in favour of its speedy termination and with all their powers to utilise the political and economic crisis created by the war to arouse the people and thereby to hasten the downfall of capitalist class

RE

rule ". On the very eve of war the terms of this pledge were re-affirmed at a huge Trafalgar Square demonstration where Keir Hardie and Arthur Henderson were among the speakers. Similar demonstrations were held in many big towns.

But before the end of August the Labour Party had decided to support the Government's recruiting campaign, and, far from attempting to "arouse the people" the Labour Party and the Trade Union Congress decided:

"That an immediate effort be made to terminate all existing disputes, whether strikes or lock-outs, and wherever new points of difficulty arise during the war a serious attempt should be made by all concerned to reach an amicable settlement before resorting to strikes or lock-outs."

These capitulations left the workers leaderless and bewildered and did perhaps more than anything else to convince them of the correctness of the official propaganda about the character of the war. Of all the European Socialist Parties only the Bolsheviks carried on the struggle against war on revolutionary lines. Elsewhere such opposition was confined to small groups and to individuals like Rosa Luxemburg and Karl Liebknecht in Germany, Connolly in Ireland and John McLean in Scotland. In England opposition to the war often took the peculiar form of pacifism.

The resolution quoted above was soon strengthened by direct agreements with the Government for the prevention of strikes and by the surrender of Trade Union safeguards that had taken generations of struggle to secure. Compulsory arbitration was enforced and strikes were declared illegal in a number of industries. Under the Defence of the Realm Act (D.O.R.A.) a complete censorship was imposed which confined the Left press to propaganda of the most general kind and even then left it open to frequent attacks and suppression. Later when the Liberal Government was replaced by 'National' coalition, leading members of the Labour Party, including Henderson and Clynes, became members of these governments alongside of Churchill, Lloyd George, Carson and Bonar Law.

The surrender of the Trade Union machinery into the hands of the Government facilitated the making over of the whole economy of the country for war. Government control was established over shipping and railways and over the raw materials most important for war purposes, such as cotton, iron and steel. A large measure of State capitalism accelerated the progress towards monopoly and the concentration of capital noted already as one of the features of Imperialism. Great trusts and combines, especially in the metal and chemical (i.e., explosives and poison gas) industries were fostered by the super-profits earned by the largest concerns. Capital was freely watered and a large proportion of the profits, in order to avoid taxation, were used for the construction of new plant and factories which in many cases were of little use in time of peace. Other factories were constructed by the Government and sold after the war to the combines for a fraction of the original cost.

The war thus gave industry an artificial prosperity which prepared the way for the great depression which followed. The transition from boom to slump was all the more acute because the industrial production of the war years was concentrated upon goods of no general utility and was based upon credit. Nearly £7,000,000,000 was added to the National Debt between 1914 and 1918, leaving a permanent burden upon industry which became relatively heavier as prices fell from the heights to which wartime inflation raised them. The general effect of the War was therefore to increase the concentration of British capitalism without increasing its efficiency or real strength.

During the first few months of the War strikes almost ceased, prices rose rapidly, while wages lagged far behind. There was considerable unemployment till recruiting and the needs of war industries had cancelled out the effects of the initial dislocation. In February new signs of life appeared in the great engineering centre of the Clyde, under the leadership of the Shop Stewards' Movement which had taken the position left empty by the official Union leadership. The wartime strikes were at first entirely unpolitical, that is, they were directed not against the War but against economic grievances. Later, when the struggle against conscription, which was introduced by instalments between the autumn of 1915 and the spring of 1916, began, and, even more, after the Russian Revolution, they took on a more political character. From the start, however, many of the leaders like McLean, were avowed revolutionaries and anti-militarists.

The February strikes on the Clyde won from the Government a wage advance of 1d. an hour. They also inspired it to pass the Munitions Act, by which a number of industries were proclaimed as war industries and strikes in them made illegal. The Act was challenged successfully in July 1915 by 200,000 miners in South Wales who struck for a week and won a new agreement.

The Clyde continued to be the main centre of agitation. The Shop Stewards had organised themselves into a body called the Clyde Workers' Committee which rapidly became the spokesman for the whole area. A rent strike, supported by well-timed industrial action, put an end to the worst exactions of the Glasgow landlords and forced the Government to pass a Rent Restriction Act. All through 1915 there were constant strikes which neither Government nor Union officials could prevent. Early in 1916, and largely owing to weaknesses within the Committee, the Government was able to intervene. The Committee's paper *The Worker* was suppressed, and the most active leaders of the agitation were deported to other areas or imprisoned, John McLean receiving a sentence of three years. From this time Sheffield became the main storm centre.

In November 10,000 men struck successfully to secure the release of a worker who had been conscripted into the Army. The greatest strike of all took place in May 1917 when 250,000 engineers from almost every centre in

England ceased work in protest against the dilution of labour and a proposed extension of conscription. The Government arrested the strike leaders and the breaking away of some of the less strongly organised towns led to defeat after a struggle lasting two weeks.

By this time the news of the Russian Revolution had become known everywhere, and great mass meetings and demonstrations left no doubt as to the sympathy of the British workers. So strong was this that at a Convention held at Leeds in the beginning of June, 1,150 delegates were present representing every section of the Labour Movement. More remarkable still was the spectacle of MacDonald and Snowdon taking a leading part in the proceedings and helping to pass resolutions in favour of the setting up of workmen's and soldiers' councils (which people in Britain were just beginning to learn to call Soviets) all over the country. Another indication of the changed feelings of the people was Henderson's decision that the time had come when it was wise for him to resign from the War Cabinet. The reactionaries, who had been able to retain control at the Leeds Convention by a cleverly calculated shift to the Left, remained strong enough to prevent its decisions being carried out, and when the Bolsheviks seized power in November they adopted an openly hostile attitude to the new Soviet Republic. Among the rank and file support continued to grow, though it had little opportunity to take any practical form till after the Armistice. The Shop Stewards' Movement was, however, active in propaganda to secure support for the Bolshevik appeal for peace.

In 1919 there was widespread opposition to the action of Lloyd George's Government in sending an expedition to Archangel against the Bolsheviks. In many cases soldiers ordered to this new front mutinied and refused, and there were even mutinies among the troops already there. The formation of a national 'Hands off Russia' Committee forced the Government to withdraw its forces and cease from direct intervention. It continued to support with money and supplies the White armies who were fighting against the Soviet Government in many parts of Russia.

This indirect intervention reached its highest point when Poland was encouraged to invade Russia in 1920. The British workers replied by setting up Councils of Action, and the refusal of the London dockers to load the s.s. *Jolly George* with munitions for Poland caught the imagination of the whole country and carried the agitation to its greatest heights. In August, when the Poles were being driven back, Lloyd George threatened the Soviet Government with war unless their troops withdrew. Immediately this threat became known a special conference of the Labour Party and the T.U.C. met and decided in favour of a general strike to prevent war. Lloyd George at once abandoned his attitude and advised the Poles to make peace.

In Ireland the reaction to the war was somewhat different. While Redmond and the bourgeois Nationalists supported England and turned themselves into recruiting agents, the left wing of the Volunteers and Connolly opposed the war and prepared for an armed rising. They were ready, if necessary, to seek German aid as the United Irishmen had sought that of France. At the same time, Connolly had no illusions about German Imperialism, and his attitude was crystallised in the famous slogan: "We serve neither King nor Kaiser, but Ireland."

Within the Volunteers there were further differences, one section led by Pearse wishing to strike as early as possible and a second following MacNeill preferring to remain passive in the hope of extorting concessions after the war. The differences reached such a pitch that when a rising was decided upon at Easter 1916, MacNeill sent out a countermanding order with the result that the rebel forces were completely disorganised. Even so, and although the rising was almost confined to Dublin, it took 20,000 troops a week to suppress it. Pearse, Connolly and most of the other leaders were taken prisoner and executed.

The crushing of the Easter Rising proved to be the beginning rather than the end of the rebellion in Ireland. During the next two years the Labour and National movements grew steadily. In 1918 an attempt to extend conscription to Ireland was defeated by a General Strike. The new movement developed, however, largely under the eadership of the Sinn Fein Party, a bourgeois Nationalist organisation that was opposed to English rule but had taken no part in the 1916 rebellion. The Sinn Fein leaders were careful to prevent any class or agrarian element from intruding itself into the guerilla war which lasted from 1919 to 1921. For this reason a gap was made between the masses and the leadership of the rebellion and the way was opened for the Treaty of December 1921 by which the Free State was set up. The essence of the Treaty was that the dominant sections of the Irish bourgeoisie were granted certain, for them, valuable concessions by the English Government, and, in return, undertook the task of suppressing the genuine movement of revolt among the workers and peasants, which was showing signs of growing out of control and was as dangerous to them as to the English.

The end of the War came at a time when the situation was full of anxiety for the Government. Opposition to war and sympathy for the Russian Revolution were increasing. The Shop Stewards were perfecting a national organisation. A serious naval mutiny was only just prevented by concessions, and, in September, the London police struck for higher wages. It was this general unrest, generally felt and much more serious than the surface reactions indicate that impelled the Labour Party to prepare its first avowedly Socialist programme, *Labour and the New Social Order*. It was true that its Socialism was extremely vague and remote, but it served as a focus and at the same time for a distraction to the universal desire of the people for a different life.

No sooner was the War ended than a regular epidemic of mutinies broke out in the Army. The first began at

Shoreham only two days after the Armistice and before long the revolt had spread to scores of camps in France and all over the South of England. The most determined units were hastily demobilised and the political inexperience of the leaders prevented the mutinies from having more than local success, but they caused the greatest alarm in the ranks of the Government.

No one sensed the changed atmosphere better than Lloyd George, with his almost uncanny capacity for gauging the temper of the masses. His appreciation of the danger of revolution is shown by a memorandum, drawn up a little later, in which he declared:

"Europe is filled with revolutionary ideas. A feeling not of depression, but of passion and revolt reigns in the breasts of the working class against the conditions that prevailed before the War. The whole existing system, political, social and economic, is regarded with distrust by the whole population of Europe."

It was this sense of urgency which led him to seek a snap decision in the Khaki Election of 1918, held while the soldiers were still in the main unable to vote and thousands of the newly enfranchised electors were not yet on the register. He prepared a programme in which social demagogy (houses for all and a land fit for heroes) was blended with a more deliberately evil attempt to turn the existing unrest into hatred of Germany. Under these conditions an overwhelming success was inevitable, though the Labour Party polled two and a quarter million votes and returned fifty-seven Members. Lloyd George obtained his majority, and, with it, what could be construed as a mandate for the crazy and disastrous Versailles settlement, the full results of which have not even yet been exhausted.

3. EPILOGUE

It is probable that the historian of the future will see in the World War neither the beginning nor the end of an age, but rather a turning point, marking the passing over of European Imperialism into decline. For the War has been followed by a period of permanent crisis in capitalism, a period in which the booms and slumps of the old trade cycle give way to alternations of profound depression with partial recoveries in which the boom is replaced by a condition of unhealthy stimulation oddly mixed with stagnation, a period when even in the most prosperous years unemployment never falls below the levels which in pre-war days marked the worst slumps. It is impossible in this Epilogue to do more than pick out a very few of the most outstanding events and tendencies of this period.[1]

The War decided nothing though it changed many things. It left unsolved all the major antagonisms of Imperialism and added a quite new antagonism, that between the world of capitalism and the world of socialism, in the form of the first workers' State, the Union of Socialist Soviet Republics. But it produced also important changes in the relative strengths of the Imperialist Powers, changes nearly all of which accentuated existing antagonism. In the first place, the Versailles Treaty, marking the victory of the older Powers, Britain and France, over the rising Power, Germany, gave additional grounds for the same animosities that had led to war in 1914. At Versailles, Germany was stripped of all her colonies, much of her coal and iron, all her navy and most of her merchant fleet, while a huge indemnity was imposed under the guise of reparations. The object of the Treaty, the permanent crippling of Germany as an economic and military rival, proved unattainable, but the attempt came within a little of destroying the whole fabric of European capitalism.

The full fruits of victory did not, however, go to Britain and France. Entering the War late, the U.S.A. secured

[1] This is the less to be regretted because much of the ground has recently been excellently covered by R. Palme Dutt in his *World Politics*, 1918–36, and by Allen Hutt in *The Post-War History of the British Working Class*.

RI

the maximum profits with the minimum damage and emerged with a vastly strengthened economic machine and as the world's creditor, a position previously enjoyed by Britain. Whereas before 1914 much British capital was invested in America, after 1918 Britain was only one of the many countries to which America had granted loans totalling thousands of millions of pounds. The years after 1918 saw, therefore, a growing antagonism between the two. If Versailles was to some extent a British victory, American money power found expression in the Washington Naval Treaty of 1921 in which she secured a nominal equality but actual superiority of naval strength and later in the hard conditions for the settlement of British debts as compared to those granted to other countries.

Thirdly, the decline of capitalism and the chaos of post-war Europe led to an intensification of the class struggle, to revolutions and attempted revolutions in Germany and a number of other countries, which failed partly because of the forcible intervention of the victorious Powers and partly because of the tactics adopted by the Social Democrats and the immaturity of the revolutionary forces grouped together in the newly formed Communist or Third International.

In England as elsewhere the first years after the War were years of industrial and political ferment. The movement in support of Soviet Russia already referred to had as its background a whole series of strikes in which miners, railwaymen, engineers and textile workers were especially prominent. But the movement was masked by the short replacement boom which followed the end of the War. Nevertheless, the period was one advance, and the Government and the ruling class were forced to make concessions and to use the utmost cunning, as in the case of the miners and the Sankey Commission.

By the summer of 1920 falling prices and rising unemployment heralded the end of the boom, which had no real basis in the state of the world market. In February 1921 there were over a million unemployed; by June over two million. The crisis gave the signal for the beginning of the great counter-offensive of British capitalism now emboldened by the receding of the revolutionary wave throughout Europe. Both employed and unemployed were engaged in continuous struggles in which the young Communist Party began to play a part, winning its first successes and making its first mistakes in the difficult passage from the narrow isolated tradition of the pre-war Socialist groups. In April 1921 the betrayal of the miners on 'Black Friday' left the working class badly divided and doomed to meet the attacks of the employers section by section.

The ruling class was able to defeat these sections, but its own position was one of great difficulty. India and Egypt were in revolt, guerilla war in Ireland went on up to the end of 1921, exports fell rapidly as the crisis spread from continent to continent, the coal industry being especially affected. Further, British industry was meeting the competition of new rivals in Japan, China and India.

Then, in 1924, came an apparent turn of events, the crisis eased, Europe seemed to be settling down to a relative tranquillity. But this period of stabilisation was based not upon a real return to prosperity but on the unstable foundation of American credits. Beginning with the adoption of the Dawes Plan, a rationalised method of extracting reparations from Germany, an immense flow of surplus capital set in from America to Europe. With this capital, the industrial plants of the main European countries were modernised, world trade began to revive, and the politicians began to talk of a return to normality. In fact, the whole revival was a sham, because the interest on all these loans was only paid by further borrowing: the scheme only continued to work so long as the flow of credit continued unbroken. When it ceased, a crisis on a scale never before known began.

Nor did the period of stabilisation mean a lessening of class conflicts, since the second base of the revival was a direct attack on both wages and working conditions. Returning to the Gold Standard in 1925, British capitalism prepared a frontal attack on the miners, the strongest and at the same time the most exposed section of the working class. Baldwin, the representative of heavy industry at its most aggressive, who had replaced Lloyd George and MacDonald as Prime Minister, declared frankly, "all the workers of this country have got to take reductions in wages". The blow at the miners had to be postponed till May 1926 only because of the support they received from the other sections of the organised workers.

The General Strike of May 1926 is now a matter of history: so, too, is both the response of the rank and file and the manner in which the General Council of the T.U.C. called off the Strike and left the miners to go down to defeat alone after a lock-out lasting into December. If the General Strike stands out among the great events in the history of the British workers, its lessons were lost upon the T.U.C. leaders. After 1926 the main drive of the employers was for the rationalisation of industry, a process that in some cases meant the modernising of plant but more often meant getting more output from a smaller number of workers. Instead of resisting this, the T.U.C. actually supported it, accepting the invitation of Sir Alfred Mond (of Imperial Chemicals) to enter negotiations about the best way to rationalise industry without industrial friction. The result was that while production increased unemployment remained at the same high level and real wages tended to fall. There was a vast piling up of stocks of every kind of commodity, and especially in primary products, since the gap between what the masses produced and what they consumed grew continually wider. The crisis of 1929, inevitable once the stream of American loans stopped, was thus made more severe.

Anticipating the coming catastrophe, the ruling class manœuvred the second Labour Government into office early in 1929. It made a pitiful showing, standing impotently by while the total of registered unemployed rose to nearly three millions. In 1931, faced with a sensational drop in exports, a sudden calling in of short-term loans due to the financial collapse in Germany, with a budget that would not balance and insistent demands from the bankers for economy measures at the expense of the workers, the Labour Government resigned.

A National Government was formed, in which MacDonald, Thomas and Snowden took posts, and in the General Election which followed the Labour Party suffered a crushing defeat. The National Government initiated a policy of cuts in wages and unemployment benefit, only carried through after a struggle in which terrific demonstrations by the unemployed and a mutiny in the North Sea Fleet at Invergordon were the outstanding features. The Government was copied in its wage reductions by the railways and many other sections of employers. In spite of these expedients, Britain was forced off the Gold Standard and had to discard free trade and set up a complete system of tariffs. Recovery only took place very slowly and at a low level.

The crisis was not confined only to Britain. Throughout the world production fell by an average of 42 per cent, a fall six times greater than in any pre-war slump. World unemployment rose to an estimated thirty millions in 1932. And with the crisis came the destruction of the carefully constructed European settlement on the basis of the Versailles Treaty. Reparations payments had to be suspended, while Germany and Central Europe moved rapidly towards Fascism, the last defence of capitalism in decline.

When the Nazis came to power in Germany in 1933 a new world grouping began. On the one side were the Fascist Powers—Germany, Italy and Japan, in serious difficulties and looking to war as the only way of escape and on the other, France and the other relatively prosperous States, fearing a war in which they had everything to lose and little to gain. The Soviet Union, anxious for peace for quite different reasons, became a centre around which the peace-desiring Powers tended to group themselves. As the danger of war became more acute a new arms race began on a scale far exceeding that of the years to 1914. With rearmament came another unhealthy boom period, based on the abnormal stimulation of the heavy industries.

In this situation the British National Government has played an ambiguous rôle. On the one hand it fears war as a danger to its overblown Empire and sees danger in the demands of Fascism; on the other, it hopes to buy off the Fascist Powers, to satisfy their demands at someone else's expense and so keep its possessions intact. In addition, it dislikes the friendly relations which France has established with the Soviet Union and is consequently seeking to drive a wedge between them and, if possible, to establish a new grouping of Britain, France and Germany.

The result has been that British policy has been one of continued shuffle, of compromise and retreat before aggression, of the betrayal of peace. In 1932 Japan was encouraged to seize Manchuria. In 1935 the Anglo-German Naval Agreement gave Hitler British support for the rearmament of Germany and Italy was allowed to conquer Abyssinia under the nose of the League of Nations. In 1936 the war of Germany and Italy upon the Spanish people was only possible because Britain prevented France from taking counter measures. In 1937 Japan, made bold by previous success and by a military alliance with Germany, has commenced a new war upon China.

The world stands in the shadow of a war more terrible than that of 1914. If war comes the British Government must bear a heavy share of the responsibility. It is not even now[1] too late for the danger to be averted if the British people, and above all the working people who form the overwhelming majority of the population and who are always the worst sufferers in any war, are able to unite in sufficient strength to force the Government

[1] October, 1937.

to stop encouraging aggression and take their stand with France and the Soviet Union for world peace. This book ends at one of the most critical moments in our history, when more than ever before their own fate and the fate of the world lies in the capacity of the people for right judgment followed by right action.

NOTE ABOUT BOOKS

IN SPITE OF its title, this book is not so much a History of England as an essay in historical interpretation. It sets out to give the reader a general idea of the main lines of the movement of our history, and to do this a great mass of detail has been sacrificed and events of considerable importance have been of necessity omitted or have received the most cursory treatment. Further, it is intended for the general reader rather than for the specialist, and makes no pretence of being the result of original research: it would, indeed, be quite impossible for any one writer to attempt to cover the whole field of English History in such a way. Whatever value this book may have must lie rather in the interpretation than in the novelty of the facts it presents.

In a work of this character, a formal bibliography would be out of place. I have preferred to give a short annotated list of books which may be of use to the reader who wishes to carry his studies further. Most of these books have been selected as being likely to help the reader along the line which I have attempted to sketch out. This does not mean that they are all written from a standpoint which I believe to be correct: the great majority are not. But I do believe that from the facts they contain the reader will be able to form his own conclusions as to the correctness or otherwise of the general view of history which underlies my essay. Finally, I have tried to confine my list to books which will not be too technical or too detailed for anyone who is a newcomer to the study of history. This accounts for what may seem the curious omission of a number of standard works of unquestioned authority.

Many of the books mentioned below have bibliographies to which reference can be made.

Among medium length books, *A Short History of the English People* by J. R. Green remains, in spite of many details which have been found to be inaccurate, the classic example of a Liberal History. G. M. Trevelyan's *History of England* is a more recent work similar in scope. *A History of English Life* by A. Williams-Ellis and F. J. Fisher is a Socialist work notable for its wealth of pictorial diagrams illustrating social and economic changes. For economic history W. Cunningham's *The Growth of English Industry and Commerce* and J. F. Thorold Rogers' *The Economic Interpretation of History* contain a wealth of information. Both need to be read with some caution, and the historical sections of K. Marx's *Capital* supply a valuable check and corrective here. *English Economic History, Select Documents* by A. E. Bland, P. A. Brown, and R. H. Tawney is a useful compilation of illustrative material.

Constitutional history, always a stronghold of academic pedantry, can be illuminating when rescued from the isolation in which it is usually studied. Here, G. B. Adams' *Constitutional History of England* and *The Constitutional History of England* by F. W. Maitland may be consulted.

For agriculture, Lord Ernle's *English Farming Past and Present* is valuable, while *The Decisive Wars of History* by Captain B. H. Liddell Hart is a brilliant introduction to military history, a subject far too neglected by the Liberal historians of the recent past.

Since this book is a history of England, events in Ireland, Scotland and the British Empire have only been discussed when they have a direct bearing on the main theme. On Ireland Mrs. J. R. Green's *Irish Nationality* and J. Connolly's classic *Labour in Irish History* should be read in conjunction with Elinor Burns' more recent *British Imperialism in Ireland*. G. M. Thompson's *A Short History of Scotland* is a readable if somewhat biased recent work. For the Empire, J. F. Horrabin's *A Short History of the British Empire*, R. P. Dutt's *Modern India* and the monographs prepared by the Labour Research Department are all valuable.

By far the most illuminating short book on British pre-history is *The Personality of Britain* by Cyril Fox. *The Origin of the Family*, by F. Engels, though not dealing specifically with Britain, should be consulted for background. *Roman Britain* by R. G. Collingwood and *The Romanisation of Roman Britain* by R. B. Haverfield are temperate surveys of an obscure period. For the transition from tribal to feudal society P. Vinogradoff's *The Growth of the Manor* is an admirable work whose author comes at times very close to the standpoint of historical materialism. In the first volume of *The Political History of England* edited by W. Hunt and R. L. Poole, T. Hodkin outlines the events up to the Norman Conquest vividly even if he is sometimes uncritical of his sources. There is a translation of the *Anglo Saxon Chronicle* in the Everyman Library.

For the medieval period G. G. Coulton's *Social Life in Britain from the Conquest to the Reformation* and *The Medieval Village* are invaluable, the latter being specially good on the relations between church and peasantry. E. Power's *Medieval People* is useful for the growth of the wool trade, and G. M. Trevelyan's *England in the Age of Wycliffe* for the rising of 1381 and the Lollards.

On the Tudor Period, the Reformation and the rise of Puritanism, A. F. Pollard's *Factors in Modern History* and R. H. Tawney's *Religion and the Rise of Capitalism* and *The Agrarian Problem in the Sixteenth Century* may be consulted. K. Kautsky's *Thomas More and his Utopia* contains much interesting matter, but his generalisations must be treated with caution as many of them apply to Germany rather than to England. G. C. Perry in his *History of the Reformation in England* summarises the orthodox Anglican version. The extremely picturesque and often most inaccurate writings of J. A. Froude have a special interest today because his open and delighted imperialism often leads to an unexpected frankness.

G. M. Trevelyan's *England Under the Stuarts* is an excellent example of the faults and virtues of Liberal history. F.

Guizot's *History of the English Revolution*, old-fashioned in many respects, is valuable because as a Frenchman he had an instinctive understanding of what a revolution is like. C. H. Firth, F. H. Hayward and H. Belloc have written strongly contrasting lives of Cromwell, and the second chapter of T. H. Wintringham's *Mutiny* has a good account of the Levellers. O. Airey's *Charles II* gives a lively description of the transition period between 1660 and 1688. *The Rise of European Liberalism* by H. J. Laski is a brilliant analysis of the growth of the political theories appropriate to bourgeois society.

Life and Work in Modern Europe by G. Renard and G. Weulersse covers the development from domestic to capitalist industry during the Seventeenth and Eighteenth Centuries. On Eighteenth Century politics J. Morley's *Walpole*, J. B. Namier's *The Structure of Politics at the Accession of George III* and *That Devil Wilkes* by R. W. Postgate provide interestingly contrasted viewpoints. *The First American Revolution* by Jack Hardy attempts a Socialist analysis of one of the outstanding events of history.

Among the many books on the Industrial Revolution *The Town Labourer* and *The Village Labourer* by J. L. and B. Hammond and *The Condition of the Working Class in England in 1844* by F. Engels are still outstanding. E. Halévy's *A History of the English People* gives a general description of this country at the time of the Napoleonic War. His conclusions should be treated with extreme caution. The contemporary writings of Burke, Paine and Cobbett are of considerable historical value.

Of Nineteenth Century England E. Wingfield-Stratford's *Victorian Trilogy* gives perhaps the best panoramic view. The last and best volume, *The Victorian Aftermath* carries the picture to the eve of the World War. C. R. Fay's *Life and Labour in the Nineteenth Century* is good in its accounts of industrial conditions and developments but less satisfactory in the chapters dealing with the working-class movement. For this, *The History of Trade Unionism* by S. and B. Webb,

This Final Crisis by A. Hutt, *From Chartism to Labourism* by T. Rothstein and *Revolution from 1789 to 1906*, a collection of documents, by R. W. Postgate should be consulted. There is no one book which covers the whole ground satisfactorily. The *Correspondence* of Marx and Engels is a mine of information on all aspects of Nineteenth Century history.

For the late Nineteenth Century and the period of the World War, in addition to many of the books mentioned above, Lenin's *Imperialism* and the collection published under the title *Lenin on Britain* are invaluable. Good too, in spite of some curious lapses of judgment, is Ralph Fox's *The Class Struggle in Britain in the Epoch of Imperialism*, unfortunately unfinished.

The International Anarchy, 1904–1914 by G. Lowes Dickenson is a well documented account of the events leading the World War. *A History of the World War* by Captain B. H. Liddell Hart is likely to remain the standard technical work on its subject.

INDEX